# MODELING IN RESOURCE MANAGEMENT AND ENVIRONMENT THROUGH GEOMATICS

## About the Authors

**Prof. H.S. Sharma** (*b.* 1945) holds postgraduate and doctoral degrees in Geography from the University of Saugar, Madhya Pradesh. He has travelled widely across the U.K., the U.S.A., Germany, Holland, Canada, Norway, Seychelles and Malaysia and has over 75 papers and a dozen books to his credit. He has supervised nearly three dozen Ph.Ds.

Prof. Sharma has successfully conducted several research projects sponsored by the U.G.C., Ministry of Environment and Forests, DRDO, New Delhi, and NORAD, Norway. He is a former director of the Indira Gandhi Centre for Human Ecology, Environment and Population Studies, (HEEPS), Academic Staff College, and Dean, Faculty of Science, University of Rajasthan, Jaipur. He is a member of many national and international associations.

Recipient of the UGC Career Award in 1979, Gold Award, Vijaishri Award and the ISEER Award, Dr. Sharma is former Professor of Geography, and a Chancellor's nominee in the Syndicate, University of Rajasthan. He is the President of the Commonwealth Human Ecology Council (Chec-India) and National Association of Geographers, India (NAGI). Professor Sharma has also been nominated as a member on Court of Visva Bharti, Shanti Niketan (W.B.) by His Excellency, the President of India for three years (2010).

**Dr. P.R. Binda,** is a Cartographer, Department of Geography, niversity of Rajasthan, Jaipur. Dr. Binda passed his M.A. in Geography and awarded Ph.D. degree from University of Rajasthan, Jaipur. He is associated with National and International research projects. He is incharge of GIS cartographic laboratory in the Department of Geography, University of Rajasthan, Jaipur. He has visited Norway in 1995.

# Modeling in Resource Management and Environment Through Geomatics

*Training Programme on Modeling in Resource Management and Environment through Geomatics*
*by Department of Geography,*
*University of Rajasthan, Jaipur during*
*1st December to 30th December 2006*

**H.S. Sharma**
*Course Coordinator*
**P.R. Binda**
*Course Co-Coordinator*

CONCEPT PUBLISHING COMPANY, NEW DELHI 110 059

**Cataloging in Publication Data—DK**
*Courtesy:* D.K. Agencies (P) Ltd. <docinfo@dkagencies.com>

**Training Programme on Modeling in Resource Management and Environment through Geomatics (2006 : Jaipur, India)**

Modeling in resource management and environment through geomatics: Training Programme on Modeling in Resource Management and Environment through Geomatics by Department of Geography, University of Rajasthan, Jaipur during 1st December to 30th December 2006 / [edited by] H.S. Sharma, P.R. Binda.

p. cm.
Lecture notes.
Includes bibliographical references.
Includes index.
ISBN 13: 9788180694875
ISBN 10: 8180694879

1. Natural resources—India—Management—Simulation methods—Congresses. 2. Environmental management—India—Simulation methods—Congresses. 3. Geomatics—India—Congresses. I. Sharma, H. S. (Hari Shanker), 1945- II. Binda, P. R. III. Title.

DDC 910.285 22



ISBN 13: 978-81-8069-487-5
ISBN 10: 81-8069-487-9

First Published 2007



*Published and Printed by*
Ashok Kumar Mittal
**Concept Publishing Company**
A/15-16, Commercial Block, Mohan Garden
New Delhi-110059 (INDIA)

*Phones* : 25351460, 25351794
*Fax* : 091-11-25357103
*Email* : publishing@conceptpub.com

# Preface

Geomatics encompasses Remote Sensing, Global Positioning System (GPS), Geographical Information System (GIS), Satellite Communication and Information Technology. Geoinformatics has become an important requirement for the generation of geographic data bases for resource inventory, assessment, management and their applications.

During last 20 years there has been a tremendous increase in remote sensing technology along with Geographical Information System, Networking, Modeling and so on. At the same time, there has been development in the areas of geomatics techniques such as GPS, GPR which have contributed immensely to the growth and development of remote sensing and GIS in the country.

As most of the natural resources are interdependent and coexist in nature, they need to be considered collectively for their utilization. This fact has led to the development of the concept of integrated assessment of natural resources. Attempts have been made in India to integrate the information on various natural resources including forest cover as derived from remote sensing data along with the socio-economic factors such as social and demographic profiles, economic status and other data such as slope aspect, drainage etc., in a GIS environment to generate specific action plan on a watershed basis for sustainable development.

In short period of about two and a half decades space-borne remote sensing has emerged as a unique and powerful system providing information on natural resources of the world at global/regional/local levels with no regards to political boundaries.

Keeping above facts in mind the geoinformatics education programme in India should encompass besides satellite remote sensing, other like satellite communication, satellite meteorology and disaster management. The application of this technology should be popularized and man power be generated through training in this field.

With these above considerations a proposal was submitted to Department of Science and Technology, Government of India, New Delhi for funding a month Training Programme on Modeling in Resource Management and environment through Geomatics to provide basic training to young research scholars and teachers of geography, geology and cognate discipline.

The volume consists of 29 selected lecture notes in the form of chapters on various aspects of modeling in resources management and environment using geomatics delivered by resource persons during training programme from 1st December to 30th December, 2006.

J.R. Sharma has traced the development of Indian Space Programme in chapter first. He has emphasized that India has established space system that form an important element of the national infrastructure. Remote sensing and application potential has been discussed by M.P. Punia in chapter two. S.K. Pathan in chapter three has discussed application of geoinformatics in urban and regional planning with special reference to Indore city of M.P. Digital image processing and geomatics and Radiometric corrections have been studied by M.P. Punia in chapter four. A case study of Land Resource Management using remote sensing and GIS has been analyzed by Sandeep Goyal in chapters five and six. In chapter seven T.I. Khan analyses environmental impact assessment. S.K. Chattopadhyay and Mahamaya Chattopadhyay in chapter eight discuss RS and GIS application in generation and synthesis of environmental statistics taking a case study of Ittikara river basin of Kerala. M.S. Nathawat and Kirti Avishek in chapter nine discuss Landscape Ecological Assessment using Hemoroby Model. M.S. Nathawat in chapter ten discusses Environmental Modeling through geomatics. Smt. Rajashree V. Bothale in chapter eleven gives an overview of geographical information system. GIS application has been discussed by B.K. Bhadra in chapter twelve. A.K. Bera has given an overview of data base organization and creation in GIS in chapter thirteen. Surparn Pathak in chapter fourteen has given an analysis of data display and presentation. Grid analysis has been discussed by Dibyendu Dutta in chapter fifteen. V.M. Bothara in chapter sixteen discusses manipulation and analysis in GIS. Bio-diversity assessment through geo-informatics has been examined by Sarnam Singh in chapters seventeen and eighteen. N.R. Patel in chapter nineteen has discussed spatial decision support system in crop management. He further discusses Drought Monitoring by Satellite Remote Sensing in chapter twenty. Application of Remote Sensing and GIS has been discussed by N.R. Patel in chapter twenty-one. Hema Yadav in chapter twenty-two discusses application of GIS in preparation of National Agricultural Market Atlas. In chapter twenty-three Ali Mohmmed discusses the role of geomatics in land resource and Land capability analysis. He further in chapter twenty-four examines environmental pollution and threat to food security. Application of RS-GIS in road Mapping has been examined by Mahamaya Chattopadhyay in chapter twenty-five. S.K. Chattopadhyay in chapter twenty-six has introduced the concept fractal of analysis and its application in geomorphology. S.R. Singh Yadava has examined application of Remote Sensing in Natural Resources Management in chapter twenty-seven. M.B. Singh in chapters twenty-eight and twenty-nine has discussed Wasteland Management and role of geomatics and Modeling in transport and topology using geomatics respectively.

We take this opportunity to express our gratitude to Prof. S.C. Kalwar, then Head of the Department of Geography and present Head of the Department of Geography Dr. R.D. Gurjar for their administrative and academic support.

We also take this opportunity to express our gratitude to Dr. N.K. Jain, Vice Chancellor, University of Rajasthan, Jaipur for his continual support through out the training programme. The financial support by DST, New Delhi for conduct of a training programme specially to Dr. D.R. Ram, Director, ESS Division that lead to the genesis of this book is gratefully acknowledged. We extend our sincere thanks to all the resource persons and all contributors who despite their busy schedule have extended help as per our lecture programme.

Last but not the least we thank the authors and publishers whose published work have been discussed and used in this volume.

*Editors*
**H.S. Sharma**
**P.R. Binda**

# Contents

# List of the Tables

# List of the Figures

# List of the Contributors

**Dr. A.K. Bera,** Scientist, RRSSC/ISRO, Jodhpur

**Prof. Ali Mohammad,** Department of Geography, Aligarh Muslim University, Aligarh (U.P.)

**Dr. B.K. Bhadra,** Scientist, RRSSC/ISRO, Jodhpur

**Dr. D. Dutta,** Scientist, RRSSC/ISRO, Jodhpur

**Prof. H.S. Sharma,** Prof. of Geography (Retd.) University of Rajasthan, Jaipur

**Dr. Hema Yadav,** Deputy Director, Agricultural Marketing Centre, Bambala, Tonk Road, Jaipur

**Dr. J.R. Sharma,** Director, RRSSC, Jodhpur

**Prof. M.B. Singh,** Department of Geography, Banaras Hindu University, Varanasi-221005, INDIA

**Dr. M.P. Punia,** Head, Remote Sensing Division, BITS, Jaipur

**Prof. M.S. Nathawat,** Head, Remote Sensing Department, Birla Institute of Science and Technology, Ranchi

**Dr. Mahamaya Chattopadhayay,** Centre for Earth Sciences Studies, Akkulam, Trivananthapuram-695031, Kerala

**Dr. N.R. Patel,** Scientist, Indian Institute of Remote Sensing, Dehradun

**Smt. Rajshree V. Bothale,** Scientist, RRSSC/ISRO, Jodhpur

**Dr. S. K. Pathan,** Head, FLPG, Space Application Centre, Ahmedabad

**Dr. S.R. Singh Yadava,** Head,Department of Geography, Udai Pratap College, Varanasi.

**Dr. Sandeep Goyal,**B-6 M.P.C.S.P, Scientific Residential Complex Near Hindustan Petrolium, Gautam Nagar, Bhopal

**Dr. Sarnam Singh,** Scientist,'SG' Indian Institute of Remote Sensing, Dehradun

Dr. Srikumar **Chattopadhayay,** Centre for Earth Sciences Studies, Akkulam, Trivananthapuram-695031,Kerala

**Shri Suparn Pathak,** Scientist, RRSSC/ISRO, Jodhpur

**Dr. T.I. Khan,** Indira Gandhi Centre for HEEPS, University of Rajasthan, Jaipur

**Vinod M. Bothale,** Scientist, RRSSC/ISRO, Jodhpur

# 1

# Indian Space Programme
## Towards National Development

*J.R. Sharma*

The Indian Government established the Department of Space in 1972 to promote development and application of space science and technology for socio-economic benefits. Indian Space Research Organisation (ISRO), is the primary agency under Department of Space, for executing space programmes. During the seventies, India undertook demonstration of space applications for communication, broadcasting and remote sensing; designing and building experimental satellites—Aryabhata, Bhaskara, APPLE and Rohini and experimental Satellite Launch Vehicles—SLV-3 and ASLV. Today, India has established space systems that form an important element of the national infrastructure.

### National Systems Using Space Technology

| *INSAT* | *IRS* |
|---|---|
| * Telecommuications | * Natural Resources Management |
| * Broadcasting (TV, Radio) | * Natural Resources Information System |
| * Business Communication | —Water |
| * Mobile Communication | —Forest |
| * Telemedicine | —Crop |
| * Search and Rescue | —Land |
| * Satellite Navigation | —Minerals |
| * Meteorology | —Environment |
| | —Ocean |
| * Disaster Management Support | |
| * Village Resource Centres | |

### *Indian National Satellite (INSAT) System*

Commissioned in 1983, INSAT is a multipurpose satellite system for telecommunications, television broadcasting, meteorology, disaster warning and search and rescue. Besides telecommunications and other regular broadcasting services, INSAT is widely used for interactive educational television, developmental communication and telemedicine. Meteorological imaging and direct-to-community broadcast capabilities of INSAT help in issuing warnings on impending cyclones. INSAT also carries transponders dedicated to search and rescue operations as part of international COSPAS/SARSAT programme.

### *Indian Remote Sensing Satellite (IRS) System*

Commissioned in 1988, India now has the world's largest constellation of remote sensing satellites. The system offers space-based data in a range of spectral bands, spatial resolutions and swaths. The data is used for several applications covering agriculture, water resources, urban development, mineral prospecting, environment, forestry, drought and flood forecasting and ocean resources.

### *Launch Vehicles*

India has developed and commissioned Polar Satellites Launch Vehicle (PSLV) and Geosynchronous Satellite Launch Vehicle (GSLV). PSLV can launch 1400 kg. Class remote sensing satellites into an 820 km polar Sun Synchronous Orbit (SSO). It can also place a satellite weighing about 1100 kg in Geosynchronous Transfer Orbit (GTO) or a 3500 kg class satellite in Low Earth Orbit (LEO). GLSV is capable of launching 2000 kg class satellites into GTO. GSLV Mark-III, to place 4000 kg class satellites in GTO, is under development.

A variety of sounding rockets have also been developed for conducting scientific and technological experiments.

### Space Science

India has flown Gamma-Ray and Retarding Potential Analyser payloads on two of its SROSS satellites launched in 1992 and 1994. IRS-P3, launched in 1996 carried an X-ray astronomy payload. Chandrayaan-1, which envisages orbiting a spacecraft at a height of 100 km in the polar orbit around the moon for physical and chemical mapping of the moon's surface, is planned in 2007-08. An exclusive astronomical satellite, ASTROSAT, is also planned. Several ground-based facilities for space sciences, including a Mesosphere Stratosphere Troposphere (MST) Radar, have been set up in India.

### Infrastructure for Space Development

India has established a strong infrastructure for executing its space programme. They include facilities for the development of satellite and launch vehicles and their testing;

launch infrastructure for sounding rockets and satellite launch vehicles; telemetry, tracking and command network; and data reception and processing systems for remote sensing. A number of academic and research institutions as well as industries participate in the Indian Space Programme. Several Indian industries have the expertise to undertake sophisticated jobs required for space systems.

### Space Services from India

Indian space capabilities are available to international customers through Antrix Corporation of the Department of Space. Presently, these include the reception of Indian Remote Sensing Satellite data, launch services, lease of transponders on INSAT and providing TTC support.

### International Co-operation

International co-operation has been the hallmark of Indian space programme. India participates in major space fora including the UN, IAF, COSPAR and CEOS. India has set up the Centre for Space Science and Technology Education in Asia and the Pacific (CCSTE-AP), which is sponsored by the United Nations. India offers training in space applications to personnel from developing countries under the programme Sharing of Experience in Space (SHARES). ISRO and the French Space Agency CNES have undertaken a joint atmospheric satellite mission Megha-Tropiques to be launched in 2008-09.

### Space Centres in India

#### New Delhi

- DOS Branch Secretariat
- ISRO Branch Office
- Delhi Earth Station

#### Jodhpur (Rajasthan)

- Western RRSSC

#### Udaipur (Rajasthan)

- Solar Observatory

#### Mt. Abu (Rajasthan)

- Infrared Observatory

#### Lucknow (Uttar Pradesh)

- ISTRAC Ground Station

**Dehradun (Uttaranchal)**

- Indian Institute of Remote Sensing
- Northern RRSSC

**Ahmedabad (Gujarat)**

- Space Applications Centre
- Physical Research Laboratory
- Development and Education Communication Unit

**Nagpur (Maharashtra)**

- Central RRSSC

**Mumbai (Maharashtra)**

- ISRO Liaison Office

**Aluva (Kerala)**

- Ammonium Perchlorate Experimental Plant

**Thiruvananthapuram (Kerala)**

- Vikram Sarabhai Space Centre
- Liquid Propulsion System Centre
- ISRO Inertial System Unit

**Mahendragiri (Tamil Nadu)**

- Liquid Propulsion Facilities

**Bangalore (Karnataka)**

- Space Commission
- Department of Space and ISRO Headquarters
- INSAT Programme Office
- NNRMS Secretariat
- Civil Engineering Division
- Antrix Corporation
- ISRO Satellite Centre
- Laboratory for Electro-Optic Systems
- ISTRAC
- Southern RRSSC
- Liquid Propulsion Systems Centre

**Hassan (Karnataka)**

- Master Control Facility (MCF)

**Sriharikota (Andhra Pradesh)**

- Satish Dhawan Space Centre, SHAR

**Tirupati (Andhra Pradesh)**

- NMRF

**Hyderabad (Andhra Pradesh)**

- National Remote Sensing Agency

**Port Blair**

- Down Range Station

**Kharagpur (West Bengal)**

- Eastern RRSSC

**Shillong**

- North Eastern Space Applications Centre

**Indian Satellites Launched so far**

| *S. No.* | *Name* | *Date of Launch* | *Weight (Kg)* | *Launch Vehicle* |
|---|---|---|---|---|
| 1. | Aryabhata | 19.04.1975 | 358 | C-1 Intercosmos, USSR |
| 2. | Bhaskara-1 | 07.06.1979 | 444 | C-1 Intercosmos, USSR |
| 3. | RTP | 10.08.1979 | 35 | SLV-3, India |
| 4. | RS-1 | 18.07.1980 | 35 | SLV-3, India |
| 5. | RS-D1 | 31.05.1981 | 38 | SLV-3, India |
| 6. | Apple | 19.06.1981 | 670 | Ariane, Europe |
| 7. | Bhaskara-2 | 20.11.1981 | 436 | C-1 Intercosmos, USSR |
| 8. | INSAT-1A | 10.04.1982 | 1150 | DELTA, USA |
| 9. | RS-D2 | 17.04.1983 | 41.5 | SLV-3, India |
| 10. | INSAT-1B | 30.08.1983 | 1194 | Space Shuttle, USA |
| 11. | SROSS-1 | 24.03.1987 | 150 | ASLV, India |
| 12. | IRS-1A | 17.03.1988 | 980 | Vostok, USSR |
| 13. | SROSS-2 | 13.07.1988 | 150 | ASLV, India |
| 14. | INSAT-1C | 22.07.1988 | 1190 | Ariane, Europe |

*(Contd.)*

*(Contd.)*

| *S. No.* | *Name* | *Date of Launch* | *Weight (Kg)* | *Launch Vehicle* |
|---|---|---|---|---|
| 15. | INSAT-1D | 12.06.1990 | 1293 | Delta, USA |
| 16. | IRS-1B | 29.08.1991 | 990 | Vostok, USSR |
| 17. | SROSS-C | 20.05.1992 | 106 | ASLV, India |
| 18. | INSAT-2A | 10.07.1992 | 1906 | Ariane, Europe |
| 19. | INSAT-2B | 23.07.1993 | 1932 | Ariane, Europe |
| 20. | IRS-1E | 20.09.1993 | 845 | PSLV, India |
| 21. | SROSS-C2 | 04.05.1994 | 113 | ASLV, India |
| 22. | IRS-P2 | 15.10.1994 | 904 | PSLV, India |
| 23. | INSAT-2C | 07.12.1995 | 2050 | Ariane, Europe |
| 24. | IRS-1C | 28.12.1995 | 1250 | Molniya, Russia |
| 25. | IRS-P3 | 21.03.1996 | 920 | PSLV, India |
| 26. | INSAT-2D | 04.06.1997 | 2070 | Ariane, Europe |
| 27. | IRS-1D | 29.09.1997 | 1200 | PSLV-C1, India |
| 28. | INSAT-2DT | Procured in Orbit from Arabsat in January, 1998 | | |
| 29. | INSAT-2E | 03.04.1999 | 2550 | Ariane, Europe |
| 30. | IRS-P4 | 26.05.1999 | 1050 | PSLV-C2, India |
| 31. | INSAT-3B | 22.03.2000 | 2070 | Ariane, Europe |
| 32. | GSAT-1 | 18.04.2001 | 1530 | GSLV-D1, India |
| 33. | TES | 22.10.2001 | 1108 | PSLV-C3, India |
| 34. | INSAT-3C | 24.01.2002 | 2750 | Ariane, Europe |
| 35. | Kalpana-1 | 12.09.2002 | 1060 | PSLV-C4, India |
| 36. | INSAT-3A | 10.04.2003 | 2950 | Ariane, Europe |
| 37. | GSAT-2 | 08.05.2003 | 1825 | GSLV-D2, India |
| 38. | INSAT-3E | 28.09.2003 | 2775 | Ariane, Europe |
| 39. | Resourcesat-1 | 17.10.2003 | 1360 | PSLV-C5, India |
| 40. | Edusat | 20.09.2004 | 1950 | GSLV-F01, India |

## International Satellites Launched by India

| *S. No.* | *Name* | *Date of Launch* | *Weight (Kg)* | *Launch Vehicle* |
|---|---|---|---|---|
| 1. | DLR-TUBSAT, Germany | 26.05.1999 | 45 | PSLV-C2 |
| 2. | KITSAT-3, Republic of Korea | 26.05.1999 | 110 | PSLV-C2 |
| 3. | BIRD, Germany | 22.10.2001 | 92 | PSLV-C3 |
| 4. | PROBA, Belgium | 22.10.2001 | 94 | PSLV-C3 |

## Indian Satellite Launch Vehicles

### *SLV*

| | | |
|---|---|---|
| Height | : | 22 m |
| Lift-off weight | : | 17 t |
| Propulsion | : | All Solid |
| Payload mass | : | 40 kg. |
| Orbit | : | Low Earth |

***ASLV***

| | | |
|---|---|---|
| Height | : | 23.5 m |
| Lift-off weight | : | 39 t |
| Propulsion | : | All Solid |
| Payload mass | : | 150 kg |
| Orbit | : | Low Earth |

***PSLV***

| | | |
|---|---|---|
| Height | : | 44 m |
| Lift-off weight | : | 295 t |
| Propulsion | : | Solid and Liquid |
| Payload mass | : | 1400 kg |
| Orbit | : | 820 km Sunsynchronous Polar<br>(1050 kg in Geosynchronous Transfer Orbit) |

***GSLV***

| | | |
|---|---|---|
| Height | : | 49 m |
| Lift-off weight | : | 414 t |
| Propulsion | : | Solid, Liquid and Cryogenic |
| Payload mass | : | 2000 kg |
| Orbit | : | Geosynchronous Transfer |

## 2

# Remote Sensing and Application Potential

*M.P. Punia*

---

### Remote Sensing Systems

Earth resources Satellites, both manned (*e.g.*: Soyuz *I* Salut) and unmanned *e.g.*:

- Landsat, SPOT, IRS;
- Polar orbiting and geostationary environmental satellites;
- High altitude aircraft;
- Conventional aircraft;
- Balloons;
- Rockets (*e.g.* for stratospheric studies);
- Helicopters;
- Data collection platforms.

### Major Components of Remote Sensing System

There are four major components of a remote sensing system *viz.*:

1. Radiation sources
2. Target
3. Sensor
4. Transmission Path

#### *Radiation Source*

The sun with a surface temperature of almost 6000° K radiates enormous amount of energy at wavelengths with the maximum concentration of energy occurring at a wavelenth of about 0.5 micro meter. Thus during day light hours the maximum energy incident on the earth and reflected from earth is in the visible band with a maximum energy peak at 0.5 micro meter.

### *Target*

The portion of the earth's surface reflection or emission measured by the remote sensing system.

Object of Earth surface interact with incident radiation and modify the radiation by reflection/absorption and transmission through. The reflection and emission by earth object in different wavelengths gives useful information about the object which in turn help in identification of these objects. These characteristics are called spectral characteristics of the object.

### *Sensor*

Remote sensing system are designed to record radiation in one or more parts of EM spectrum. Imaging sensor is a device that receives EM Radiation and converts it into signal that can be recorded and displayed as numerical data or an image.

### *Transmission Path*

Transmission through media's of different densities such as from air into water. Transmission is called volume phenomenon because these are determined by the internal characteristic of the smaller, *viz.* Density and Condition.

## Electromagnetic Radiation (EMR)

The earth's surface receives only a fraction of total incident solar radiation. Most of this radiation is either absorbed or scattered or reflected back into the space by the upper atmosphere of the earth. The shortwave radiation consisting of x-rays, Gamma rays, Ultraviolet rays and other radiation harmful to humans and other living organisms is absorbed by the ozone layer in the atmosphere and allows only the longer wave radiation of visible, infrared, microwave, radiowaves and so on. The visible light as we see is constitutes only a small portion of the EM spectrum.

## Electromagnetic Energy

Electromagnetic energy refers to the energy that moves with velocity of light (3 × 108m/sec) in a harmonic wave pattern (equally and repetitively spaced in time) and has two force fields electric and magnetic that are orthogonal to each other.

It is possible to categories EM energy according to its position along a continuum of wavelengths, generally referred as Electromagnetic spectrum. It is a continuum sequence of EM energy arranged according to wavelength or frequency.

The earth's atmosphere absorbs energy in the gamma-ray, x-ray and most of the ultraviolet region, therefore these regions are not used for remote sensing. Remote Sensing deals with energy in visible, infrared, thermal and microwave regions. These regions are further sub-divided into bands, such as blue, green, red, infrared, thermal, microwave, etc.

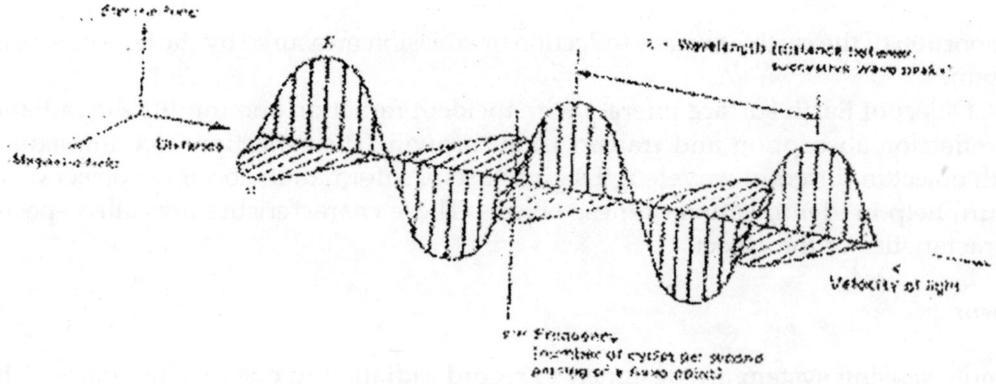

Basic radiation laws—Sun is the strongest source of radiant energy for Remote Sensing. All objects above O°K emit EM radiation at all wavelengths due to conversion of heat energy into EM energy. Blackbody is a hypothetical ideal radiator that totally absorbs and remits all energy incidents upon it. Emission of radiation depends upon two parameters—Temperature (T) and emissivity (0) of the material.

### *Stefan-Boltzman Law*

All bodies with temp above 0°k emits EM radiation. The energy radiated by an object at a particular temperature is given by:

$$M = \sigma T^4$$

$\sigma$ is the Stefan-Boltzmann constant $5.67 \times 10^{-8}$ $W/m^2/K^4$

T—absolute temp, M (radiant existence) $w/m^2$

As 'M' varies with forth power of 'T', the objects even with close difference in temperature can be distinguished ITom Remote Sensing measurements.

### Wien's Displacement Law

Maximum spectral radiant exitance of a blackbody is inversely proportional to its temperature.

$$M\lambda_{max} = \frac{A}{T}$$

where A - Wine's constant 2898 μm oK

As the temperature of a Blackbody increases, the dominant wavelength of emitted radiation shifts towards shorter wavelength.

***Planck's Law***

The total energy radiated in all directions by unit area in unit time in a spectral band (Spectral radiant existence $M\lambda$) for a given body is given by

$$M\lambda_{max} = \frac{Cl}{\lambda 5 e^{(C2/\lambda T\text{-}1)}}$$

Where, Cl - First radiation constant 3.74 × 10 - 16 *w/m*[2]
C2 - Second radiation constant $1.44 \times 10^{-2}$ mK

**EM Radiation and the Atmosphere**

All EM radiation (detected by the sensor from the object of interest) has to pass through atmosphere. The water vapor, oxygen, ozone, $CO_2$, aerosols present in the atmosphere influence EM radiation through the mechanism of scattering and absorption.

***Scattering***: It is unpredictable diffusion of radiation by particles present in the atmosphere. It reduces the image contrast and changes the spectral signature of ground objects. The atmospheric scattering can be categorised as:

| *Rayleigh's* | *Mie's* | *Non-Selective* |
|---|---|---|
| When diameter of molecules or particles is much less than wavelength of radiation $R_s \propto 1/\lambda^4$ Lesser the wavelength more is the scattering. Haze appears on the image. It causes a bluish grey cast on the image, thus reducing the contrast. | When diameter of molecules or particle approximately equals to wavelength of radiation, *e.g.* water vapour, dust particles $M_s \propto 1/\lambda^2$ | When diameter of particles is several times more than radiation wavelength, *e.g.* water droplets. Scatters all wavelengths of visible light with equal efficiency. It justifies the reason why cloud appears white in the image. |

***Absorption***: In contrast to scattering, atmospheric absorption results in the effective loss of energy as a consequence of the attenuating nature of atmospheric constituents *viz.* molecules of ozone, $CO_2$ and water vapor.

**Electromagnetic Radiation—Interaction Mechanism**

EM energy that encounters matter (Object) is called incident radiation. Interaction which can change following properties of incident radiation:

Intensity, Direction, Wavelength, Polarisation, Phase etc.

Energy balance equation for radiation at a given wavelength (J.) can be expressed as—

| EI | =ER | +EA | +ET |
|---|---|---|---|
| (Incident) | =Reflected | +Absorbed | +transmitted |

Proportion of each traction (ER/EA/ET) will vary for different materials depending upon composition and condition. Within a given feature type, these proportions vary at different wavelengths thus helping in discrimination of different objects.

***Spectral reflectance characteristics of earth's surface features*:** It can be quantified by the proportion of energy reflected (spectral reflectance) by features at different wavelengths. The spectral reflectance of an object is the ratios of ER (λ) and EI (λ).

A graph of spectral reflectance of an object as a function of wavelength is termed as spectral reflectance curve.

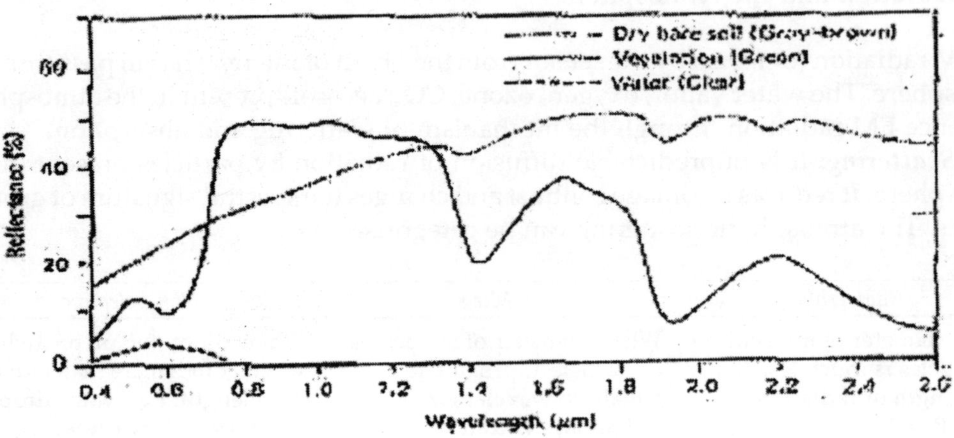


**Sensors**

***(a) Linear Imaging and Self-Scanning Sensor-I (LISS I)***

| | |
|---|---|
| Resolution | 72.5m |
| Band width (micro meter) | 0.45 - 0.52, 0.52 - 0.59, 0.62 - 0.68, 0.77 - 0.86 |
| Swath | 148 Km |
| Quantization level | 7 bit |

***(b) Linear Imaging and Self-Scanning Sensor-II (LISS II)***

| | |
|---|---|
| Resolution | 36.25 m |
| Band width (micro meter) | 0.45 - 0.52,0.52 - 0.59, 0.62 - 0.68, 0.77 - 0.86 |
| Swath | 74km |
| Quantization level | 7 bit |

***(c) Linear Imaging and Self-Scanning Sensor-III (LISS III)***

| | |
|---|---|
| Resolution | 23m |
| Band width (micro meter) | 0.52 - 0.59, 0.62 - 0.68, 0.77 - 0.86, 1.55 - 1.77 |
| Swath | 141 km |

| | |
|---|---|
| Quantization level | 7 bit |
| Signal to noise ratio | > 128 |

***(d) Panchromatic sensor (PAN) - This payload is on board IRS 1C and ID satellites***

| | |
|---|---|
| Resolution | 5.8m |
| Band width (micro meter) | 0.50 - 0.75 |
| Swath | 63 to 70 km |
| Quantization level | 6 bit |
| Steering | :t 26 degree |
| Signal to noise ratio | >64 |

***(e) Wide Field Sensor (WIFS)***

| | |
|---|---|
| Resolution | 188 m |
| Band width (micro meter) | 0.62 - 0.68, 0.77 - 0.86, 1.55 - 1.75 (Only in IRS P3) |
| Swath | 812 km |
| Quantization level | 7 bit |
| Signal to noise ratio | > 128 |

***(f) Modular Upto Electronic Scanner (MOS)***

| | |
|---|---|
| Resolution (Mas A + B + C) | 1569 × 1395m , 523 × 523m; 523 × 644 m |
| Bands | 4, 13,1 |
| Spectral range | 755 - 768, 408 - 1010, 1500 - 1700 |
| Swath | 195 km, 200 km, 192 km |

***(g) Ocean Color Monitor (OCM)***

| | |
|---|---|
| Resolution | 360 m across track and 236 m along track |
| Bands width (nano meter) | 402 - 422, 433 - 453, 480 - 500, 500 - 520, 545 - 565, 660 - 680, 745 - 785, 845 - 885 |
| Swath | 1420 Km. |
| Quantization level | 12 bits |
| Steering angle | + 20 degree |

**Resolution**

1. Spatial Resolution,
2. Temporal Resolution,
3. Spectral Resolution, and
4. Radiometric Resolution.

### *1. Spatial Resolution*

Is the resolving ability of a sensor that could separate the two objects on the ground by radiometrically. The radiometry of a satellite data system is dependent upon the ability of the optical system of a satellite and the amount of data that sensor system could store in the digital format. For example, an eight bit data can represents 256 gray levels! colours. Bit is a binary representation of zerøs and ones which is corresponding to absence and presence of data. The more the bits, the greater the gray levels.

### *2. Temporal Resolutions*

Recording the changes of a terrain at different periods of time, in which imageries of the area of interest were taken at different intervals of time.

### *3. Spectral Resolution*

Among the three kinds of the resolutions, spectral resolution is the most important in the image interpretation. The reflected! emitted radiation of the terrain is recorded on a specific bands, *i.e.* range of wave frequencies. Each one of these bands can transmit a particular frequency of electromagnetic radiation and can record a specific thematic information such as vegetation, soils, water bodies, geology etc. for example, band No. 4, which is a near infrared region, characteristics of maximum chlorophyll reflection and absorption by water bodies, hence facilitates the delineation of water bodies and land boundaries and also good for geological and geomorphological studies.

### *4. Ratiometric Resolution*

It characterizes the ability to distinguish the finer variation of the reflected for emitted radiation from different objects. It is represented by the number of levels which can be realized between minimum and maximum values of received radiation.

## Scanning Systems

***Cross-Track Scanning System***: The widely used cross-track scanning systems employ a faceted mirror that is rotated by an electric motor, with a horizontal axis of rotation aligned parallel with the flight direction. The mirror sweeps across the terrain in a pattern of parallel scan lines oriented normal (perpendicularly) to the flight direction. Energy radiated or reflected from the ground is focused onto the detector by secondary mirrors.

$$= \tan\left(\frac{\text{angular field of view}}{2}\right) \times \text{altitude} \quad (1.5)$$

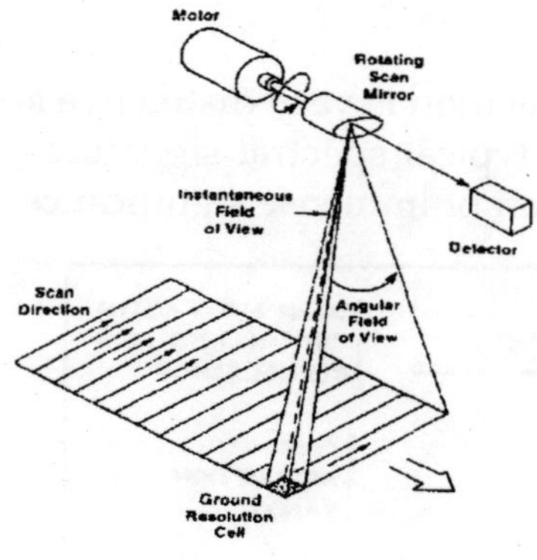


A. CROSS-TRACK SCANNER

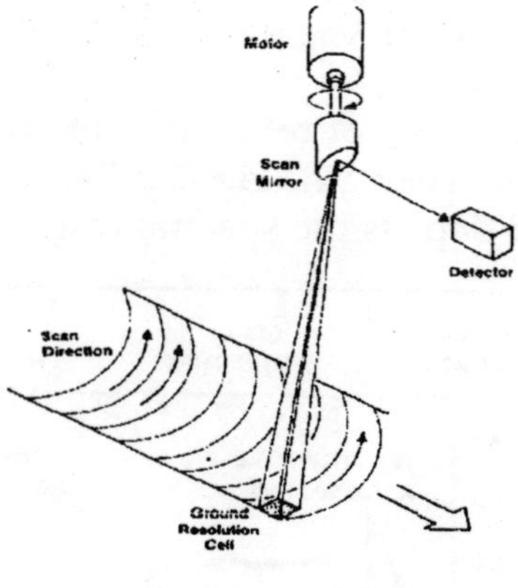


B. CIRCULAR SCANNER

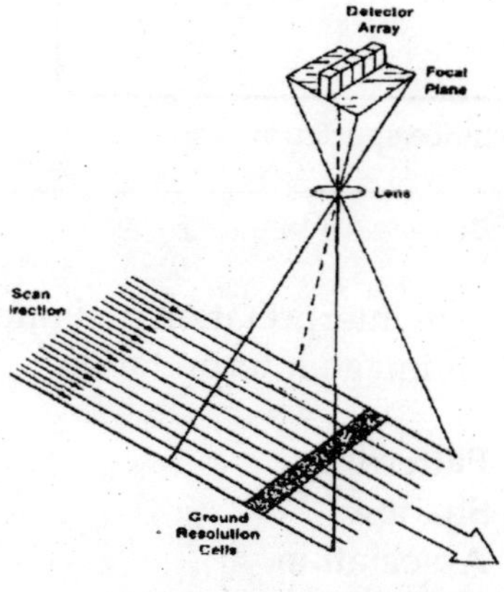


C. ALONG-TRACK SCANNER

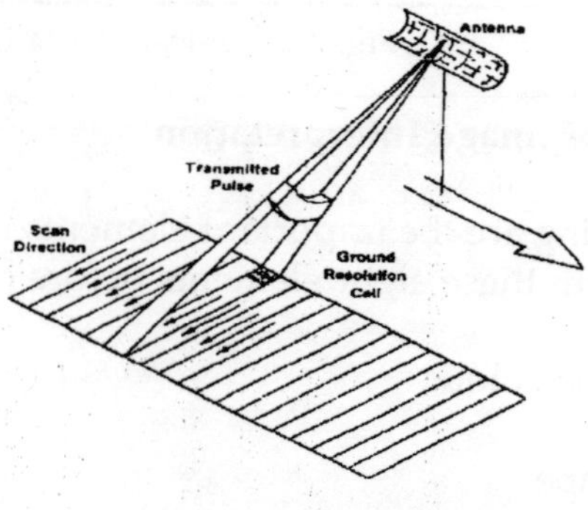


D. SIDE SCANNING SYSTEM

Scanning Systems for Acquiring Remote Sensing Images

## Spectral Signature

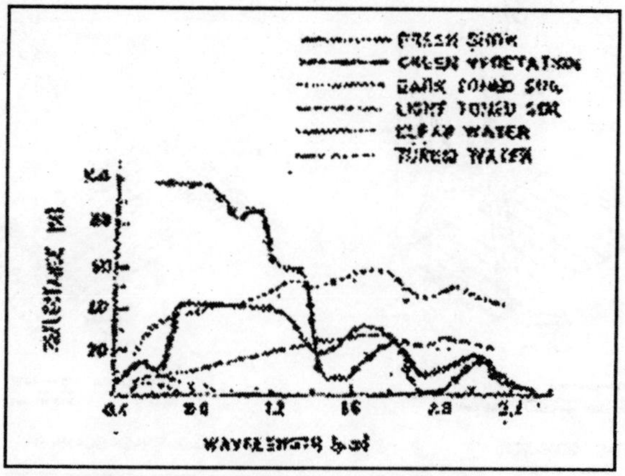

**Fig. 2.1:** Comparison of reflectance spectra of a few land covers

## Spectral Signature of Vegetation

The spectral signature of reflectance of green vegetation is very distinctive and quite variable with wavelength. Fig. 2.2 Represents a typical spectral signature of green vegetation and depicts the spectral response region of immense significance.

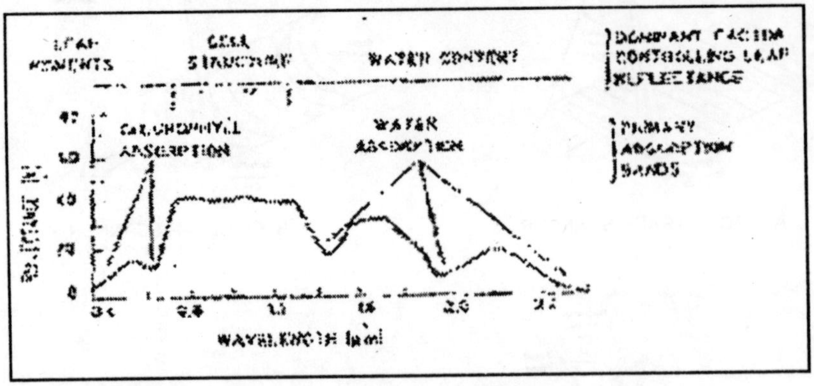

**Fig. 2.2:** Typical vegetation reflectance spectrum

## Elements of Image Interpretation

The following are the important elements in the image interpretation and one should familiar with these eight elements before starting an image interpretation.

(i) Tone/colour
(ii) Size
(iii) Shape
(iv) Texture
(v) Pattern
(vi) Shadow
(vii) Association
(viii) Site/Location

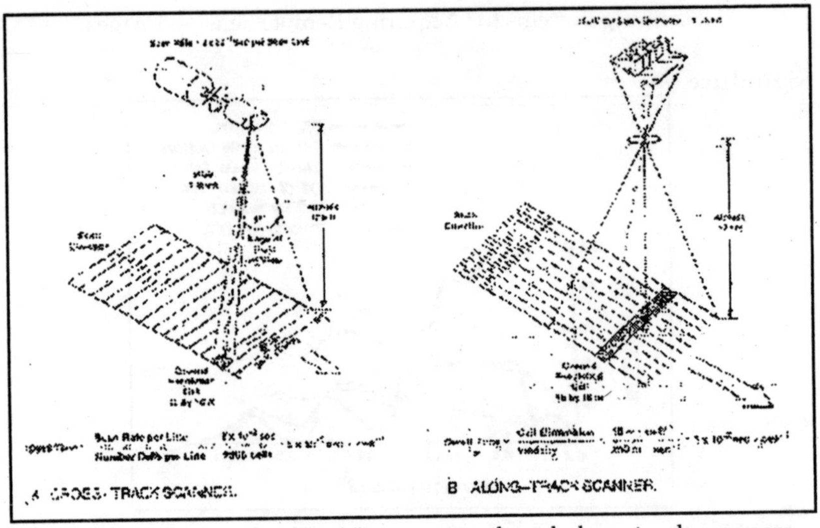

**Fig. 2.3:** Dwell time calculated for cross-track and along-track scanners

***Circular Scanning System:*** In a circular scanning system, the scan motor and mirror are mounted with a vertical axis of rotation that sweeps a circular path on the terrain. Only the forward portion of the sweep is recorded to produce images. An advantage of this system is that the distance between scanner and terrain is constant and all the ground resolution cells have the same dimensions. The major disadvantage is that most image processing and display systems are designed for linear scan data; therefore, the circular scan data must be extensively reformatted prior to processing.

***Along-Track Scanning System***: For scanner systems to achieve finer spatial and spectral resolution, the dwell time for each ground resolution cell must be increased. One method is to eliminate the scanning mirror and provide an individual detector for each ground resolution cell across the ground swath. The detectors are placed in a linear array in the focal plane of the image formed by a lens system.

***Side Scanning System***: The three types of scanners just described are passive systems, since they detect and record energy naturally reflected or radiated from the terrain. Active systems, which provide their own energy sources, operate primarily in the side-scanning mode. A radar system that transmits pulses of microwave energy to one side of the flight path (range direction) and records the energy scattered from the terrain back to the antenna. Another system is side-scanning sonar, which transmits pulses of sonic energy in the ocean to map bathymetric features.

# 3

# Application of Geo-Informatics in Urban and Regional Planning with Specific Reference to a Case Study

*Subhan K. Pathan*

## Introduction

Rapid urbanisation and consequent haphazard growth of cities is a global phenomenon and India is no exception. This is resulting in deterioration of loss of agricultural lands, open spaces, loss of water bodies, depletion of ground water aquifer zones, air pollution, water contamination, health hazards and many micro-climatic changes. It is, therefore, desirable to plan for the city and its region in an integrated manner so that in due course as the city grows the periphery can emerge into the whole. In doing so, one cannot only save a good amount of productive agricultural land but also avoid all natural hazards. In the preparation of environmentally compatible urban and regional plan, it is a prerequisite to understand linkages and interactions that exist between different components of the urban environment. Secondly, the data collected on different aspects of the urban environment has to be translated into useful information for the purpose of urban development. Thirdly, there is also a need to aggregate this information according to administrative/natural and hierarchical units. Basic caveat for this is the availability of systematic, detailed, reliable, timely and accurate information on various facets of urban environment. Experiences gained so far show certain shortcomings in regard to acquisition of statistics, processing, generation of graphic outputs and their storing in the existing conventional system. Such a lacuna impedes efficient and meaningful planning, implementation of programmes and their monitoring. Moreover, by the time the plan is made using conventional surveys, the data becomes old and the plan may not be suitable for implementation. It is in this context, the Orbital Remote Sensing (ORS) data and Geographic Information System (GIS) techniques play a major role by providing reliable, accurate, timely, periodic data and methods of integration of spatial and non-spatial data to create various planning scenarios for decision making. This type of planning scenarios helps planners and administrators to view various advantages and disadvantages of different perspectives and select best perspective for implementation and monitoring (Pathan *et al.*, 1987, 1991, 1993 and 1997).

In view of different advantages of Orbital Remote Sensing data and GIS techniques, a project on the preparation of "Development Plan of Indore for the year 2011" and "Perspective Plan of Indore Metropolitan Region for the year 2025 has been taken up by Space Applications Centre (SAC), ISRO, Ahmedabad jointly with Directorate of Town Planning Department, Bhopal, Indore Municipal Corporation (IMC), Indore Development Authority (IDA), Indore and Madhya Pradesh State Remote Sensing Applications Centre (MPRSAC), Bhopal.

## Objectives

The prime objective of the study is to prepare an environmental begin urban development plan for the city of Indore and its region. Hence the goals to formulate a plan is to focus on all physical, geographic, historic and cultural characteristics of the city and environs, harmonisation of sectorial development plans and evolve development portfolio on the basis of carrying capacity of the region. Therefore, the detailed objectives of the study are:

- To carry out a detailed analysis of Indore city and its environs in order to project the regional perspective of the region.
- To carry out demographic analysis for identifying areas required for future urban development.
- To prepare thematic maps, *viz.* urban land use, urban sprawl, surface water bodies, hydrogeomorphological, ground water prospects, slope, flood, erosion, earthquake hazards and transportation network maps.
- To carry out the suitability analysis and environmental sensitivity with the help of multivariate analysis.
- To prepare regional and development plans for the city of Indore.

## Study Area

Development of a metropolis influences not only the surrounding urban fringe but in a wider sense it affects the regional and subregional activities and economy. The productivity of the region and subregion strengthen the economy of the metropolis and as a result, structure of the urban centre develop and provide the opportunities for increasing employment, specialised services and facilities. Hence, it is evident that planning for an urban area cannot be considered in isolation and the physical development should go hand in hand to match the changing demands and pattern of activities and functions.

Indore, the premier city of Madhya Pradesh and Divisional Head Quarter, is situated almost centrally on the fertile Malwa with its cardinal points 22°43′N latitude and 76°42′E longitude with an altitude of 1805 feet above mean sea level. It is the largest city of "Indore Agro-Industrial Region" consists of seven districts, *viz.* Indore,

Ujjain, Dewas, Ratlam, Mandsaur, Dhar and Jhabua. Since ancient times the city occupies an important place in the trade and commerce of the Central India. The former Holkar state established a custom free zone at Indore which strengthened economic linkages of the city with neighbouring states at Dewas, Gwalior etc. Its Regional road pattern fans out in all directions. The city is, served by a broad gauge and metre gauge railway line.

The city occupies relatively plain having a very gentle slope towards North. Hinterland of the city is also flat but dotted with some hillocks like Bijasan, Gadha Tekri, Bhuri Tekri, Deoguradia and depression at Sirpur Tank. Thee are no physical constrains except Pipaliyapala Tank on the South-Eastern side and Sirpur Tank in the South-West which will limit the growth of the city. The drainage of the city is provided by two small rivers, Khan and Saraswati. Khan river, a tributary of Kshipra rises near Umaria village about 11 km south of Indore and flows through the heart of the city. It has been dammed near the Navlakha Garden, where it intersects the Agra-Bombay Road, (NH-3). Further three km down, it is joined by the Saraswati, a small stream which rises near Machla village. The heart of the city, known as Rajwada area is located near the confluence (at Krishnapura Bridge). The preparation of development plan of the city not only depend on the problems of the city but also the acute problems in its hinterland. Hence, the entire Indore Planning area (about 650 sq. km) has selected for the study.

## Data Used

Indian Remote Sensing Satellite LISS-III and Panchromatic data of multidate along with collateral data has been primarily used for the preparation of thematic maps. Multi-date satellite data has been used for the preparation of urban sprawl map.

## Methodology

Population data pertaining to 1971, 1981 and 1991 census have been collected and population projections for the year 2011 have been made by adopting standard statistical techniques such as Ratio method, exponential and conversion methods. Further, the entire area is divided into different groups of villages envisaging high, medium and low growth rates. Population projections under each scenario are made by analyzing the observed trends from the year 1971, 1981 and 1991. The projections obtained geometrical method has been adopted for the study.

The total study area is covered in 9 SOI topographic maps at 1:50,000 scale. Though the extent of the area is partial in some of the toposheets, a standard registration procedure has been adopted. IRS-1C merged (LISS-III with PAN) data products were generated by taking intensity from Panchromatic data, hue and saturation from LISS-III data (Figure 3.1). Various enhanced techniques have been applied to improve the contrast between the features on this merged data. Visual interpretation techniques were used to prepare various thematic maps on the basis of the image characteristics. Land use classification developed by Anderson (Anderson *et al.*, 1976) has been modified to suit with the Indore Planning area.

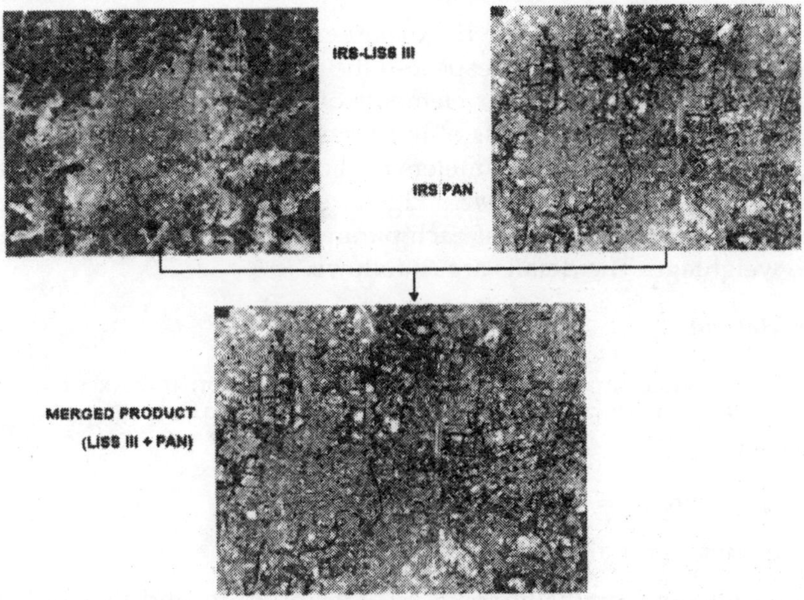


**Fig. 3.1:** IRS-1C Merged Data Product

A spatial framework has been created by dividing the entire area into 5′ × 5′ graticule (network of latitude and longitudes) grids to capture thematic maps in GIS environment. A composite urban land development unit map has been prepared by using integration analysis. A multivariate weighted index approach has been followed to identify the area for construction and conservation activities. The details of this method are as under.

### *Urban Land Use Suitability Analysis*

One of the classic problems in decision theory or multi-parameter analysis (Urban land use survey handbook, 1987) is the determination of the relative importance (weights) of each parameter with respect to the other. This is a problem which requires human judgement supplemented by mathematical tools. As all parameters of the land cannot be weighted equal for the suitability assessment, it is essential that a weighted method needs to be employed where the relative importance of the parameters defines the weightage. A number of methods are available to deal with such problems. Saaty's analytic hierarchy process (Saaty, T.L., 1980) is a most-widely accepted method for scaling the weights of parameter by constructing a pair-wise comparison matrix of parameters whose entries indicate the strength with which one element dominates over another *vis-a-vis* the relative criterion. The pair-wise comparison of parameters results into the "importance matrix" which is based on a scale of important intensities and is generated by a group of experts.

The importance matrix for eleven physical paramters was generated based on Saaty's guidelines. The importance level has been assigned based on the consensus reached through discussion and also the experience of town planning officials. The importance of each parameter with respect to the other parameter is determined and generated a 11 * 11 matrix. The other elements of the matrix are determined by the reciprocality of the matrix. Four types of importance matrices were generated based upon giving important different parameters in each matrix. The importance matrices were analysed using two methods *viz.* "Eigen vector" method and "Least square" method to arrive at the weightages of each parameter and nullify the biasness while assessing the weightage. The details are as follows.

### *Eigen Vector Method*

In this method the basic input is the pair-wise comparison matrix of n parameters constructed based on the Saaty's scaling ratios, which could be of the order (n × n), and is in the form of:

$$A = [aij], \text{ where } i, j = 1, 2, 3..., n \qquad (1)$$

Where aij = wi/wj for all i and j.

The matrix A has generally the property of reciprocality and also the consistency. This is, mathematically,

$$aij = 1/aji, \qquad (2)$$

and

$$aij = aik/ajk \text{ for any } i, j \text{ and } k. \qquad (3)$$

Thus, multiplying equation (1) with the weighting vector – W of (n × 1) size yields

$$(A - nI)\,W = 0 \qquad (4)$$

Where I is an identity matrix of (n × n). According to the matrix theory if the comparison matrix A has the property of consistency, the system of equations has a trivial solution. The matrix A is, however, a judgment matrix and it may not be possible to determine the elements of A accuracy to satisfy the property of consistency. Therefore, it is estimated by a set of linear homogeneous equations:

$$A^*\,W^* = \text{max}W^* \qquad (5)$$

Where A* is the estimate of A and W* is the corresponding priority vector and max is the largest eigen value for the matrix A. The equation no. 5 yields the weightages W which are normalised to unity for further purposes.

### *Least Square Method*

Another method for determining weightage of parameter is the weighted least square method is proposed by Chu *et al.* This method involves the formation of constrained optimisation problem and solving for the weighting vector-W. Consider the elements aij of Saaty's importance matrix. It is desired to determine weights, wi such that for a given aij,

aij = Wi/Wj, for all i and j.

These weights can be obtained by solving the constrained optimisation problem:

n n
Min. z = ä ä (aij Wj – Wi)2
i = 1 j = 1

n
such that ä Wi = 1
i = n

and additionally each

Wi > = 0 for all i = 1, 2, ... n.

For minimising z, the Lagrangian function L is formed as follows:

n n n
L = [ä ä (aij Wj – Wi)2 + 2 (ä Wi – 1)
i = 1 j = 1 i = 1

where 'L' is the Lagrangian multiplier. Differentiating equation 12 with respect to W1 and solving the resulting set of linear equations yield the weightages for different parameters.

Applying the above two methods, the actual weightages are derived for the said parameters. However, the weightages derived using the eigen vector method has been adopted for land use suitability analysis and rare presented Table 3.1.

**Table 3.1:** Weightages Derived for the Eleven Parameters

| *No.* | *Parameters* | *M-1* | *M-2* | *M-3* | *M-4* |
|---|---|---|---|---|---|
| 1. | Soil depth | 0.058 | 0.235 | 0.150 | 0.100 |
| 2. | Soil Texture | 0.047 | 0.068 | 0.068 | 0.068 |
| 3. | Slope | 0.132 | 0.150 | 0.090 | 0.090 |
| 4. | Flood hazard | 0.092 | 0.113 | 0.090 | 0.090 |
| 5. | Water bodies | 0.135 | 0.076 | 0.076 | 0.076 |
| 6. | Land use/cover | 0.100 | 0.068 | 0.100 | 0.200 |
| 7. | Ground water prospects | 0.068 | 0.146 | 0.100 | 0.100 |
| 8. | Earthquake | 0.085 | 0.053 | 0.103 | 0.103 |
| 9. | Road network | 0.135 | 0.024 | 0.150 | 0.010 |
| 10. | Railway station | 0.055 | 0.017 | 0.027 | 0.027 |
| 11. | Land values | 0.100 | 0.100 | 0.050 | 0.050 |

Model-1 (M-1): Road network and Waterbody/watershed buffer parameters have been given more importance,
Model-2 (M-2): Slope Road network and soil depth have been given more importance,
Modal-3 (M-3): Road network and soil depth have been given more importance, and
Model-4 (M-4): Land use have been given more importance.

After determining the weightages for the parameters, a rank to each category for all the parameters has been assigned. The ranks to the individual categories are assigned in such a way that higher the rank, higher is the suitability and lesser are the limitations. Lower is the rank, lower the priority for urbanisation and higher are the limitations for development. So, the categories of parameters considered for suitability are studied carefully and arranged in four ranges for the assignment of ranks. Urban land use suitability indices have been obtained by multiplying weightages with rank numbers of each category and by summing up the values of all categories. The entire area is then evaluated with respect to environmental sensitivity analysis. The details of this analysis is summarized below.

### *Environmental Sensitivity Analysis*

The data on air quality (RPM, $NO_x$, $SO_2$, SPM), ground water quality (pH, Coliform, Nitrate, BOD and TDS) and surface water quality (pH, Coliform, Nitrate, Ammonia, TKN, DO, BOD and TDS) has been collected from 31 stations well distributed through out the study area.

The location of 31 observation points has been digitized in GIS environment and integrated air and water quality data to these stations. Then a surface analysis has been carried out using TIN analysis techniques. From the surface analysis, each parameter has been classified into three ranges and assigned a rank depending upon its sensitivity to the environment (Table 3.2).

**Table 3.2:** Criteria Table for Defining Rank

| *No. Parameters* | *Range of Value Defining* | | |
|---|---|---|---|
| | *Rank-1* | *Rank-2* | *Rank-3* |
| **Air Quality** | High | Medium | Low |
| 1. RPM | 0-100 | 100-150 | 150-1200 |
| 2. $NO_x$ | 0-15 | 15-20 | 20-60 |
| 3 $SO_2$ | 0-15 | 15-25 | 25-60 |
| 4. SPM | 0-100 | 200-350 | 350-1200 |
| **GW Quality** | High | Medium | Low |
| 1. pH | <6.5 | 6.5-8.5 | >8.5 |
| 2. Coliform | 6-7 | 7-8 | 8-12 |
| 3. Nitrate | 0-4 | 4-10 | >10 |
| 4. BOD | 0-1 | 1-2 | >2 |
| 5. TDS | 0-500 | 500-2000 | >2000 |
| **SW Quality** | High | Medium | Low |
| 1. pH | 7-8 | 8-8.5 | 8.5-9.5 |
| 2. Coliform | 0-50 | 50-500 | >500 |
| 3. Nitrate | 0-5 | 5-10 | 10-100 |
| 4. Ammonia | 0-1 | 1-1.5 | 1.5-12 |
| 5. TKN | 0-3 | 3-10 | 10-33 |
| 6. DO | 8-6 | 6-4 | <4 |
| 7. BOD | 0-2 | 2-10 | >10 |
| 8. TDS | 0-500 | 500-2000 | >2000 |

Indices for each parameter has been generated by multiplying individual category ranks. Higher the index value lower the quality. The details are as under.

Air Quality Index (AQI) = $RPM_{rank}$ $*NO_{x\ rank}$ $*\ SO_{2\ rank}$ $*SPM_{rank}$

Ground Water Quality Index (GQI) = $pH_{rank}$ $*Coliform_{rank}$ $*Nitrate_{rank}$ $*BOD_{rank}$ $*TDS_{rank}$

Surface water Quality Index (SQI) = $pH_{rank}$ $*Coliform_{rank}$ $*Nitrate_{rank}$ $*BOD_{rank}$ $*TDS_{rank}$

Integrated all three air, ground water and surface water quality layers in GIS. Environmental Sensitivity has been calculated by multiplying the each parameter quality index with another.

Environment Sensitivity Index (ESI) $AQI_{rank}$ $*GQI_{rank}$ $*SQI_{rank}$

This environment sensitivity index (ESI) has been classified into three categories High, Medium and Low to represent environment sensitivity zones.

### *Integrated Analysis*

An integrated analysis to find out the final suitability of land for urbanization has been carried out by union of urban suitability layer with environment sensitivity layer. After critically evaluating each composite unit, the area has been divided into four classes. The first two suitability classes are suggested for urban development and the rest are suggested for conservation under greenbelt. On the basis of four suitability classes, the extent and spatial distribution of existing land use pattern, urban sprawl, socio-economic constraints, infrastructural facilities, financial allocations etc. the development plan is prepared.

## Results

### *Population Changes in Study Area*

The study of demographic pattern plays a major role in the preparation of sustainable urban development plan. This type of study helps to assess the past and present growth trends and to estimate the future growth. The knowledge of basic demographic trend, in the area to be planned, is very essential to perceive the problems and exact needs of the area. It gives the idea about living conditions of the people and their immediate needs of basic amenities which planner should attend while preparing development plan. Therefore, the analysis of demographic factors in relation to various urban functions facilitate the requirement or need for housing, industry, commerce, amenities and recreation.

### *Growth of Population*

The population data collected from the year 1971 to 2001 census has been studied critically and is presented in Table 3.3.

**Table 3.3:** Population and Growth Rate of Indore Planning Area

| *Year* | *Indore Municipal Corporation* | | *Indore Planning Area* | |
|---|---|---|---|---|
| | *Population* | *Growth rate in per cent* | *Population* | *Growth rate in per cent* |
| 1971 | 537000 | | 646744 | |
| 1981 | 829327 | 54.44 | 949921 | 46.87 |
| 1991 | 1091618 | 31.63 | 1271218 | 33.82 |
| 2001 | 1626297 | 48.98 | 1893865 | 48.98 |

It has been observed from the above table that he percentage increase of population in 1981, over population of 1971 was 46.87 per cent. The population growth from 1981 to 1991 has observed as 33.82 per cent and between 1991 to 2001 as 44.98 per cent. It has also been observed from these figures that increase in population of 1991-2001 was tremendous. The high rate of growth of population during this period is mainly attributable to the rapid industrial and commercial development in Indore planning area.

### *Population Projection for the 2011*

The population projections for the Indore Planning Area up to the year 2011 were made on the basis of different standard statistical procedures such as Arithmetic, Geometric and Incremental increase methods. The projections obtained from geometric method were adopted for the study to calculate the additional requirements of land for the year 2011. It has been observed that the population of Indore city is likely to be about 27.12 lakh by 2011.

Migration is also an important and a dynamic factor in projecting the future population. However, there are no figures, which can suggest the migration rate or its pattern. But there are enough evidences to show that migration is indeed a very important criteria for projecting the population. Many people from small to medium towns come to Indore. Moreover, people from one area cross over to another area in the same city due to Indore. Moreover, people from one area cross over to another area in the same city due to many reasons. Though these are not seen in overall figures, but have a major effect on the housing and residential patterns of the city. Such micro level changes and habits have not been taken into consideration as the figures of growth of population incorporate these figures.

### Population Density

The population density of the Indore Planning Area as per 2001 census is as high as 2109 persons per sq. km. particularly in the CBD area. This figure is too high even when compared to the population density figures of other cities in Madhya Pradesh State and Indore District. Spatial distribution of population density of Indore city, ward-wise has been studied. It has been observed that the density is ranging from a meagre 100 persons/ha in the peripheral areas to as high as 2000 persons per ha in the core of the city. Therefore, there is tremendous pressure on the existing land and needs to be regularised in the development plan.

### *Urban Sprawl Analysis*

The history of spatial expansion (physical growth) of a city could be explained in terms of waves of urban growth. The magnitude and direction of waves depends upon various exogenous and endogenous factors (Geddes, Patrick, 1915). The physical growth of Indore city from the year 1975 to 2000 has been studied with the help of multidate remote sensing data, *viz.* IRS LISS-II, IRS LISS-III and IRS PAN data employing both visual and digital techniques and with limited field checks.

Urban sprawl map of Indore city was prepared using Survey of India topographical maps and multi-date remote sensing data. This map depicts details on physical growth of the city and direction of growth. It has been observed that the rate of the growth of the city was higher during the period 1996-2000 compared to the growth rates during the period 1991-1996. The average annual growth rate from 1996 to 2000 is 40.52 per cent. Spatial distribution of urban sprawl is shown in Figure 3.2.

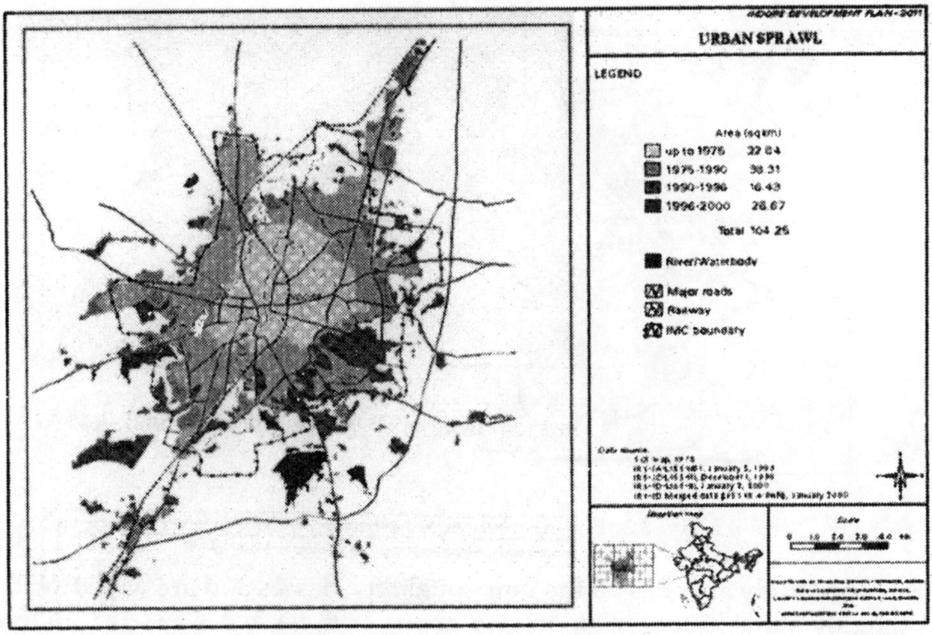


**Fig. 3.2:** Urban Sprawl Map of Indore City

### *Determination of Area Required for Urban Development*

The actual population for the year 2001 was collected from Indore Municipal Corporation, Indore and calculated the additional population for the year 2011. It has been observed that the difference in the population between 2001 and 2011 is about 6 lakh. On the basis of 100 persons per hectare, the requirement of additional area for the year 2011 has been determined. As per the calculation the additional area required for urban development for the year 2011 is about 5000 ha. To meet the additional demand, an integrated analysis has been carried out as per the procedure mentioned in methodology.

### *Urban Land Use Suitability*

The urban land use suitability maps prepared using four different models along with environmental sensitivity areas (Figure 3.3) in the entire Indore Planning Area were discussed with government officials and local corporators of Indore Municipal Corporation along with important personalities of the city. Model-1 mentioned in the methodology has been taken up as the final suitability (Figure 3.4) and adopted for land use allocations. The observations made from this map are as under.

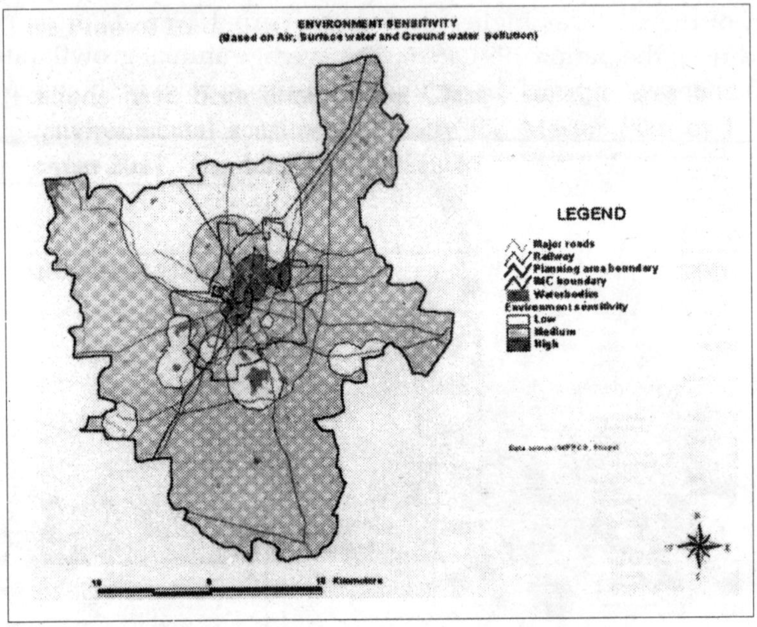


**Fig. 3.3:** Environmental Sensitivity Areas

The entire study area has all the four suitability classes and are well distributed. Class-I (Highly suitable) cover an area of about 4996 ha and Class-II (Moderately suitable) cover an area of about 25020 ha area. Areas under class-III (Less suitable) is about 38653 ha and constitutes the areas where there is poor accessibility, good ground water prospects and natural hazards such as erosion, earthquake, flooding etc. Class-IV is about 6024 ha and the area has productive agricultural lands away from the IMC with very poor accessibility and good ground water potential. Hence, Class-III and ClassIV have been strictly identified for conservation purpose.

## Land Use Plan of Indore City

Land use allocations have been done taking Class-I suitable area both in terms of urban suitability and environmental sensitivity. Finally, the Master Plan of Indore city has been prepared for the year 2011. The details are presented in Figure 3.5.

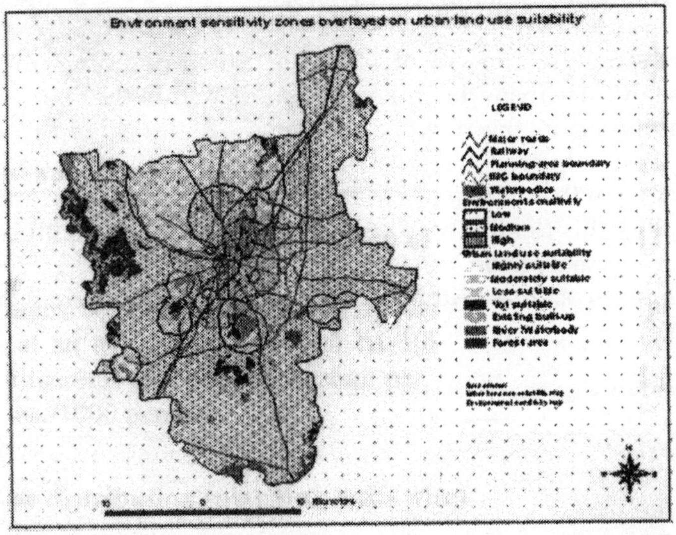


**Fig. 3.4:** Urban Land Use Suitability (Physical parameters versus Environment sensitivity zones)

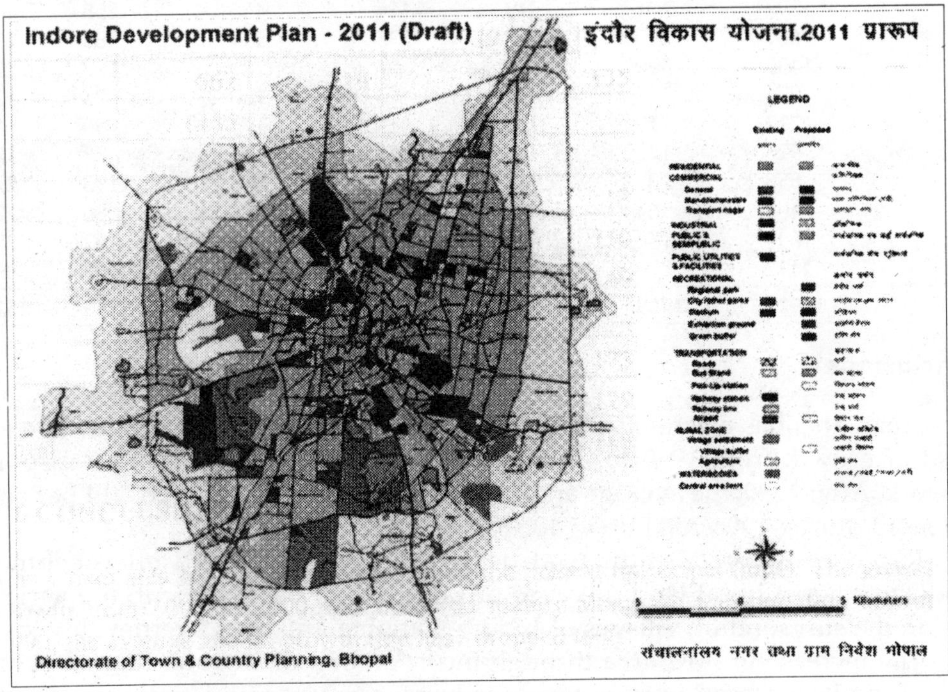


**Fig. 3.5:** Master Plan of Indore City—2011

The plan envisages compact development of planning units. It is proposed to develop the planning units at an average rate of 10.0 ha./1000 person. In Development Plan-1991 the average land utilization rate was 9.7 hectare per 1000 persons and present land utilization rate is only 6.0 ha./1000 persons.

### *Land Use Distribution (Planning Units-Wise)*

The overall city structure consists of 11 reconstituted planning units. Each planning unit derives its land-use from the linkage it builds within the framework of total land use pattern envisaged in the development plan. At the time of demarcation, road alignment may be readjusted and uses on either side of the proposed road alignment will be irrespective of the ownership of land and land use will be as it is shown in this plan conceptually. This flexibility is kept due to practical difficulties and economical alignment of roads based on detailed physical survey for implementation. The proposed distribution of areas within each planning unit in different land use categories is given in Table 3.4.

**Table 3.4:** Land Allocation at Planning Unit Level (Area in Hectare)

| *Planning Unit to* | *Residential* | *Comm. Utilities* | *PSP and Utilities* | *Industrial* | *Transportation* | *Recreational* | *Total* |
|---|---|---|---|---|---|---|---|
| (1) | (2) | (3) | (4) | (5) | (6) | (7) | (8) |
| 1. | 310 | 89 | 72 | 3 | 260 | 40 | 826 |
| 2. | 1799 | 101 | 49 | 1416 | 456 | 258 | 4034 |
| 3. | 662 | 210 | 79 | 135 | 499 | 62 | 1366 |
| 4. | 1455 | 399 | 108 | --- | 229 | 127 | 2565 |
| 5. | 974 | 39 | 73 | --- | 140 | 23 | 1277 |
| 6. | 712 | 19 | 335 | 13 | 175 | 100 | 1309 |
| 7. | 928 | 125 | 81 | 250 | 94 | 73 | 1703 |
| 8. | 558 | 231 | 337 | 49 | 468 | 1195 | 2710 |
| 9. | 401 | 64 | 41 | --- | 106 | 86 | 712 |
| 10. | 1694 | 156 | 203 | 173 | 278 | 162 | 2808 |
| 11. | 2432 | 276 | 539 | 129 | 919 | 993 | 5908 |
| **Total** | **11925** | **1709** | **1917** | **2168** | **4380** | **3119** | **25218** |

## Conclusions

The Urban area has extended well beyond the present municipal limits. The general trend of growth from 1990 to 2000 was observed mainly along the transportation network. After 1990, the average annual growth rate has dropped to 7.14 per cent, but increased during 1996-2000 up to 40.58 per cent.

Rapid commercial/industrial development has caused encroachment on productive agricultural land. Because of rapid urban development, the agricultural land in the surrounding villages of Indore Planning area was irretrievably lost.

The increase in IMC area through incorporation of surrounding rural areas in the IMC limits has been a process and can be seen as an administrative response to an essentially economic phenomenon.

The existing built-up area (as on 2001) with respect to the total area of each village in Indore planning area has been studied and the net area available for development in each village has been calculated. Additional area required for urban development for the year 2011 has been determined on the basis of population trends, distribution, density and the net area available in each village for development. The projected population of the year 2011 will be 27,12,528. Thee will be an increase of about 8.18 lakh population by the year 2011. A population density of 150 persons/ha (carrying capacity of the region) has been considered for calculating the area required for urbanisation. It works out to about 5457 ha area. It means that an area of about 5457 ha additional area is required for urban development to meet the demands up to the year 2011. It is observed that the highly suitable area in Indore planning area is 4996 ha and moderately suitable area is 25020 ha.

RS and GIS techniques based approaches have improved the preparation of development plans of Town Planning Department of Government of Madhya Pradesh. The information system created using RS and GIS based methodologies has facilitated working out sustainability of urban environment and generating alternate planning scenarios. The information system has flexibility to accommodate any new data and provides integration as well as updation. It allows aggregating the information at any level, *i.e.* Development authority of Regional level. The planning departments are planning to use land use, urban sprawl and urban land use suitability information while issuing permissions for urban development as well as maintain the sustainability of land through time.

## REFERENCES


Anderson, J.R., Hardy, E.E., Roach, J.T. and Witmer, R.E., 1976. A Land Use and Land Cover Classification System for Use with Remote Sensor Data: Geol. Survey Professional Paper 964, p. 28, USGS Publication, Virginia.

Geddes, Patrick, 1915. "Cities in Evolution", Williams and Nergate Limited, London.

Pathan *et al.*, 1997, "Revised Development Plan of Ahmedabad Urban Development Authority Area—2011, Volume 1: Remote Sensing and GIS Approach", Technical Report No. SAC/RSAG/TR/12/August, p. 176.

Pathan, S.K., *et al.*, 1989. "Urban Land Use Mapping and Zoning of Bombay Metropolitan Region Using Remote Sensing Data", *Photonirvachak,* Journal of Indian Society of Remote Sensing, Vol. 17, No. 13, Dehradun, India, pp. 11-22.

Pathan, S.K., Shukla, V.K., Patel, R.G., Patel B.R. and Mehta, K.S., 1991. Urban Landuse Mapping: A Case Study of Ahmedabad City and Its Environs, *Photonirvachak,* Journal in Indian Society of Remote Sensing, Vol. 19, No. 2, 1991, pp. 95-112.

Pathan, S.K., Navalgund, R.R. and Pramod Kale, "Potential of GIS Network for Perspective Planning—A Case Study", Proc. of Western Regional Convention 93, Computer Society of India, December 1993.

Saaty, T.L., *The Analytic Hierarchy Process.* A McGraw Hill, New York Publication of 1980.

*Urban Land Use Survey Handbook, 1987.* Water and Soil Miscellaneous Publication No. 105, Wellington, New Zealand.

## ANNEXURE

### GIS Basics and Applications

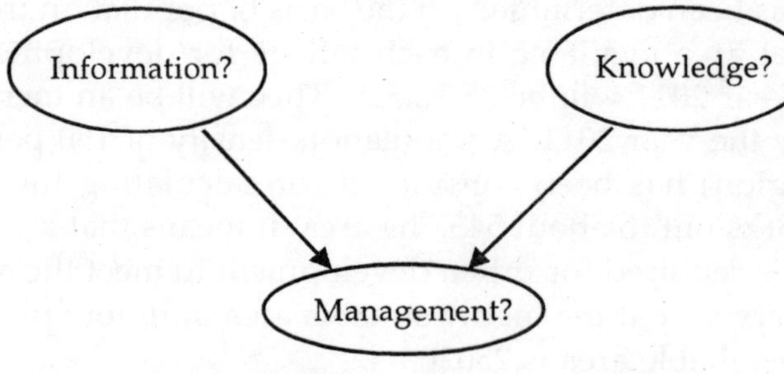


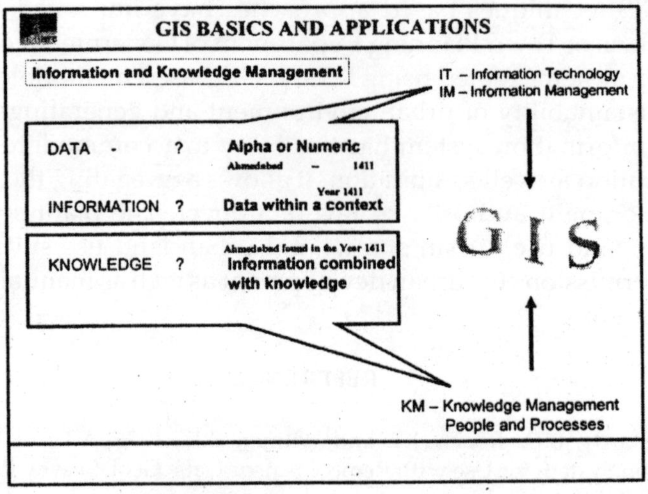


### Geographic Information System (GIS)

- Geo-Information System
- Geologic Information System
- Geo-data Information Systems
- Geo Spatial Information System

→ Geography — **GIS**

### GIS

- A Geographic Information System uses geographically referenced data as well as non-spatial data and includes operations which support spatial analysis.
- In GIS, the common purpose is decision-making, for managing use of land, resources, transportation, retailing, oceans or any spatially distributed entities.
- The connection between the elements of the system is geography, *e.g.* location, proximity, spatial distribution.

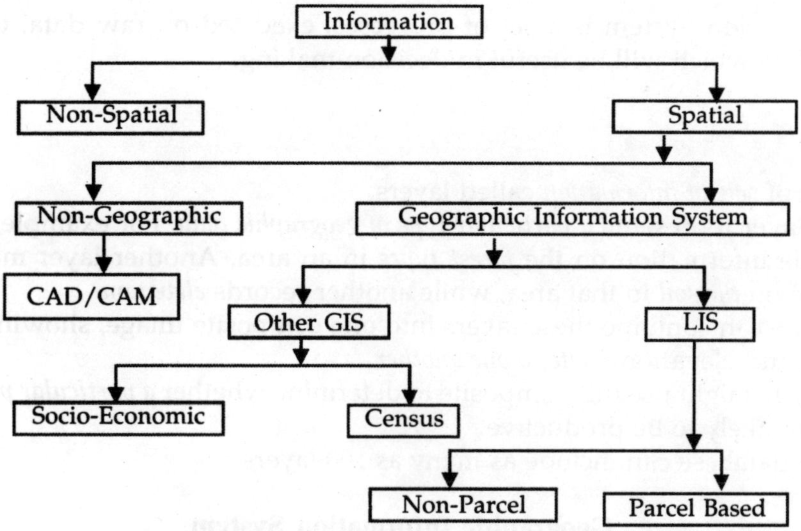


**Taxonomy of Information System**

**GEOGRAPHIC INFORMATION**

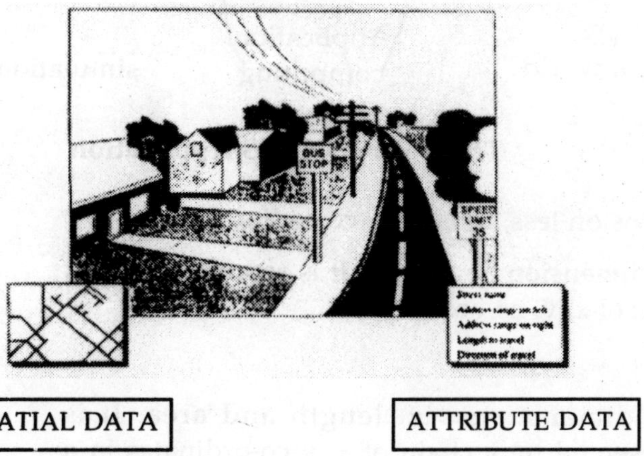


## Geographic Information System

- A particular form of Information System applied to geographical data
- A System is a group of connected entities and activities which interact for a common purpose:

  For ex.: A car is a system in which all the components operate together to provide transportation.

- An Information System is a set of processes, executed on raw data, to produce information which will be useful in decision-making.

## GIS

GIS consist of *sets of information* called layers.

Each layer represents a *particular type of geographic data.* For example, one layer may include information on the *forest types* in an area. Another layer may contain information on *the soil* in that area, while another records *elevation.*

The GIS can combine these layers into one composite image, showing how the forest, soil, and elevation *relate to one another.*

Foresters might use this composite to determine whether *a particular patch* of this area is more likely to be productive.

A GIS database can include as many as 100 layers.

**Geographic Information System**

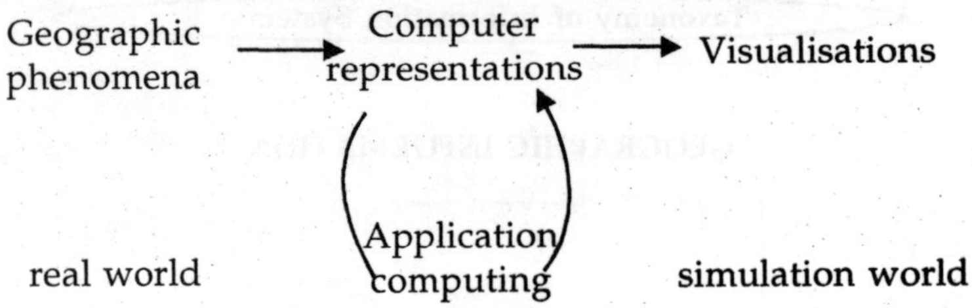


**Three Ways of GIS Application**

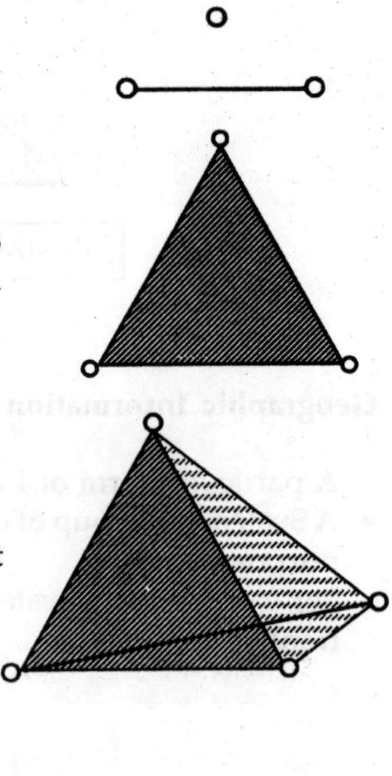

**Point** Dimension less, it has x, y co-ordinates only.

**Line** One dimension *i.e.* length. It is represented by a Chain of x, y, co-ordinates.

**Polygon** Two dimensions viz. length and area. It is represented by a chain of x, y co-ordinates in a closed loop.

**Surface** Three dimensions *i.e.* length, area and volume. It is represented by x, y and z co-ordinates.

**2-D GIS :** Representation of x, y co-ordinates of the surface.

**2.5-D GIS:** Representation of x, y and 'z' co-ordinates of the surface (z value at a given point).

**3-D GIS:** Representation of x, y and 'z' co-ordinates of the surface in all directions (Cuboidal structure)

**3.5-D GIS:** Representation of x, y, z co-ordinates of the surface along with time.

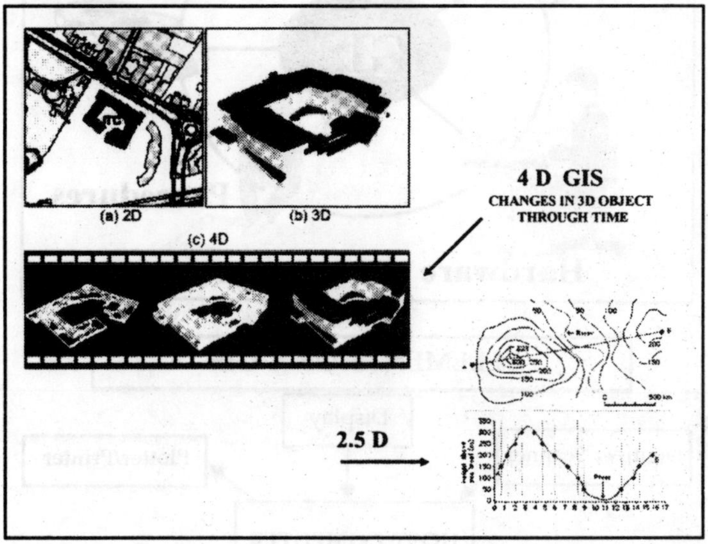


## Geographic Information System (GIS)

It is an automated tool to ......

- Capture
- Storage
- Retrieve
- Manipulate (Integration)
- Both spatial and aspatial data
- To create various planning scenarios
- For decision making

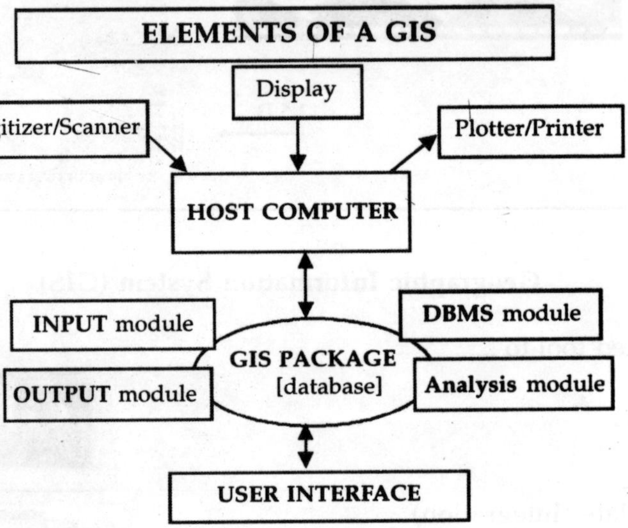


**What is a Map?**

"A map is a selective, symbolised and collective picture of some spatial distribution of earth's surface as seen from about at a reduced scale."

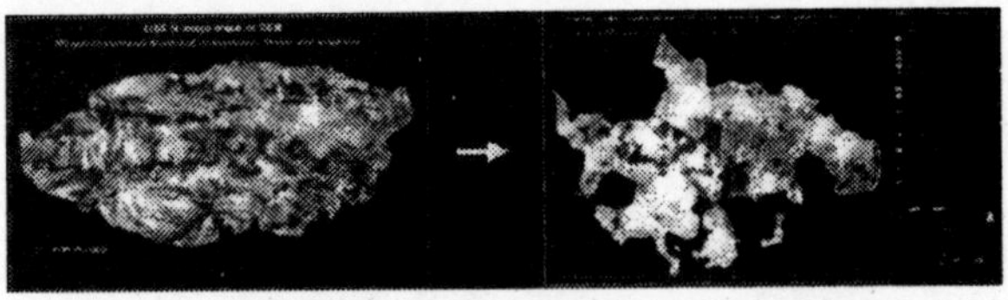

- Subjective abstraction of some real world features
- Communicates locational and descriptive information
- Portrays spatial relationships

**GIS: Thematic maps in GIS**

Several types of thematic map are important in GIS:

A choropleth map uses reporting zones such as countries or census tracts to show data such as average incomes, per cent female, or rates of mortality.

— the boundaries of the zones are established independently of the data, and may be used to report many different sets of data

An area class map shows zones of constant attributes, such as vegetation, soil type, or forest species

— the boundaries are different for each map as they are determined by the variation of the attribute being mapped, *e.g.* breaks of soil type may occur independently of breaks of vegetation

An isopleth map shows an imaginary surface by means of lines joining points of equal value, "isolines" (*e.g.* contours on a topographic map)

— used for phenomena which vary smoothly across the map, such as temperature, pressure, rainfall or population density

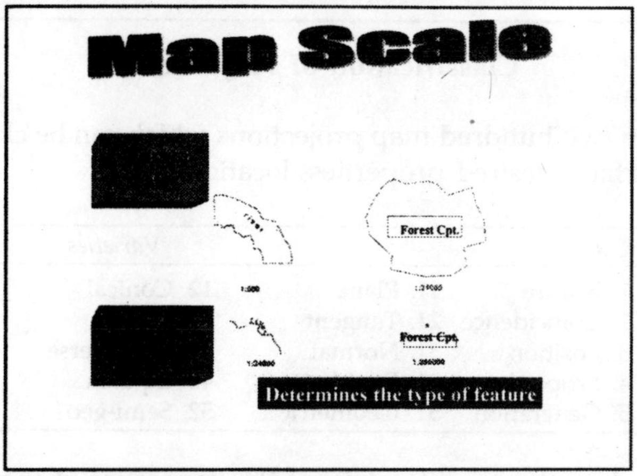


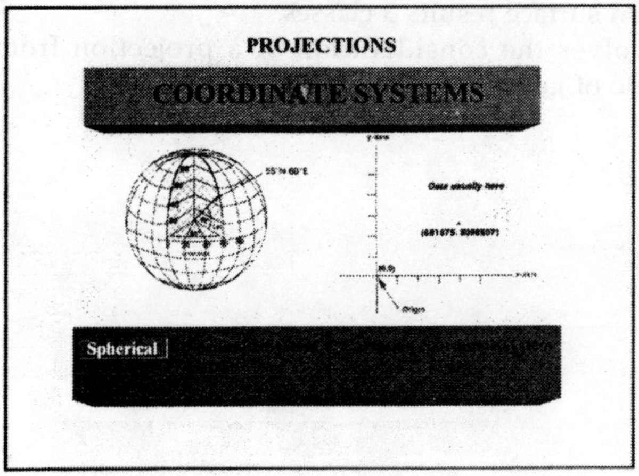

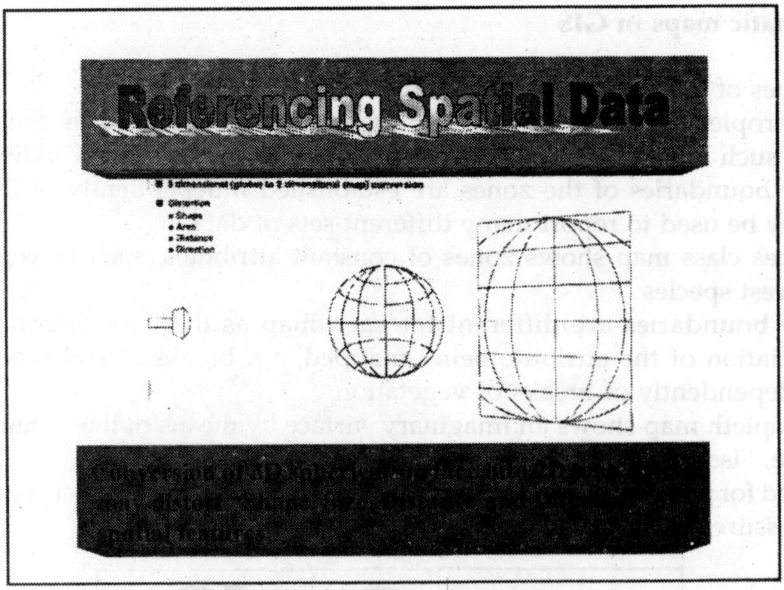


## Classification of Projections

There are more than two hundred map projections which can be classified depending upon projection surface, desired properties, location etc.

| *Projection* | *Class* | | *Varieties* | |
|---|---|---|---|---|
| Projection Surface (Extrinsic problem) | 1. Nature | 11. Plane | 12. Conical | 13. Cylindrical |
| | 2. Coincidence | 21. Tangent | 22. Secant | 23. Polysuperficial |
| | 3. Position | 31. Normal | 32. Transverse | 33. Oblique |
| Projection Process (Intrinsic problem) | 4. Properties | 41. Equidist | 42. Eq-area | 43. Conformal |
| | 5. Generation | 51. Geometric | 52. Semi-geo | 53. Conventional |

**Extrinsic:** Involves the consideration of the properties of the projection surface relative to the datum surface results 3 classes.

**Intrinsic:** Involves the consideration of a projection from its cartographic properties and mode of generation results two classes.

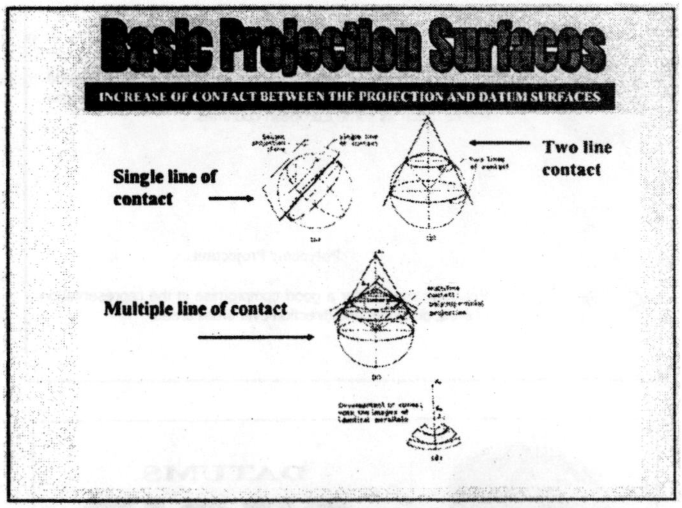


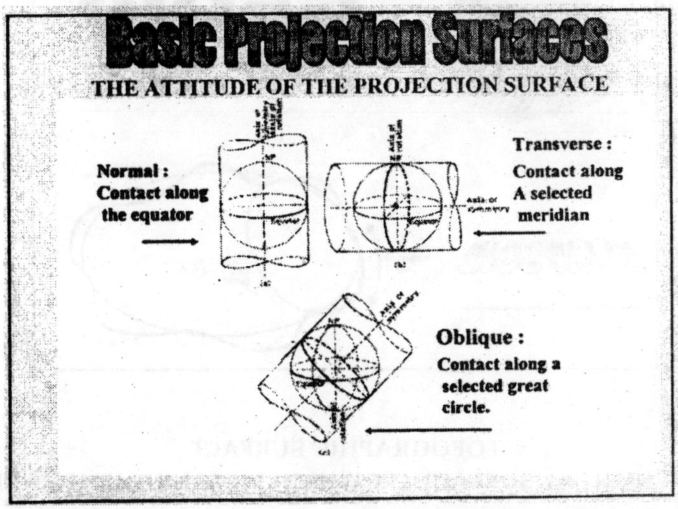


**Cylindrical Projection**

The shape of the continents near the middle of the cylinder would be relatively free of distortion, but the regions near the poles would be stretched out of proportion.

**Azimuthal Projection**

Azimuthal projection maps are useful for viewing the polar regions of the world, because the poles usually appear near the center of the map, with longitudinal lines meeting at the poles and spreading away from each other as they move away from the poles. The polar regions are relatively free of distortion, but the distortion increases as the longitudinal lines move toward equatorial areas.

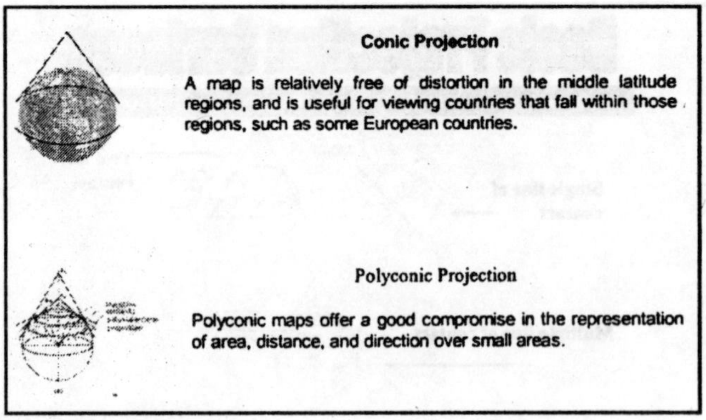


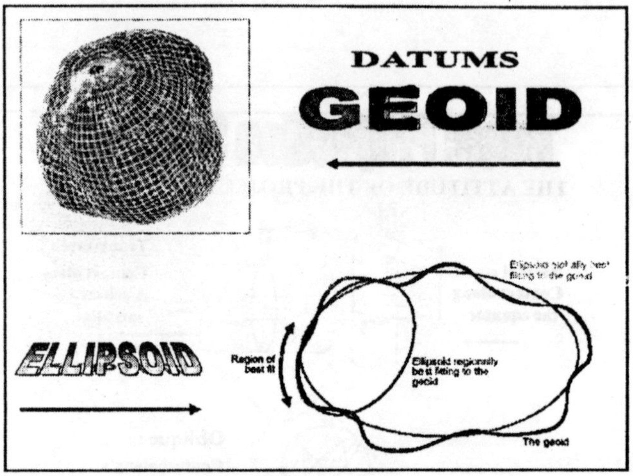


**TOPOGRAPHIC SURFACE**
**EARTH'S PHYSICAL SURFACE ON WHICH MEASUREMENTS ARE MADE**

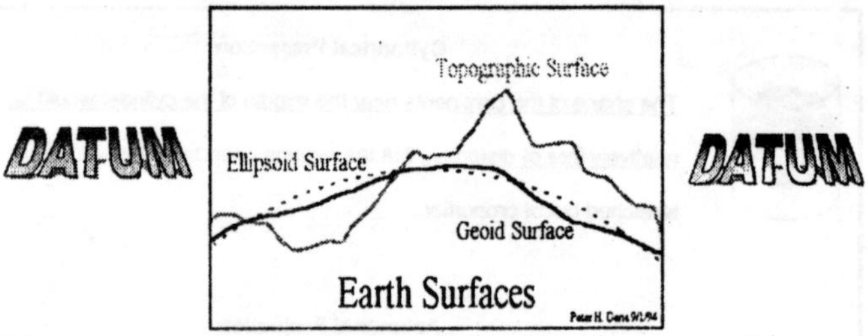


**GEOID**

Equipotential Surface

Complex Surface

Geoid as a reference Datum for Measurement of Heights

**Reference Ellipsoid**

Mathematical Surface with Defined Geometrical Figure

Defined by Semi Major AXIS (a) and Flattening (f)

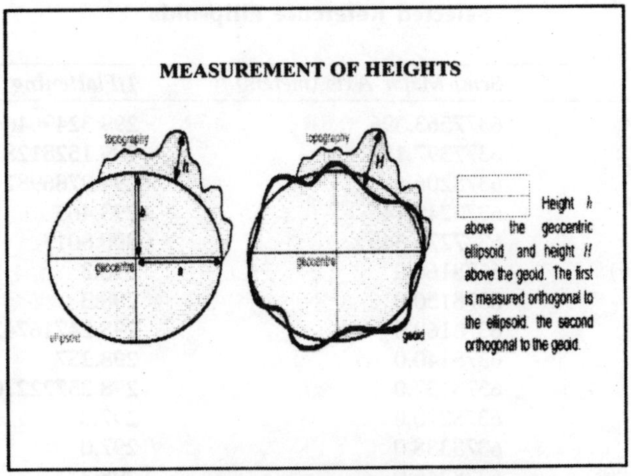


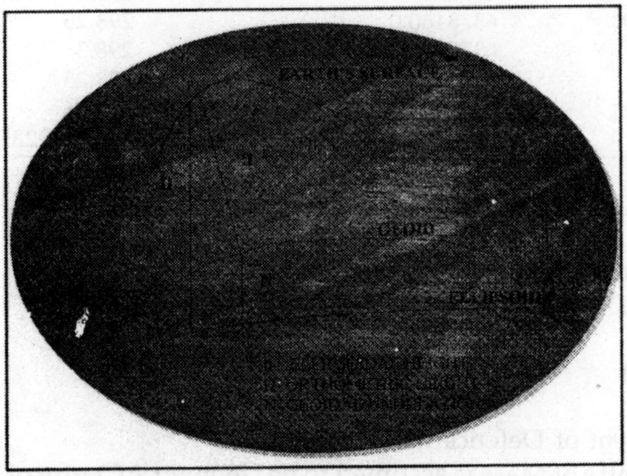

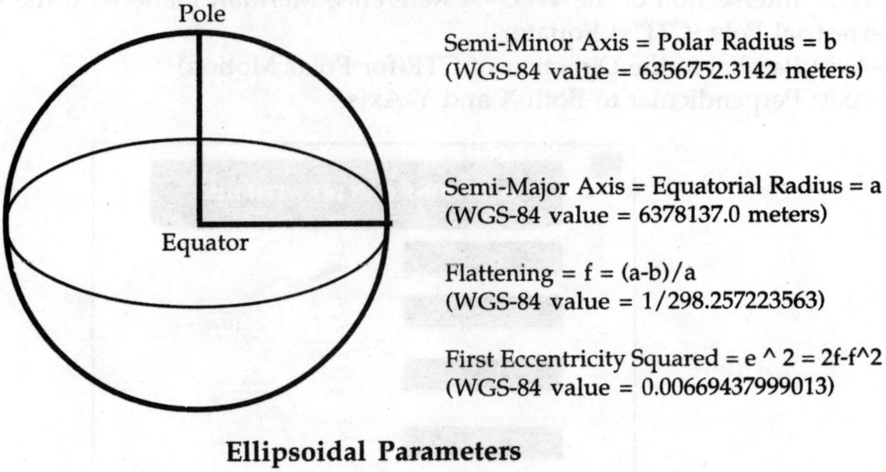


**Ellipsoidal Parameters**

**Selected Reference Ellipsoids**

| *Ellipse* | *Semi-Major Axis (meters)* | *1/Flattening* |
|---|---|---|
| Airy 1830 | 6377563.396 | 299.3249646 |
| Bassel 1841 | 6377397.155 | 299.1528128 |
| Clarke 1866 | 6378206.4 | 294.9786982 |
| Clarke 1880 | 6378249.145 | 293.465 |
| Everest 1830 | 6377276.345 | 300.8017 |
| Fischer 1960 (Mercury) | 6378166.0 | 298.3 |
| Fischer 1968 | 6378150.0 | 298.3 |
| G R S 1967 | 6378160.0 | 298.247167427 |
| G R S 1975 | 6378140.0 | 298.257 |
| G R S 1980 | 6378137.0 | 298.257222101 |
| Hough 1956 | 6378270.0 | 297.0 |
| International | 6378388.0 | 297.0 |
| Krassovsky 1940 | 6378245.0 | 298.3 |
| South American 1969 | 6378160.0 | 298.25 |
| WGS 60 | 6378165.0 | 298.3 |
| WGS 66 | 6378145.0 | 298.25 |
| WGS 72 | 6378135.0 | 298.26 |
| WGS 84 | 6378137.0 | 298.257223563 |

**Modified Everest Datum**

Origin of the Co-ordinate System is in Kalianpur (M.P.)
The a and f Were Derived by Everest in 1830.

**WGS-84 Ellipsoid**

The U.S. Department of Defence has Established.
Origin: Earth's Centre of Mass is assumed to be Geometric Centre of WGS-84 Ellipsoid.
X-Axis: Intersection of the WGS-84 Reference Meridan Plane with the Conventional Terrestrial Pole (CTP's) Equator
Z-Axis: Parallel to the Direction of CTP(for Polar Motion)
Y-Axis: Perpendicular to Both X and Y-Axis.

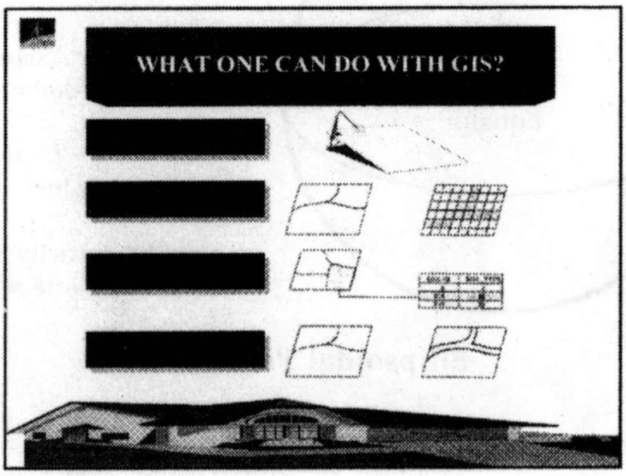

## GIS

A GIS is designed to accept geographic data from a variety of sources, including:

- Maps,
- Satellite/Aerial photographs, and
- Printed text and Statistics.

GIS sensors can scan some of this data directly—for example, a computer operator may feed a map or photograph into the scanner, and the computer "reads" the information it contains. The GIS converts all geographical data into a digital code, which it arranges in its database. Operators program the GIS to process the information and produce the images or information they need.

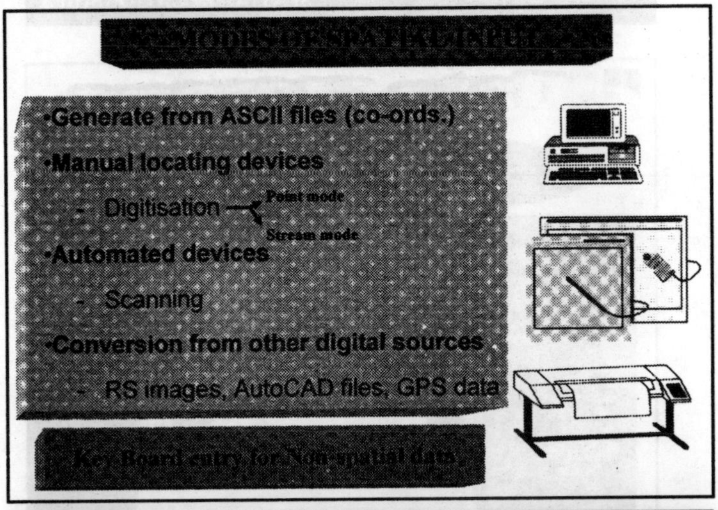


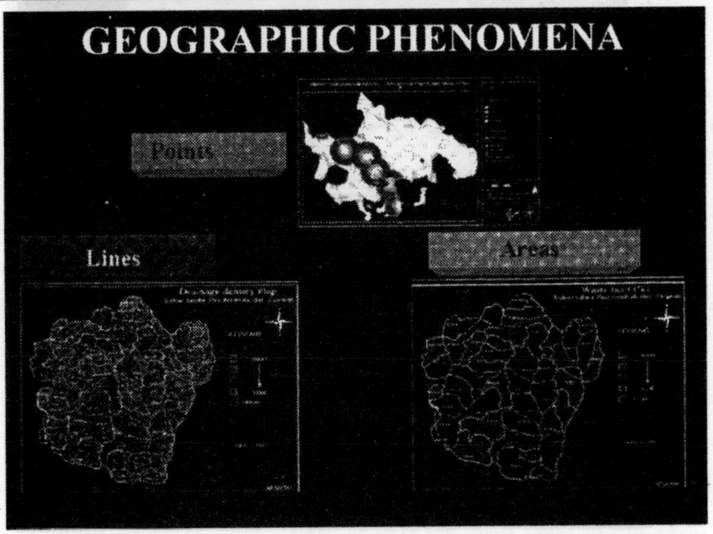

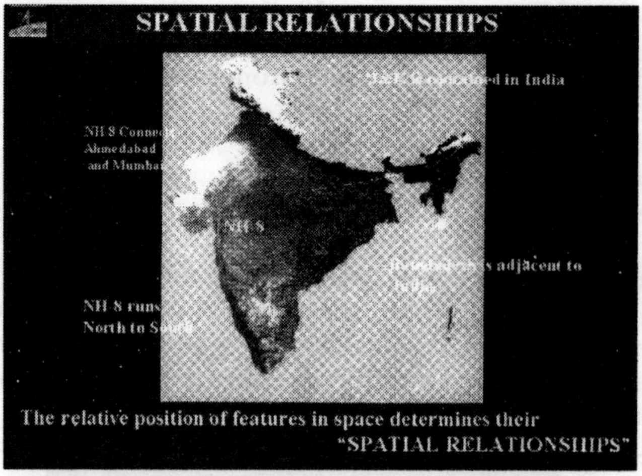
SPATIAL RELATIONSHIPS
Ahmedabad
NH 8
NH 8 runs
The relative position of features in space determines their
"SPATIAL RELATIONSHIPS"

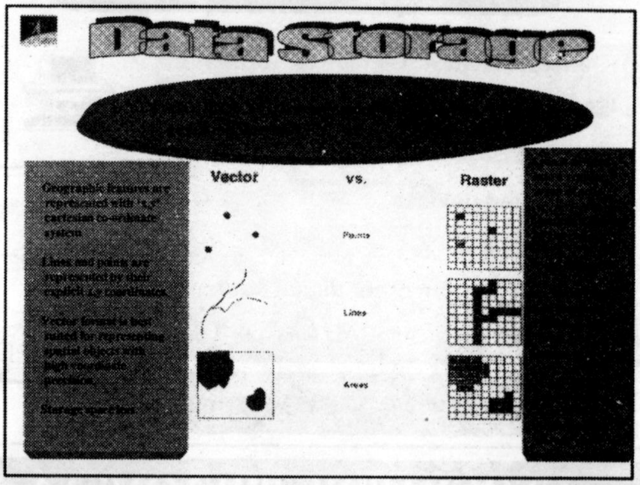
Data Storage
Vector
vs.
Raster
Points
Lines
Areas

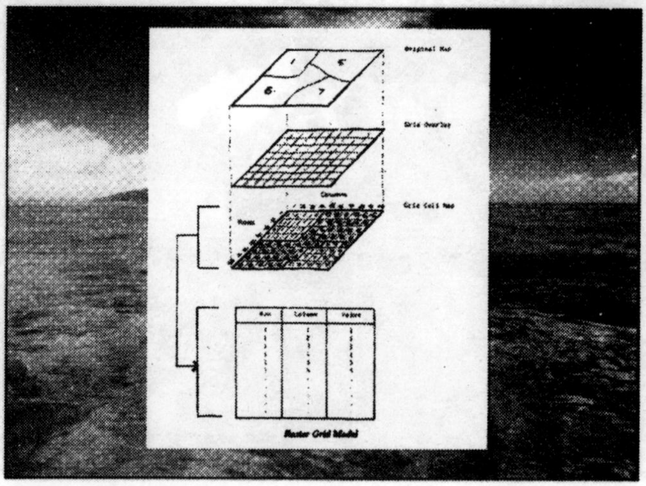
Original Map
1
5
6
7
Grid Overlay
Columns
Grid Cell Map
Rows
Raster Grid Model

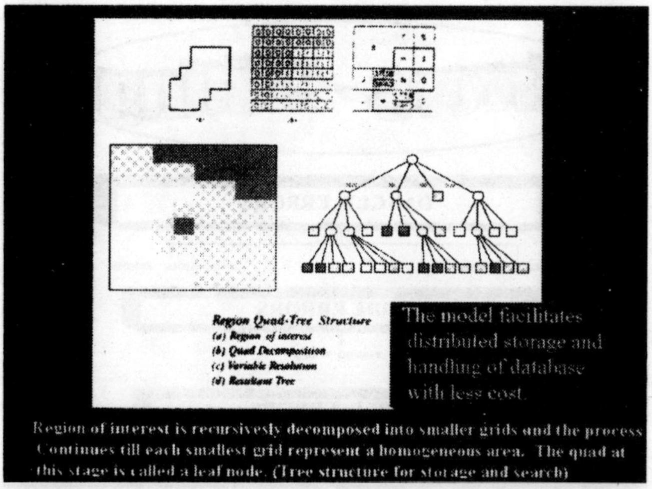
Region Quad-Tree Structure
(a) Region of interest
(b) Quad Decomposition
(c) Variable Resolution
(d) Resultant Tree
The model facilitates distributed storage and handling of database with less cost.
Region of interest is recursively decomposed into smaller grids and the process Continues till each smallest grid represent a homogeneous area. The quad at this stage is called a leaf node. (Tree structure for storage and search)

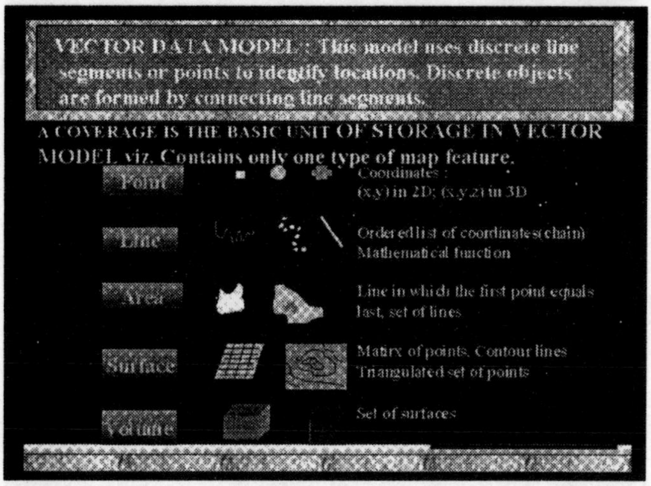
VECTOR DATA MODEL : This model uses discrete line segments or points to identify locations. Discrete objects are formed by connecting line segments.
A COVERAGE IS THE BASIC UNIT OF STORAGE IN VECTOR MODEL viz. Contains only one type of map feature.
Point
Coordinates : (x,y) in 2D; (x,y,z) in 3D
Line
Ordered list of coordinates(chain) Mathematical function
Area
Line in which the first point equals last, set of lines
Surface
Matrix of points, Contour lines Triangulated set of points
Volume
Set of surfaces

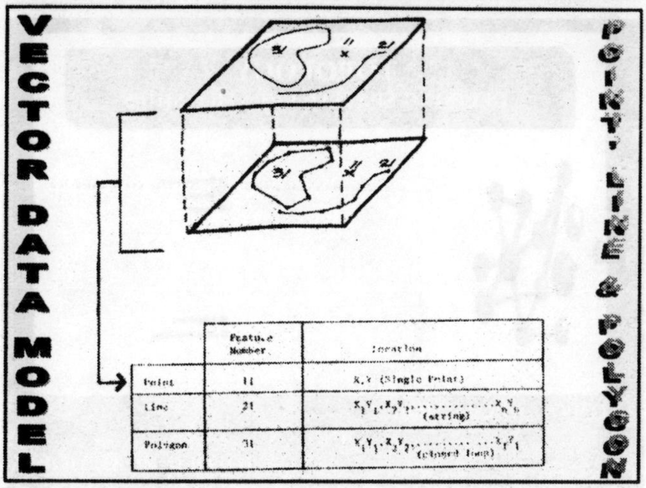
VECTOR DATA MODEL
POINT, LINE & POLYGON
Feature Number
Location
Point
11
X,Y (Single Point)
Line
21
(string)
Polygon
31
(closed loop)

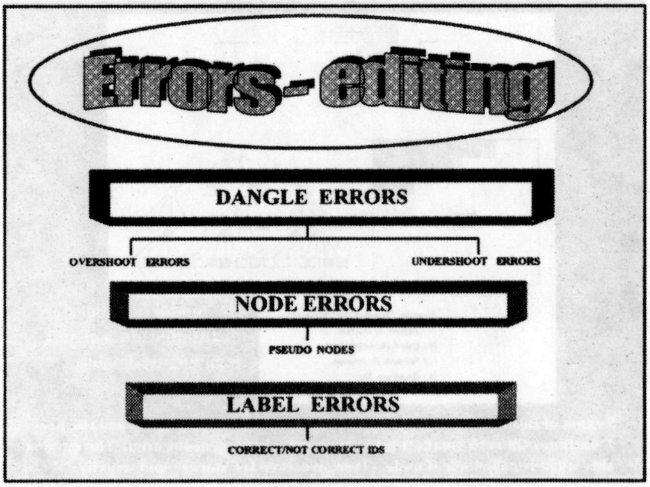
Errors - editing
DANGLE ERRORS
OVERSHOOT ERRORS
UNDERSHOOT ERRORS
NODE ERRORS
PSEUDO NODES
LABEL ERRORS
CORRECT/NOT CORRECT IDS

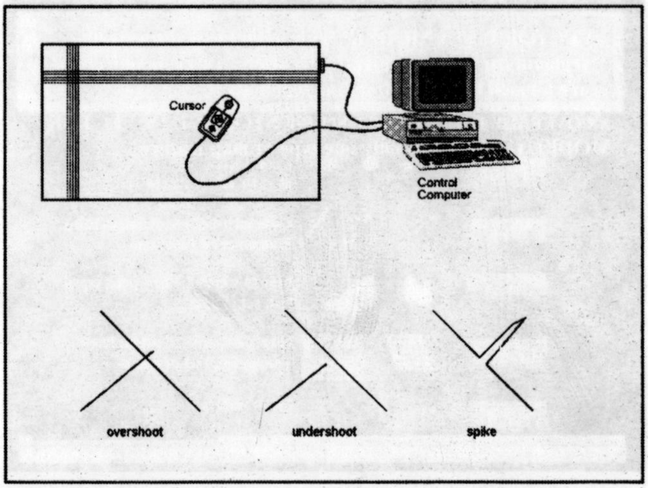
Cursor
Control Computer
overshoot
undershoot
spike

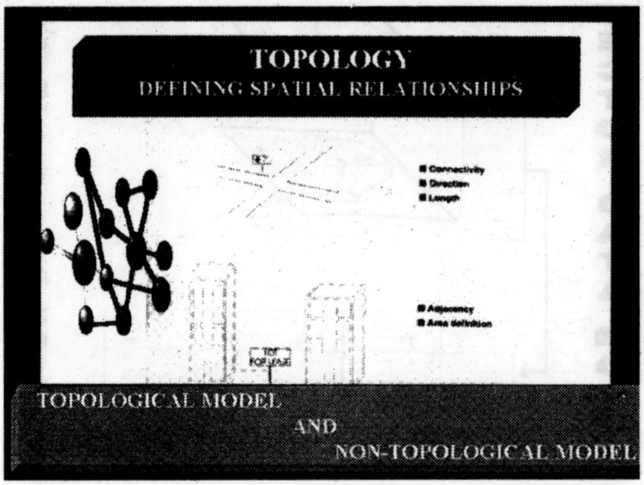
TOPOLOGY
DEFINING SPATIAL RELATIONSHIPS
Connectivity
Direction
Length
Adjacency
Area definition
TOPOLOGICAL MODEL
AND
NON-TOPOLOGICAL MODEL

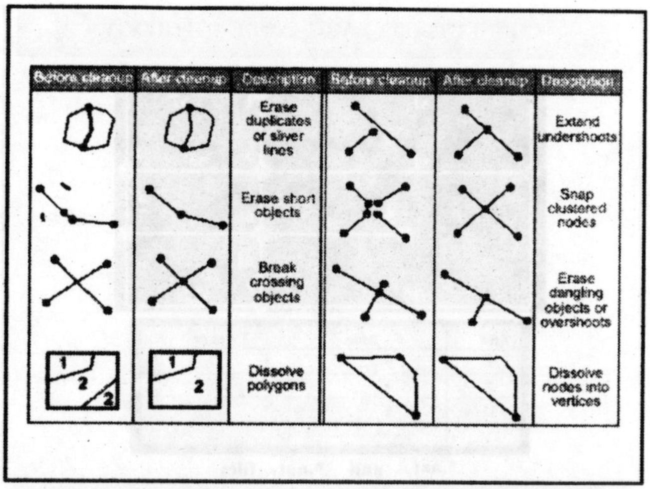
Before cleanup
After cleanup
Description
Before cleanup
After cleanup
Description
Erase duplicates or sliver lines
Erase short objects
Break crossing objects
Dissolve polygons
Extend undershoots
Snap clustered nodes
Erase dangling objects or overshoots
Dissolve nodes into vertices
1
2
2
1
2

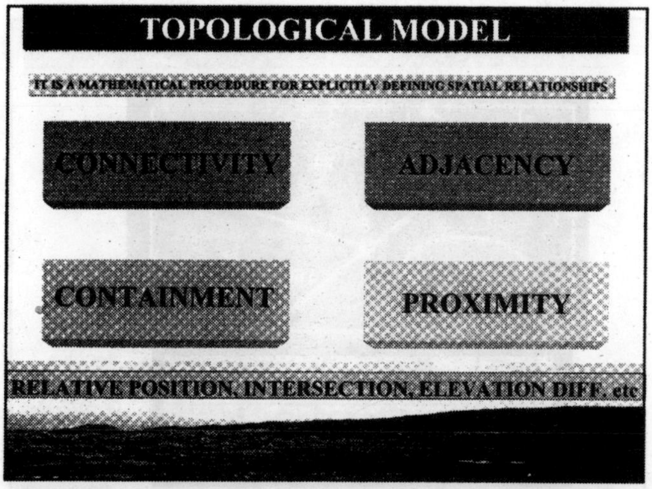
TOPOLOGICAL MODEL
IT IS A MATHEMATICAL PROCEDURE FOR EXPLICITLY DEFINING SPATIAL RELATIONSHIPS
CONNECTIVITY
ADJACENCY
CONTAINMENT
PROXIMITY
RELATIVE POSITION, INTERSECTION, ELEVATION DIFF. etc

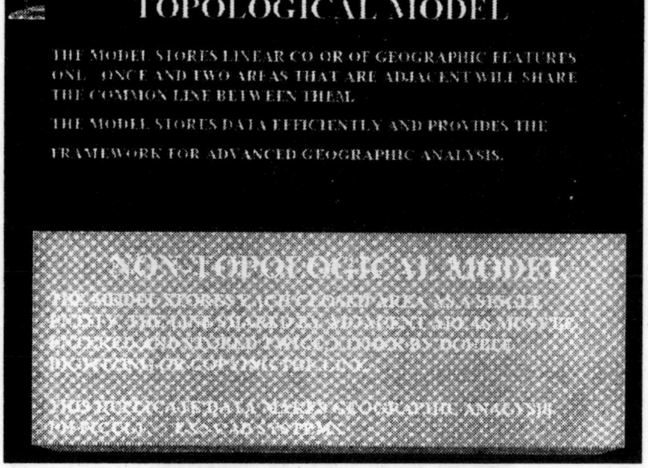
TOPOLOGICAL MODEL
THE MODEL STORES LINEAR CO OR OF GEOGRAPHIC FEATURES ONL ONCE AND TWO AREAS THAT ARE ADJACENT WILL SHARE THE COMMON LINE BETWEEN THEM.
THE MODEL STORES DATA EFFICIENTLY AND PROVIDES THE FRAMEWORK FOR ADVANCED GEOGRAPHIC ANALYSIS.
NON TOPOLOGICAL MODEL

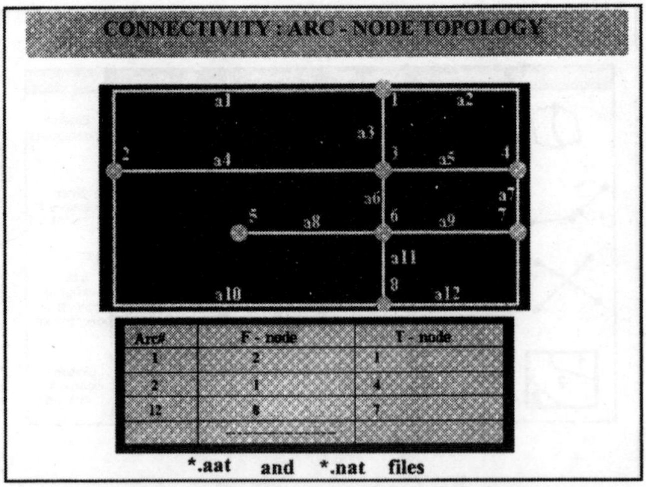


| Arc# | F - node | T - node |
|---|---|---|
| 1 | 2 | 1 |
| 2 | 1 | 4 |
| 12 | 8 | 7 |
| | ------------ | |

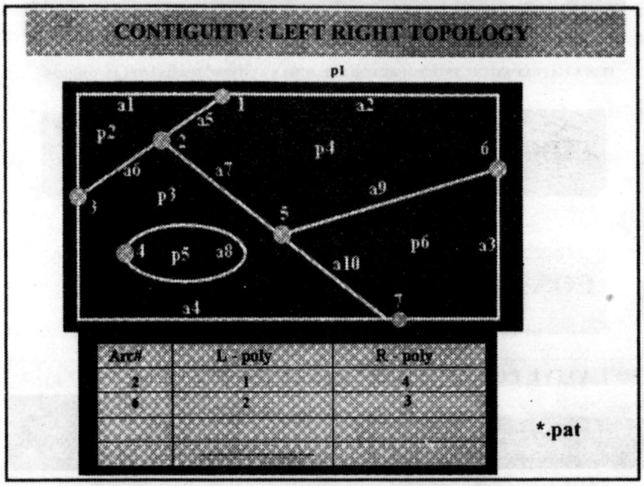


| Arc# | L - poly | R - poly |
|---|---|---|
| 2 | 1 | 4 |
| 6 | 2 | 3 |
| | | |
| | ------------ | |

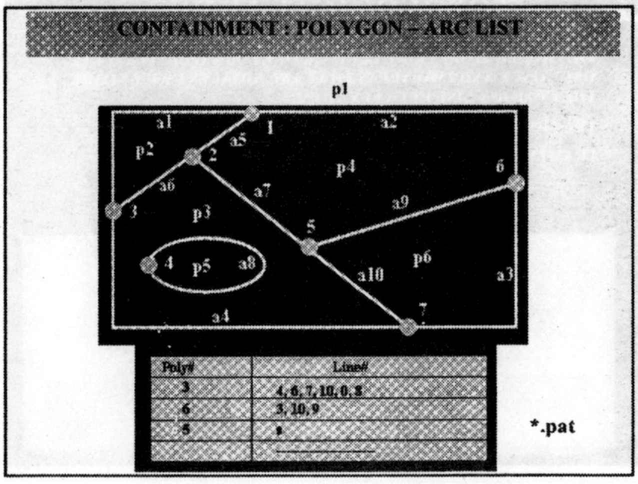


| Poly# | Line# |
|---|---|
| 3 | 4, 6, 7, 10, 0, 8 |
| 6 | 3, 10, 9 |
| 5 | 8 |
| | ------------ |

| *Raster Model* | *Vector Model* |
|---|---|
| Tells what occurs everywhere, at each place in the area | Tells where everything occurs, gives a location to every object |
| Its suffers to present precise details of measured quantities due to its discretization. | Its is precise and has no no approximate errors for the measured quantities like area, length and perimeter. |
| Points, lines, polygons are not recognised as objects in their own merit. | Point, lines and polygons are recognised in their own merit (accuracy is high) |
| Computation faster | Computation slow |

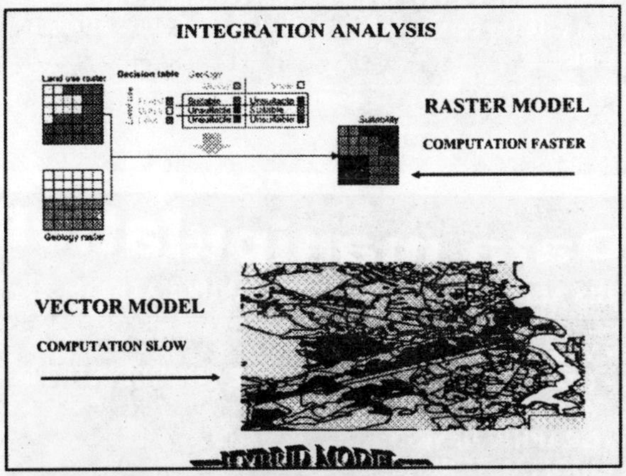


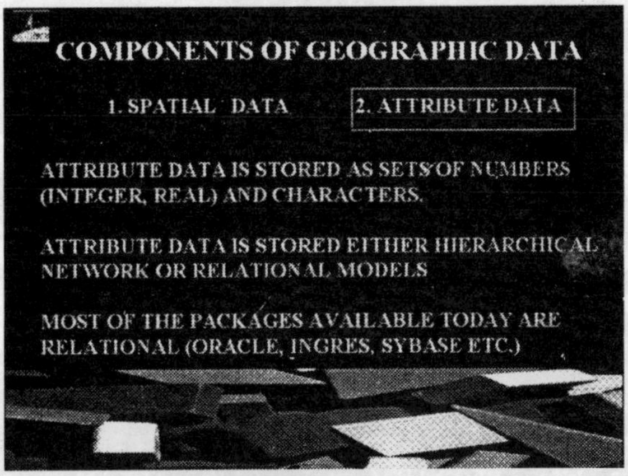

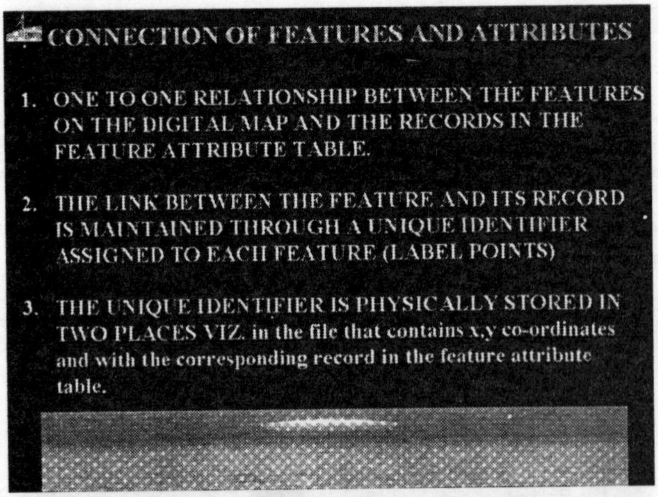
CONNECTION OF FEATURES AND ATTRIBUTES
1. ONE TO ONE RELATIONSHIP BETWEEN THE FEATURES ON THE DIGITAL MAP AND THE RECORDS IN THE FEATURE ATTRIBUTE TABLE.
2. THE LINK BETWEEN THE FEATURE AND ITS RECORD IS MAINTAINED THROUGH A UNIQUE IDENTIFIER ASSIGNED TO EACH FEATURE (LABEL POINTS)
3. THE UNIQUE IDENTIFIER IS PHYSICALLY STORED IN TWO PLACES VIZ. in the file that contains x,y co-ordinates and with the corresponding record in the feature attribute table.

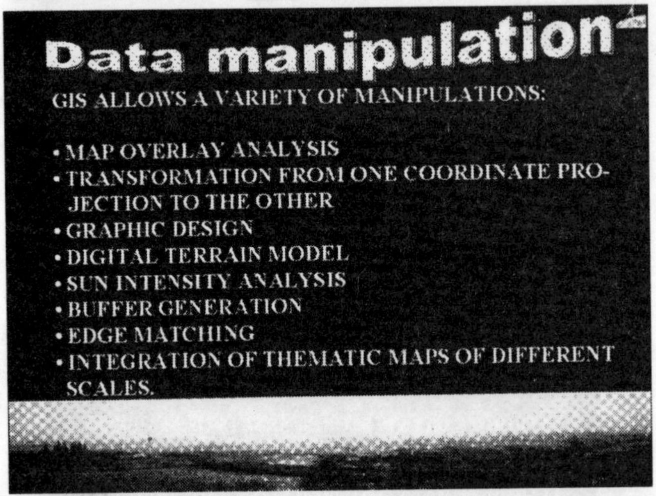
Data manipulation
GIS ALLOWS A VARIETY OF MANIPULATIONS:
• MAP OVERLAY ANALYSIS
• TRANSFORMATION FROM ONE COORDINATE PROJECTION TO THE OTHER
• GRAPHIC DESIGN
• DIGITAL TERRAIN MODEL
• SUN INTENSITY ANALYSIS
• BUFFER GENERATION
• EDGE MATCHING
• INTEGRATION OF THEMATIC MAPS OF DIFFERENT SCALES.

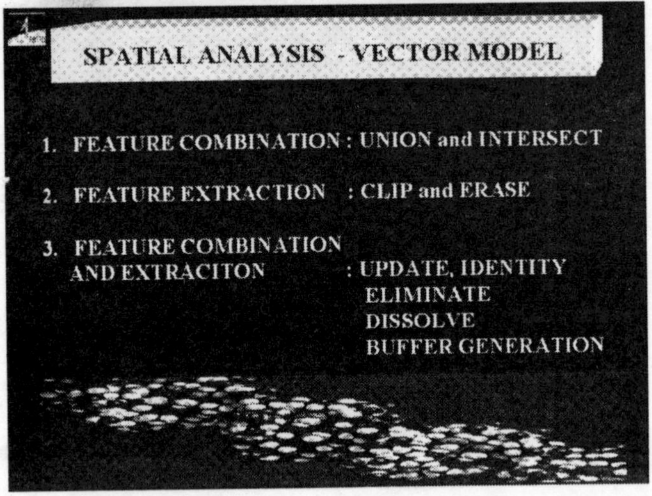
SPATIAL ANALYSIS - VECTOR MODEL
1. FEATURE COMBINATION : UNION and INTERSECT
2. FEATURE EXTRACTION : CLIP and ERASE
3. FEATURE COMBINATION AND EXTRACITON : UPDATE, IDENTITY
ELIMINATE
DISSOLVE
BUFFER GENERATION

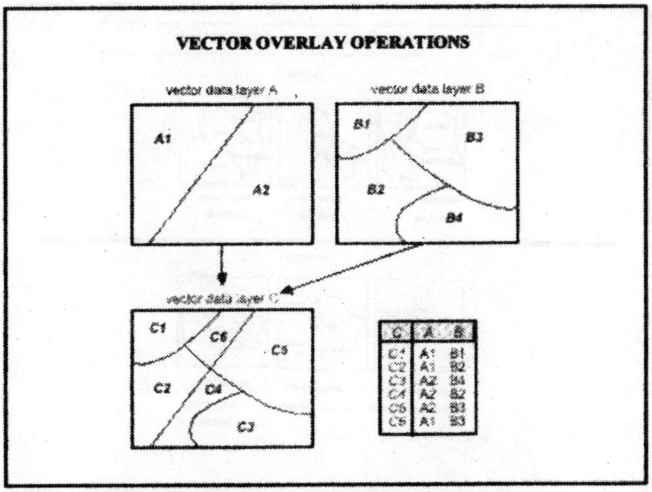
VECTOR OVERLAY OPERATIONS
vector data layer A
vector data layer B
A1
A2
B1
B2
B3
B4
vector data layer C
C1
C2
C3
C4
C5
C6
C A B
C1 A1 B1
C2 A1 B2
C3 A2 B4
C4 A2 B2
C5 A2 B3
C6 A1 B3

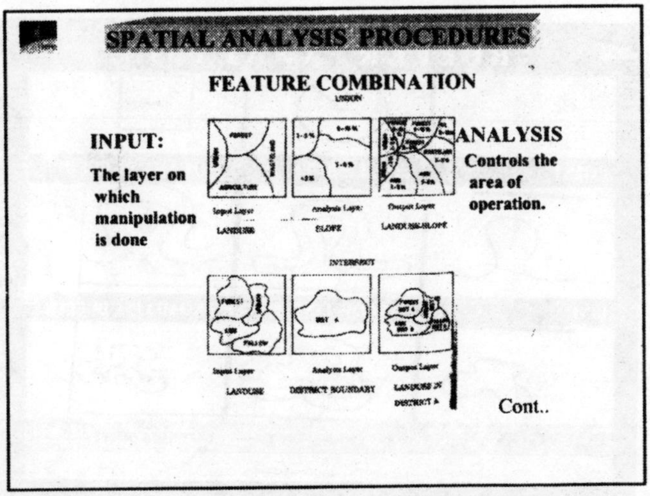
SPATIAL ANALYSIS PROCEDURES
FEATURE COMBINATION
INPUT:
The layer on which manipulation is done
ANALYSIS
Controls the area of operation.
Input Layer
Analysis Layer
Output Layer
DISTRICT BOUNDARY
Cont..

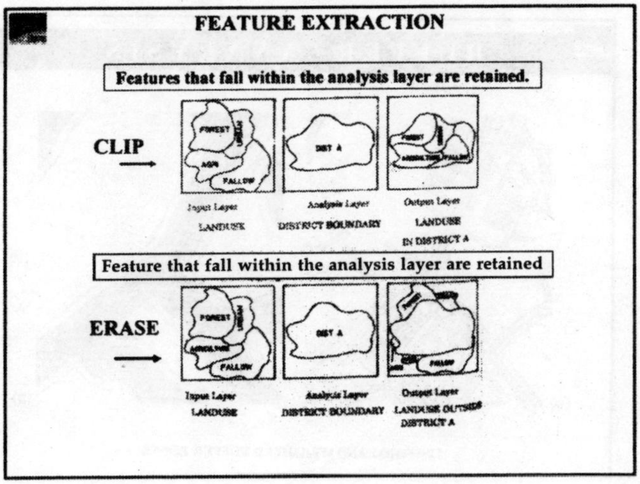
FEATURE EXTRACTION
Features that fall within the analysis layer are retained.
CLIP
Input Layer
LANDUSE
Analysis Layer
DISTRICT BOUNDARY
Output Layer
LANDUSE
IN DISTRICT A
Feature that fall within the analysis layer are retained
ERASE
Input Layer
LANDUSE
Analysis Layer
DISTRICT BOUNDARY
Output Layer
LANDUSE OUTSIDE
DISTRICT A

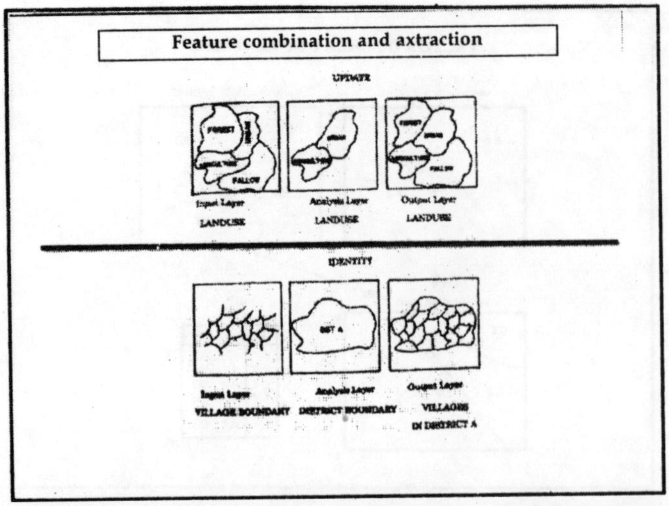
Feature combination and axtraction
UPDATE
FOREST
FALLOW
Input Layer
LANDUSE
Analysis Layer
LANDUSE
Output Layer
LANDUSE
IDENTITY
Input Layer
VILLAGE BOUNDARY
Analysis Layer
DISTRICT BOUNDARY
Output Layer
VILLAGES
IN DISTRICT A

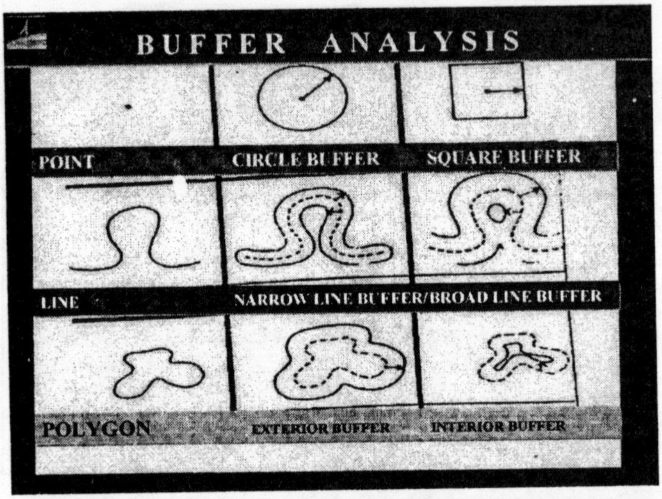
BUFFER ANALYSIS
POINT
CIRCLE BUFFER
SQUARE BUFFER
LINE
NARROW LINE BUFFER/BROAD LINE BUFFER
POLYGON
EXTERIOR BUFFER
INTERIOR BUFFER

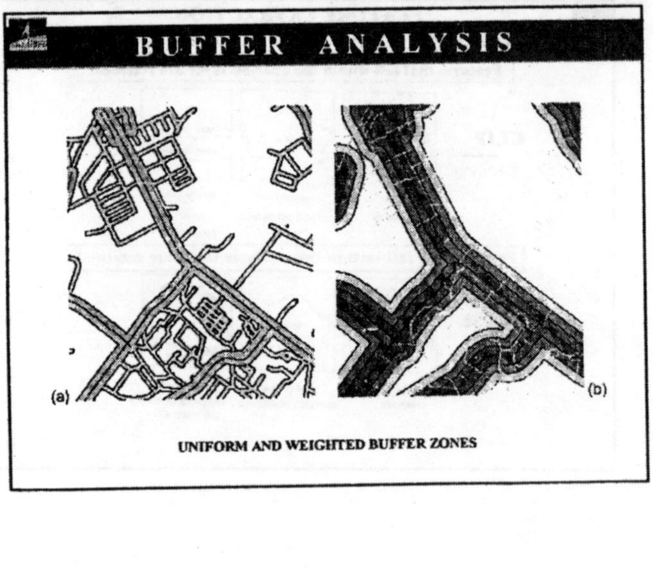
BUFFER ANALYSIS
(a)
(b)
UNIFORM AND WEIGHTED BUFFER ZONES

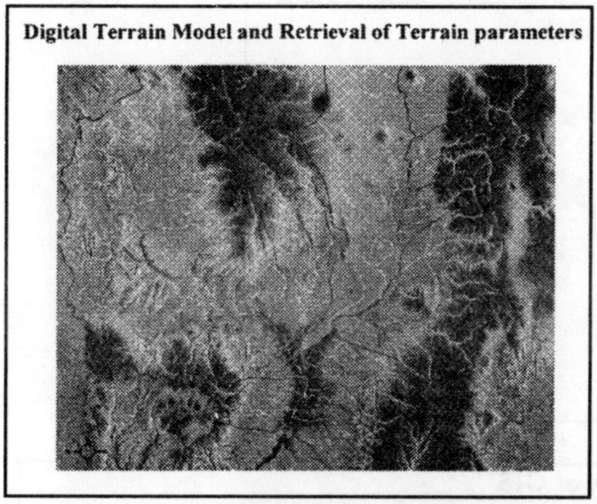
Digital Terrain Model and Retrieval of Terrain parameters

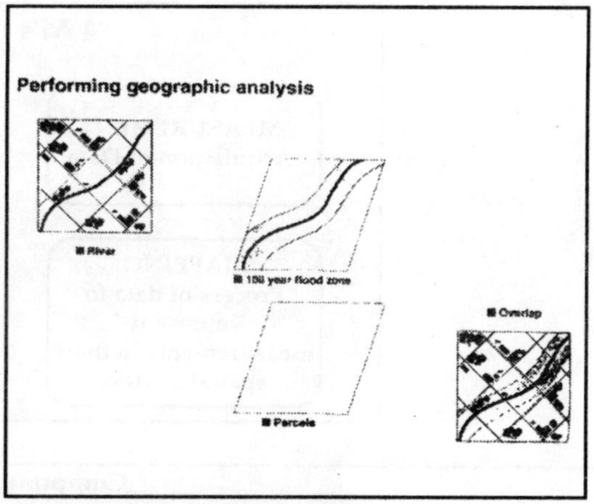
Performing geographic analysis
River
100 year flood zone
Overlap
Parcels

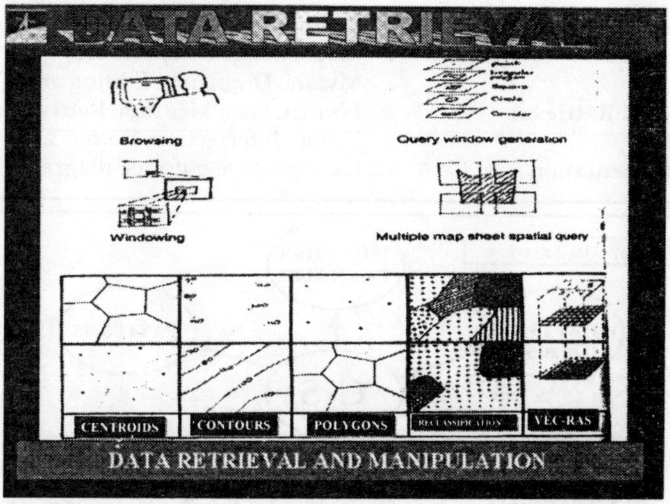
DATA RETRIEVAL
Browsing
Query window generation
Windowing
Multiple map sheet spatial query
CENTROIDS
CONTOURS
POLYGONS
RECLASSIFICATION
VEC-RAS
DATA RETRIEVAL AND MANIPULATION

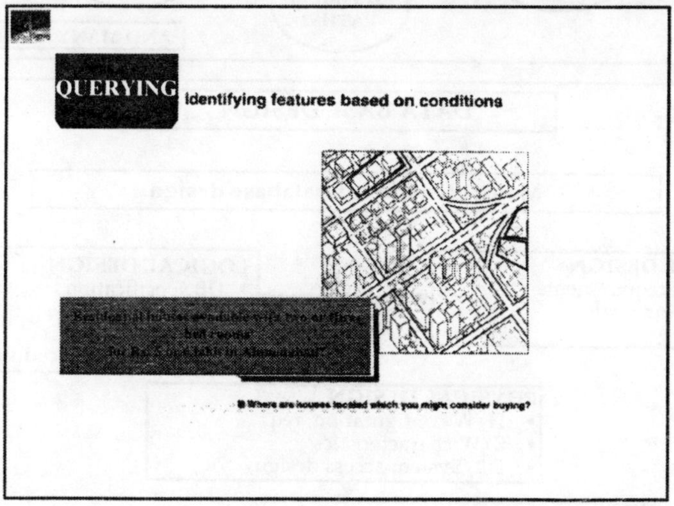
QUERYING
identifying features based on conditions
Where are houses located which you might consider buying?

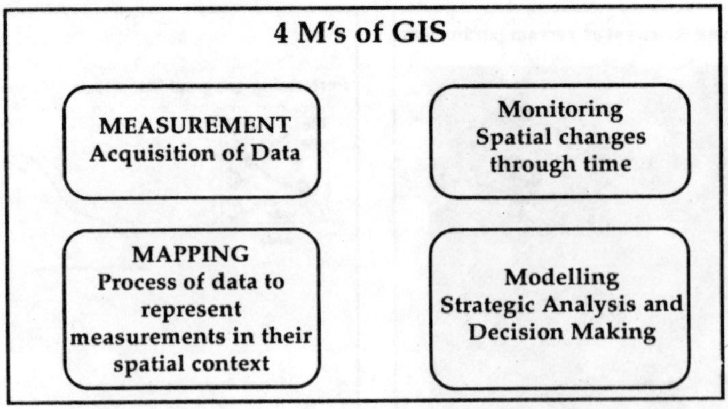


**Components of GIS**

- **The end use or Management** : Evaluation, Selection, Organisation and use
- **Data Acquisition** : Maps, Images, Reports etc.
- **Data Input** : Mylars, Digitizing, Editing and Transformation
- **Data Storage and Retrieval** : Format, Size, Medium, Retrival unit etc.
- **Data Analysis** : Union, Intersection, Buffer, Criterions etc.
- **Information Presentation** : Cartographic outputs, diagrams etc.

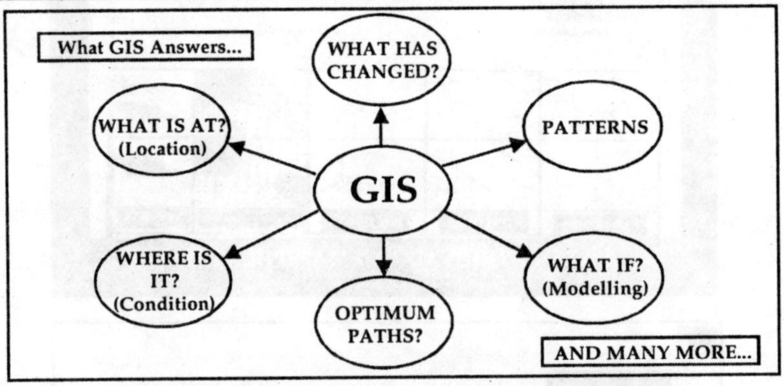


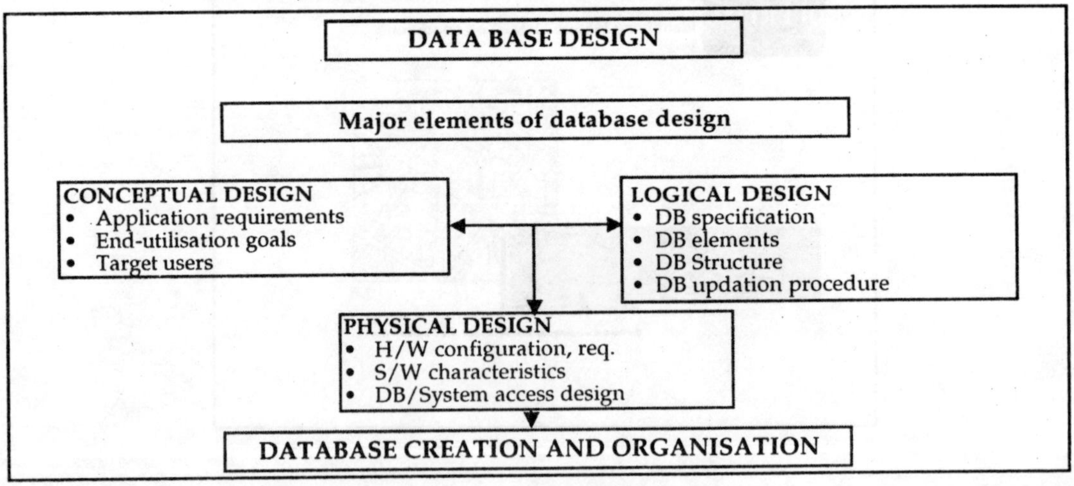

# 4

# Digital Image Processing: Part 1

## Geometric and Radiometric Corrections

*M.P. Punia*

### Introduction

When image data is recorded by sensors on satellites and aircraft, it can contain errors in geometry and in the measured brightness values of the pixels. The latter are referred to as radiometric errors and are mainly due to the instrumentation used to record the data and from the effect of the atmosphere. Image geometry errors can arise in many ways. The relative motions of a satellite, its scanners and the earth, for example, can lead to errors of a skewing nature in an image product. Non-idealities in the sensors themselves, the curvature of the earth and uncontrolled variations in the position and attitude of the remote sensing platform can all lead to geometric errors of varying degrees of severity.

### Radiometric Corrections

Radiometric correction of remotely sensed data normally involves the processing of digital images to improve the fidelity of the brightness value magnitudes (as opposed to geometric correction which involves improving the fidelity of relative spatial or absolute locational aspects of image brightness values). The main purpose for applying radiometric corrections is to reduce the influence of errors or inconsistencies in image brightness values that may limit one's ability to interpret or quantitatively process and analyze digital remotely sensed images. Throughout this section, radiometric errors and inconsistencies will be referred to as "noise", which could be considered any undesirable spatial or temporal variations in image brightness not associated with variations in the imaged surface.

## Geometric Corrections

### *Sources of Geometric Distortion*

The following are some of the sources of geometric distortion seen in image data:

(i) Rotation of the earth during image acquisition
(ii) Curvature of the earth,
(iii) Sensor non-idealities,
(iv) Variations in platform altitude, attitude and velocity,
(v) Panoramic effects related to the imaging geometry, and
(vi) Wide field of some sensors.

### *Earth Rotation Effects*

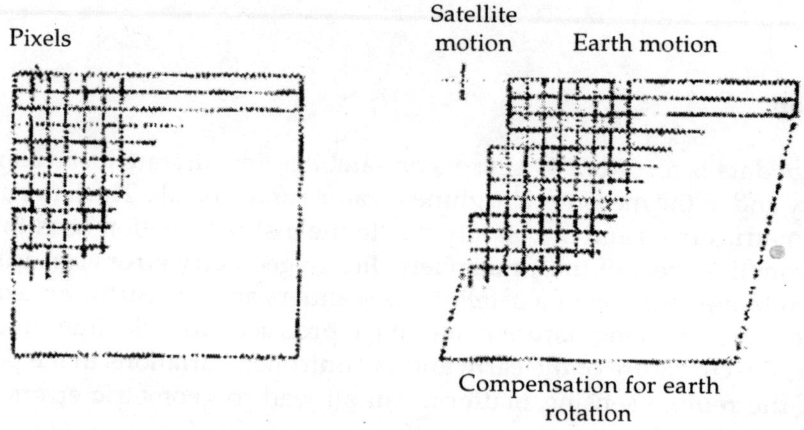


**Fig. 4.1 and Fig. 4.2:** The effect of earth rotation on scanner imagery. A Image formed according to Fig. 4.1 in which lines are arranged on a square grid; b Offset of successive lines to the west to correct for the rotation of the earth's surface during the frame acquisition time

### *Panoramic Distortion*

In case of scanners used on spacecraft and aircraft as remote sensing platforms the angular IFOV is constant. As a result the effective pixel size on the ground is larger at the extremities of the scan than at nadir as illustrated in Fig. 3. In particular, if the IFOV is $\exists$ and the pixel dimension at nadir is $p$ then its dimension in the scan direction at scan angle of 2 as shown is $P2 = \exists\, h \sec^2 2 = P \sec^2 2$.

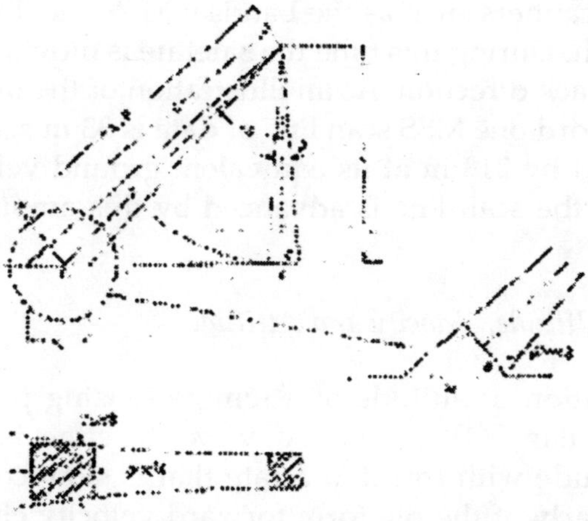

**Fig. 4.3:** Effect of scan angle on pixel size at constant angular instantaneous field of view

*Earth Curvature*

Aircraft scanning systems, because of their low altitude (and thus the small absolute swath width of their image data), are not affected by earth curvature. Neither are space systems such as Landsat and SPOT, again because of the narrowness of their swath. However wide swath width spaceborne imaging systems are affected. For NOAA with swath width of 2700 km and an altitude of 833 km it can be shown that the deviation of the earth's surface from a plane amounts to about 2 - 3 per cent over the swath, which seems insignificant. However, it is the inclination of the earth's surface over the swath that causes the greater effect. The increase in pixel size can be computed by reference to the geometry of Fig. 4.4.

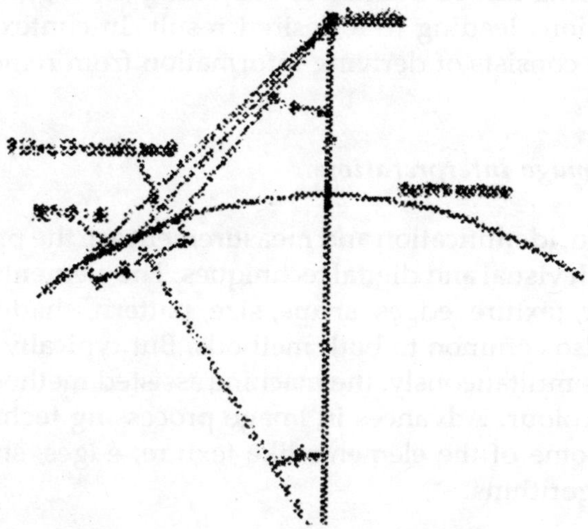

**Fig. 4.4:** Effect of earth curvature on the size of a pixel in the scan direction (across track)

Mechanical line scanners such as the Landsat MSS and TM require a finite time to scan across the swath. During this time the satellite is moving forward leading to a skewing in the along track direction. As an illustration of the magnitude of the effect, the time requires to record one MSS scan line of data is 33 m sec. During this time the satellite travels forward by 213 m at its equivalent ground velocity of 6.450 km/sec. As a result the end of the scan line is advanced by this amount compared with its start.

*Variations in Platform Altitude, Velocity and Attitude*

Variations in the elevation or altitude of a remote sensing platform lead to a scale change at constant angular IFOV and field of view; the effect is illustrated in Fig. 4.5a for an increase in altitude with travel at a rate that is slow compared with a frame acquisition time. Similarly, if the platform forward velocity changes, a scale change occurs in the along track direction. This is depicted in Fig. 4.5b.

*Aspect Ratio Distortion*

The aspect ratio of an image (that is, its scale vertically compared with its scale horizontally) can be distorted by mechanisms that lead to overlapping IFOvs. The most notable example of this occurs with the Landsat multi-spectral scanner. Samples are taken across a scan line too quickly compared with the IFOV. This leads to pixels having 56 meter centres but sampled with an IFOV of 79 m. Consequently the effective pixel size is 79 m × 56 m and thus is not square.

## Digital Image Processing: Enhancements and Image Analysis

Digital image processing can be defined as subjecting the digital image to a series of mathematical operations leading to a desired result. In context of remote sensing, digital interpretation consists of deriving information from remotely sensed. Images using a computer.

### *Visual and Digital Image Interpretation*

Detection, recognition, identification and measurement are the primary tasks of image interpretation for both visual and digital techniques. The elements of image interpretation like tone, colour, texture, edges, shape, size, pattern, shadows and context (site or association) are also common to both methods. But typically a human interpreter can use all the clues simultaneously, the machine assisted method is mostly limited to use of only tone or colour. Advances in image processing techniques are removing this limitation and some of the elements like texture, edges, shapes can be used in image processing algorithms.

### *Media and Format of Digital Images*

(a) Bands interleaved by pixels, (b) Bands interleaved by line, and (c) Band sequential as explained below:

(a) *Bands interleaved by pixels (BIP)*: In this format each successive pixel contains data for all bands.
(b) *Band-interleaved by lines (BIL)*: In this case each successive scan line contains data for all the bands.
(c) *Band sequential (BSQ)*: In this format each successive band is stored as complete file.

## Digital Image Processing

The four important categories are (a) image restoration, (b) image enhancement, (c) image transformations, and (d) image analysis.

***Image restoration***: Image restoration is concerned with restoring distorted image to a faithful representation of the original scene. Geometric distortion, degradation and noise are induced in the imaging process are corrected by using procedures for geometric and radiometric corrections.

### *Contrast Stretching*

Enhancement can be divided Into 3 categories:

—Radiometric or grey level stretching.
—Spatial filtering, image convolution, edge enhancement and Fourier analysis.
—Colour enhancement on 2 or more image channels such as Principle Component Analysis (POA), Arithmetic combination and IHS transformations.

### *Grey Level Thresholding*

It is a simple look up table, which partitions the grey levels in an image into one of two categories those below a user selected threshold and those above, *i.e.* two regions of interest which can be used as template.

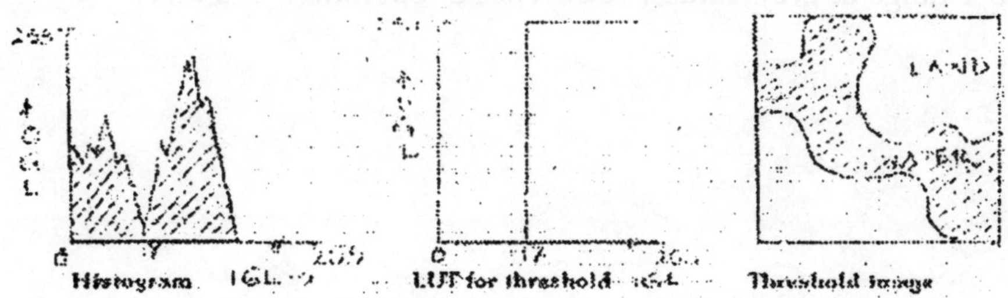


Histogram    LUT for threshold    Threshold image

The binary class of threshold image must be converted to bitmap (mask or template) by using the function **THR.** Two methods of performing.

***Density Slicing***

It is a process of grouping the grey levels of an image into a number of ranges. Each grey level is reassigned a unique grey level or colour. It is most easily performed in video using pseudo-colour table modification functionality of program DCP. Theoretically, density slices are decided by viewing the histogram distribution of the image of interest.

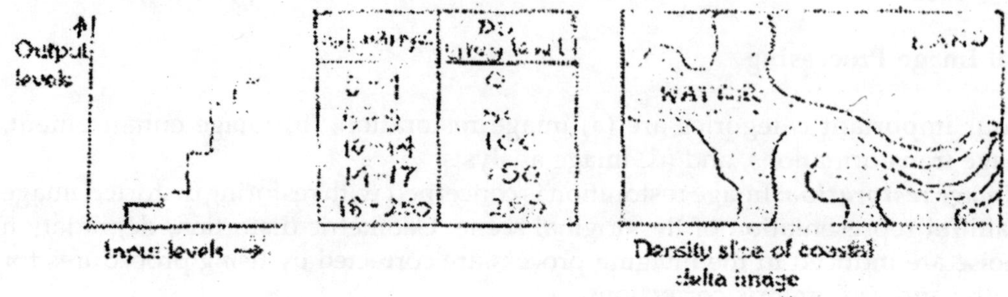


**Pseudo-colour table**

| *Image grey Levels* | *PCT red value* | *PCT green value* | *PCT blue value* | *Colour* |
|---|---|---|---|---|
| 0-4 | 255 | 0 | 255 | Purple |
| 5-9 | 0 | 0 | 255 | Blue |
| 10-14 | 0 | 100 | 255 | Mid-blue |
| 15-17 | 0 | 255 | 255 | Cyan |
| 18-255 | 18-255 | 18-255 | 18-255 | Grey |

It is an effective technique for visually demonstrating discrete temperature ranges for TIR imagery.

The pixel values in the majority of digital scenes occupy a relatively small portion of the possible range of image values, resulting in low contrast display. A contrast stretch enhancement expands the range of pixel values so that they are displayed over a fuller range of grey values. Four types of operations are there.

- **No stretch:** The intensity values are directly sent to display device, full dynamic range is not used, Reduces user's ability to discriminate image detail.

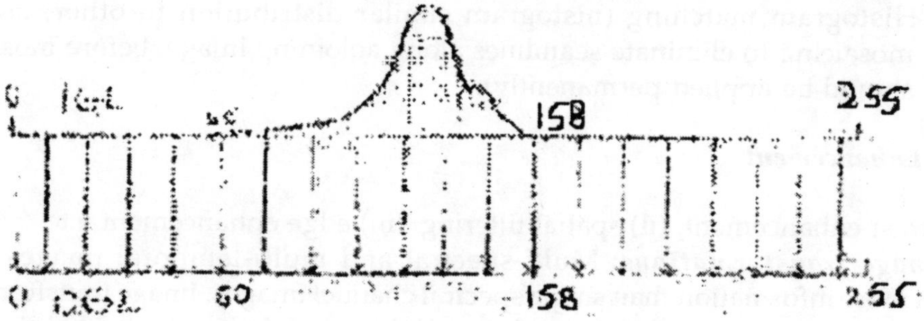


- **Linear stretch :**

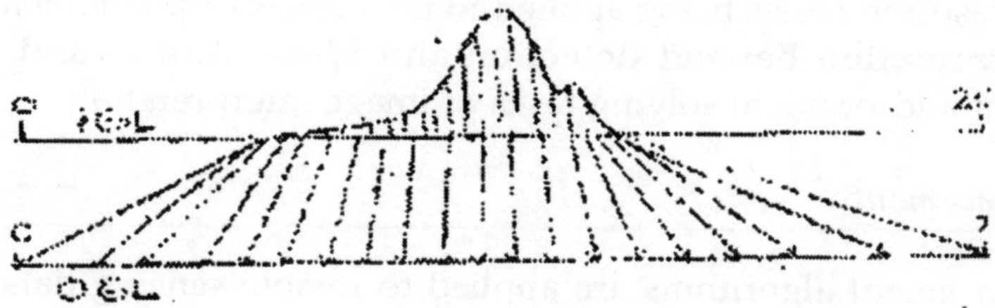

- **Histogram equalised stretch**

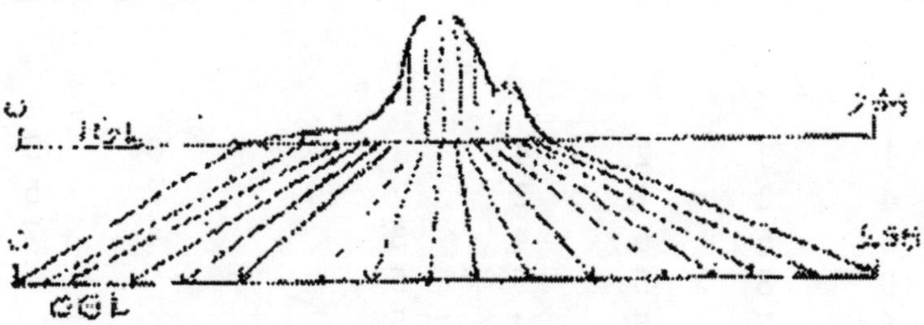

- **Special or Piecewise stretch:**

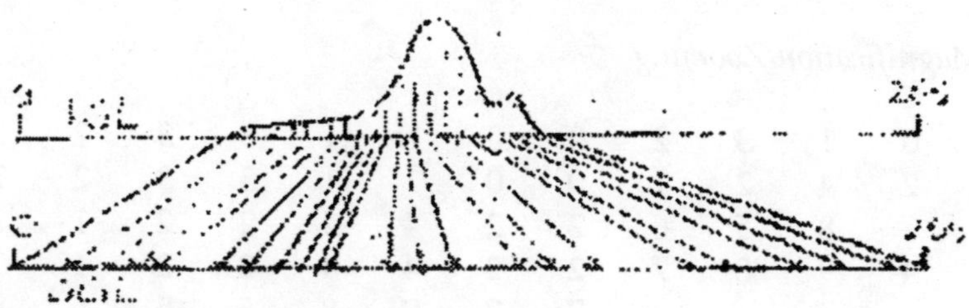

—Histogram equalization
—Histogram normalization (Gaussian distribution)
—Histogram matching (histogram similar distribution to other, useful for mosaicing to eliminate seamlines along adjoining image, before mosaicing it should be applied permanently).

### *Image Enhancement*

(i) contrast enhancement, (ii) spatial filtering, (iii) edge enhancement, etc.

***Image transformations***: Multi-spectral and multi-temporal images usually contain more information than single spectral channel images. Image transforms effect a reduction in data set size while retaining the essence of the extractable information.

***Image analysis:*** Analysis procedure involve those processes which when completed, result in labels being applied to the objects or phenomena. This is taking image interpretation beyond detection and identification and constitutes the measurement and problem solving tasks of image interpretation.

### *Image Enhancement*

Image enhancement algorithms are applied to remote sensing data to improve the appearance of an image for visual analysis or machine analysis.

#### ***1. Image reduction and magnification***

*1.1 Reduction*

| 0 | 1 | 3 | 2 | 4 | 3 |
|---|---|---|---|---|---|
| 2 | 4 | 2 | 1 | 2 | 2 |
| 7 | 8 | 5 | 6 | 4 | 3 |
| 4 | 9 | 8 | 5 | 5 | 5 |
| 4 | 8 | 7 | 5 | 4 | 5 |
| 4 | 6 | 7 | 5 | 4 | 6 |

Original Image

| 0 | 3 | 4 |
|---|---|---|
| 7 | 5 | 4 |
| 4 | 7 | 4 |

Image reduction

*1.2 Magnification/Zooming*

| 0 | 1 | 3 | 2 |
|---|---|---|---|
| 2 | 4 | 2 | 1 |
| 7 | 8 | 5 | 6 |
| 4 | 9 | 8 | 7 |

Original Image

| 0 | 0 | I | 1 | 3 | 3 | 2 | 2 |
|---|---|---|---|---|---|---|---|
| 0 | 0 | 1 | 1 | 3 | 3 | 2 | 2 |
| 2 | 2 | 4 | 4 | 2 | 2 | 1 | 1 |
| 2 | 2 | 4 | 4 | 2 | 2 | 1 | 1 |
| 7 | 7 | 8 | 8 | 5 | 5 | 6 | 6 |
| 7 | 7 | 8 | 8 | 5 | 5 | 6 | 6 |
| 4 | 4 | 9 | 9 | 8 | 8 | 7 | 7 |
| 4 | 4 | 9 | 9 | 8 | 8 | 7 | 7 |

Magnified Image

**Spatial Filtering**

Filtering is an enhancement operation that alters pixel values on the basis of the grey values of its surrounding neighbours. For this reason it is considered as a spatial operation. Spatial operations are called filters because like their real counterparts they. 'shift' only the image frequencies considered to be important. High pass filters allow only the high frequency information of an image to be sieved into a new image channel. High frequency images contain all of the local details in an image (*i.e.* its edge). Whereas, low pass filters pass only low frequency information producing images that appear smooth or blurred in comparison to the original data.

The general concept for any filter is to define a filter window, (kernel) the dimension being an odd number of pixels and lines. Each pixel of this window containing a coefficient or weighting factor representative of some mathematical relationship. A filtered image is generated by multiplying each coefficient in the window by the grey level in the original image corresponding to the window's current location and assigning the result to the control pixel location of the window in the filtered channel. The window is moved throughout the image one pixel at a time. This window multiplication process is known as convolution.

The edge pixels along the perimeter of an image is replicated during filtering as follows:

| | | | | | | | | | | |
|---|---|---|---|---|---|---|---|---|---|---|
| 25 | 31 | 29 | 33 | 25 | 25 | 31 | 29 | 33 | 33 | |
| 24 | 29 | 33 | 35 | 25 | 25 | 31 | 29 | 33 | 33 | X and Y dimension of the window can be 1 to 33 |
| 20 | 27 | 34 | 37 | 24 | 24 | 29 | 33 | 35 | 35 | |
| | | | | 20 | 20 | 27 | 34 | 37 | 37 | |
| | | | | 20 | 20 | 27 | 34 | 37 | 37 | dimensions must be odd |
| Original Image | | | | edges replicated for 3*3 filtering | | | | | | |

*Spatial frequency*

It is the number of changes in BV per unit distance for any part of the image. If there are very few changes in BV over a given area, it is known as "low frequency" area and if there are large changes known as "high frequency". As spatial frequency describes the BV over a region, it is essential to adopt spatial approach for extracting quantitative spatial Information.

A linear spatial filter is a filter for which the $BV_{i,j,}$ in the output image is a function of some weighted average of BV's located in a particular spatial pattern around the i,j location in the input image. The process of evaluating the weighted neighbouring pixel values are called two-dimensional convolution. It emphasizes high spatial frequency, may sharpen the edge of the image where as emphasizing the low spatial frequencies may be used to reduce noise in an image.

***Low frequency filtering in the spatial domain (LPF)***: Low frequencies describe gradual grey level changes over a large number of pixels (*i.e.* water bodies, large fields and forest cover) Image enhancements that de-emphasise or block the high spatial frequency detail are low-frequency or low pass filters. The size of the convolution mask or kernel (n) is usually 3 × 3, 5 × 5, 7 × 7, 9 × 9 and so on.

| mask A = | 1 | 1 | 1 |
|---|---|---|---|
| | 1 | 1 | 1 Coefficients of low frequency |
| | 1 | 1 | 1 mask is set to 1 |

The coefficients $C_j$, in the mask are multiplied by the following individual $BV_i$ in the input image. The spatial moving average then shifts to the next pixel, where the average of all nine BV's are computed. This operation is repeated for every pixel in the input image. Such image smoothing is useful for, removing periodic salt and pepper effect.

Examples area average filter (FAV), Gaussian filter (FGA), median filter (FME), mode filter (FMO).

*Average filter (FAV)*

It computes the mean of the grey levels within a kernel and eliminates noise. Filter window need not be square. Input and output channel can be same.

*Distance weighted filter/Gaussian filter (FGA)*

Used as a low pass filter if only one SIGMSQ (Gaussion filter parameter) is specified. It can also used as band pass filter to detect sudden intensity changes, if 2 SIGMSQ values are specified. FGA computes the weighted sum of grey levels within kernel surrounding central pixel. The weights are results of the Gaussian function with given deviation. Kernel will be a square of size (2 × SIGMSQH).

$$G\,(_{i,J} = \exp\,(-((i-u)^2 + (j-v)^2)/2*\text{sigma}^2)) \qquad \begin{matrix}121\\242\\121\end{matrix}$$

where $(_{i,j})$ is a pixel within filter window, (u,v) is the centre of kernel and sigma square is a parameter.

Filter weight $(W_{i,J})$ are the normalised values of $G(_{i,j})$ over the entire kernel, hence sum of all weights is 1. Grey level of a filtered pixel is sum of $w(_{i,j}) * v(_{i,j})$ over the window where, $v(_{i,j})$ is the original value at location $(_{i,j})$. It replicates edge pixel values to give sufficient data.

- Adjusting the kernel coefficients based upon its proximity to pixel being altered,
- Weightage decreases away from the centre.
- Smooth more gently than FAV.

*Median filter (FME)*

It computes the median value (the middle value in an ordered set of values, below and above which there is an equal number of values within a filter window surrounding all pixels. Result is smoothening of the image and preservation of edges. Maximum filter size allowed is 7 × 7 and window need not be square.

*Mode filter (FMO)*

—It is primarily used to clean up thematic maps for presentation purpose.
—It computes the modes of grey values within the kernel.
—It replaces small islands by their large surrounding themes.
—Maximum filter size allowed is 7 × 7, filter window need not be square.
—Edge pixels are replicated.

### *High Frequency Filtering in Spatial Domain (HPF)*

High frequencies describe rapid grey value changes from one pixel to the next (*e.g.* lithological contracts, drainage networks, roads and naturally occurring boundaries). This very rapid changes represent high spatial frequencies called edges. Products are known as edge detection images. It enhances features less than half of size of the kernel and de-emphasises features that are more than half the kernel size. High pass filtering is applied to imagery to remove the slowly varying components and retain only the high frequency local variations. High frequency filtered image have an arrow intensity histogram. Hence most high-frequency filtered images must be contrast stretched, prior to visual analysis. These filters accentuate or sharpen edges and can be produced using the following convolution masks.

$$\text{mask E} = \begin{matrix} -1 & -1 & -1 \\ -1 & 9 & -1 \\ -1 & -1 & -1 \end{matrix} \qquad \text{mask F} = \begin{matrix} 1 & -2 & -1 \\ -2 & 5 & -2 \\ 1 & -2 & -1 \end{matrix}$$

Examples area edge sharpening filter (FSHARP, Pre-witt edge detector (FPRE), Sobel edge detector (FSOBEL).

### *Edge Enhanced Images*

As edge enhanced image removes low frequencies and the images gives a confusing look. For this a portion of the original image is added back to the high pass image through ARI (40% is normally suggested). The combination of the original image plus the edge detection image is called edge enhanced image. While adding grey value range may exceed the 8 bit, channel limit. So to scale the output result is necessary parameters AUTO and R VAL) of program ARI or write in a 16 bit channel. PCI program FSHARP computes the result of performing a high pass differential edge detection filter and then adds this result back to the original image to produce the final edge enhanced image.

*Programmable filter (FPR)/Laplacian filter*

Performs programmable filtering on image data. It averages image data according to user specified weights. Filter dimension must be odd and possible upto 33 × 33 Kernel Size. A matrix of real weights should be specified by the user within the kernel filtered pixel value will be sum of weighted values divided by the sum of all filter weights. If the sum of the filter weights is zero, then the weighted SUM of grey values in the kernel is computed for the central pixel Parameters to be set are FILE, DBIC, DBOC, FLSZ, MASK, FLTFIL, MRnn. FLTFIL specifies the name of the text file, MRnn filters matrix row elements, 11 or fewer real values. Number of elements and rows should be equal to FLSZ. All rows should have same number of elements and must be odd number.

| | | | | | |
|---|---|---|---|---|---|
| 0 | 1 | 0 | -1 | -1 | -1 |
| 1 | -4 | 1 | -1 | 8 | -1 |
| 0 | 1 | 0 | -1 | -1 | -1 |

*Pre witt edge detector*

It creates an image where edges are shown. It computes the root mean square of two templates. Most popular 3 × 3 edge detection filter. Parameters to be set are FILE, DBIC, DBOC, FLSZ, FACTOR (gain).

| | | |
|---|---|---|
| -1 | 0 | 1 |
| -1 | 0 | 1 |
| -1 | 0 | 1 |
| | X | |

*Sobel edge detector (FSOBEL)*

| | | |
|---|---|---|
| 1 | 1 | 1 |
| 0 | 0 | 0 |
| -1 | -1 | -1 |
| | Y | |

It creates an image where edges are shown. It also computes the root mean square of two 3 × 3 templates. Parameters required are same as in prewitt edge detector.

| | | | | | |
|---|---|---|---|---|---|
| -1 | 0 | 1 | 1 | 2 | 1 |
| -2 | 0 | 2 | 0 | 0 | 0 |
| -1 | 0 | 1 | - 1 | - 2 | - 1 |
| | X | | | Y | |

*Edge sharpening filters (FSHARP)*

It uses a subtractive smoothing method. First an average filter is applied. The output image retaining all low frequency information but has high frequency features attenuated. Average image is subtracted from the original one and resultant difference image only have edges and lines. This difference image is then added back to the original to give edge enhanced image. Dimension of kernel must be odd, maximum filter size is 33, window need not be square. For 8 .bit channel if the result is less than '0' it will be truncated to zero. Similarly, values more than 255 will be truncated to zero.

***Edge Enhancement***

*Linear*

Based upon application of running difference operation. Original image is shifted by one pixel and the difference with original is tested. If no change DN = 127, for negative change DN = 30 and positive change DN = 200 is assigned. The result is an image with grey background and black and white lines surrounding the edges. The algorithm for enhancing horizontal, vertical and diagonal edges are as follows:

| | | |
|---|---|---|
| Horizontal | — | $BV_{i,J} = BV_{i,j} - BV_{i,j}$ |
| Vertical | — | $BV_{i,j} = BV_{i,j} - BV_{i,j}+_1$ |
| Diagonal | — | $BV_{i,j} = BV_{i,j} - BVi+_{ij}+_I$ |

By selectively applying these enhancements, it is possible to enhance only vertical, horizontal or diagonal edges.

Second method is by convolving the original data with a weighted mask of optimum size compass gradient masks can be used to perform two-dimensional discrete differentiation edge enhancement.

| | | | | | | | |
|---|---|---|---|---|---|---|---|
| North = | 1 | 1 | 1 | South = | -1 | -2 | -1 |
| | 1 | 2 | 1 | | 1 | 2 | 1 |
| | -1 | 1 | -1 | | 1 | 1 | 1 |
| Northeast = | 1 | 1 | 1 | Southeast = | -1 | -1 | 1 |
| | -1 | - 2 | 1 | | -1 | -2 | 1 |
| | -1 | - 1 | 1 | | 1 | 1 | 1 |
| East = | -1 | 1 | 1 | West = | 1 | -1 | 1 |
| | -1 | - 2 | 1 | | 1 | -2 | 1 |
| | 1 | 1 | 1 | | 1 | 1 | 1 |
| Southwest = | 1 | - 1 | -1 | Southwest = | 1 | 1 | 1 |
| | 1 | - 2 | -1 | | 1 | -2 | 1 |
| | 1 | 1 | 1 | | 1 | -1 | -1 |

It emphasises maximum values or peaks within the image often edge enhanced output is added back to original image.

## Special Transformation

### *Principal Component Analysis*

It is also called Karhunen-Loeve Analysis. The transformation of the raw data using PCA can result in new PC image that are more interpretable than the original data. It is also used to compress the information content or reduce dimensionality content of a number of bands.

### *Vegetation Indices*

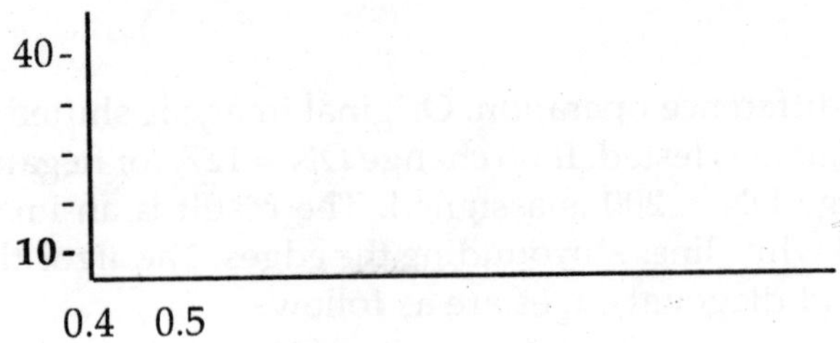


Spectral reflectance curve of vegetation

*NDVI (normalized difference vegetation index) = $\frac{IR - R}{IR + R}$

*TVI (transformed vegetation index) = NDVI + 0.5

Brightness is highly correlated with bare soil while greenness is highly correlated with legal area index,% canopy do sure and/or biomass.

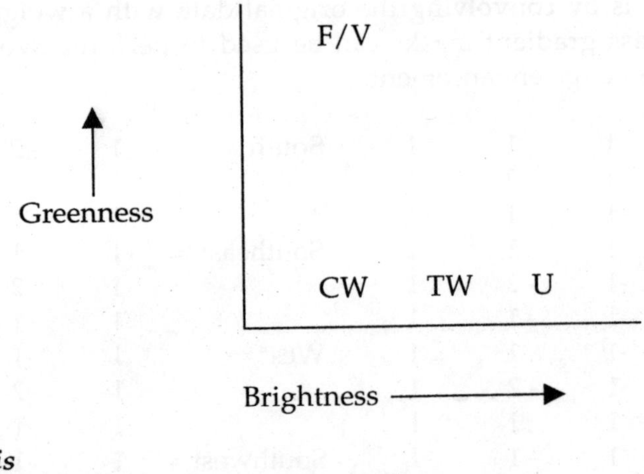


### *Image Analysis*

Image Classification: The term classification is often used in a general sense to indicate any of the decision making operations carried out in pattern recognition to allocate unknown patterns to pattern classes. The term pattern is not used in its normal sense, since in mathematical terms pattern is simply a set of numerical values, each value describing the state of a particular feature. The pattern recognition when used in digital interpretation may mean multispectral pattern recognition in addition to spatial pattern recognition. Identification of suitable bands for a classification constitutes feature selection.

### Supervised Classification

Supervised classification is the name normally used for pattern recognition. Pattern recognition is a process which is used to categorize or classify each pattern (pixel) into one of a pre-specified labels (classes). It is a two-step process in which:

(a) The classes of interest are characterized through analysis of data, which are representative of the class. This step is called training the classifier.
(b) All the data are classified by means of numerical rules (decision rules/ classifier) which utilize the class characteristics.

#### *Training the Classifier*

In this step ground truth information is used to identify areas, which correspond to various classes on the ground, and information about each class is derived from this representative set. Training Field Extraction: Use of supervised classification means that analyst should have some idea about the number of information classes present in the image. These classes are located by fieldwork or from air photographs or map interpretation and their position on image is found either by visual interpretation or by carrying out geometric correction of the image. From these identified location of training classes, statistical properties of the classes are estimated.

#### *Training Field Analysis*

The process of moving from initial training fields and their statistics to a set of refined statistics, which will be used in classification, named training field analysis, is the most difficult step in supervised classification. It involves judgement of the analyst and can also be time consuming. The reasoning behind decisions to merge or delete classes has been described as more of art than science and requires experience or expert analyst. Training field analysis on the basis of estimated statistical properties of the identified fields involves two major decisions: whether or not to merge the data from two or more training fields if they are spectrally similar, and whether or not to delete a training field if its characteristics are sub-optimal in the context of classification algorithm that will be based on this training data.

#### *Statistical Separability*

The purpose of using statistical pattern recognition techniques is to classify in presence of some uncertainty or presence of some overlap between the classes. In such a situation it is necessary to know the probability of error or confidence in classifier. If this could be computed before the classification step, it could be used in designing a more effective classifier. One way could be to classify the training data, which in practice will give lower than actual error rate for the entire data. Another approach is to use an independent data set for error estimation. In this case, higher errors could be simply due to non-representativeness of the ground truth classes. Third approach is to use indirect measures of probability or error, which is generally done through measures of statistical separability among classes.

*Classification procedures using spectral information*

Minimum distance classifier Parallelepiped Classifier.
Maximum Likelihood Classifier

Hybrid methods: A hybrid classifier is one, which incorporates two, or more decision rules (classification algorithms) and tries the cheapest one first. An example is use of simple classifier such as parallelepiped for identifying well separated classes and use of computationally expensive procedure of MXL for those cases where pixel falls in two or more parallelepipeds.

***Decision-tree Classifiers***

Generally one or few features can distinguish different patterns. However, these features may not be the same for each pair of patterns. The decision tree classifier is an attempt to use a "stratified" or "layered" approach to problem of discrimination. The computation time for this approach increases only linearly with number of features in contrast to MXL where it increases as square of number of features. The design of decision tree classifiers is an area of research as manual method of design may be too difficult or time consuming.

***Unsupervised Classification***

The unsupervised classification techniques are two-step approach to pattern classification in which the first step aims to find *out* natural groupings in the data without any priori information about the ground classes. These natural groupings are called "spectral classes". In the second step, these spectral classes are assigned to ground or information class using ground/field information. These techniques are very useful in a number of situations.

**Post Classification Analysis**

The post-classification step in digital image analysis can include one or more of the following procedures:

(a) *Accuracy Estimation*: Includes procedures, which are useful in estimating accuracy of a thematic map generated from digital analysis.

(b) *Area Estimation*: Includes step of estimation of aerial extent of land cover categories from Digital thematic map.
(c) *Statistical analysis with collateral data*: Includes regression of ground observed variables with satellite observed radiances or estimated reflectance.
(d) *Resolving mixed pixels into component classes*: Includes procedures for obtaining individual components making up coarse resolution data like NOAA-A VHRR.
(e) *Post-classification smoothing*: Includes removing small and unmapable unit for display of smoothed classified image.
(f) *Import into GIS* for further analysis and integration
(g) *Generation of hardcopy*: Processing to generate colour or black and white hardcopy from thematic map and can include enhancements (black and white/colour), annotating the image, overlaying vector information, scaling and output generation.

**Utility of Remotely Sensed Data for Various Applications**

Since the launch of Landsat and subsequently the IRS series multispectral data have been subjected to intensive study and experimentation by many resource scientists. Considerable progress has been made in operational use of remote sensing technology in several countries including India for various applications such as geology/ geomorphology, mineral and petroleum exploration, soils, crop identification and acreage estimation, soil mapping, land 'degradation, forest management, vegetation mapping, hydrology and water resources, cartography, land use, urban planning, marine resources and oceanography etc.

RESOURCES MAPPING
GEOLOGICAL MAPPING
GEOMORPHIC MAPPING
SOIL MAPPING
LAND COVER MAPPING
FOREST MAPPING

# 5

# A Case Study on Land Resource Management Using Remote Sensing and GIS

*Sandeep Goyal*

Remote Sensing technique provides accurate, reliable and spatially comprehensive data on various natural resources at regular interval, thus proved to be the most effective tool for mapping and monitoring of natural resources. Remote sensing is the process of sensing, identification and delineation of various objects from a distance without directly coming physically into contact with them (Gautam, N.C., 1993). In other words 'Remote Sensing' is the science of deducing inferences about objects from measurements made at a distance, without coming into physical contact with the objects under study. The term remote sensing is used more commonly to denote identification of earth features by detecting the characteristic electromagnetic radiation that is reflected/emitted by the earth surface. Remote Sensing, due to its synoptic coverage and repetitive availability of data is a proven tool for generation of spatial information about geology, geomorphology, soil type and land use/land cover practices. It is largely concerned with the measurement of electromagnetic radiation from the sun, radiated, emitted or scattered by the different objects on the surface of earth. Due to different physical and optical properties of the objects, different objects reflect different amounts of energy in different wavelength ranges of electromagnetic spectrum. In addition, objects emit radiation depending on their temperature and emissivity. If the reflectance or emittance of any object at different wavelengths is studied it gives a reflectance or emittance pattern, which is a characteristic of that object, known as "Spectral signature". The "Spectral signature" enables, in principle, to identify the objects. Visual perception of objects is the best example of remote sensing. The light that reflected from the object falling on the human eye sees an object. Modern remote sensing is an extension of this natural phenomenon. However, apart from visible range of spectrum, the electromagnetic radiation extending from the ultraviolet to the far infrared (IR) and the microwave regions are also used for remote sensing of the earth resources.

A remote sensing system consists of two parts, *i.e.* data acquisition and data analyses. Data acquisition system consists a sensor to collect the radiation and a platform an aircraft, a balloon, rocket, satellite or even a ground-based sensor-supporting stand on which a sensor can be mounted. In a satellite based remote sensing system, the sensor detects electromagnetic radiation reflected, emitted or scattered by the various objects on the surface of the earth in different wavelength ranges known as bands. This quantum of energy detected by the sensor is converted into a digital number or DN value and transmitted back to ground station. Initially this data is in the grey level format but to enhance the interpretability the different band data is passed through three primary colour filters, *i.e.* red, blue and green to generate False Colour Composite. These FCC images can be put to analyses either in a hardcopy format or in a softcopy. Hardcopy photographs are interpreted visually whereas softcopy can be analysed digitally using computers and digital image processing system to produce thematic maps and other resource information. The information thus generated in the form of various layers can be effectively superimposed on each other for further analyses using GIS.

In the present study the study area pertains to the watershed of Chundi River. The Chundi watershed, with Chundi as a major consequent stream flows east-west having a catchment area of 532.35 sq. km impressively decorated with undulated moderately high denudational hills in the east and south-west and vast flat weathered buried bedrock surface termed as pediplain, spread over the rest of the region. The boundary of the watershed is formed by water-divide of the Chundi river system. It is located between 23°31′06″ to 23°45′06″ N latitude and 81°14′30″ E to 81°40′ 43″ E longitude covering a total area 532.35 sq. km. Geographically the Chundi watershed is bounded by the watersheds of Odari Nadi in east, Halphal and Gorna Nala in north and south and by the Son river in the west, where it meets the Son.

Administratively the maximum area of Chundi watershed lies in Gohaparu and Jaishinghnagar blocks of Shahdol district of Madhya Pradesh covering an area of 263.69 and 226.52 sq. km respectively. A small portion on the western border of the Chundi watershed lies in the adjacent Bharatpur tehsil of Sarguja district, Chhattisgarh covering an area of 42.14 sq. km. The Chundi river bisect the administrative boundary between Gohaparu and Jaisinghnagar blocks of Shahdol district. Jaisinghnagar block lies in the northern side of Chundi river whereas southern side is occupied by the areas of Gohaparu block. The major towns of the Chundi watershed are Jaisinghnagar and Khannaudhi.

In the present study IRS-1C LISSIII geocoded images (paper prints) pertaining to Survey of India toposheet nos. 64E/2, 64E/5, 64E/6 and 64E/10, on 1:50,000 scale were visually interpreted to generate various thematic maps. For the evaluation and management of land resources of Chundi watershed the thematic maps of land use/land cover, geology, geomorphology etc. have been generated using satellite images. The other information such as relief and slope etc. were gathered from the toposheets and converted in digital layers using GIS.

Management of land resources infers proper land utilisation in such a way that the yield is optimised and also it prevents the soils or land from further degradation. Therefore, it is necessary to evaluate the landuse/land cover of the region and land capability of the Chundi watershed for its proper management. These landuse and land cover units have a defined land capability on the basis of which it is to be decided that what should be the proper use of each land parcel in such a way that it will yield to its maximum capability without any further degradation. Soil permeability is also an important factor for watershed management to assess the groundwater conditions. Soil permeability is also discussed in this chapter.

Land utilisation covers two aspects, *i.e.* landuse and land cover. Landuse refers to the various uses under which land is brought by a multitude of human activities whereas land cover refers to the natural covering or setting of land without interference of any human activity. For the evaluation and management of the Chundi watershed, the study of landuse/land cover is one of the most important variables.

The distribution of wasteland and degraded forest in the country accounts to 20 per cent of total geographical area and Madhya Pradesh (unified) comprises 15 per cent of its total geographical area as wastelands, whereas in Chundi watershed approx. 25 per cent of land is under wasteland and degraded forest. In the present study an integrated approach has been adopted to evaluate every parcel of lands for adoption of a suitable landuse management practice. Capabilities of GIS are utilised adopting Boolean Logic Model with equal weightage and table criteria approach, for integration of thematic information and generation of land resource management plan. The thematic layers, which are considered for land resource management, are Lithology, Geomorphology, Landuse/Landcover, Soil, Slope, Land Capability and Groundwater Potential. These layers are integrated using 'CROSS' operation of ILWIS 2.2 GIS packages resulting in Composite Land Development Unit (CLDU) map. Each CLDU explains a unique combination of Lithology, Geomorphology, Landuse/Landcover, Soil, Shape, Land capability and Groundwater potential. 970 such combinations are found after integration. These combinations are grouped in a tabulated form and suitable action is suggested for each group of combination. Land resource management is divided in three parts, *i.e.*:

1. Agriculture Land Management
2. Waste Land Management
3. Forest Land Management

**Agriculture Land Management**

Conventional cropping pattern and agricultural practices do not seem adequate during the periods of weather aberrations. Apart from that as per the land capability classification system capability classes I to IV along with gentle to moderate slope, supporting Lithology, Geomorphology and suitable groundwater condition are found suitable for agricultural practices beyond that they are unsuitable for conventional agriculture use. Chundi watershed comprises 13.54 sq. km of land, which is under cultivation despite of unsuitable conditions, which results in poor production. Similarly, some areas are under-utilised due to social and economic problems. Therefore, all such areas and conditions are studied are fully to suggest optimum utilisation of each land unit. Various actions suggested for optimum utilisation of land. These actions are as follows:

### *Double Crop*

Double cropping system is very common agriculture practice in the areas where required soil moisture for growing a crop is available for about 200 days or more in a year. The moisture retaining capacity of soil should also be good.

### *Agro-Horticulture*

Agro-Horticulture is a modified system of Farm-Forestry or Agro-Forestry. This system plays an important role in cropping areas where productions of annual crop were insufficient. In this system plantation of fruit bearing trees is done along with existing cropping system. Most of the fruit bearing trees are woody perennials with deep roots, which take a minimum number of years to bear fruit. Trees are to be distributed evenly over the area to optimise growing space and light for both trees and under-storey crop. Adoption of this system helps in increasing of organic matter content of the soil through the addition of leaf litter and other plant parts, which improves soil fertility. Tree growth also helps in checking of soil erosion and increase infiltration of rainwater, which improves soil moisture. Although initial expenditure to establish this is high in comparison to normal cropping, but once trees start bearing fruits, it gives good annual return on a regular basis. Until the farmer starts getting returns from the horticulture component, inter-cropping can compensate the income and at later stages, cropping can be practised with judicial management of trees.

### *Agro-Forestry*

Agro-forestry is similar system as agro-horticulture; the difference lies in selection of tree species. In this system fast growing trees of forestry importance such as Su-babool, Jangal Jalebi etc. are chosen for plantation. Similar to the previous system the trees are planted in such a way that it provides sufficient space for individual growth and proper light for under-story crops. This pattern not only helps in providing fuel and timber but also fodder for the livestock. Regular management of this system includes thinning and pruning of trees to create appropriate condition for the understorey crop to be growing. Then the under-stony crop is established and intensively managed to provide short-term income. This system helps in improving soil fertility by increasing the organic matter content of soil. It also helps in checking the soil erosion and improves the soil moisture content.

Few areas with soil erosion problem are suggested for ***Agro-forestry with soil conservation*** measures are also suggested. These soil conservation measures are required in the initial stage of tree farming and once the system is established and trees are grown-up, they themselves check the soil erosion. Some land parcels are also suggested for ***Agro-forestry on farm bunds*** by plantation of trees on farm bunds.

### *Dry Land Horticulture*

Dry land horticulture is a system in which, fruit bearing trees which do not require very good soil moisture are adopted for plantation or in other words the dryland species, *e.g.* Ber, Amla and Custard apple etc. are the varieties which can be adopted for this purpose. Marginal crop areas having skeletal soil and moderate to poor ground water potential are not suitable for crop production, are to be converted into dryland horticulture. Initially crop can be grown as a usual practice as an understorey to compensate the income to the farmer but once the trees are grown up farming practice should be stopped. Because in such areas farming will lead to further degradation of land which may be irrecoverable in the long run. This practice can also be effectively used for reclamation of ***culturable wastelands***.

### *Farm Forestry*

Farm forestry is a type of agroforestry and is applied where the soil is with the land capability VI and VII and ground water conditions are moderate to poor or poor to nil. The difference in farm forestry and agro forestry lies in selection of crops and tree species. In this system dry land species of trees are chosen for plantation. The tree species suitable in Chundi watershed area for farm forestry are Babool *(Acacia Nilotica)*, Gumhar *(Gmelina arborea)*, Su babul *(Leucaena leucocephala)* etc. The selection of under-storey crops are also from dry land agriculture species such as fast growing legumes, Jwar, Bajra etc. This pattern helps in providing fuel, timber and fodder for the livestock. Regular management of this system includes thinning and pruning of trees to create appropriate condition for the understorey crop to be growing. This system helps in improving soil fertility by increasing the organic matter content of soil. It also helps in checking the soil erosion and improves the soil moisture content.

### *In-situ Soil Conservation*

*In-situ* soil conservation is the practice used for soils which are suitable for agriculture as per the land capability is concerned but there is some limitation with soil such as erosion proneness, wetness limitation or soil depth limitation. Soil conservation measures such as vegetative bunding, using of organic manure etc. are being used to prevent from further degradation of soils and increase sustainability and production.

### *No Action*

There are areas which are already utilised optimally as per their conditions and capability. Such areas are being left as no action required, only the present landuse system should be maintained.

## Wasteland Management

India is having 510488.76 sq. km wastelands are culturable or recoverable which suitable management practices. Similarly Madhya Pradesh (unified) is having 69713.75 sq. km of wastelands which are recoverable. Wasteland management envisages not only the reclamation of the present wasteland but also checks the further degradation of land units, which may increase the extension of wasteland.

Chundi watershed comprise of 63.95 sq. km of area under wasteland category of landuse/land cover classification. All of these wastelands are culturable in nature and using suitable management techniques these areas can not only be reclaimed but also can be productive for bio-mass production. Different wastelands are suggested for various actions as per their respective prevailing conditions. The actions suggested are given below:

***Ley Farming***

Ley farming is the activity under which in the initial year land is utilised for pasture development using grass-legume mixture or lay as a farm crop. The grass has valuable quality of improving soil structure whereas the legume enriches the soil nitrogen. In the later years once the soil fertility is improved this land can be utilised for agricultural activity, along with reseeding of lays at a regular interval. In other words the term "Ley Farming" cannotes a system where a farm or a group of fields is cropped entirely with lays, which are reseeded at regular interval (R.P. Singh *et al.*, 1990). Ley farming helps in soil conservation improvement in structure and fertility of soil. It acts as a soil-fertility regenerating system especially with respects to nitrogen. For example, "Stylosanthes Hamata" is a protein rich pasture legume which is widely used as pasture legume ley. This helps in providing fodder for the livestock of the neighbouring hamlets. For getting the optimum yield it requires regular management pattern. As a management practice open grazing should not be allowed in these areas. In place of this the fodder should be cut when the grass in fully-grown up and fed to cattle. Uncontrolled grazing can totally damage this system.

**Fuelwood Plantation**

Fuelwood plantation is a management practice which can be applied to either community waste lands or even private holding wastelands which are culturable having good to moderate groundwater potential. This system helps in providing fuel and fodder to the neighbouring areas. It also caters to the timber requirement up to a great extent for the surrounding hemlets. The species which are to be selected should be locale specific and suitable to climatic conditions of the area. The species which are adopted for this system are usually fast growing. As a regular management practice the areas under this system should be protected for grazing and uncontrolled tree shedding.

***Pasture Development***

"Native pastures in India are very poor in productivity. They almost lack any vegetative cover. In essence, they are exercise ground for cattle rather than pasture lands. Multifarious problems are associated with low productivity. Some of which are technical and others are social (R.P. Singh *et al.*, 1987). Most of the pasturelands have been under pressure of regular uncontrolled grazing for years without any input or management. This leads these land units to convert as land with or without scrub. To develop the pastures lands the first and foremost step is to identify suitable grasses and legumes which are high productive and suitable to climatic conditions of the area.

As per the researches done by Central Research Institute for Dryland Agriculture (CRIDA) or other agricultural research centres it has been found that in rain fed areas legumes from genera *Dolichos, Macropiytilium, Leucaeua, Clitoria, Desmodium, Cassia, Stylosathes* etc. can be grown. But out of these *Stylosanthes* is the ideal legume which was found to be excellent in regard to persistence, nutritive values and palatability. Similarly, the grasses from *Dichanthim, Cenchrus, Lasiurus, Chloris, Paspalum* etc. are suitable. Out of these species *Cenchrus ciliaris* is high yielding and suitable in all conditions.

### *Silvipasture*

Silvipasture is an integrated landuse management system in which the fast growing trees of forestry importance are grown up in such a way to provide conditions for under story cropping grasses and legumes. In other words silvipasture is an agro-forestry practice specifically designed and managed for the production of trees, tree products and forage for the livestock. In the some parts of the globe livestock management is also included with silvipasture and termed as "Silvopasture". Silvipastoral systems are designed to produce a high volume timber component. While providing short-term cash flow from the forage development. Towards the management part of this system the timber component should be fast growing deep rooted and drought tolerant whereas the forage component must be highly productive, having high nutritive value and compatible with the climatic conditions of the area.

### *Pasture Development with Gully Control Measures*

Wastelands under gullied/ravenous land category are required to be controlled on topmost priority. Due to head ward erosion gully formation moves very fast in the head ward direction and can grab the cultivated areas under their grip. Gully control measures are to be applied to such areas. The most suitable and commonly used practice is Gully-plugging. Gully-plugging can be done either using Gabbean structure or ordinary rock fill. Gabbean structures slightly costlier than rock fill but more stable and useful. In the Gabbean structures a wire mesh is wrap over the rock fill to provide the stability using this structure the gully heads are to plug as the first step. Later pasture development can be practiced. Pasture development helps in checking the soil erosion and all useful due to forage production.

### *Pitting Followed by Plantation*

Stony waste areas where the soil cover is very less to adopt any management practice can be effectively reclaimed up to a certain extent using pitting followed by plantation.

In this system in the initial year pits are dig and left for one or two rainy season. This helps in development of some soil moisture. In later years plantation of dry land tree species can be done in these pits. At places if required soil can be transported from neighbouring areas. For filling this pit during the plantation to support the plant survival.

**Forest Land Management**

Good forests are must for maintaining the ecological balance. Wildlife protection is providing climatic conditions and checking of land degradation. It is therefore necessary to apply suitable management techniques to conserve and develop forest. Various management techniques such as Afforestation, Gap plantation etc. have been suggested as per suitable conditions.

***Nursery Development***

Nursery development is the most important management practice in the forest management activity. For any management practice such as gap plantation, afforestation or silvipasture etc. the first and fore most requirement is plant siblings. It is not economically viable to transport the plant from a centralised nursery to all the areas. Therefore, small patches of degraded or blank forest areas having good to very good ground water conditions can be developed as nursery. While developing the nursery it is to be kept in view that the plants should be locale specific and suitable to climatic conditions of the area.

***Gap Plantation***

Gap plantation as the term reveals is the plantation of suitable trees in gaps developed in the forest due to tree cutting and degradation of forests. It is a modified Afforestation technique applied to open/degraded forest areas. To achieve the best result of this system it is necessary to select plants which are similar to existing naturally grown species. Such areas should be protected from grazing and other encroachment. As an initial step pits have to be made ready before rainy season and then after initial precipitation the plantation is to be done.

***Afforestation***

Afforestation is the most commonly used forest management practice in which plantation of forest importance trees is done in the forest blank or in the forest encroachment areas. Similarly, as Gap plantation initially the pitting is done as a first step before the monsoon. After the initial showers plantation is done. The areas which are under afforestation are to be protected from grazing and encroachments. It has been observed that in some areas where good amount of rootstock is available, the natural growth from the rootstock after protection of these areas shows better results then plantation. It is also necessary to choose fast growing and climatically suitable species for afforestation.

### *Cattle Protection Trench*

Areas which are presently under plantation are under the continuous threat of grazing. It is necessary to protect these areas using cattle protection trenches. These trenches are about 1.5 m width and about one metre deep so that the cattle cannot cross these trenches and the area is protected.

### *Forest Protection*

The dense forest areas are needed to be conserved from natural hazards such as soil erosion. Keeping this in view the dense forest areas of Chundi watershed, which are having moderate to very steep slopes are suggested for forest protection. Under this management practice the higher slope areas are to be protected against soil erosion by soil conservation measures and contour bunding.

### *No Action*

The dense forest areas which are having very gentle to gentle slope do not need any other management practice except conservation therefore kept under no action.

Criteria tables for different land management actions suggested as per suitability are given as annexure.

## REFERENCES

Bahera, G. *et al.*, 1995, *"Integrated Mission for Sustainable Development – Technical Guidelines"*, NRSA, Department of Space Publication, Hyderabad.

Burrough, P.A., 1990, *Priciples of Geographical Information Systems for Land Resources Assessment*, Clarendon Press, Oxford.

Champion, H.G. *et al.*, 1968, *"Revised Forest types of India"*, Government of India Publications, Delhi.

Rao Mukund, Jayaraman, V. and Chandrasekhar, M.G., 1994, *"Organising Spatial Information Systems Around a GIS Core – Database Organisation and Integrated Analysis using GIS"*, Special publication, NNRMS, Indian Space Research Organisation, Bangalore, Vol. SP-70-94.

## ANNEXURE

**Criteria Table for Agriculture Land Management**

| *Landuse* | *Landcap* | *Geomorphology* | *Slope* | *GWP* | *Lithology* | *Soil* | *Remark* |
|---|---|---|---|---|---|---|---|
| **1. Action Suggested: Double Crop** | | | | | | | |
| Kharif Crop | IIe, | IFV, BPP-M | 2 | Very Good to Excellent | Alluvium, Sandstone | Fine Loamy Typic Haplustalf Fine Loamy Typic and Ultic Paleustalf | — |
| Kharif Crop | IIIw | IFV, BPP-M, BPP-S | 2, 3 | Good, Very Good and Very Good to Excellent | Alluvium, Sandstone | Coarse Loamy Aeric Fluquent and Fine Loamy Aquic Ustochrept. | — |
| **2. Action Suggested: Agrohorticulture** | | | | | | | |
| Double Crop | VIIes | BPP-M, BPP-S | 2, 3 | Moderate to Poor and Poor | Sandstone | Loamy Skeletal Typic and Lithic Ustorthent | Rain water harvesting structures suggested in adjacent areas. |
| Fallow Land | IIe, IIIes, IIIw | IFV, BPP-M, BPP-S | 2 | Good, Very Good and Very Good to Excellent | Alluvium, Sandstone | Fine Loamy Typic Haplustalf and Typic and Ultic Paleustalf, Coarse Loamy Aeric Fluquent and Fine Loamy Aquic Ustochrept. | — |
| Kharif Crop | IIe, IIIes, IVes, VIes, VIIes | IFV, BPP-M, BPP-S, BP | 2, 3 | Good, Very Good and Very Good to Excellent | Alluvium, Sandstone and Basic Intrusive | Fine Loamy Typic Haplustalf and Typic and Ultic Paleustalf, Loamy Skeletal Lithic and Typic Ustorthent | — |
| **3. Action Suggested: Agroforestry** | | | | | | | |
| Fallow Land | IIe, IIIes, IIIw | IFV, BPP-M, BPP-S | 2, 3 | Moderate to Poor and Poor | Alluvium, Sandstone | Fine Loamy Typic Haplustalf, Fine Loamy Typic and Ultic Paleustalf, Coarse Loamy Aeric Fluquent | — |
| Kharif Crop | IIe and VIes with Good | BPP-M, BPP-S, BP | 2, 3 | Moderate to Poor | Alluvium, Sandstone and Basic | Fine Loamy Typic Haplustalf and Typic and | — |

*(Contd.)*

*(Contd.)*

| *Landuse* | *Landcap* | *Geomorphology* | *Slope* | *GWP* | *Lithology* | *Soil* | *Remark* |
|---|---|---|---|---|---|---|---|
| | GWP | | | | Intrusive | Ultic Paleustalf, Loamy Skeletal Lithic and Typic Ustorthent | |
| Kharif Crop | IIIes, IIIw, and IIe with Poor GWP VIes with Moderate to Poor GWP | BPP-M, BPP-S, BP, LR, DH | 2,3,4 | Moderate to Poor and Poor | Sandstone and Basic Intrusive | Fine Loamy Typic Haplustalf and Typic and Ultic Paleustalf, Coarse Loamy Aeric Fluquent, Loamy Skeletal Lithic and Typic Ustorthent | Agroforestry along with **Soil Conservation Measures** and on higher slopes with **Contour Bunding** |
| Kharif Crop | VIes | BP, LR | 2,3,4 | Poor | Basic Intrusive | Loamy Skeletal Typic Ustorthent | Agroforestry along with **Vegetative Barrier.** |
| **4. Action Suggested: Dry Land Horticulture** | | | | | | | |
| Kharif Crop | VIIes | BPP-S, BP, LR, DH | 2,3,4 | Moderate to Poor | Sandstone and Basic Intrusive | Loamy Skeletal Lithic and Typic Ustorthent | — |
| **5. Action Suggested: Farm Forestry** | | | | | | | |
| Fallow Land | VIes, VIIes | BPP-M, BP | 2,4 | Moderate to Poor and Poor | Sandstone and Basic Intrusive | Loamy Skeletal Lithic and Typic Ustorthent | — |
| Kharif Crop | VIIes | BP, DH, LR | 2,3,4 | Poor | Sandstone and Basic Intrusive | Loamy Skeletal Lithic and Typic Ustorthent | Contour Bunding may be added on higher slopes. |
| **6. Action Suggested: In situ Soil Conservation** | | | | | | | |
| Double Crop | IIe, IIIes, IIIw, IVes | IFV, BPP-M, BPP-S, BP | 2,3 to | Moderate Poor and Poor | Alluvium, Sandstone and Basic Intrusive | Fine Loamy Typic Haplustalf and Typic and Ultic Paleustalf, Coarse Loamy Aeric Fluquent, Fine Loamy Skeletal Typic Ustorthent | Rain Water harvesting structures suggested in adjacent areas to increase irrigation and for sustainability. |
| **7. No Action** | | | | | | | |
| Double Crop | IIe, IIIes, IIIw, IVes | IFV, BPP-M, BPP-S, BP | 2,3 | Very Good to Excellent, Very | Alluvium, Sandstone and Basic | Fine Loamy Typic Haplustalf, Fine Loamy | — |

*(Contd.)*

*(Contd.)*

| *Landuse* | *Landcap* | *Geomorphology* | *Slope* | *GWP* | *Lithology* | *Soil* | *Remark* |
|---|---|---|---|---|---|---|---|
| | | | | Good, and Good | Intrusive | Typic and Ultic Paleustalf, Coarse Loamy Aeric Fluquent, Fine Loamy Skeletal Typic Ustorthent | |

**Criteria Table for Wasteland Management**

| *Landuse* | *Landcap* | *Geomorphology* | *Slope* | *GWP* | *Lithology* | *Soil* | *Remark* |
|---|---|---|---|---|---|---|---|
| **1. Action Suggested: Ley Farming** | | | | | | | |
| Land with Scrub and Land without Scrub | IIe, IIIes, IIIw, IVes, VIes | IFV, BPP-M, BPP-S, BP | 2, 3 | Very Good to Excelent, Very Good and Good | Alluvium, Sandstone and Basic Intrusive | Fine Loamy Typic Haplustalf and Typic and Ultic Paleustalf, Coarse Loamy Aeric Fluquent, Fine Loamy Skeletal Typic Ustorthent | — |
| **2. Action Suggested: Fuel Wood Plantation** | | | | | | | |
| Land with Scrub and Land without Scrub | VIIes | CB, BPP-M, BPP-S and BP | 2 | Very Good and Good | Alluvium, Sandstone and Basic Intrusive | Fine Loamy Skeletal Typic Ustorthent, Loamy Skeletal Lithic and Typic Ustorthent | |
| **3. Action Suggested: Pasture Development** | | | | | | | |
| Land with Scrub and Land without Scrub | IIe, IIIes, IIIw, IVes, VIes, | IFV, BPP-M, BPP-S, BP | 2 | Moderate to Poor and Poor | Alluvium, Sandstone and Basic Intrusive | Fine Loamy Typic Haplustalf and Typic and Ultic Paleustalf, Coarse Loamy Aeric Fluquent, Fine Loamy and Loamy Skeletal Typic Ustorthent | — |
| **4. Action Suggested: Silvipasture** | | | | | | | |
| Land with Scrub and Land without Scrub | IIe, IIIes, IIIw, IVes, VIes | IFV, BPP-M, BPP-S, BP, DH, LR | 3,4,5 | Moderate to Poor and Poor | Alluvium, Sandstone and Basic Intrusive | Fine Loamy Typic Haplustalf and Typic and Ultic Paleustalf, Coarse Loamy Aeric Fluquent, Fine Loamy and Loamy Skeletal Typic Ustorthent | — |

*(Contd.)*

*(Contd.)*

| *Landuse* | *Landcap* | *Geomorphology* | *Slope* | *GWP* | *Lithology* | *Soil* | *Remark* |
|---|---|---|---|---|---|---|---|
| **5. Action Suggested: Dry Land Horticulture** | | | | | | | |
| Land with Scrub and Land without Scrub | VIIes, | BPP-M, BPP-S, BP, DH, LR | 2,3, 4,6 | Moderate to Poor and Poor | Sandstone and Basic Intrusive | Fine Loamy and Loamy Skeletal Typic Ustorthent and Loamy Skeletal Lithic and Typic Ustorthent | — |
| **6. Action Suggested: Pasture Development with Gully Control Measures** | | | | | | | |
| Gullied/ Ravenous Land | — | — | — | — | — | — | Gully control measures such as gully plugging, Gabbean Structures etc. required to be applied. |
| **7. Action Suggested: Pitting followed by Plantation** | | | | | | | |
| Stony Waste | — | — | — | — | — | — | Pitting to be done in the first year and plantation in the following years. |

**Criteria Table for Forest Land Management**

| *Landuse* | *Landcap* | *Geomorphology* | *Slope* | *GWP* | *Lithology* | *Remark* |
|---|---|---|---|---|---|---|
| **1. Action Suggested: Nursery Development** | | | | | | |
| Open/ Degraded Forest, Forest Blank, Scrub Forest, Crop Land in Forest | II, III, IV, VI | IFV, BPP-M, BPP-S, BP | 2,3 | Good, Very Good and Very Good to Excellent | Alluvium, Sandstone and Basic Intrusive | Small patches are to be used to avoid transportation of plants for afforestation and gap plantation. |
| **2. Action Suggested: Gap Plantation** | | | | | | |
| Open/ Degraded Forest | II, III, IV, VI, VII | BPP-M, BPP-S, BP, DH, LR | 2 | Good, Moderate to Poor and Poor | Sandstone and Basic Intrusive | — |
| Scrub | II, III, IV, | IFV, BPP-M, | 2,3,4 | Good, | Sandstone | — |

*(Contd.)*

*(Contd.)*

| *Landuse* | *Landcap* | *Geomorphology* | *Slope* | *GWP* | *Lithology* | *Remark* |
|---|---|---|---|---|---|---|
| Forest | VI | BPP-S | | Very Good and Very Good to Excellent | and Basic Intrusive | |
| Open/ Degraded Forest, Scrub Forest | II, III, IV, VI and VII with slope class 3 | BPP-M, BPP-S, BP, DH, LR | 3,4 | Good, Moderate to Poor and Poor | Sandstone and Basic Intrusive | Gap Plantation along with **Soil Conservation Measures.** |
| Open/ Degraded Forest | VII | DH, LR | 4 | Poor | Sandstone and Basic Intrusive | Gap Plantation along with **Contour Bunding.** |
| Open/ Degraded Forest | VI, VII | DH, LR | 5, 6 | Moderate to Poor and Poor | Sandstone and Basic Intrusive | Gap Plantation along with **Contour Bunding.** |
| **3. Action Suggested: Afforestation** | | | | | | |
| Forest Blank | II, III, IV, VI, VII | BPP-M, BPP-S, BP, DH, LR | 2, 3 | Good and Very Good | Sandstone and Basic Intrusive | — |
| Double Crop in Forest, Kharif in Forest | II, III, IV | BPP-M, BPP-S, BP | 2, 3 | Good and Very Good | Sandstone and Basic Intrusive | — |
| Forest Blank | II, III, IV, VI, VII | BPP-M, BPP-S, BP, DH, LR | 2, 3, 4, 5, 6 | Moderate to Poor and Poor | Sandstone and Basic Intrusive | Afforestation with **Soil Conservation Measures up to** slope class 3, and **Contour Bunding** at higher slopes. |
| Double Crop in Forest, Kharif in Forest | II, III, IV, VI, VII | BPP-M, BPP-S, BP, DH, LR | 2, 3, 4 | Moderate to Poor and Poor | Sandstone and Basic Intrusive | Afforestation with **Soil Conservation Measures.** |
| **4. Action Suggested: Cattle Protection Trench** | | | | | | |
| Plantation | II, III, VI | BPP-M, BPP-S | 2 | - | Sandstone and Basic Intrusive | Protection against grazing and encroachment. |
| **5. Action Suggested: Silvipasture with Cattle Protection Trench** | | | | | | |
| Scrub Forest | III, IV, VI, VII | BPP-S, BP, DH, LR | 2,3,4 | Moderate to Poor and Poor | Sandstone and Basic Intrusive | — |
| **6. Action Suggested: Forest Protection** | | | | | | |
| Dense Forest | III, IV, VI, VII | BPP-S, BP, DH, LR | 4 and above | — | — | Protection against Soil erosion on higher slopes. |
| **7. No Action** | | | | | | |
| Dense Forest | II, III, IV, VI, VII | IFV, BPP-M, BP, BPP-S, DH, LR | 2,3 | — | — | — |

# 6

# Modeling Concepts for Land Resource Management through Geomatics

*Sandeep Goyal*

Due to population explosion, there is an excessive demand of more land for agriculture and non-agricultural practices. Forests are degraded due to human encroachments, deforestation and increase in grazing. More and more marginal and sub-marginal lands are being brought under cultivation. Cultivation of such land is not only un-economical in long run but also can lead to serious imbalance of the eco-systems. To prevent from such a threatening situation, it is therefore, necessary to evaluate the land conditions and adopt suitable land use practices as an alternate. Geomatics plays an important role to provide spatial information on various parameters and their integrated modeling to generate sustainable development plan.

All the aspects of land resource management such as agriculture land management, *i.e.* wasteland management and forestland management need to be taken up for sustainable development. Boolean logic model approach is found suitable for generation of land resource management plan. This chapter also includes a case study showing details of various land management activities suggested in a watershed.

## Modeling Concepts

The most persistent and pervasive term in GIS is 'Modeling' or in other words 'Integration'. Modeling/Integration in GIS is the synthesis of spatial and non-spatial information within the framework of an application study. Therefore, these information sets are converted into digital format in the form of primary and derived layers to make use of capabilities of GIS.

The most important part of the study is to extract needful information from the map layers to generate analytical models, which support in decision making. The capabilities of GIS are used along with different decision support methods to achieve the result in the form of natural resources evaluation and management plan.

Integration in GIS involves a conjunctive analysis of multi-parameter data. These multi-parameter data include different thematic spatial inputs such as landuse, soils, slopes, lithology etc. and other non-spatial data sets. Integration of these data sets in GIS is carried out to obtain composite information and equally significant would be to derive relevant information out of this composite information. GIS with its processing capabilities can be put to use either by defining logical set of conditions or by relative significance for each data set or parameter in use. For Land resource management the first approach is found most suitable. The fundamental aspect of integration is 'Criterion Definition'.

***Criterion Definition***

Defining the relationship amongst the different parameters in the same units or scale is called as criterion definition. A criterion defines the logic for the analysis of the composite information-set. The criterion is basically a logical grouping of the parameter values into distinct classes for an end-objective. The model may be as simple as re-classification of the parameter values. This is an important aspect of modeling as most of the GIS data sets are represented in different scales and relationships are not well defined. For example, if a soil map and a land use map have been integrated then the relationships of the different land use and soil categories need to be defined. There could be as many criterions as objectives but it is necessary to adopt a systematic logical and rational approach to arrive at an optimal solution. For example, the integration of land use and soil information could be modeled to identify suitability for a crop and also suitability for plantations. However, decision on the actual use would be based on the optimality of the solutions. The relationship definition in all these multi-parameter integration is highly subjective and consensus rarely exists concerning the relationship. Therefore, criterion can either be a simple statement that would describe a true condition or it could be a set of simple statements bundled together to form a tabular description. On this basis criterion can be categorised into **Statement criterion** and **Table criterion.**

A statement criterion is where the relationships of the parameters are defined as a statement. For example, if in an area the soil is moderate to deep, groundwater potential is moderate and present landuse\land cover is wasteland, then the best utilisation of that unit can be a grassland or afforestation. This can be given in a statement as below:

If,
SOIL = Moderate to Deep,
And LANDUSE = Wasteland
And GROUNDWATER = Moderate
Then,
Optimal Solution = Grassland or Afforestation

In this method, the criterion is class dependent and thus the relationship of the parameters within the class is defined. As a result, the relationship across the classes is not defined, thus making the criterion too rigid. For example, the above criterion statement only defines the relationship for moderate to deep soils, wastelands and moderate potentials of groundwater and does not define what happens to shallow soils, forest/agriculture and other land use and poor or good groundwater potential categories. As a result, the integration would be limited by the definition and would not be all encompassing. However, this method is most appropriate where there is no ambiguity in the relationship of the parameters.

A table criterion is a more organised and systematic definition of the relationship amongst all parameters and its categories. The table criterion lays down all possible combinations or relationships and thus provides a total solution from the data set hence it has been used in the present study. The table criterion is basically a matrix of parameters and the solution class categories. For example, land capability determination as is used by the All India Soil and Landuse Survey (AISLUS, 1970). The criterion is based on six parameters categorised into eight capability classes (table 6.1). The criterion table defines the logic of the integrated analysis and provides the **framework** for obtaining systematic outputs. Therefore, in criterion definition the **relative importance** of each parameter is undefined and thus an implicit equality of parameter importance is assumed.

**Table 6.1:** Land Capability Determination

| *Parameters* | *Capability Classes* | | | | | | | |
|---|---|---|---|---|---|---|---|---|
| | I | II | III | IV | V | VI | VII | VIII |
| **Slope%** | 0-1 | 0-1 | 1-3 | 3-5 | 5-10 | 5-10 | 10-15 | >15 |
| **Depth** | >100 | 45-100 | 22.6-46 | 7.5-22.5 | 7.5-22.5 | <7.5 | <7.5 | — |
| **Erosion** | None-Moderate | Moderate | Moderate-Severe | Severe | Severe-V. Severe | V. Severe | V. Severe-Excessive | Excessive |
| **Salinity/ Alkalinity** | None | Moderate | Moderate | Strong | — | Severe | V. Severe | — |
| **Texture** | SI-L | SI-L | SI-L | S-LS | — | Sandy | Sandy | — |
| **Permeability** | Rapid | Rapid-Moderate | Moderate-Slight | Moderate-Slight | — | Slight | Slight | None |

## *Integration Model for Land Resource Management*

Various modeling techniques and methods are evolved and used by researchers for the integration of various types of spatial and non-spatial data. These techniques ranges from simple methods of synthesis of information from the geographical database and querying of information to multivariate methods of statistical analysis and spatial analysis using neighborhood junctions and interpolation methods. Different workers have attempted to define the classification of these models based on different properties. Graeme, F. Bonham-Carter (1994) distinguished GIS models based on the type of relationships (Table 6.2).

**Table 6.2:** Classification of GIS Models Based on Relationship

| *Class* | *Type of Relationship* | *Example* | |
|---|---|---|---|
| | | *Field of Application* | *Model* |
| Technical | Physical/chemical principles | Groundwater flow | Equation of motion |
| Hybrid | Semi-empirical | Sediment transport | Transport equations |
| Empirical | Heuristic of statistical | Mineral prediction | Statistical regression |

"Amongst the variety of complex modeling techniques that can be implemented using the GIS tools, broad distinction can be drawn between those concerned with what is or what could be and those concerned with what should be. This distinction can be expressed in terms of descriptive and prescriptive models. As the application of modeling technique moves from relatively passive forms of query to more active and deliberate forms of decision making and problem solving, the techniques involved tend to be more prescriptive" (Mukund, Rao, 1994).

The most commonly used models are Boolean Logic Model, Fuzzy Logic model, Multi Criterion Evaluation Model/Weighted Index Model etc. All of these techniques have their own merits and demerits for a chosen study. It is found that for land resource management of Boolean Logic Model is very suitable. In Boolean Logic equal weightage of parameters and table criterion method is applied.

***Boolean Logic Model***

In this model the rules of Boolean logic are applied on the attributes and spatial properties of a geographical data. In Boolean algebra operations AND, OR, XOR, NOT are used to see that whether a particular condition is true or false. Various combinations for two objects are represented in a truth table (Table 6.3).

**Table 6.3:** Truth Table Showing Combinations of Two Objects

| *A* | *B* | *NOT A* | *A AND B* | *A OR B* | *A X OR B* |
|---|---|---|---|---|---|
| 1 | 1 | 0 | 1 | 1 | 0 |
| 1 | 0 | 0 | 0 | 1 | 1 |
| 0 | 1 | 1 | 0 | 1 | 1 |
| 0 | 0 | 1 | 0 | 0 | 0 |

Here 1 represents true whereas 0 represents false.

This can also be portrayed visually using Venn diagrams. If set A is the set of items having attribute A, set B is the set of items having attribute B, and set C is the set of items having attribute C then statements A AND B, A OR B, A X OR B, A NOT B, A AND B OR C will return items that have attribute combinations covered by the shaded portions of the respective Venn diagrams (Figure 6.3).

To explain the Venn diagram, an example can be stated as given below:

If,

A = Single Crop (Landuse), B = Good (Groundwater Prospect) and C = II or III (Land Capability)

**Venn Diagrams**

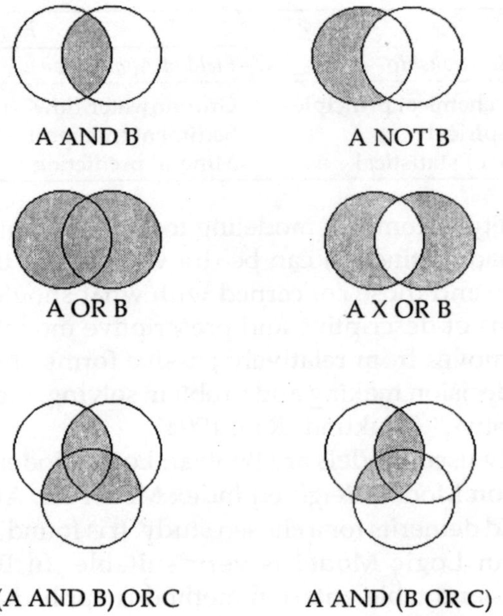


Now, X = A AND B — Finds all mapping units, which have single crop and good groundwater condition.

X = A OR B — Finds all mapping units, which either have single crop or good groundwater condition.

X = A X OR B — Finds all mapping units which either have single crop or good groundwater condition but not in combination.

X = A NOT B — Find all mapping units, which have single crop but not good groundwater condition.

X = (A AND B) OR C — Return all mapping units, which have single crop, and having good groundwater condition or land capability II or I.

X = A AND (B OR C) — Return all mapping units, which have single crop and having either good groundwater condition or land capability I or II.

As Boolean logic works on true-false conditions, hence it cannot be applied with unequal weightage approach. It can either be applied to attributes of any spatial layer using Single Parameter Weightage or it can be applied to spatial properties of different layers using Equal Weightages. For land resource management several layers and parameters need to be integrated, therefore, while applying Boolean Logic Model, equal weightage approach is most suitable.

According to the aspects of integration, another important aspect is defining a criterion. Boolean logic can either be applied to a statement criterion or a table criterion.

In the present study table criteria approach has been adopted. To explain the table criteria approach an example can be stated as given in Table 6.4.

**Table 6.4:** Table Criteria Approach

| *Parameters* | *Management Practice Suggested for Land Resource Management* | |
|---|---|---|
| | *Double Crop* | *'Alley Cropping* |
| Landuse | Kharif Crop | Kharif Crop |
| Land Capability | II or III | IVes |
| Groundwater Prospects | Moderate | Moderate to Poor |
| Slope | 0% to 3% (Class 1 or 2) | 5% to 10% (Class 4) |

The table in Boolean Logic Model can be expressed as follows:

- **Double Crop** = (Landuse = 'Kharif Crop') AND [(Land capability = II) OR (Land capability = II)] AND (Groundwater Prospects = 'Moderate') AND [(Slope = 1) OR (Slope = 2)].
- **Alley Cropping** = (Landuse = 'Kharif Crop') AND (Land capability = IVes) AND (Groundwater Prospects = 'Moderate to Poor') AND (Slope = 3).

This means that the mapping units having kharif crop and land capability II or III and moderate ground water conditions and slope that is nearly level to very gently sloping, are suitable for Double Crop. Similarly, the mapping units having kharif crop and land capability IVes, moderate to poor ground water conditions and a slope that is moderately sloping can be suggested for Alley Cropping.

This model with table criterion method assuming equal weightage to each parameter can be applied for land resource management activity. In this approach each combination set is converted into a logical statement using Boolean operation to achieve the result as on optimal solution. A case study showing application of this model is described in the following chapter.

## REFERENCES

Burrough, P.A., 1990, *Priciples of Geographical Information Systems for Land Resources Assessment*, Clarendon Press, Oxford.

Graeme, F. Bonham-Carter, 1994, *"Geographic Information System for Geoscientists: Modelling with GIS"*, Pergamon, Ottawa.

Rao Mukund, Jayaraman, V. and Chandrasekhar, M.G., 1994, *"Organising Spatial Information Systems Around a GIS Core – Database Organisation and Integrated Analysis using GIS"*, Special publication, NNRMS, Indian Space Research Organisation, Bangalore, Vol. SP-70-94.

# 7

# Environmental Impact Assessment

*T.I. Khan*

Environment Impact Assessment 'EIA' is formal technic, used to predict the environmental consequences of a proposed major development project, for example, building a hydroelectric dam or a factory, irrigating a large valley, or developing a harbor, mining etc.

An EIA concentrate on problems, conflicts and natural resources constraints which might affect the viability of a project. It also predicts how the project could harm to people, their homeland, their livelihoods, and the other nearby developmental activities. After predicting potential impacts, the EIA identifies measures to minimise the impacts and suggests ways to improve the project's viability.

The aim of an EIA is to ensure that potential impacts are identified and addressed at an early stage in the project's planning and design. To achieve this aim, the assessment's findings are communicated to all the relevant groups who will make decisions about the proposed project ; the project developers and their investors, as well as regulators, as well as regulators, planners and the politicians. Having read the conclusions of an environmental Impact Assessment, project planners and engineers can shape the project so that its benefits can be achieved and sustained without causing adverse impacts.

EIA helps officials make decision about a project and it helps the project's proponents achieve following aims more successfully:

(a) A project that has been designed suit the local environment is more likely to be completed on time and within budget, and is more likely to avoid difficulties along the way.
(b) A project that conserves the natural resources it relies upon will continue to be sustained by the environment for years to come.
(c) A project that yields its benefits without causing serious problems is more likely to bring credit and recognition to its proponents.

Thus, an Environmental Impact Assessment predicts the likely environmental impacts of projects, finds ways to reduce unacceptable impact and to shape the project so that it suits the local environment and presents these predictions and options to decision-makers.

Like economic analysis and engineering feasibility studies, EIA is a management tool for officials and managers who must make important decision about major development projects.

All developers are familiar with economic and engineering studies. These tools provide the basic for designing robust, economically-viable projects. EIA is now seen as an equally important tool in designing a viable project.

In recent years, major projects have encountered serious difficulties because insufficient account has been taken of their relationship with the surrounding environment. Some projects have been found to be unsustainable because of resource depletion. Others have been abandoned because of public opposition, financially encumbered by unforeseen costs, held liable for damages to natural resources and even been the cause of disastrous accidents.

Given this experience, it is clearly very risky to undertake finance, or approve a major project without first taking into account its environmental consequences and then siting and designing the project so is to minimise adverse impacts. For instance, the following questions need to be asked about any major project.

(a) Can it operate safely without serous risk of dangerous accidents or long-term health effect?
(b) Can the local environment cope with the additional waste and pollution it will produce?
(c) Will its proposed location conflict with nearby land uses, or preclude later developments in the surrounding areas?
(d) How will it affect local fisheries farms or industry ?
(e) Is there sufficient infrastructure such as roads and sewers to support it?
(f) How much water, energy and other resources will it consume, and are these in adequate supply?
(g) What human resource will it require or replace, and what social effects may this have on the community?
(h) What damage may it inadvertently cause to national assets such as virgin forest, tourism areas, or historical and cultural sites?

**Precise**

It is important that an Environmental Impact Assessment does not try to cover too many topics in too much detail, it has to be very precise.

At an early stage, the scope of the EIA should be limited to only the most likely and most serious of the possible environmental impacts. Some EIA have resulted in large and complex reports running in the serval thousand pages. Such extensive work is unnecessary, and can be counter-productive, because the EIA's findings must be readily accessible an immediately useful to decision makers and project planners.

When mitigation measures are being suggested, it is again important to focus the study only on workable, acceptable solutions to the developer or the Government.

When it is time to communicate, the conclusions, the EIA should provide a summery of information relevant to the needs of each group for making its decision. Supporting data should be provided separately.

**Constitution of EIA Team**

Just as it is important not to waste time and effort on irrelevant issues, it is also important to be selective when involving people in the EIA process. Generally, there categories of participants are needed to carry out an EIA:

(a) Those appointed to manage and undertake the EIA process (usually a co-ordinator and a staff of experts).
(b) Those who can contribute facts ideas or concerns to the study, including scientists, economists, engineers, policy makers and representative of interested or affected groups.
(c) Those who have direct authority to permit, control or alter the project that is, the decision makers including for example, the developer, aid agency or investors, competent authorities regulators and politicians.

**Information**

An EIA should be organised so that it directly supports the many decisions that need to be taken about the proposed project. It should start early enough to provide information to improve basic designs, and should progress through the several stages of project planning. In a typical sequence:

(1) When the developer and investors first broach the project concept, they consider likely environmental issues.
(2) When the developer is looking for sites or routes, environmental considerations are used to aid the selection process.
(3) When the developer and investors are assessing the project's feasibility, an EIA is in progress, helping them to anticipate problems.
(4) When engineers are creating the project design, the EIA identifies certain standards for the design to meet.
(5) When a permit is requested a completed EIA report, is submitted, and also published for general comment.
(6) When the developer implements the project, monitoring or other measures provided for in the EIA are undertaken.

**Mitigation of Impacts**

To help decision-markers, the EIA must be designed so as to present clear choices on the planning and implementation of the project, and it should make clear the likely results of each option. For instance, to mitigate adverse impacts, the EIA could propose, pollution control technology or design features, the reduction treatment or disposal of wastes and compensation or concessions to affected groups.

To enhance environmental compatibility the EIA could suggest:

- Several alternative sites.
- Changes to the project's design and operation.
- Limitations to its initial size or growth.
- Separate programmes which contribute in a positive way to local resources or to the quality of the environment.

And to ensure that the implementation of an approved project is environmentally sound, the EIA may prescribe.

- Monitoring programmes on periodic impact reviews.
- Contingency plans for regulatory action.
- The involvement of the local community in later decisions

**Presentation**

The objective of an EIA is to ensure that environmental problems are foreseen and addressed by decision-makers. To achieve this, decision makers must fully understand the EIA's conclusions. Most decision-makers are unlikely to use information, no matter how important it is, unless it is presented in terms and formats immediately meaningful:

- Briefly present 'hard' fact and predictions about impacts, comment on the reliability of this information, and summarise the consequence of each of the proposed options.
- Write in the terminology and vocabulary that is used by the decision-makers; and the community affected by the project.
- Present the essential findings in a concise document, supported by separate background materials where necessary.
- Make the document easy to use-providing visuals whenever possible.

**Environmental Impact Assessment Process**

***Before Starting the EIA***

Despite its usefulness in finding ways to make project successful, the full scale EIA process is not necessary for all kinds of development project. For a major project, an EIA may use considerable resources and expertise. If a detailed EIA is not needed, these resources can be put to better use elsewhere.

There are two 'tiers' of assessment which should be applied to the project before proceeding with a full scale EIA. Screening and preliminary assessment. Where these first tiers of assessment are a regulatory requirement, the developer normally does the work and submits the results to the regulatory agency. The agency may then decide that either there is nothing to be concerned about or the evaluation should proceed to me next tier.

The advantage of a tier approach is that the extent of the inquiry expands with the advancing development of the project plans. 'Screening' is appropriate when the project is only a rough concept. Later when the project is under more general discussion, a 'Preliminary assessment' can look deeper into possible sites and potential impacts. Then, just before the preliminary stages of feasibility and design work get underway, a full 'EIA study' can commence, so that it can influence the detailed decisions to come. This tier approach also ensures that Impacts are examined at a very early stage in the project planning, and not later when sites or designs are already decided by other factors.

### *Screening*

Screening is the first and simplest tier to project evaluation. Screening helps of clear types of projects which is past experience are not likely to cause serious environmental problems. The exercise may take one of the following several forms.

(1) Measuring against simple criteria such as size or location
(2) Comparing the proposal with lists of project types rarely needing an EIA (*e.g.* schools) or definitely needing on (*e.g.* coal mines).
(3) Estimating general impacts (*e.g.* increased infrastructure needed) and comparing these impacts against set thresholds.
(4) Doing complex analyses, but using readily available data.

### *Preliminary Assessment*

If screening does not clear a project, the developer may be required to undertake a preliminary Assessment. This involves sufficient research data and expert advice to identify the project's key impacts on the local environment, to predict the extent of the impacts and briefly evaluate their importance to decision-makers.

The preliminary assessment can be used to assist early project planning for instance to narrow the discussion of possible sites and it can serve as an early warning that the project may have serous environmental difficulties. It is in the developer's interest to do a preliminary assessment, since in practice, this step can clear projects of the need for a full EIA.

### *Formation of an EIA Team*

If after reviewing a preliminary assessment the competent authority deems that a full EIA is needed the next step for the project developer is the preparation of the EIA. This entails:

1. Commissioning and briefing an independent co-ordinator and expert study team (the disciplines that will be represented are decided after the 'scooping' stage, but the team always includes a communications expert).
2. Identifying the key decision-markers who will plan, finance, permit and control the proposed project, so as to characterise the audience for the EIA.

3. Researching laws and regulations that will affect these decisions.
4. Making contact with each of the various decision-markers.
5. Determining how and when the EIA's findings will bė communicated.

**Scooping**

The first task of the EIA study team is 'Scooping' that EIA. The aim of scooping is to ensure that the study addresses all the issues of importance to the decision-makers. First of all the study team's outlook is broadened by discussions with the project proponents, decision-makers, the regulatory agency, scientific institutions, local community representatives and others to include all the possible issues and concerns raised by these various groups. Then the study team selects primary impacts for the EIA to focus on, choosing on the basis of magnitude geographical extent, significance to decision-makers, or because of special local sensitivities (*e.g.* soil erosion, the presence of an endangered species, or a nearby historical site.)

**Main EIA**

After 'scooping', the main EIA attempts to answer five questions:

(i) What will happen as a result of the project?
(ii) What will be the extent of the changes?
(iii) Do the changes matter.?
(iv) What can be done about them?
(v) How can decision-makers be informed of what needs to be done?

After controls on the project's impacts are proposed in answer to question (iv), the study team may again ask: "What will happen as a result of the (now revised) project?" Thus the EIA often becomes a cyclical process of asking and further asking the first four questions, until decision-makers can be offered workable solutions.

***Identification***

The answer to the first question—"What will happen as a result of the project?" has already been partly discussed, but only in general terms; if 'preliminary assessment' has been done, it will have broadly reviewed the project's effect; also, 'scooping' will have focused the study on the most important issues of decision-makers. Taking these findings into account, the full EIA study now formally identifies those impacts which should be assessed in detail. This identification phase of the study may use these or other methods:

1. Compile list of key impacts—*e.g.* changes in air quality, noise levels wildlife habitats, species diversity, landscape views, social and cultural systems, settlement patterns and employment levels—from other EIAs for similar projects. This should draw on as many examples of similar projects as possible.

2. Name all the project's 'sources' of impacts (*e.g.* smoke emissions, water consumption, construction jobs) using checklists or questionnaires; then list possible 'receptors' in the environment (*e.g.* crops, communities using the same water for drinking migrant labourers) by surveying the existing environment and consulting with interested parties. Where the 'sources' may affect the 'receptors,' a potential impact is suspected.
3. Identify impacts themselves through the use of checklists, matrices networks, overlays, models and simulations.

***Prediction***

The next step, called prediction, answers the EIA's second question: 'What will be the extent of the changes'. As for as is practicable, prediction scientifically characterises the impact's causes and effects, and its secondary and synergistic consequences for the environment and the local community. Prediction follows an impact within a single environmental parameter (*e.g.* a toxic liquid effluent) into its subsequent effects in many disciplines (*e.g.* reduced water quality, adverse impacts on fisheries, economic effects on fishing villages, and resulting socio-cultural changes). Prediction draws on physical, biological, socio-economic, and anthropological data techniques. In quantifying impacts, it may employ mathematical models, physical models, socio-cultural models, economic models, experiments or expert judgements.

To prevent unnecessary expense, the sophistication of the prediction methods used should be kept in proportion to the 'scope' of the EIA. For instance, a complex mathematical model of atmospheric dispersion should not be used if only small amount of relatively harmless pollutant is emitted. Simpler modes are available and are sufficient for the purpose, Also it is not necessary to undertake expensive analyses if they are not required by the decision-makers for whom the EIA is being done.

All prediction techniques, by their nature involve some degree of uncertainty. So along with each attempt to quantify an impact, the study team should also quantify the prediction's uncertainty in terms of probabilities or margins of error.

It has been shortcoming of many EIAs that social and cultural impacts are not given the prominence they deserve in describing the extent of changes expected to result from a major development project. This has been due to the bias of physical and biological scientists against the comparatively younger disciplines of cultural anthropological and sociology. This is an unfortunate bias, since socio-cultural impacts are the ones that the local community will feel most acutely in their everyday lives. A consideration of socio-cultural impacts should be integrated, whenever possible, into every discussion of physical biological change, and not just treated separately in minor chapter or appendix.

***Evaluation***

The third question addressed by the EIA—'DO the changes matter?'—is answered in the next step. Evaluation, so called because it evaluates the predicted adverse impacts to determine whether they are significant enough to warrant mitigation. This judgement of significance can be based on one or more of the following:

(a) Comparison with laws, regulations or accepted standards.
(b) Consultation with the relevant decision-makers.
(c) Reference to pre-set criteria such as protected sites, features for species.
(d) Consistency with government policy objectives.
(e) Acceptability to the local community or the general public.

**Mitigation**

If the answer to the third question is 'Yes', the changes do 'What can be done about them?' In this phase, the study team formally analyses Mitigation. A wide range of measures are proposed to prevent, reduce, remedy or compensate for each of the adverse impacts 'evaluated' as significant. Possible mitigation measures include:

(a) Changing project sites, routes, processes, raw materials, operating methods, disposal routes or locations, timing, or engineering designs.
(b) Introducing pollution controls, waste treatment monitoring, phased implementation, landscaping, personnel training, special social services or public education.
(c) Offering (as compensation) restoration of damaged resources, money to affected persons, soncessions on other issues, or off-site programmes to enhance some other aspect of the environment or quality of life for the community.

All mitigation measures cost something, and this cost must be quantified too.

These various measures are then compared, trade-offs between alternative measures are weighed, and the EIA study team proposes done or more 'action plans,' usually combining a number of measures. The action plan may include technical control measures, an integrated management scheme (for a major project), monitoring, contingency plans, operating practices, project scheduling, or even joint management (with affected groups). The study team should explicitly analyse the implications of adopting different alternatives, to help make the choices clearer for decision-makers. Several analytical techniques are available for this purpose as given below:

(1) Cost/benefit analysis, in which all quantifiable factors are converted to monetary values, and actions are assessed for their effect on project costs and benefits (Be cautioned, however, that the unquantifiable and qualitative aspects can be equally important, and often need to be taken into account in the decision-making process).
(2) Explaining what course of action would follow from various broad 'value judgement' (*e.g.* that social impacts are more important than resources).
(3) A simple matrix of environmental parameters versus mitigation measures, containing brief descriptions of the effects of each measure.
(4) Pair-wise comparisons, whereby the effects of an action are briefly compared with the effects of each of the alternative action are briefly compared with the effects of each of the alternative actions, one pair at a time.

### Documentation

The last step in the EIA process, which answers the last question—'How can decision-makers be informed of what needs to be done?' is the Documentation of the process and the conclusions. Recall that the purpose of an EIA is to ensure that potential problems are foreseen and addressed in the project's design. Many technically first-rate EIA studies fail to exert their importance and usefulness because of poor documentation. The EIA can achieve its purpose only if its findings are well communicated to decision-makers.

Generally, to produce effective communications, one must identify the target audience or audiences, and then shape and style the publication to meet their specific needs. In documenting an EIA this means identifying the key decision-makers, perceiving the questions they will be asking and providing them with straightforward answers, formatted for easy interpretation to their decision-making (*e.g.* tables, graphs summary points). Successful EIA documentation is more readily produced if the audience and their needs are established at the start of the EIA and then made to affect how the research is focused and reported. It is the job of the study team's communications expert to make this happen.

So that decision-making can look more deeply into particular issues, the EIA report should also include a record of the EIA process and the judgements made by the study team. An EIA report should contain:

(a) An executive summery of the EIA findings.
(b) An description of the proposed development.
(c) The major environmental and natural resource issues that needed clarification and elaboration.
(d) The project's impacts on the environment (in comparison with a baseline were identified and predicted).
(e) A discussion of options for mitigating adverse impacts and for shaping the project to suit is proposed environment, and an analysis of the trade-offs involved in choosing between alternative actions.
(f) An overview of gaps or uncertainties in the information.
(g) A summary of the EIA for the general public.

All of this should be contained in a very concise, easy-to-ready document, with cross references to background documentation, which is provided in an appendix (The short document is sometimes called an 'Environmental Impact,' especially when it is submitted as part of a permit application.)

### Using the Results

Decisions based on the EIA are usually made by persons who have not been closely involved with the day-to-day progress of the EIA study. Their first consideration of the project may well be the moment they pick up and skim through the EIA report. The EIA will hopefully tell them all they need to know about 'what will happen as a result of the project,' the 'extent of the changes,' 'whether the changes matter,' and 'what can be done about them.' But the decision-makers themselves must also consider political realities when selecting a course of action. Only decision-makers are in a position to balance the project's needs and problems with the other needs and problems over which they have jurisdiction. They must take into account not only the facts of the situation, but also people's perceptions.

If the project is accepted perhaps with recommended modifications, then the decision-maker may need to take two further actions:

(1) Prepare a plan for reducing conflicts about the project, this may include public participation in planning, public eduction, and actions to compensate affected groups.
(2) Allocate institutional responsibilities for overseeing the proponents adherence to its environmental requirements, for incorporating environmental management into further planning and for enforcing any restrictions or carrying out any monitoring Sometimes the competent authority sends the EIA to a review panel for comment on its adequacy and quality, before reaching its decision. The decision-maker may call for further study to answer additional questions about the project. The decision-maker may also ask that an opportunity be provided for public review and involvement. The competent authority simply places copies of the report on public display, and invites the public to comment. The EIA team may then be asked to re-draft the EIA to take account of the comments made, before a decision is taken. In cases where the decision-maker chooses to reject the proposed project altogether, there should be an appeal process open to the project developers.

The EIA's usefulness does not end with the decision on a course of action about the project. It still have several further contributions to make to the project's success *e.g.:*

(1) If the project goes ahead with recommended changes, the EIA's findings should be used to help shape the project to suit the environment, by influencing engineering designs. Decisions that need to be made in the latter phases of project planning, such as precisely where to route supporting road or rail links, should be based on the EIA.
(2) The EIA's precautions on environmental impacts can be part of the brief for tendering on contracts, and should be re-drafted an environmental safety guidance for workers.

Lastly, after the project is completed, a 'post audit' (Environmental audit) can be done to determine how close the EIA's predictions were to the project's real impacts. This forms a valuable record for other doing EIAs on similar projects in the future.

# 8

# RS-GIS Application in Generation and Synthesis of Environmental Statistics

## A Case of Ittikara River Basin, Kerala

*Srikumar Chattopadhyay* and *Mahamaya Chattopadhyay*

### Introduction

Meaningful dialogue on development can hardly take place today without reference to environment. It is now increasingly realised at different levels that integration of environmental issues within the development framework, more specifically, ecologic-economic integration is necessary to trade the path of sustainable development. The World Commission on Environment and Development (WCED, 1987) report "Our Common Future" called for a fundamental reordering of global priorities. The inescapable links between environmental, economic and social concern are well illustrated. The Earth Summit at Rio in 1992 brought out the 'Agenda 21' which had clearly identified specific action points. Database development was one of the key elements for all the programmes envisaged under 'Agenda-21'. The Millennium Development Goals (MDGs) adopted by the United Nations General Assembly in 2000 have identified environmental sustainability as one of the objectives. The World Summit on Sustainable Development (WSSD) held at Johannesburg in 2002 reaffirmed the importance of the MDGs and also stressed in creating database to cater to the needs at various levels.

Decision making process is often beset due to lack of data and where data are available there is a problem of compatibility and scale. Further, micro level data are not always available at the desired scale, which compels decision maker to use macro level data. With growing concern about environmental degradation and high incidence of poverty, it is increasingly felt that disaggregate data at the ground level are necessary in order to overcome human tragedies. Poor people living in precarious conditions are the most vulnerable to storms, floods and sudden sea surge which are made worse by deforestation, soil erosion and climate change. The human tragedies behind the statistics are a compelling reminder that environmental and social progress are not luxuries that can be set aside when the world is experiencing economic and political problems (The World Watch Institute, 2003). The 13th Stockholm water symposium, while charting the future course of action stressed on hard facts at the ground level, which will not only help balancing various issues related to river basin management, but also to cope with perceptual gaps and growing complexity (IWA, 2003).

Remote Sensing and Geographic Information System (GIS), two IT tools widely used in recent years have opened up new opportunities for data generation. Remotely sensed data are more and more used due to increased quality of data, improved analytical procedure and specificity of questions. Recent application of remote sensing for the environmental study includes changes in landuse, production ecology, quality of ecological structures and geomorphological and geological investigations. The match between remote sensing and environment is in principle a very promising one (Stein and Meer, 2001). There are some basic issues interfacing environment and remote sensing. These are:

(i) Spatial correspondence between environmental aspects and remote sensing data.
(ii) Easy identification of problems and development in the environment through remote sensing, which otherwise would have been difficult.
(iii) Increased details due to increase in the spectral resolution helping in-depth analysis of the ecological complexities.
(iv) Time-series nature of remote sensing data enabling monitoring of dynamic processes in space and time.

Geographic Information System (GIS) on the other hand helps integration of data from diverse sources and create various scenarios to arrive at proper decisions. Spatial and attribute data can be linked through GIS and a digital database can be developed.

Both RS and GIS are enabling tools to equip the society with more and more in-depth information base. Spatial dimension of environment and development issues can no more be ignored and RS-GIS application is therefore a felt need of society. The present paper attempts to demonstrate applicability of RS-GIS in generation and synthesis of environmental statistics.

**Methodology**

Primary data had been generated through fieldwork, sample analysis in the laboratory and satellite image analysis. Data on geology, soil, rainfall, temperature, humidity, surface and sub-surface water were obtained from respective departments and survey organizations. The IRS-1C PAN images were used for extracting information on various themes. Map themes, image characteristics and identification particulars are tabulated to high light applicability of remote sensing.

Data on demographic, socio-economic, settlement and other facilities were collected from concerned departments and panchayat offices. Geographic Information

System (GIS) had been applied for data analysis and synthesis. An experimental work on grid cell based environmental data generation had been attempted. All data are available in digital form. A Flow Chart has been worked out to indicate various steps in data generation.

**Study Area: A Brief Introduction**

The Ittikara drainage basin occupies the southern part of Kollam district and a small portion of Thiruvananthapuram district. It extends from 8°44′10′′ N to 9°0′50′′ N latitudes and 76°37′ E to 77°2′20′′ E longitudes. Ittikara river is an important west-flowing stream with a length of 56 km and a catchment area of 650 km$^2$. The river Ittikara originates from the low hills of Karakunnu (250m above Mean Sea Level) adjacent to Madathara in the foothill region of the Western Ghats and flows through the Yeroor Reserved Forest area in a straight north-westerly course where streams of various orders are formed and join the main river. After flowing through the midland terrain, the river debouches into the Paravur *kayal* (estuary/back water) in the south-western portion of Kollam district. Climatologically, the basin area falls under the realm of sub-tropical region. Annual average rainfall is 2353 mm. Average temperature of the area is more than 20°C throughout the year. Administratively, Ittikara basin encompasses seven blocks covering 32 panchayats and one municipality. It has a total population of 10.40 lakhs. Landscape analyses involving identification of terrain units as per morphogenetic/geomorphological processes have been carried out for the basin. There are 11 units identified in the basin area. The rock types exposed within the drainage basin, include Precambrian crystallines, Neogene and recent to sub-recent sediments. The oldest and the most widespread rocks Grid based data and maps are the Precambrians, consisting of migmatised khondalites, charnockites, patches of garnet-biotite gneiss and garnet-quartz-feldspar neosomes. Morphometric analysis shows that the river Ittikara is a 6th order stream with 2 fifth order, 16 fourth order stream with 2 fifth order, 16 fourth order, 25 third order, 218 second order and 902 first order sub-basins. Average drainage density is 1.47 km/km$^2$.

Landuse pattern of the basin has been analysed in detail. Decadal changes in landuse pattern have been amplified through landuse maps of 1967 and 1989 data and further ascertained by interpreting PAN image data of 1999 and field check during 2002. Sub-basinwise analyses for different 3 basins pertaining to three physiographic units have also been incorporated.

Environmental evaluation of the basin has also been done with emphasis on the trend of deforestation rate, soil degradation, rate of reclamation of paddy fields, and sand and clay mining. Increased rate of depletion of forests had impacted the perennial nature of streams. Apart from these, morphographic factors such as lower topographic slope and reduced drainage density are also responsible for the poor water quality due to sluggish flow of river. This basin was taken up to demonstrate utility of RS-GIS in environmental data generation and synthesis.

**Results and Discussion**

Environmental statistics have been generated under the components of land, water, landuse, environmental issues and human settlement. Data are presented through tables (38 nos) and maps (29 nos).

*Land*

Relief, landform, slope, geology and soil types are studied under land component. Seven tables and five maps are prepared. Distribution of area under different altitudes indicates that around 78 per cent of the total area of the basin lies below 100 m altitude. Landforms in this basin have developed under marine/estuarine, fluvial and denudational processes. Altogether 11 units are identified. Terrain units under denudational processes cover as much as 83 per cent of the total area of the basin. Among the units under denudational processes, moderately undulating terrain has the highest coverage (25.5%) followed by gently sloping terrain (14.5%) and steep rolling terrain (14%). It is important to note that even in a basin of around 400 m altitude as much as 9 per cent of area falls under erosion scarp. Distribution of area under various slope categories indicates that around 33 per cent of the total basinal area fall in the slope category of 15 per cent to 25 per cent. Rock types found in this basin are khondalite, garnet-biotite gneiss, laterite and warkalli formations. Panchayat-wise distribution of area under each rock type has been worked out. Laterite is confined to the central part of the basin. Panchayats lying to the eastern part are under khondalite type of rock. There are six soil types covering this basin. Soils are deep to very deep and well drained. A small patch in the western part of the basin is characterised by sandy and excessively drained soils. Panchayat-wise distribution of area under each soil type has been computed. There are 10 panchayats with two soil types and two panchayats with three soil types. Rest 20 panchayats each has one soil type each. Capability classes of these soil types are class-III and class-IV and there are limitations of erosion (e), wetness/drainage (w) and soil (s) (Table 1.7).

*Water*

The water component of environment has been presented through six tables and four maps. Data on rainfall, temperature and relative humidity are collected from three stations distributed in and around the basin. There are two rain gauge stations at Nilamel and Paravur within the basin limit maintained by the Hydrology division of the Kerala State Irrigation Department. Punalur station located outside the basin boundary of Ittikara which is maintained by India Meteorological Department is also taken into consideration for the analysis to arrive at a better and realistic evaluation. Average normal annual rainfall in Punalur is 2661 mm. The normal monthly maximum temperature varies from 29.9°C in July tc 36.4°C in March and the normal monthly minimum temperature varies from 19.4°C in January to 23.8°C in May. Average monthly temperature and humidity data available for Punalur indicate that the average monthly maximum temperature (1990-1994) varied from 30°C in July to 36.5°C in April and the average monthly minimum temperature varied from 19.7°C in January to 24.6°C in April. Average relative humidity recorded at 8.30 hrs. varied from 78.2 per cent in January to 93.4 per cent in July and at 17.30 hrs. it varied from 46 per cent in February to 80.4 per cent in June and July. Rainfall data analyse of three stations bring out that mean annual rainfall was the highest in Punalur. This station had also recorded the highest rainfall of 5076.7 mm in 1946. The range between the lowest and the highest rainfall in 80 years period is also the highest (3133.5 mm) in Punalur.

The Isohyet map shows that rainfall increases from south to north and from west to east. Average annual rainfall increases from 1800 mm in the western coastal stretch to 3600 mm in the eastern border. Distribution of water bodies is given to provide a spatial perspective. The western part of the basin is dominated by water logged areas. The confluence of the river to the sea is artificially created as the normal confluence is blocked due to sand deposits. There are ponds of different sizes distributed throughout the basin.

Monthly drainage discharge data recorded in the gauging station of Ayur during 1972-1992 showed that annual discharge recorded wide variations from 93.88 $m^3$/sec in 1982 to 553.11 $m^3$/sec in 1992. The year of 1982 was a drought year, when the whole State experienced dry condition with very low rainfall. Monthly discharge indicates wide variations between monsoon and non-monsoon months.

Data pertaining to depth to water table have been computed in order to understand the status of groundwater condition. Average depth varied from 2.91 m below ground level (bgl) in Ezhukone to 15.77 mbgl in Ittikara during the period from April 2001 to January 2002. Water table rose to the maximum level during the month of November 2003 in all 15 locations except Kulavettur, where the maximum level was in the month of August 2001. Fluctuations in depth to water table between two series of observations (1994-95 and 2001-2002) have been computed for all four months of April, August, November and January. The April data indicated that water table in 2001 had gone down compared to 1994 in three stations only and in all other stations the water table was up. The highest rise (+2.64 m) was in Ayur. So far as the August data were concerned, as many as six stations recorded negative trend or fall in water table in August 2001 compared to August 1994. Seven stations showed negative trend in November and in the case of January only one station had recorded fall in water table.

Comparing the fluctuations experienced by 15 observation stations over this period of 1994-95 and 2001-2002, it can be inferred that water table had gone down in Chadayamangalam, as it showed negative trend in the months of April, August and November. Data pertaining to January was not available for this station.

Fall in water table is a manifestation of over exploitation of groundwater and fall in river water level can be attributed to indiscriminate sand mining and excavation of wetland for clay. Chadayamangalam is one such area where all these activities are noticed. Water table contour for the month of April 2001 and August 2001 are presented.

***Landuse***

Landuse component has been presented through 15 tables and 10 maps. Landuse data have been computed for the Ittikara basin as a whole and also for three sub-basins, namely, Palliman Ar (stream), Kulanji Thodu (stream) and Man Ar (stream). There were 11 landuse categories identified in 1967 covering the entire basin. The category of settlement with mixed tree crops covered around 73.8 per cent of the total basinal area in 1967. Area under paddy fields which accounted for 13 per cent of the total basinal area in 1967 had come down to 11 per cent in 1989 and to 8.36 per cent in 2002. This indicates diversion of prime agricultural land for other purposes. Area under settlement with mixed tree crops had decreased from 73.8 per cent in 1967 to 69 per cent in 1989 and to 57.4 per cent in 2002. Decrease in area under this category points out that mixed tree crops are being replaced by other types of landuse categories. Rubber plantation is one such category that had grown from 2.67 per cent coverage to 18.03 per cent coverage in this period from 1967 to 2002. Spatial distribution of natural vegetation cover and landuse pattern in the entire basin for the years of 1967, 1989 and 2002 are given. The trend of change and expansion of rubber is quite evident from these maps. Landuse data for Palliman Ar sub-basin show that area under paddy decreased from 18 per cent in 1967 to 7 per cent in 2002. Area under settlement with mixed tree crops had initially increased in the period from 1966-67 to 1988-89 and subsequently showed a decreasing trend. Sizable growth was recorded in area under rubber plantation. The trend is more or less similar in Kulanji Thodu sub-basin also. It can be deciphered from the datra that rate of decrease in paddy area had come down from 25 per cent in the period of 1966-67 to 1988-89 to 19 per cent in the period of 1988-89 to 2002. The area under rubber has grown from 2.41 per cent to 51.8 per cent of the total area of this sub-basin during the same period.

The Man Ar sub-basin is located to the eastern part of the basin, which is dominated by natural forest. Landuse dynamics within the forest area is well exemplified in this basin. Around 52 per cent of the total area of this basin was under forest cover in 1966-67 and by the year 2002 the forest cover had come down to 32 per cent. Area under paddy declined from 6.25 per cent in 1966-67 to 4.8 per cent in 1988-89 but by 2002 paddy area increased by 0.50 per cent.

Another feature of landuse change in this basin is decline in area under rubber in the period from 1988-89 to 2002. Landuse maps of 1967, 1989 and 2002 indicate the trend in landuse change. Paddy fields marked in 1967 are diverted to settlement with mixed tree crops along the periphery and new areas particularly within the forest were brought under paddy cultivation, which was evident by comparing landuse maps of 1967, 1989 and 2002. Fragmentation of forest area is also well manifested in these maps.

Agricultural statistics were computed based on the data available from the Panchayat Development Reports. All panchayats in Kerala started preparing their development reports with all necessary details since 1996. In fact, there are now 999 Panchayat Development Reports (PDR) covering each panchayat prepared during the period 1996-2001. Some of the panchayats have repeated the exercise for the 10th

Plan period (2001-2006) also. Crop statistics used in this report were collected from PDRs available in the State Planning Board, Government of Kerala.

Panchayat-wise distributions of area under seasonal crops, tree crops and plantation crops have been computed. Area under seasonal crop varies from as low as 71 ha in Eravipuram to 2090 ha in Neduvathur. Paddy is cultivated in all the panchayats, in varying proportions. Tapioca and banana are other two important seasonal crops. There are only three panchayats in this basin namely, Thrikkovilavattam, Neduvathur and Velinallur, where areas under seasonal crops account for more than 50 per cent of the gross cropped area (area under seasonal crops + area under tree crops). Majority of the panchayats are in the category of 30 per cent - 40 per cent.

Coconut is the major tree crop, grown in all the panchayats. Eravipuram is the only panchayat where coconut covers 100 per cent area under tree crops. Cashew and arecanut are other tree crops with limited coverage. There are only three panchayats where areas under tree crops are less than 50 per cent of the gross cropped area. Tree crops account for more than 50 per cent of the gross cropped area in all other panchayats. Very high concentration of tree crops are found in three patches: (i) along the coast (Eravipuram), (ii) in the midland (Veliyam and Ummannur panchayats) and (iii) in the highlands adjoining the forest areas (Chithara and Alayamon panchayats).

Rubber is the major plantation crop raised in all the panchayats except four panchayats (Mayyanadu, Eravipuram, Thrikkovilvattom and Neduvathur). Areas under plantation crops have been computed in terms of total area of the panchayat. The coverage varies from less than 1 per cent in Chathannur and Kottamkara panchayats to 56 per cent in Chithara panchayat. High concentration is found in the south-eastern part except Kadakkal panchayat.

### *Environmental Issues*

Data and maps on environmental issues have been generated through synthesis of various maps, and using mapped and attribute data applying GIS. Maps depicting individual themes are overlayed to arrive at synthesised maps depicting the final output. Erosion is one of the major environmental problems encountered in large parts of this river basin as that in the State of Kerala as a whole due to undulating nature of topography. Man Ar sub-basin being in the hilly part was chosen for this exercise.

Individual factor maps are prepared depicting slope, source and junction points, and landuse for the forest and non-forest areas. Units or grades identified under each of these factors are given a specific rating for erosion proneness. To begin with, a map is prepared showing slope with five erosion proneness grade from very low to very high. Areas of no erosion (valleys) are also shown. Source and junction points of streams are considered along with slope in the next step (step 1) as depicted in the map. Landuse data are considered in the final step (step 2) and erosion proneness of the basin is assessed. Landuse/land cover protects soil from erosion and therefore, it acts as modifier. There are only few patches of high erosion prone areas. Majority of the areas are subjected to low and moderate erosion. Usual soil protection measures can ameliorate the situation in this basin.

Laterite soils are acidic in nature with pH values of less than 6. Six types of soils marked in this basin have various pH range. Swampy and marshy soils designated by K04 type records pH value of 2.4 to 3.2. Tidal influence on soil formation in the presence of high organic matter results in low pH or alkaline degraded condition.

River water pollution is emerging as a serious problem encountered in the State. Monitoring of river water in various stretches under different landuse categories is a part of continuous research programme of CESS (Soman and Mahamaya, 2002). Three sample points were selected in this basin and water samples were collected during October 2002 for physico-chemical analysis. These sample points are under different type of topography and landuse. Sample site 1 represents relatively highland topography with dominant landuse of forest vegetation while sample 2 is in the midland stretch with dominance of mixed agriculture and sample 3 is in the lowland stretch influenced by wetland ecosystem, dense settlements and intensive agriculture. Water sample of the river stretch within the forest segment is found to be non-polluted, when compared to other stretches. High DO value and low BOD value indicate good quality of water. However, it may be noted here that as a whole water quality is generally good and pollution level is marginal in this river.

Landuse change, particularly in forest area, is an important component to assess environmental condition. In view of its importance, specific studies are conducted in the Man Ar sub-basin. Change detection has been attempted only in the forest area. Total area of the Man Ar sub-basin is 94.38 km$^2$, of which 49.40 km$^2$ were classified under forest and the rest 44.98 km$^2$ were non-forest as on 1966-67. Within this 49.40 km$^2$ forest area there were 0.45 km$^2$ of area under settlement with mixed tree crops. Forest areas were given for various plantations of oil palm, rubber, eucalyptus and *Acacia-Manjium* in the intervening period from 1966-67 to 2002. *Acacia-Manjium* was introduced after 1988-89. Major change in forest area took place in the period from 1966-67 to 1988-89. However, there were changes after 1988-89 also. This is a matter of serious concern as in spite of increasing awareness about forest conservation reduction in forest area still continues.

Landuse conversion matrix shows the nature of conversion that each category of landuse had experienced during the period from 1989 to 2002. Rubber is one such category that replaced forest, oil palm and eucalyptus. Spatial distribution of landuse changes during the periods of 1967 to 2002 and 1989 to 2002 are given.

Synthesising all data an environmental appraisal map is prepared applying GIS. This map shows areas affected by sea erosion, sea wall, water logged area, reclaimed area, deforested area, sites of clay and sand mining and even garbage dumps within the forest area (detected through field investigation). Purpose of this map is to provide a comprehensive picture, which is one of the principal objectives of this project. Issues like coastal erosion, sand mining, clay mining, reclamation of paddy fields, unabated deforestation, fall in groundwater table in some sites are of serious nature and deserve proper attention. Water pollution is not so serious in this basin primarily due to high rainfall and absence of industrial effluents.

Various environmental problems faced by different panchayats are listed. Certain problems like reclamation, sand and clay mining, soil erosion etc. are common in more than one panchayats and there are certain problems confined to only specific sites. Loss of stream perenniality in Ittiva panchayat is a serious issue. This hydrological change can be attributed to deforestation or change in forest landuse. Similarly, fall in groundwater level in Chadayamangalam panchayat deserves special attention. These findings in specific sites, though of lower magnitude, are important indicators for future management planning. If adequate measures are not taken immediately, these problems can spread over to other panchayats also. Based on the nature and intensity of problem each panchayat can be prioritized for ameliorating measures.

To understand the extent of population pressure, data pertaining to certain selected demographic particulars like total population, density of population, households etc. are provided. Spatial distribution of population shows high concentration in the western part. Population density is very high in all the panchayats except Kulathupuzha, which is largely covered under forest. It is possible to link high population concentration with environmental degradation in certain sectors like land reclamation, sand and clay mining, deforestation and water quality. Panchayat-wise distributions of BPL families are also given. A final table showing biophysical characteristics, landuse, population and environmental issues have been worked out to provide a comprehensive picture of the basin.

***Environmental Data Generation: A Grid Cell Approach***

This is an experimental exercise to demonstrate GIS application in database preparation from the mapped data. A set of 10 maps were prepared. Information for each grid cell of 500m × 500m size covering each of these 10 maps was extracted from these maps. Each grid cell can be accessed through grid number and environmental data can be obtained. Parameters considered for this database are relative relief, slope, drainage density, geology, terrain, soil, vegetation and landuse (13 types). Significance of this exercise lies in storage, retrieval and easy accessibility to database for any desired grid cell location.

**Salient Points Emerged from the Study**

(1) This study has brought out ground level environmental data and an environmental atlas for the Ittikara basin of Kerala covering selected parameters showing land, water, landuse and environmental issues.

(2) This basin is dominated by undulated topography; however, due to dense vegetation cover (both natural and man-made) high erosion prone areas are limited. Land reclamation (diversion of paddy fields to other uses) is marked in almost all the panchayats. Soil acidity is a problem in the marshy/swampy areas lying adjacent to the western part of the basin.

(3) Sea erosion, excessive sand and clay mining, loss of river perenniality, fall in ground water table and landuse conversion particularly deforestation are major environmental issues highlighted in this study.

(4) Remote sensing is found to be useful to extract environmental data pertaining to coastal erosion, terrain condition, landuse and landuse change detection, surface water condition, deforestation and land reclamation.

(5) Supplementary data pertaining to geology, soil, vegetation type, ground water condition, drainage discharge and topographic parameters are necessary to complete the database on biophysical components of environment. Large volume of primary data have been generated and presented both in tabular and map form.

(6) Application of GIS is found to be useful for assessing erosion proneness, landuse change detection, preparation of environmental appraisal map and deciphering spatial relationships on various environmental issues.

(7) Mapping of environmental data provides site-specific condition and spatial perspective of the concerned theme. The environmental atlas, covering factor maps and synthesised maps presented here appear to be a handy tool for environmental management planning.

(8) The exercise of environmental data extraction using grid cell approach is a potentially significant attempt to work out a comprehensive methodology for environmental data generation.

(9) This study has demonstrated the utility of spatial data preparation by using RS and GIS in the context of a specific river basin. Problems of environmental degradation faced by different panchayats have been identified. Spatial association of various factors can be easily assessed by comparing the maps.

(10) This study is of evolving nature. There is scope for further refinement by using digital image processing technique and to work out spatial models based on multi-factor data. It is possible to work out various scenarios by adding or deleting or altering the rating of a variable. An appropriate decision support system can be worked out through the process of iteration. Environmental data, due to its spatial dimensions can be presented through maps. Attribute tables can be linked up with the maps as and when required. This will provide a comprehensive picture essential for the planners, decision makers, administrators, academicians and researchers.

(11) With specific example this study has demonstrated the utility of methodology followed here and also the need for generating environmental maps and using them to comprehend the environmental condition both at macro level (basin-wise) and micro level (sub-basin and panchayat-wise).

## REFERENCES

International Water Association, IWA (2003). Water 21, October, 2003, pp. 15-16.

Kerala State Landuse Board (1995). Land Resources of Kerala State. Government of Kerala, Thiruvananthapuram, p. 290.

Soman, K. and Mahamaya Chattopadhyay (2002): Impact of landscape change on water quality—A case study from Kerala, India. In Collection of Marine Research Works, Vol. XII, Suppl. Issue, pp. 39-50.

Stein, A. and Meer, Vander F. (2001). Statistical sensing of the environment. Special Issue, *ITC Journal*, Issue 2, pp. 111-113.

The World Watch Institute (2002). State of the World, 2002. W.W. Norton and Co. New York, p. 265.

The World Watch Institute (2003). Vital Signs, 2003, UNEP, W W Norton and Co. New York, p. 153.

United Nations (1992). Earth Summit—Agenda-21. The United Nations Programme of Action from Rio, p. 279.

## Acknowledgements

This project was funded by the Central Statistical Organisation, Government of India, New Delhi. Authors are grateful to Dr. M Baba, Director CESS for his permission to execute this project. Thanks are also due to Dr. K. Soman, Head Resource Analysis Division, CESS for providing required facilities.

# 9

# Landscape Ecological Assessment Using Hemoroby Model

## An Approach Using Integrated GIS Technique

*M.S. Nathawat* and *Kirti Avishek*

### Introduction

As the percentage of urban dwellers increase day by day there has been a drastic change in the ecosystem pattern of the third world countries. Remote sensing and GIS have been particularly useful in determining the impact of ecosystem changes due to anthropogenic factors including the economic changes and demographic conditions. Remote Sensing has been defined as the practice of deriving information about the earth's surfaces using images acquired through overhead perspective, using electromagnetic radiations in one or more regions of the electromagnetic spectrum, reflected or emitted from the earth's surface. Researchers have used GIS to aid in satellite based mapping of land cover of different kinds of landscape (Stow, 1993). Geographical Information System GIS) is a specialized computer programs designed to analyze the spatially referenced data. Major barrier to progress in landscape ecology are problems of data collection and analysis when we focus at landscape or ecosystem level. The recent emphasis of larger study areas over longer time scales have coincided with the development of GIS (Lavers, 1993). The urban expanse is occurring at a cost of agricultural land as they share the boundaries with human settlement areas. Likewise the study area chosen has also witnessed vast expanse on urban land use and their consequent changes leading to environmental damages including *landscape ecological degradation.* An *Environmental information system* aimed at being a useful decision support tool should contain a spatial and thematic description of the compartments of the landscape ecological system. Only then can the effect of changing natural environment can be assessed and the productive and regenerative potential of the landscape be preserved. Remote sensing and GIS have been particularly useful in determining the impact of ecosystem changes dur to *anthropogenic factors* including the economic changes and demographic conditions.

### What is Landscape Ecology?

Landscape has been derived from a German word "Landschap or Landschafte" is not only confined to what is reflected in English literature as scenic aesthetic landscape perception. Different technical disciplines notably agriculture, forestry, waste disposal, country planning, water supply, remote sensing to name few have contributed purposeful management of landscape denoted as Landschafte Gestaltung (Landscape management).

The term Landscape was first of all introduced by *Alexander Von Humboldt*, the pioneer of geobotany and physical geography and defined landscape as total character region of earth. According to *Vink (1983)*, landscape is defined as, *"the study of relationships between phenomenon and processes in the geosphere including communities of plant, animal, and man"*. Haekal in 1866 defined ecology as the science the investigates the relation between the organism and its environment. In *1939 Carl Troll* used the term *Landscape ecology* as the interdisciplinary science dealing with the interrelation between human society and landscape.

*Forman and Godron (1986) gave a technical definition of landscape ecology as, "the study of the structure, function, and change in the heterogeneous land area composed of interacting ecosystem."*

### What are the Elements of Landscape

Zonneveld (1979) used the following terms to describe the landscape:

- ***Ecotope***: The smallest holistic land unit characterized by homogeneity of at least one land attribute of geosphere.
- ***Land Facet***: A combination of ecotypes forming a pattern of spatial relationship, being related to at least one attribute.
- ***Land System***: A combination of land facet to form one mapping unit.
- ***Main Landscape***: A combination of land system in one geographical region.

Zonneveld described ecotope as the basic unit of landscape. This term *"ecotope"* is a synonym for *"biotope"* used by Neer (1967). However, Forman and Gordon used the term Landscape element as the basic unit of landscpae. *An ecotope is defined as 'a physically limited ecological unit, whose composition and development are determined by abiotic, biotic and anthropogenic aspects together'.*

Ecotopes are more or less homogeneous units on the scale of the landscape, identifiable by their similarities and differences in geomorphological and hydrological characteristics, vegetative structure and land use.

### Landscape System

1. ***Natural System***: (i) Forest, (ii) Water, (iii) Plantation, (iv) Hill.
2. ***Anthropogenic System***: (i) Built up.

Based on the above classification the Landscape of the study area is classified at Ecotope level and is shown in Table 9.1.

**Table 9.1:** Ecotope Classification (1976)

| *Landscape System* | *Land Facet* | *Ecotope Level* | *Symbol* |
|---|---|---|---|
| **1. Natural System** | Forest Sub-System | Fairly Dense Sal | FDS |
| | | Dense Sal | DS |
| | | Eucalyptus only | E0 |
| | | Eucalyptus and Sal | ES |
| | Plantation Sub-System | Trees | T |
| | | Shrubs | S |
| | | Bamboo | B |
| | | Agriculture | AF |
| | | Other Plantation | OP |
| | Water Sub-System | Fish ponds | FP |
| | | Other Ponds | OP |
| | | Lakes | LA |
| | | Tanks | TA |
| | | Rivers | RI |
| | | Reservoirs | RE |
| | Hill Sub-System | Residual Hills | RH |
| | | Stony Mounds | SM |
| **Anthropogenic System** | Built Up System | **Residential** | |
| | | • High Density | HDR |
| | | • Medium Density | MDRV |
| | | • Low Density | LDRV |
| | | • Rural | RRS |
| | | **Industry** | |
| | | • Stone Quarry | ISQ |
| | | • Industrial Unit | IIU |

## Landscape Ecological Modeling Concept as the Basis of Environmental Remote Sensing and GIS

An environmental information system aimed at being a useful decision support tool should contain a spatial and thematic description of the compartments of the landscape ecological system. Only then can the effect of changing natural environment can be assessed and the productive and regenerative potential of the landscape be preserved. Mainly in the study of environmental system where processes are stirred by several influencing factors, GIS is providing a tool to arrive at a proper conclusion. Data are collected by ground survey and they incorporated into GIS to determine the causal relation. GIS supported process, related with the environmental data can be gained in much shorter time than the conventional method. The benefits are that the environmental data are getting cheaper, retaining or even surpassing the quality of conventional method. The landscape has been classified into two major categories as Natural and Anthropogenic. Further it was classified into the land facet level as given below.

## Landscape Modeling Using Hemoroby Index

### *Concept*

Human activities lead to landscape change. To ensure the function of life support systems and to prevent its degradation it is necessary to monitor these changes and to evaluate their impact. The term hemoroby comes from a Greek word 'hemeros' (cultivated, tamed, refined). It was introduced in ecology by Jalas in order to classify plant species according to degree of share in neophytic regions. *According to Sukopp the degree of hemoroby is, "an integrative measure for the impacts of all human interventions on ecosystem, whether they are intended or not"*. The degree of hemoroby increases with the increase in human influence. *Centre for Environmental Research, Germany.* They defined hemoroby over her as an index to assess the impacts. The concept of hemoroby deals with assessing the impacts of human on the landscape.

### *Degree of Hemoroby*

The degree of hemoroby has been classified into seven levels. Table 9.2 shows the different categories of hemoroby along with the Land use type that has to be associated with it.

**Table 9.2:** Degree of Hemoroby

| *Degree of Hemoroby* | *Symbol* | *Degree of Naturalness* | *Land Use Type* |
|---|---|---|---|
| Ahemorobe | AH | Natural | ××××××××××××× |
| Oligohemorobe | OH | Close to natural | Mixed forest |
| Mesohemorobe | MH | Semi-natural | Deciduous woods, Bushes, Hedges, Three row |
| b-euhemorobe | BEH | Relatively far from natural | Fruit rows, ponds, drainage, river, grassland. |
| a-euhemorobe | AEH | Far from natural | Rural settlement, parks, play grounds |
| Polyeuhemorobe | PH | Strange to natural | Railways, roads |
| Metahemorobe | MAH | Artificial | Urban settlement, Industrial sites, liquid dumps. |

### *Hemoroby Index*

Based on the human impact the hemoroby index is calculated as follows:

$$M = 100\xi\,(f^m/m)\,h$$

Where, m = number of categories of hemoroby
Fm = proportion of area of category hemoroby
H = hemoroby factor (linear from h = 1 and h = m for maximal hemoroby)
M = hemoroby index

Thus $M_{max}$ = 100 if the whole area has maximal hemoroby, *i.e.* all LU types are classified as Metahemorobe. If there is no human impact than $M_{min}$ = 0.

**Data Base Used**

***Primary Data/Spatial Data***

1. *Satellite imagery*
   Satellite: IRS-Resource SAT
   Sensor: LISS III (Multispectral)
   Path/ROW: 105/56
   Date of Acquisition: March 02, 2004
   Bands: 2(Green), 3(Red), 4(NIR), 5(MIR)
   Scale: 1:50,000
2. *Survey of India Toposheet*
   No.: 73E/2, 3, 4, 6, 7, 8, 11, 12
   Scale: 1:50,000

***Secondary/Collateral Data***

1. Census Data: 1991 and 2001 Data
2. Block Maps:
   Kanke, Ratu and Namkum Block Map from Census Department, Patna, Bihar.
3. Photographs of landscape:
   To show the onsite degration of landscape due to man.

**Flow Diagram:** The entire methodology has been shown as a flow diagram in Fig. 9.1.

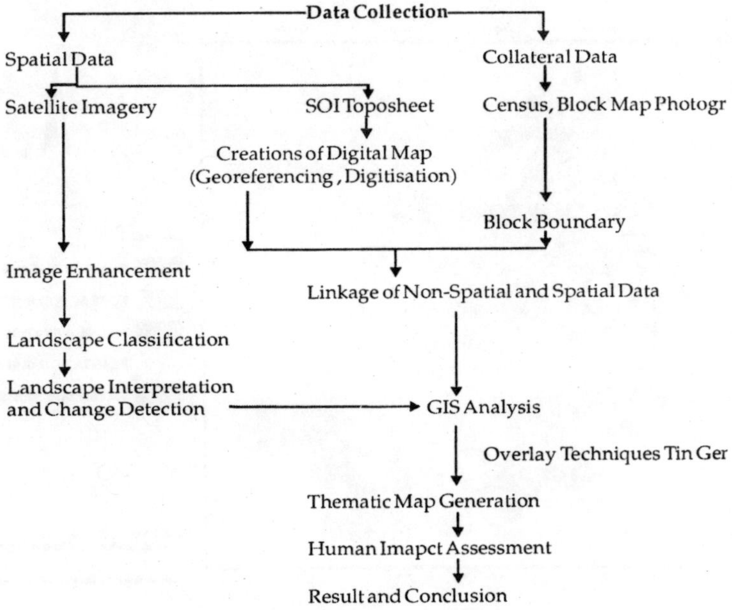


**Fig. 9.1:** Flow Diagram of Methodology

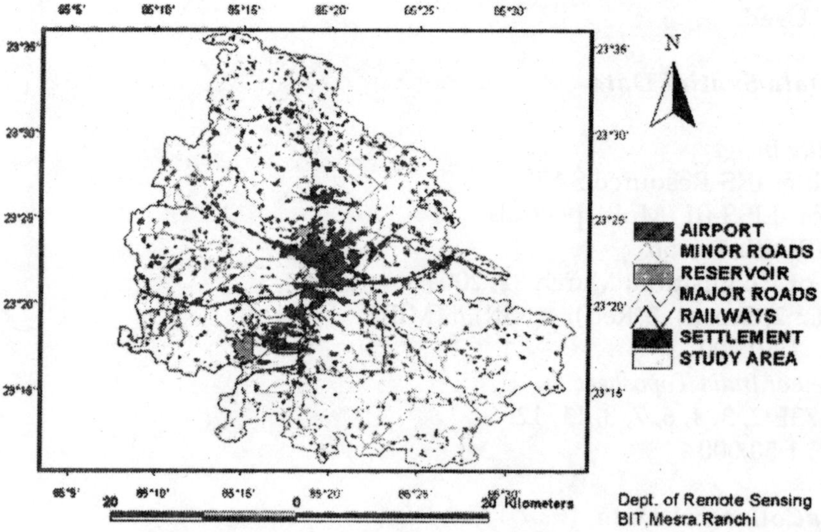


**Plate 1:** Base Map of Study Area

Plate 2 show the *Land Facet Level Map* and it can be interpreted that anthropogenic system consisting of built up areas is located at the centre of the map. This area is the Central Business District of the study area. However, small patches of settlement can be observed in the entire maps, these are rural areas of the region. Forest system can only be seen at the extremes and nowhere near the urban pockets. It can also be seen that urban pockets will expand at the cost of plantation sub-system, either grasslands or croplands.

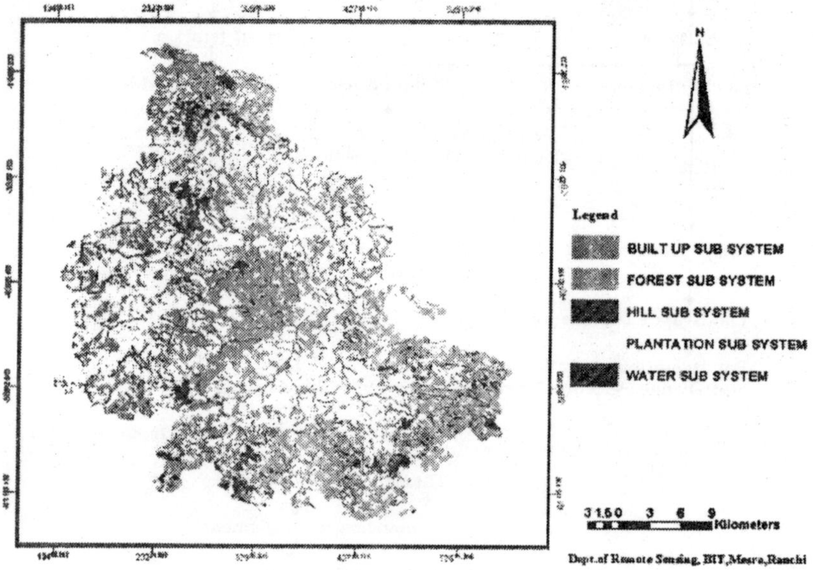


**Plate 2:** Land Facet Map

**Table 9.3:** Ecotope Classification according to 2004 Imagery

| *Landscape System* | *Land Facet* | *Ecotope* | *Symbol* | *Area km²* |
|---|---|---|---|---|
| Natural System | Forest Sub-system (FSS) | Fairly Dense Sal | FDS | 31.01 |
| | | Dense Sal | S | 44.46 |
| | | Eucalyptus | E | 1.4 |
| | | Eucalyptus and Sal | ES | 2.4 |
| | | Forest Blanks | FB | 6.48 |
| | | Uplands with Sal | US | 29.56 |
| | | Degraded Sal | DSF | 28.12 |
| | Plantation Sub-system (PSS) | Other trees | OT | 17.00 |
| | | Shrubs | SH | 2.87 |
| | | Bamboo | B | 0.05 |
| | | Acacia | AC | 1.8 |
| | | Acacia and Eucalyptus | AE | 2.5 |
| | | Agriculture | A | 246.7 |
| | | Grasslands | GL | 120.0 |
| | | Gulmohar | GUL | 0.19 |
| | | Eucalyptus and Pine | EP | 0.33 |
| | | Follow Land | FL | 22.45 |
| | Water Sub-system (WSS) | Ponds | P | 5.89 |
| | | Reservoirs | RE | 4.34 |
| | | Lakes | L | 0.18 |
| | | Rivers | RI | 69.63 |
| | | Fish ponds | FP | 0.011 |
| | Hill Sub-system (HSS) | Residual Hill | RH | 8.75 |
| | | Stony Mounds | SM | 35.88 |
| | | Hilly Plantation | HP | 2.87 |
| Anthropogenic System | Built Up System (BUS) | Open/Other lands | OL | 94.95 |
| | | **Residential:** | | |
| | | Rural Residential | RRS | 25.96 |
| | | High Density | HDR | 30.53 |
| | | Medium Density | MDRV | 60.27 |
| | | Low Density | LDRV | 51.72 |
| | | **Industrial:** | | |
| | | Industrial Units | IIU | 2.02 |
| | | Stone Quarry | ISQ | 1.6 |
| | | Railways/Roads | IR | 3.63 |

Plate 3 shows a higher level classification than Land Facet and depicts the Ecotopes generated from the study area. From this Ecotope Map it can be easily interpreted as Highly Density Residential (HDR) area is located at the centre of the study area which is the central business district. This map can act as a baseline map for subsequent changes at ecotopic level. The expansion of one ecotope at the cost of other ecotope can be visualized using this map.

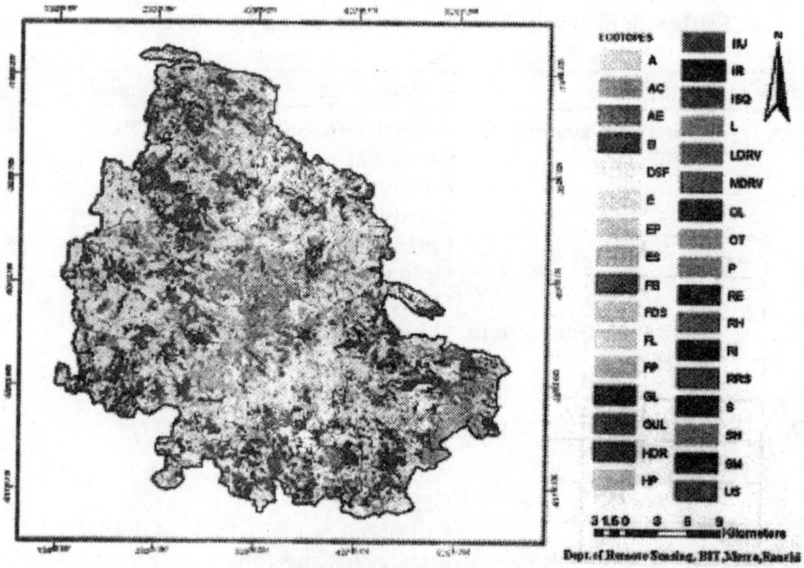


**Plate 3:** Ecotope Map

Table 9.4 shows the classification of ecotopes on the basis of the hemoroby type. Each ecotopes were then nomenclatured based on the hemoroby category and the resultant areas of each hemoroby type was obtained as shown in Table 9.5.

**Table 9.4:** Ecotopes and Corresponding Hemoroby Symbols

| *S.No.* | *Ecotopes* | *Hemoroby Symbol* | *S.No.* | *Ecotopes* | *Hemoroby Symbol* |
|---|---|---|---|---|---|
| 1 | S | OH | 18 | HP | MH |
| 2 | E | OH | 19 | RI | BEH |
| 3 | ES | OH | 20 | L | BEH |
| 4 | US | OH | 21 | P | BEH |
| 5 | DSF | MH | 22 | FP | BEH |
| 6 | FB | MH | 23 | RE | BEH |
| 7 | OT | MH | 24 | SM | OH |
| 8 | SH | MH | 25 | RH | OH |
| 9 | B | MH | 26 | OL | BEH |
| 10 | AC | MH | 27 | RRS | AEH |
| 11 | A | AEH | 28 | HDR | MAH |
| 12 | AE | MH | 29 | MDRV | MAH |
| 13 | FL | AEH | 30 | LDRV | MAH |
| 14 | GL | BEH | 31 | IIU | MAH |
| 15 | EP | MH | 32 | ISQ | MAH |
| 16 | GUL | MH | 33 | IR | PH |
| 17 | FDS | OH | | | |

**Table 9.5:** Area of Hemoroby

| *S.No.* | *Hemoroby* | *Area* |
|---|---|---|
| 1. | Oligo Hemoroby | 152.77 $km^2$ |
| 2. | Meso Hemoroby | 65.67 $km^2$ |
| 3. | Beta Hemoroby | 288.68 $km^2$ |
| 4. | Alpha Hemoroby | 498.97 $km^2$ |
| 5. | Poly Hemoroby | 3.62 $km^2$ |
| 6. | Meta Hemoroby | 152.91 $km^2$ |

**Table 9.6:** Landscape Interpretation

| *Landscape System* | *Image Interpretation* |
|---|---|
| Forest sub-system | Dense forests are identified by dark red color patterns. In the case of degraded forest there was small patches of dark red color. The blanks in the forest show creamy patches in the dark red/background. However the categorization of FDS and S was done by comparing the image layer with the toposheet. |
| Plantation sub-system | Trees are identified as dark red patches within settlements and urban areas. Differentiation between the types of trees are done by ground truthing. Agriculture has a typical light pink to light brown color. Fallow lands have light grey color. Grasslands have faint green color. Shrubs have light yellow color. |
| Water sub-sytem | River is identified as long non-linear path colored with dark blue/bright blue lines. Lake/reservoirs are identified as patterns along the river with dark to light blue. Ponds do not have any particular shape but generally oval to square and have faint blue to dark blue color. |
| Hill sub-system | Hilly structures are identified on the basis of their tone which is dark greenish blue mainly due to their composition. Residual hills are prominent circular features with higher elevations. While stony mounds are identified as all rocky structures of lesser elevation and not so prominent shape. |
| Built up system | Light grey clustering with particular patterns for the urban area. There may be brownish maroon patches for in between vegetation. For the rural settlement there occur no particular patterns of such image characteristics. |

Plate 4 is the Hemoroby Classification Map. It depicts the landscape on the basis of the naturalness that are governed by the degree of human intervention. Metahemoroby category is the class with highest human intervention and can be observed at the centre of the map as it is the urban residential areas (as per Plate 4). Oligohemoroby is the class close to natural and is seen at proximity from central urban areas. Some of the metahemoroby category is also found on the Ranchi-Tatanagar highway, Ranchi-Lohardagga highway as well as Ranchi-Patna highway. The areas adjoining metahemoroby are alphaeuhemoroby that will change to metahemoroby areas as and when expansion of anthropogenic system occurs. Based on this map decision can be made regarding the areas that need to reduce human pressures by forestation schemes. Hence this can help decision makers in proper land use planning that will ultimately stabilize the landscape.

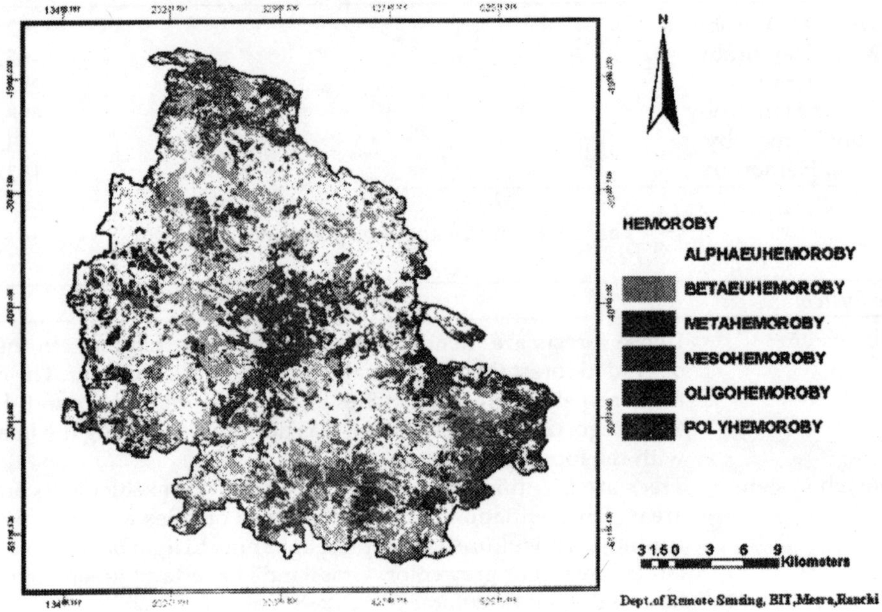


**Plate 4:** Hemoroby Map

## Hemoroby Index Calculation

Using the hemoroby index the impact of humans on the landscape was calculated to know as to what per cent of the landscape is disturbed by the human intervention.

$$M = 100\xi\ (F_m/m)\ h$$

Where,

$M$ = Hemoroby Index

$F_m$ = Proportion of hemoroby area of each category to total area.

$m$ = Number of existing hemoroby

$h$ = Hemoroby factor from 1 to m, where 1 is least impact and m is highest impact.

Hence, for the total hemoroby present:

$F_m = 0.574$

$m = 6$, $h = 1$ to 6, 1 for oligohemoroby to 6 for metahemoroby.

Therefore, putting the values in the above formulae:

$M = 100 \times 0.574$

$\mathbf{M = 57.4}$

### *Scaling of Hemoroby Index*

The hemoroby index obtained is scaled on the basis of impact. The corresponding degree of naturalness and the impact is nomenclature is obtained. Table 9.7 shows the different impact levels corresponding to the degree of impact.

**Table 9.7:** Scaling of Hemoroby Index Value

| *Impact Level* | *Index* | *Degree of Impact* |
|---|---|---|
| 1 | 0 | None |
| 2 | 1-16.67 | Minimal Impact |
| 3 | 16.68-33.35 | Limited Impact |
| 4 | 33.36-50.03 | Moderate Impact |
| 5 | 50.04-66.71 | Significant Impact |
| 6 | 66.72-83.39 | Major Impact |
| 7 | 83.40-100 | Maximum Impact |

The hemoroby index obtained is 57.4. This index gives an idea as to the extent the landscape is affected by anthropogenic factors. Hence the index defines that the landscape of Ranchi area is 57.4 per cent affected by human interventions. Its interpreted that the impact of human intervention on the landscape of Ranchi is Significant. One important drawback of this methodology is the use of Poly Hemoroby category. The linear features interpreted through the imagery is less as compared to the actual length. Hence the value obtained is less. Since the Imagery was not beneficial for interpreting all the minor roads the value obtained hence is less. If the actual length of the polyhemoroby is taken into account the index obtained will be higher.

### Conclusion

It is concluded that hemoroby method requires initial consideration regarding classification of ecotopes but later on the calculation is very simple. It has one more advantage that the individual ecotopes can be classified differently based on the degree of impact. Hemoroby map gives a clear picture about the areas that are highly human intervened to those less. Hence this map can help in proper and planned infrastructure development keeping in mind the environment of the city and state. Hemoroby index provides the planners to relocate the regions of maximum human impact by ecofriendly approach. Integrated GIS technique has been particularly helpful in very fast and effective data retrieval. Integrating GIS and hemoroby Model concept to assess the anthropogenic impact had provided better results in a short duration of time which is again an important need when dealing problems at landscape scale. These two approaches have given satisfactory results and can be employed for constant monitoring the landscape pattern and change.

# 10

# Environmental Modeling Through Geo-Informatics

*M.S. Nathawat*

## Introduction

Geoinformatics has now become a very significant technology with a variety of applications and having many advantages over conventional methods. Geoinformatics with tools like Remote Sensing (RS), Geographical Information System (GIS) and Global Positioning System (GPS) has capabilities to take up real time investigations with much precision and accuracy. Coupled with select ground investigation, Geoinformatics techniques provide fast, efficient, reliable, economic and analytical data with spatiotemporal characteristics with easy transformation to a Management Information System for planning purpose.

Author would like to give a brief review of the component of Geoinformatics for easy understanding of data being developed through its tools like Remote Sensing, GIS and GPS.

## Geoinformatics Approach for Environmental Modeling

*Definition of Remote Sensing*: It is defined as a technique for identifying, classifying and determining objects, as well as obtaining information on their physical properties through analysis of the data on the objects collected by use of remotely located sensors that do not contact physically with object. This process of gathering and recording of information without actual contact with the object or area being investigated is termed as Remote Sensing.

### *Concept*

A physical entity emanates light, which is a source of radiation. The source of radiation can be a sun and the radiated light passes over a distance, and thus is "remote" to some extent, until it encounters and is captured by a sensor, which is located on the satellites. Each sensor sends a signal to a processor the received radiations to the processing unit, which records the data and interprets this into information. Most of the information gathered is from radiations, are either reflected or transmitted from the object. This information is obtained by processing digital image processing techniques, which remove the errors and noises from the imagery. The mechanism is quiet similar to that of Human Sensory organs like ears and eyes. What we see is the radiated energy emitted by any object. These radiations from the object is collected by our eyes, processed and transformed into information in the brain.

***Remote Sensing Technique***

Remote Sensing refers to instrument-based techniques used in the acquisition and measurement of spatially distributed data/information on some property(ies) (spectral; spatial; physical) of an array of target points (pixels) within the sensed scene that correspond to features, objects, and materials, doing this by applying one or more recording devices not in physical, intimate contact with the item(s) under surveillance (thus at a finite distance from the observed target, in which the spatial arrangement is preserved); techniques involve amassing knowledge pertinent to the sensed scene (target) by utilizing electromagnetic radiation, force fields, or acoustic energy through employing cameras, radiometers and scanners, lasers, radio frequency receivers, radar systems, sonar, thermal devices, seismographs, magnetometers, gravimeters, scintillometers , and other sensing instruments.

**New developments in remote sensing are particularly taking place in the fields of radar remote sensing and the acquisition of optical data at higher spectral and spatial resolutions. Similarly, the development and availability of airborne imaging spectrometry and field spectroscopy has established these as valuable research areas.**

The different stages in Remote Sensing are shown in the diagram below:

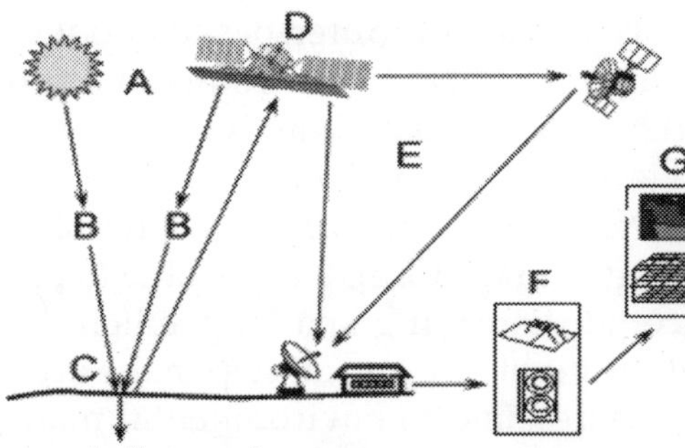


A. Energy Source.
B. Radiation and the Atmosphere.
C. Interaction with the target.
D. Recording of the Energy by Sensor.
E. Transmission, Reception and Processing.
F. Interpretation and Analysis.
G. Application.

**Fig 10.1:** Stages of Remote Sensing

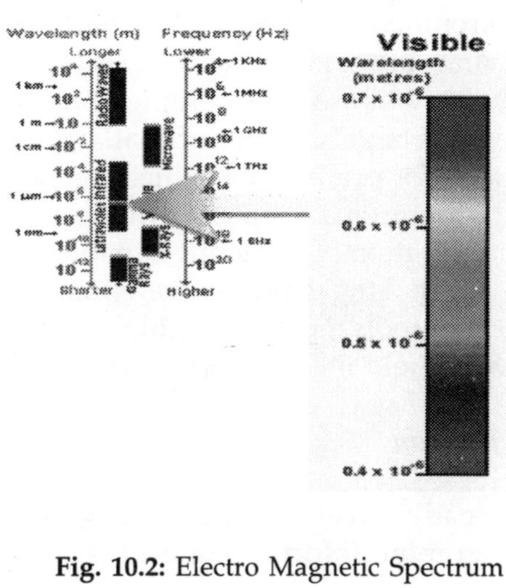


**Fig. 10.2:** Electro Magnetic Spectrum

## Satellite Data Analysis

The two major methods of data analysis for extracting resource-related information from data products, either independently or in some combination with other collateral information are:

- Visual Analysis/Interpretation
- Digital Image Processing Techniques

### *Visual Analysis*

Traditionally, visual interpretation methods have been followed for extracting information on various natural resources. Tone/color, texture, shadow, shape, size, etc. and their association are some of the basic image characteristics on which visual interpretation is based.

### *Digital Techniques*

In digital classification the computer analyses the spectral signature so as to associate each pixel with a particular feature of imagery. The reflectance value measured by a sensor for the same feature, say wheat field, will not be identical for all pixels; such response variation within a class is to be expected for any earth surface cover due to various reasons. The digital classification technique essentially partitions this feature space in some fashion so that each pixel in the feature space can be uniquely associated with one of the classes.

The Indian Remote Sensing Satellites have all the capabilities to analyze various resources at different resolutions catering to different needs of user community.

## Geographic Information Systems (GIS)

GIS has become increasingly valuable tools in the computer-based modeling of environmental processes. Spatial representation is critical to environmental problem solving, but GIS currently excels the predictive and related analytical capabilities necessary to examine complex problems at least to some extent.

The large amounts of spatial data require as input for generation of environmental models for predictions, which can be displayed in maps form. GIS are able to produce data required as input to models and excel at displaying spatial predictions. The incorporation of modeling capabilities into GIS might be a logical step in the evolution of GIS making model development is more accessible to environmental managers, and GIS tools more accessible to environmental models. Environmental modeling is a diverse field incorporating many application domains and approaches.

### *Definition*

A broadly accepted definition of GIS is the one provided by the National Centre of Geographic Information and Analysis, *"a GIS is a system of hardware, software and procedures to facilitate the management, manipulation, analysis, modeling, representation and display of georeferenced data to solve complex problems regarding planning and management of resources."* (NCGIA, 1990)

The term GIS is currently applied to computerized information storage, processing and retrieval systems that have hardware and software specifically designed to cope with geographically referenced spatial data and corresponding attribute information. The spatial data is commonly in the form of "layers" (see Figure 10.3 below), which may depict topography, water availability, soil types, forests and grasslands, climate, geology, population, landownership, administrative bounda-ries and infrastructure (highways, railroads, electricity or communications systems).

Remote sensing, geographic information systems (GIS) and agro meteorological and other environmental observations assist in acquiring and processing such data for addressing a variety of key issues related to environment and natural resources management, food production and food security, coastal zone monitoring, desertification, biological diversity, energy and climate change impact. Geo-referenced data from other sources, for example, socio-economic data, can also be combined with such environmental data for more in-depth analyses.

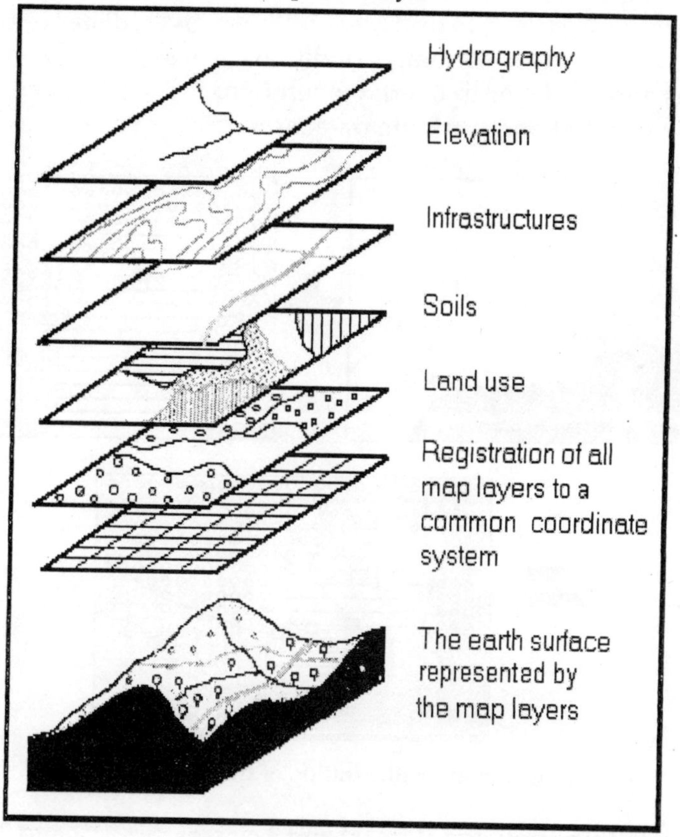


**Fig. 10.3**

Its capability of combining different map layers—in an operation known as "overlaying"—is one of the most important GIS functions.

### *Basic Functions of GIS*

Essentially, GIS provides a means of taking many different kinds of information, processing it into compatible data sets, combining it, querying and displaying the results on a map (Fig. 10.4). Some standard GIS capabilities include:

- Integrating maps based on different scales, map projections, or legends.
- Changing of scale, projections, legend, annotations, etc.
- Overlaying different types of maps of a particular area to make a new map that combines the attributes of the individual maps. For example, a vegetation map could be overlaid on a soil map, as shown in Figure 10.3. This in turn could be overlaid on a map showing length of growing season, thereby producing a land suitability map for a given crop.
- Generating buffer or proximity zones around lines or polygons on a map. This technique is used to find areas within a given distance from roads, rivers, etc., or from certain thematic conditions. These buffer zones can in turn be used as another layer in overlay operations.
- querying spatial and attribute databases.

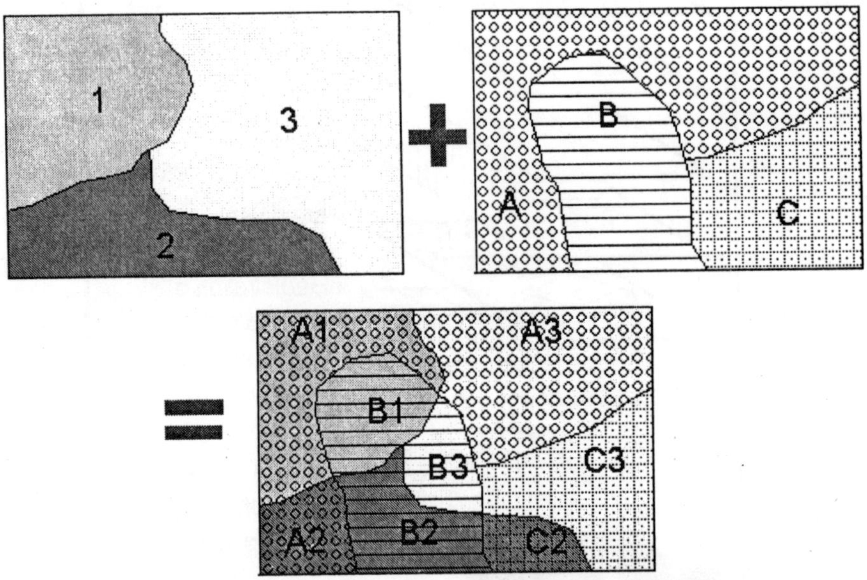


**Fig. 10.4:** Simple illustration of the overlay function.

[A map with three polygons (areas) and 3 classes, *viz.* 1, 2 and 3 is overlayed with another map again with 3 polygons and 3 classes A, B and C. The resulting "overlay" layer has 8 polygons and the class names are: A1, A2, A3, B1, B2, B3, C2 and C3.]

## Global Position System (GPS)

**NAVSTAR** (NAVigational System with Time And Ranging) **GPS** (Global Positioning System) is a space-based all weather radio navigation system. It was developed by the U.S. Department of Defense (DoD) primarily for the US military to provide precise estimates of position, velocity and time (PVT). Nevertheless, the civil application of GPS has grown at an astonishing rate. GPS has found applications in land transportation, civil aviation, maritime commerce, surveying and mapping, construction, mining, agriculture, earth sciences, electric power systems, telecommunications and outdoor recreational activities.

The GPS uses satellites and computers to compute positions anywhere on earth. The GPS is based on satellite ranging. That means the position on the earth is determined by measuring the distance from a group of satellites in space. To compute a position in three dimensions, there is a need to have four satellite measurements. The GPS uses a trigonometric approach to calculate the positions. The GPS satellites are so high up that their orbits are very predictable and each of the satellites is equipped with a very accurate atomic clock.

GPS satellites are orbited high enough to avoid the problems associated with land based systems, yet can provide accurate positioning 24 hours a day, anywhere in the world. Uncorrected positions determined from GPS satellite signals produce accuracies in the range of 50 to 100 meters. When using a technique called differential correction, users can get positions accurate to within 5 meters or less.

The GPS is divided into three major components (Fig. 10.5):

- The Space Segment
- The Control Segment
- The User Segment

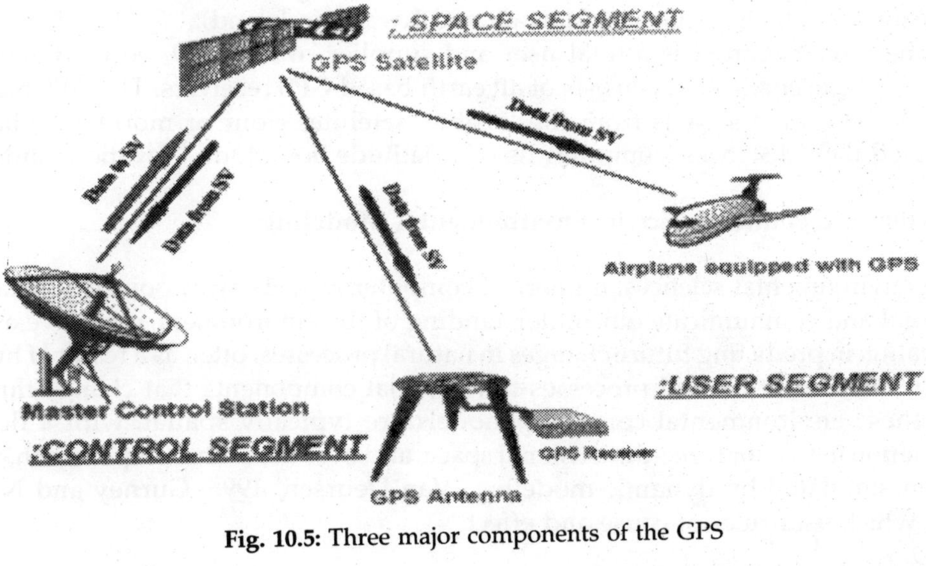


**Fig. 10.5:** Three major components of the GPS

**The Space Segment** consists of the Constellation of NAVASTAR earth orbiting satellites (Fig. 10.6). The current Defense Department plan calls for a full constellation of 24 Block II satellites (21 operational and 3 in-orbit spares). The satellites are arrayed in 6 orbital planes, inclined 55 degrees to the equator. They orbit at altitudes of about 12000 miles.

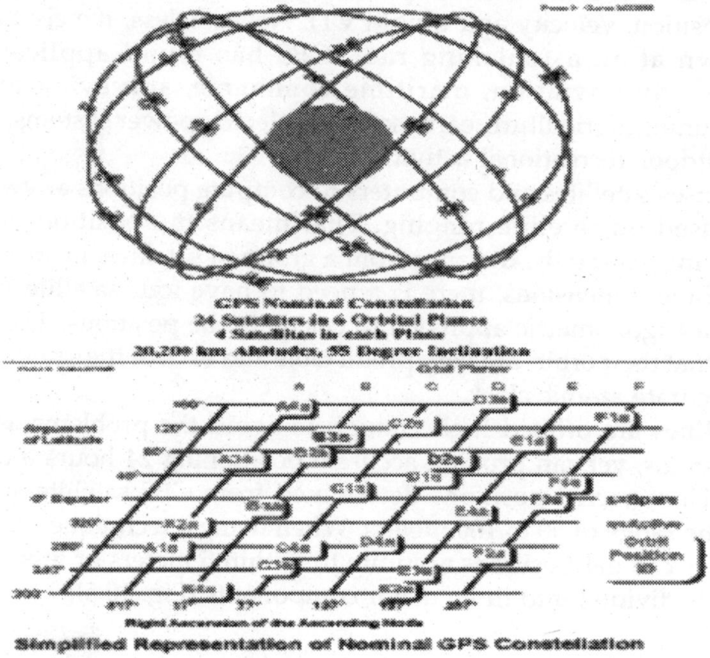


**Fig. 10.6:** The Space Segment of the GPS

The **Control Segment** consists of five monitoring stations (Colorado Springs, Ascension Island, Diego Garcia, Hawaii, and Kwajalein Island).

The **User Segment** is a total user and supplier community, both civilian and military. The user segment consists of all earth-based GPS receivers. The GPS receiver decodes the timing signals from the 'visible' satellites (four or more) and, having calculated their distances, computes its own latitude, longitude, elevation, and time.

## The Role of Geoinformatics in Environmental Modeling

In the environmental sciences, numerical computer models are a powerful means to represent and communicate our understanding of the environment, and have a wide application in predicting future changes in natural processes, often as a result of human impact. Since most natural processes have spatial components that change through time, these environmental computer models are typically spatial, with a flow of information in two- or three-dimensional space, and over time. The temporal behaviour is often simulated by dynamic modeling (Van Deursen, 1995; Gurney and Nisbet, 1998), which uses rules of cause and effect.

GIS have become increasingly valuable tools in the computer-based modeling of environmental processes. The current generation of environmental models require large amounts of spatial data as input and produce predictions which can be displayed as maps. GIS are able to produce data required as input to models and excel at displaying spatial predictions. The simplest approach to using GIS in this way is to pass files between the GIS and the modeling software. In more sophisticated approaches, the two software systems are coupled by an interface which automates the data exchange and may create the impression of a single software entity. Coupling is a pragmatic strategy which makes effective use of available technology; robust GIS modeling languages included in many GIS are a potential alternative for developing environmental models, since their concepts provide advantages over the afore-mentioned tools, when applied for environmental model construction (Karssenberg *et al.* 2001a; Karssenberg, 2002). This is because modeling languages in GIS:

1. provide functions in which commonly used spatial algorithms have been pre-programmed;
2. provide these functions in a suitable way such that they can be glued together in a model by a modeler using his or her understanding of environmental processes rather than computer expertise;
3. provide generic tools for data input, database management and visualization of data read and written by the model. Nevertheless, GIS (ESRI, 2004; Idris, 2004) have so far failed to become important tools for environmental model construction. Although they contain an extensive set of spatial analysis tools, they are not tailored to dynamic spatial modeling requiring optimization of sets of spatial functions executed in a sequence of time steps. In addition, GIS do not provide interfaces specially developed for dynamic model construction while they lack good tools for database management and visualization of temporal data, such as rain time series or time series of vegetation patterns. Even though GIS provide insufficient functionality for environmental model construction, the three conceptual advantages of GIS modeling languages over system programming languages, as noted above, still exist. This has driven specialist research groups to develop new modeling languages with sufficient functionality for dynamic model building, embedded in GIS packages act as pre- and post-processors of the model data and exible general purpose programming languages provide the implementation environment for the model itself. However, the development of coupled systems requires specialist knowledge of both development environments and of the file formats of GIS and of the model.

## Environmental Assessment

**Environment is defined as a sum total of all biotic and abiotic components that surround us and has effect on us**. The interaction and relationship between environment and man is termed as ecology. High rates of population explosion, urbanization, industrialization and the growing demand have lead to dependency on our natural resources. Our environment and its components are degrading at alarming rate. There has been a vast degree of changes in the various components of the environment due to various natural and anthropogenic processes. It is actually hard to analyze the changes and deduce the effects that the natural environment is undergoing due to systematic natural changes and anthropogenic interferences. To assess these regular changes in the environment an urgent requirement is for an operating model that can give an immediate output in matters of change—causes relationship. All Natural or Anthropogenic processes has the ability to affect the influence on human heath and the quality of living. Since our physical health acts as a major incentive to carry out an environmental assessment. **Environmental assessment is defined as a process used by decision-makers, researchers and scientists to assess, predict, and mitigate the potential impacts that any developmental project or natural disasters, natural processes and human interference might have on human health, society, ecosystem and environment.**

To assess these damages computer models play an important tool for fast retrieval of information and preventive actions. In the **environmental sciences**, numerical computer models act as powerful means to represent and communicate our understanding of the environment, and have a wide application in predicting future changes in natural processes, often resulting due to natural changes and man made interferences. Since most natural processes have spatial components that change through time, these environmental computer models are typically spatial, with a flow of information in two- or three-dimensional space, and over time.

**An operating mathematical model** is the process of use of mathematical language to describe the behaviour of a system/environment. Mathematical models are used in particular in all branches of study such biology, electrical engineering, physics, chemistry, environmental engineering, civil engineering, applied mathematics, geography and geology to name few. These operating mathematical models are used for environmental assessment, drought assessment, industrial productivity assessment, pollution forecasting and various other applications. The current lecture world focuses on the following aspects of environment using modeling:

1. Impacts of climate change on glacial ice sheets and snow transport.
2. Geomorphological development
3. Acid deposition modeling
4. Modeling of water quality and quantity.
5. Dynamics in lakes, streams and rivers.
6. Air Pollution Dynamics
7. Water Pollution Dynamics
8. Urban growth
9. Forest Degradation Dynamics.
10. Drought/Flood Assessment
11. Disaster Assessment

## Environmental Modeling

Environmental modeling is one of the scientific tools for the prediction and assessment of the rapid changing environment quality and quantity. Environmental Modeling is a well-established field of environmental research as it incorporates the use of computer aided tools and their applications. Merging of computer and their software in different fields of research, has added to yet another aspect of research and that is forecasting of environmental changes. Environmental models represent space as one, two or three dimension, and are usually dynamic and spatially distributed models. These models incorporate various aspects of the natural and manmade environment. Environmental modeling is based on the basic concept of one of systems state, of mass and energy conservation, of transformation and translocation, of species and individuals' interaction and dynamics. The different parameters that lead to environmental changes are taken into account during modeling. Parameters as constants must be set before a model can be evaluated. They may be known values (*e.g.* the charge on the electron), physically meaningful values (*e.g.* soil hydraulic conductivity), or arbitrary values used empirically within a model.

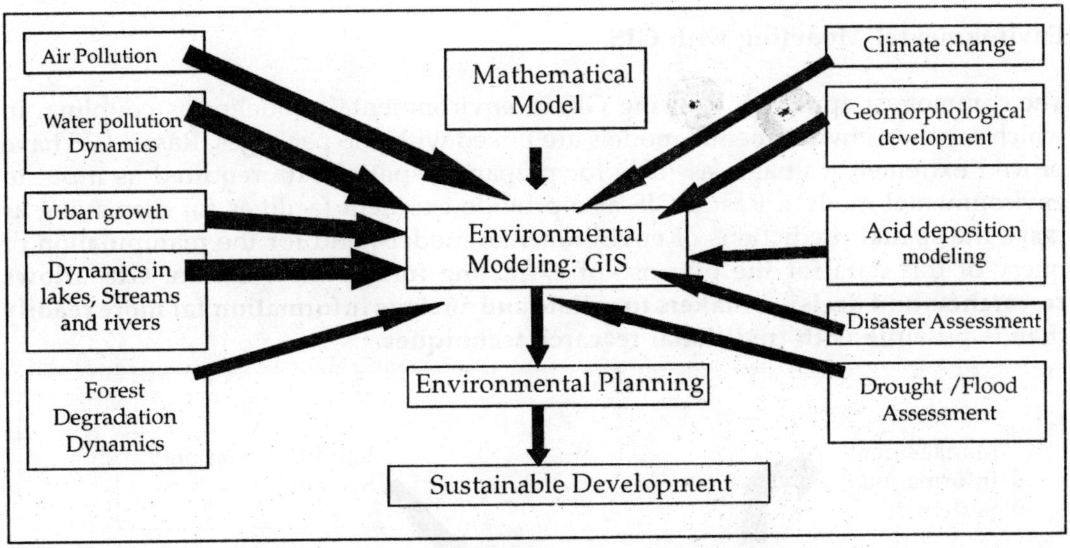


**Fig. 10.7:** Aspects of Environment using Modeling

Hence, the pre-requirements to get started with modeling are:

- Identify the problem to be studied in a particular environment/Area.
- Determine the factors that influence the area.
- Representation of these factors and their interrelationships in a mathematical way.
- Interpretation of the resultant output in reference to the real world scenario.

- Evaluation of these outputs at real-world situation.
- Re-examine the factors that were considered for a better output.

It has been evident that the mathematical modeling of physical processes has been a focus of environmental scientists since last two to three decades but implementation of these models have been a major failure. Remote Sensing and GIS software provides capabilities for spatial modeling and analysis today, these software itself were never developed keeping in mind the Environmental aspect and hence their applications has not yet found a suitable place. Environmental models have a scale range over which it is appropriate to apply them and there are pitfalls in using a model at a scale or resolution greater or smaller than that for which it was designed. GIS has the data handling capability which makes it practical to perform modeling operations over a large area whilst still maintaining the scale of detail for which the model was designed. Furthermore GIS provides a medium for linking different environment models together. Geographic Information Systems (GIS) have become increasingly valuable tools in environmental impact modeling and have been used in the evaluation of development proposals in many ways.

**Environmental Modeling with GIS**

The commonest approach to using GIS in environmental modeling is coupling, in which separate environmental models are linked with GIS packages. Raster GIS have proved extremely valuable as tools for preparing spatial data required as input to environmental models. Raster GIS also provide excellent facilities for displaying as maps the spatial predictions of environmental models, and for the manipulation or query of this data for the purpose of extracting further information. **GIS allows researchers and decision makers to collate and analyze information far more readily than is possible with traditional research techniques.**

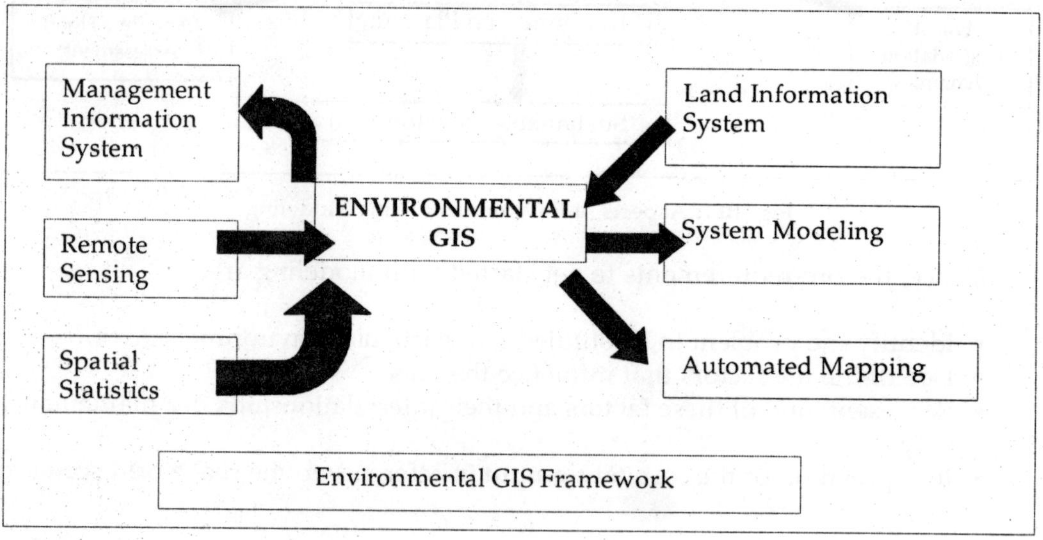


Environmental GIS Framework

**Environmental modeling** is a diverse field encompassing many application domains and countless individual approaches to conceptualizing processes. GIS-based modeling environment is not a realistic proposition. One way to proceed is to identify an existing modeling methodology, of broad appeal, which might augment current GIS capabilities.

**Environmental modeling** languages are programming languages developed for building computer models simulating environmental processes. The environmental modeling language is meant to simulate environmental processes occurring within a three-dimensional block of material such as rock, air, and/or vegetation. Within the three-dimensional block, different 'units', such as rock layers, can be distinguished, each with specific properties for the process simulated. The shape of the units and the block may be fixed or changing. It is fixed when flow of material or information within the block is modeled. Examples of such models are found in hydrology, oceanography, geochemistry, climatology, meteorology, pedology, and ecology.

They come with database and visualization routines for the data used in the models. Environmental modeling languages provide the possibility to construct dynamic models, also called forward models, which are simulations run forward in time, where the state of the model at time t is defined as a function of its state in a time step preceding t. Nowadays, these modeling languages can deal with simulations in two spatial dimensions, but existing software does not support the construction of models in three dimensions. Environmental models are currently mainly developed in general-purpose programming languages (C++, Fortran, Python, Basic), technical computing languages (MATLAB, 2004) or graphical modeling languages. General-purpose programming languages have the advantage that these enable almost any program to be made, but they are not ideal for environmental modelers who are not computer programmers mainly because the level of thinking of these languages is too strongly related to specialized computer science which may make model construction and modification cumbersome.

The graphical modeling languages are very powerful for process modeling, but their non-spatial operators do not provide the possibility of construction of models with spatial interaction. The Modeling languages in GIS:

1. Provide functions in which commonly used spatial algorithms have been pre-programmed;
2. Provide these functions in a suitable way such that they can be glued together in a model by a modeler using his or her understanding of environmental processes rather than computer expertise;
3. Provide generic tools for data input, database management and visualization of data read and written by the model.

**Cellular Automata (CA) modeling** is one such methodology which has a number of attractive features. CA is a simple yet powerful methodology for conceptualizing environmental models which has been used in a number of fields.

**Cellular Automata**

A CA model comprises a regular lattice of cells. At each time step, each cell can exist in one of a fixed number of states. Surrounding each cell is a neighbourhood of predetermined size and shape. During a time step the states of all cells are updated simultaneously as a function of states within their neighbourhoods. The strength of the CA approach is that it is inherently iterative (in contrast to the static approach of GIS) and allows the representation of a wide range of dynamic processes by relatively simple transition rules. However, even with CA-based methods there are still certain types of model which cannot be implemented. A severe limitation arises from the use of simple prescribed neighbourhoods. In reality, many environmental models require sophisticated extended neighbourhoods which may vary spatially and temporally and cannot, therefore, be prescribed. For instance, it is possible to conceptualize the likelihood of seed reaching a particular cell (which we will call the focal cell) as a function of parent plant abundance and distance distribution upwind, and of frictional land surface properties between the focal cell and seed sources.

The integration of **landscape ecology** concepts in EIA's ecological assessment brings most importantly the discussion to the need to consider the spatial dimension of our ecological environment. Ecological models and GIS technologies are the tools that allow the implementation of the concepts into practice.

**The potential use of GIS in EIA in general** and for ecological assessment in particular has been recognized and advocated. However, in today's EIA reports, the use of GIS within ecological assessment is often limited to its display functions and seldom used for its analytical capacities. A broad definition of GIS is a computer system made up of hardware, software, data and applications for managing spatial data in the form of maps, digital images and tables of geocoded data items. One main function of a GIS is to gather data that will result in the creation of a database. This database can then be the starting point for further manipulation and analysis of the data. For ecological assessment, such a database could consist of a land-cover map, a topographical map (digital elevation model), a conservation or protected-areas map, a soil map, a geology map and a climate map depending on the availability of these data. Data on climatic variables could also be relevant to perform the assessment further. The quality and accuracy of the land-cover map will be the limiting factor for the rest of the ecological assessment. At the baseline level of the EIA process, the display functions of a GIS can be used to produce background ecological maps. Ecological modeling is not restricted to GIS applications but its usefulness and potential implementation in physical planning almost make some form of spatially referenced system a requirement. The development of predictive habitat distribution models. Within ecological modeling, prediction models try to establish a relation between species occurrences and environmental variables in an attempt to characterize the habitats suitable for specific species.

**Geoinformatics** is also widely used to support the activities of other Department research groups. Other areas of interest include techniques for improved classification and visualisation of remotely sensed imagery; the integration of remotely sensed data within GIS; applications of airborne imaging spectrometry and radar polarimetry; and improved algorithms for inverse modeling.

### *Significance of GIS Integrated Technology*

The importance of GIS as an integrating technology is also evident in its pedigree. The development of GIS has relied on innovations made in many different disciplines starting from Architecture, Geography, Cartography, Photogrammetry, Remote Sensing, Surveying, Geodesy, Civil Engineering, Statistics, Computer Science, Operations Research, Artificial Intelligence, Demography, Environmental Engineering and many other branches of the social sciences, natural sciences, to engineering disciplines.

1. GIS is related with the interlinking of data's that are procured from different disciplines, but what makes a difference is that GIS is linked with Spatial reference. GIS data are geo-coded based on their positional reference and all the data's that are linked to any single entity has a geo referenced background.
2. GIS integrates technology. GIS is a sum total of different applications of disciplines that are clustered together in one platform known as GIS platform.
3. The output is displayed as maps which have an important role to play when dealing with laymans. The visual form of any data is more applicable and understandable as compared to raw form.
4. GIS plays a major role in decision making along with its visual display output (Maps). Their is an integration of different techniques such as buffering, overlay, digital elevation model that can be useful for planning and management of any area by decision makers.

### Applications of Integrated GIS Technique

**1. Natural resources management**

- Wildlife habitat management.
- Forest change detection
- Desertification
- Rain water harvesting sites
- Natural forests and sanctuaries
- Zonation of wild life species
- Wetland assessment

**2. Facilities and Infrastructure management**

- Address matching,
- Location analysis or site selection,
- Development of evacuation plans,
- Locating underground pipes and cables,

- Balancing loads in electrical networks,
- Planning facility maintenance,
- Tracking energy use,
- Construction of dams and reservoir.

**3. Land/Water Management**

- Land use planning,
- Land acquisition,
- Environmental impact policy,
- Water quality management,
- Maintenance of ownership,
- Water Quality Mapping.

**4. Environment Protection**

- Air Quality Modeling,
- Ground water Modeling,
- Noise Quality Modeling,
- Traffic Modeling.

**5. Disaster Management**

- Flood mapping,
- Drought assessment,
- Cyclonic movements,
- Earth quake assessment.

**6. Economic Development**

- Heritage site protection and development,
- Tourism site development.

## Conclusion

Geoinformatics is an integrated approach towards sustainable Environmental development. Geoinformatics is an essential tool towards modeling the environment as it incorporates the various parameters into consideration. Moreover the subject/data/parameters in geoinformatics in spatially positioned and this is one of the major benefit over other modeling tools. Proper Environmental planning can be conducted using integrated GIS approach. Hence, GIS is an essential tool for decision makers and researchers when sustainable development is the prime objective.

# 11
# Spacial Modeling of Raster and Vector Data

*Rajashree V. Bothale*

## GIS—A Tool

A GIS is a specific Information System applied to geographical data and is mainly referred to as system of hardware, software and procedures designed to support the capture, storage, management, manipulation, analysis, modeling and display of spatially-referenced data for solving complex planning and management problems.

While GIS allows the handling and manipulation of data in both spatial and non-spatial format, the power of the GIS is in the organization of Spatial Information Systems and orienting it towards decision-making or resource management. All of this is based on the concepts of technology—Spatial Science. The organization of applications around GIS requires a high-level of GIS-knowledge and visualization of integrated analysis. The design and organization of GIS is an involved activity and requires a good understating of the concepts of geography, cartography, database management, resource modeling and management etc.

## Why GIS?

Efficient means for data distribution and handling
Elimination of redundant database
Integration of data from various sources
Maximize the efficiency of planning and decision making

## Which Generic Queries GIS Can Answer?

GIS can answer queries like pertaining to—

**Location:** What exists at a particular location by name of the place, geographic co-ordinate or by interactive pointing. Thereby it can answer queries like What lies here?

**Condition**: It can find out areas where certain conditions exist. Criterias for the query can be specified. Thereby it can answer queries like Where lies this ?

**Neighborhood**: GIS allows to find out neighborhood information from a specified place, path of area. Thereby it answers queries like What lies within this distance?

**Proximity and route:** Nearest feature on the map from the particular feature can also be located. Thereby it can answer queries like Where is nearest entity from here?

**Trends:** GIS provides the changes occurring over the period of time and thereby allows to find trends.

**Modeling:** Modeling allows to solve complex problem of any application domain. Modeling for generation of land resources development plan will provide viable action plans for sustainable development of the area. Forest fire prediction models will show all probable zones, which are prone to fire. Flood hazard modeling will highlight areas, which could be inundated during flood. Network models allow planning of resource location based on demand and supply criteria. What happens if kind of scenarios can be generated using network models.

**Patterns**: GIS also help in finding out spatial patterns in the data which may lead to make some conclusions and the finding the cause for occurrence of these patterns.

## Data Structures in GIS

### *The Hierarchical Database Structure*

When the data have a parent/child or one-to many relations, such as areas for various levels of administration, soil series within a soil family, or pixels within a polygon, hierarchical methods provide quick and convenient means of data access. The main advantages of the model are its simplicity and ease of access via keys that define the hierarchy. They are easy to understand and to update and expand and can be useful for organizing data in mass storage systems.

### *The Network Database Structure*

In hierarchical structures, travel within the database is restricted to the path up and down the taxonomic pathways. In many situations much more rapid linkage is required, particularly in data structures for graphics features where adjacent items in a map need to be linked together even though the actual data about their coordinates may be written in very different parts of the database. Both redundancy and linkage problems are avoided by the compact network structure. Network database structures are very useful when the relations or linkages can be specified beforehand.

### *The Relational Database Structure*

In its simplest form the relational database structure stores no pointers and has no hierarchy. Instead, the data are stored in simple records, known as tuples, which are sets of fields, each containing an attribute; tuples are grouped together in two-dimensional tables, known as relations, somewhat in the manner of a spreadsheet program. Each table or relation is usually a separate file. The pointer structures in network structures and the keys in hierarchical structures are replaced by data redundancy in the form of identification codes that are used a unique keys to identify the records in each file.

### *Data Models in GIS*

Data input is the first step in GIS operation. Before we do this, we should know different ways of representing the data in GIS. The model in which we represent the data in GIS is termed as data model. Two basic data models are raster and vector. Application requirement will decide the representation to chose. Each data model has its advantages and disadvantages. In most of the GIS software, vector is given as a basic data model and the procedures to convert from vector to raster data model are provided.

### *Raster Model*

Representation of real world data in any of the model is nothing but the problem of explaining/representing/indicating the geographic space in the computer system. Raster method serves to quantize or divide space as a series of packets or units or grid cells of fixed or uniform size. Converting or explaining the real world data in raster is essentially storing the data at each position (grid cell). Finer the grid cell higher the amount of details in the raster data. Size of the grid cell is nothing but the resolution of the data. The grid-cell or raster model is a relatively simple approach to data representation, both conceptually and operationally. The representation of attributes is by specifying values to each grid cell. Rasters are limited by the area they can represent and also the limits of storage space. Also the fineness of the data is limited by the cell size. Thus the area coverage is trade-off with the resolution of the coverage. The storage problems are handled by resorting to compression techniques like run-length coding, block coding etc.

### *Vector Data Model*

The vector data structure represents each geographical feature by a set of coordinates. Vectors as xy coordinates define points, lines and polygons. The basic premise of the vector based structuring is to define a 2-dimensional space where features are represented by coordinates on the two-axes. Generally, representing points and lines is straightforward. Points are characterized by a x-y coordinate pair and lines by a set of x-y coordinate pairs with a specific beginning and ending vector. However, representing polygons in vector storage poses a challenge.

### *Raster Versus Vector*

As there are two characteristically different ways of spatial data representation for GIS applications, questions of preferring one method over the other arise. Some of the issues that need consideration are as follows:

(a) Vector data is precise and has no approximation errors for measured quantities like area, length, perimeter, etc. (subject, of course, to the representational accuracy of the hardware). Due to the discretization raster data suffers from such approximation errors.
(b) Generally, raster data has higher storage requirements though compression techniques can be adopted. Vector storage is relatively less.
(c) GIS manipulation operations on raster data are computationally faster and less complex than their equivalents on vector data. Imposing a structure on 2D vector data that is sufficiently formal and supports efficient searching is fairly complex.
(d) Raster data is not easily amenable to association of attribute data with spatial features such as points, lines or polygons. This is due to the fact that the basic entity in the raster approach is the grid cell and entites such as points, lines and polygons are not recognized as objects in their own merit.
(e) Raster is limited by the cell-size and sampling or dis-aggregation to a lower size is not possible. Vector structure does not impose this limitations and thus analysis, plotting etc. is more accurate in Vector structure.

## GIS Database Creation

### *Spatial Database Creation*

Based on the design, the steps of database creation are worked out and a procedure laid down. The steps for the spatial database creation include following:

(a) Creating spatial framework
(b) Master template creation
(c) Thematic map manuscript preparation
(d) Digitisation of features
(e) Coverage editing
(f) Attribute coding verification

## Non-Spatial Database Organization

Non-spatial data elements are mostly available in analog mode. Towards converting it into a digital mode, a suitable application package could be used to configure a data entry system.

# 12

# GIS Applications

*B.K. Bhadra*

## Introduction

Geographic information system (GIS) form the backbone of scientific management of natural resources. Developments in computer technology have modernized the management of geographic information and resulted in a boost in GIS applications. A variety of geographic data and tabular information generated by the different agencies on different projections, scales and accuracy can be input into a single GIS database. Using GIS different forms of data (vector, raster etc.) can be brought to a common format and analyzed for meaningful decisions. The output from GIS system can be generated on desired scales. A variety of input and output media are possible to use on a GIS system.

GIS systems support logical querying of information stored in a GIS database, *e.g.* we can find out distance between any two points/places of interest, area of a polygon; attach list of information attributes or charts, diagram, pictures, etc. with a given feature in a GIS base; find out shortest route for reaching a place (while imposing many of the pre-conditions on the route search) or analyze any other network related problems. Further, we can also find out feature sets qualifying certain conditions, *e.g.* smaller than, bigger than, equal to, less than, smallest, biggest, within a radius of given km, etc. Buffer creation along a feature is another very important utility added with the GIS.

## GIS Systems

Basic functions of GIS include capability to store voluminous data on different aspects of a theme/application, retrieval, integrate information stored in different layers, process, analyze and output analyzed information in desired scales/form in an efficient manner. Additionally, a GIS has facility for modeling, statistical analysis of stored information, map making/designing and limited scale image analysis facility.

A number of standard GIS systems and packages are available in the market. ARC/INFO, ARC/VIEW, GRASS, PAMAP, ILWIS, IDRISI, GIPSY, etc. are some of the commonly used GIS software in the country.

## GIS Applications

The awareness about advantages of GIS is increasing day by day among the decision-makers and organizations. A number of GIS studies in different thematic areas have been carried out in different application areas including geology. A number of GIS studies have been initiated by different organizations in the country on the project (experimental/operational) mode. The areas covered under various GIS application studies include Urban Information System (*e.g.* GIS for NCR and Jodhpur City Information System), Wasteland Information System, Agriculture and Soils Information System, Geological Information System (Project Vasundhara), Forest Information System, Water Resources Information System, Natural Resources Information System at district level (under NRIS project of DOS), NRDMS project of the DST, etc.

### *GIS Application Areas*

1. *Agriculture*

Crop/Non Crop
Crop Types
Crop Acreage
Crop yield
Horticulture
Plantations

2. *Soil*

Soil Types—Texture, Color etc.
Soil Suitability
Soil Moisture
Soil association

3. *Forestry*

Forest type
Extent
Density
Clearings
Encroachments
Timber Volume

Forest Fire Areas
Damage Assessment

*4. Environment*

Application Areas
Environmental Impact
Mining
River Valley projects
Urbanisation
Hazardous Waste
Thermal Power Projects
Chemical Industries
Change Detection
Coastal Erosion
Oil Slick
Forest Degradation

*5. Water Resources*

Type/Extent Water Bodies
Reservoir Volume Estimation
Ground Water Prospecting
Snow Covered Areas
Snow Melt Runoff
Reservoir Sedimentation
Water Logged Areas
Leakage Along Canals
Drainage Network
Dry *versus* Wet Sources

*6. Urban Studies*

Urban Infrastructure
Sprawl/Growth
Facilities Planning/Mapping
City Planning
Urban Landuse
Alignment for New Roads

*7. Integrated Studies*

Land Suitability Analysis
District Planning

Aftershed Prioritisation
GIS Studies

*8. Marine Studies*

Fisheries
Ocean Wind
Ocean Waves
Sea Ice
Ship Routing
Geoid

*9. Coastal Studies*

Land Use
Erosion
Wetland
Bathymetry
Aqua-culture

*10. Geological Applications*

Geological Mapping
Geomorphological Mapping
Structural Mapping
Mineral Exploration
Oil Exploration
Engineering Geology
Ground Water Studies
Geo-Environmental Studies

*11. Disaster/Natural Hazards*

Cyclones
Floods
Drought
Forest Fires
Crop Pest and Disease
Volcanoes
Earthquakes
Landslides
Coal Fires

# 13

# Data Management Models through GIS

*A.K. Bera*

Spatial databases contain many files with data on related aspects of the same entities, or of data on entities that because of their spatial proximity or connectivity have to be linked or grouped tog^ther. It is essential to organize the way these files are stored and linked in the computer to model real world phenomena and to ensure efficient storage and retrieval of data.

## Database Organization

The GIS has two distinct utilization capabilities—the first pertaining to querying and obtaining information and the second pertaining to integrated analytical modeling. However, both these capabilities depend upon the core of the GIS database that has been organized. Generally, a proper database organization needs to ensure the following:

(a) A flexibility in the design to adapt to the needs of different users.
(b) A controlled and standardized approach to data input and updation.
(c) A system of validation checks to maintain the integrity and consistency of the data elements.
(d) A level of security for minimising damage to the data.
(e) Minimizing redundancy in data storage.

The design of the GIS database will include three major elements:

(i) Conceptual design, basically laying down the application requirements and specifying the end-utilisation of the database. The conceptual design is independent of hardware and software and could be a wish-list of utilisation goals.
(ii) Logical design, which is the specification of the database *vis-à-vis* a particular GIS package. This design sets out the logical structure of the database elements and is determined by the GIS package.

(iii) Physical design, which pertains to the hardware and software characteristics and requires consideration of file structure, memory and disk space, access and speed etc.

## Database Creation

Based on the design, the steps of database creation are worked out and a procedure laid down. The procedure for the spatial database creation is described below:

(*a*) *Creating of spatial framework*: The spatial framework of the GIS database can be organized in the GIS by specifying the registration points for the total database and specifying the coordinate system of the database. Registration Points for the total area can be entered through key-board.

(*b*) *Master template creation:* As discussed earlier, a master template is created as a reference layer and consisting of the district boundary, rivers etc. This template is then used for the component themes digitization.

(*c*) *Thematic map manuscript preparation:* Based on the spatial the different theme oriented information is transferred from the base map to a mylar/transparent sheet. Spatial data manuscripts are mylars consisting features that are to be digitized. These manuscripts are prepared on a sheet-by-sheet basis for digitization. These manuscripts consist "instructions" for digitization or scanning—which include:

—Registration point locations and identifiers
—Feature codes as per the dictionary defined earlier
—Feature boundaries
—Tolerance specifications
—Any other digitization/scanning instructions.

(*d*) *Digitisation of features:* The theme features of the spatial dataset are then digitized/scanned using the GIS PACKAGE. The digitization/scanning is done for each map-sheet of the spatial reference. The master registration-point reference are used for the digitisation. The theme digitization is done as a component into a copy of the master template layer.

(*e*) *Coverage editing:* The digitized coverage is processed for digitization errors such as dangles, constituting the overshoots or undershoots, and labels for polygons. This constitutes obtaining a report of these errors and then a manual editing of these features. The editing of these features is also best carried out on a map-sheet basis. Finally, the coverage is processed for topology creation. In the case of raster GIS packages, the topology construction may not be relevant. However, a clumping process to identify the clump of rasters having similar characteristics would be essential. The tools for topology organization or the raster-polygon generation is generally available in the GIS package.

(*f*) *Attribute coding verification:* The attribute codes for the different categories need to be then verified and additional attributes—feature-name, description etc. are added into the feature database.

**Conclusions**

Some errors might occur as a result of computational miscalculations and rounding error in the GIS software. However, most database errors result from improper input.

The errors which we normally encounter are:

(a) *Entity error (positional error)*—This is primarily encountered in vector systems. Entity error can come in three different forms: missing entities, incorrectly placed entities, and disordered entities.

(*b*) *Attribute error*—Attribute error occurs in both vector and raster systems, often with the same frequency. Most often attributes are typed in, and it constitutes a major source of error. In vector systems attribute errors include using the wrong code for an attribute, as well as misspellings, which make an attribute impossible to retrieve if a query uses the correct spelling. In raster, the input most often consists of attributes, so the result of typing a wrong code number or placing it in the wrong grid location is a map that displays these incorrectly coded cells in the wrong place.

(*c*) *Entity-attribute agreement error*—Incorrectly placed attribute data gives rise to this error, (logical consistency), which also occurs in vector systems when correctly typed codes are attached to the wrong entities.

Data input is the major activity in GIS and is very crucial as the end results are totally based on the correctness of the data. The wrong or insufficient data will lead to erroneous results. Hence data input need to be followed by strict quality checks.

# 14

# Data Display Model and Presentation

*Shri Suparn Pathak*

## Introduction

After designing the database and performing series of tasks to complete the analysis, the main task is to record the analysis results and present them graphically. Usually this is done by graphical representation of data (MAP) and written description of result (INFO-REPORT). A successful map conveys several types of information such as locational information, describes the location of a particular feature on the earth's surface and their spatial relationships. A map also contains information describing the characteristics of the feature.

Design and layout must be considered when producing output. A beautiful map will help conveying the intended message with greater impact. Some of the components of good map are:

- Design the components of the map
- Using symbols effectively
- Determining the purpose of map
- Defining map parameters (size and scale)
- Designing map layout
- Preparing symbol data
- Creating a final map

## Maps

*What is a map?* A map is a geographic representation of some part of the earth's surface. Cartographic design uses symbology representing features with symbol and typography (arranging presented matter) to convey information that is both easily understood and visually appealing to the map reader.

*Map body*—The primary mapped area. You can display more than one image of your primary mapped area within your document. For example, you may want to portray change by showing several images with differing but related information, such as population maps of various years. Your map may also contain a locator map (a smaller-scale map used to help the reader in understanding where the main area of interest is located), an inset map (used to give more detailed information of an area within the main map that may not easily be understood), or an index map (often used to show where in a series of maps one map exists). All are used to assist in communicating your information to others.

The primary component of map consists of **Geographic features** and **Cartogrpahic elements**. Geographic features include area features (reprsented by polygons), linear features (represented by arcs) and point features [(x,y location) represented by point elements]. Cartographic elements helps to make the map easier to read and interpret, and these includes Titles (text), Neatlines, Legends, North arrow, Logo, etc.

## Types of maps

| *General maps* | *Thematic maps* |
| --- | --- |
| Location positional relationship and variety of features | Structures of a distribution of single attribute/ relationship. |
| *Qualitative symbology* | *Quantitative symbology* |

## Symbols

### *Types of symbol*

***Symbol defination***: A set of parameters defines each symbol. The parameters common to most types of symbols are color, pattern and size.

***Colour***: Specifys colour in three way—by colour name, by colour model and components colour value (RGP, CMY)

***Pattern***: Pattern refers to the repetition and rythem of elements in the symbol, *e.g.* dotted line can be composed of evenly spaced dots or two dots together followed by a gap.

***Size***: Size determines the width and height of text and marker or the width of line symbols or the grain of the shade patterns

These are just some of the parameters that define symbols. Other parameters apply to specific symbol types. For example, in addition to colour, pattern and size, text symbols are defined by:

***Symbole file***: ARC/INFO stores symbol definations in symbol files. Each stored symbol has a unique number referencing its own set of defination. To use a symbol, you specify the symbol set and the number of the symbol in the file, *e.g.* PLOTTER.LIN is for line symbols, PLOTTER.SHD for shade symbol, PLOTTER.MRK for marker symbols and PLOTTER.TXT for text symbol.

***Editing symbols*:** Four symbol editor provide a graphic interface that allows to quickly choose and modify a current symbol or edit an existing symbol or create a new symbol and symbol sets.

### *Creation of Map*

Major steps for map creation:

1. Define the purpose and requirement of the map.
2. Determine the size and scale of the map.
3. Design the layout of the map.
4. Prepare additional data
5. Create final map.

In **Defining the purpose and requirement of the map,** the overall aim is to define the scope of the map, establish a list of objectives and thereby develop a plan to create the map. A map is meant to communicate and it can be packed with detail or be simple in content and yet still convey its overall message. It is also important to consider the intended reader's ability to interpret the information present in the map. Thus the content of the map is determined not only by why it's being produced, but also by who will use. List of required information to display on the map.

COVERAGES/GRID/IMAGES, *e.g.* VILLAGE, ROADS, SETTLEMENT, etc.

**Size and scale of map** depends on the map's purpose and requirement.

**Optimum size:** Optimum size or aspect ratio for map looks better with width-to-height ratio of 4.3 (Robinson *et al.*). The kind of map and size also depends on the various output devices available (graphic screen, plotters or postscript printers) and the type of material used (paper or film) for output generation.

For all practical reasons map are 'scaled representation'. The scale of map is devised such that the important data is retained and presented in a map of particular size. The most commonly used scale are 1:250,000 (1cm = 2.5 km) 1:50,000 (1cm = 0.5 km), etc.

Once it is known what information the map will contain and the physical parameters of the maps are, **layout** of the information should be considered. Layout is the actual placement of both geographic features and cartographic elements in such a way so that it gives a balance and proportional look. Often, trial and error is the only way to assess the overall balance.

Before creating the map, one need to prepare many other files or data, in addition to the coverages. Most of this work relates to the symbols you choose to represent the various map features. The step commonly includes two tasks.

Specifying the symbol value used to symbolize each features in a coverage. In this a item in the attribute table is assigned the symbol value, and to symbolize the feature (either line, point or polygon) use this item.

Creating look-up tables and key files that define the symbols and text to appear in a symbol key legend.

Another way to use attributes to specify symbols is to assess a look-up table. A look-up table is an INFO data file that contains two items (relate_item and symbol). For each unique attribute value, there is a corresponding record in the look-up table associated with a specific symbol number. One can create and updata LUT table in INFO.

***Key legend:*** Legends are used to explain the map symbols. To do this, one has to create a key legend file that defines what to display in the legend. A key legend file is a text file created using the text editor of the operating system (*e.g.* vi editor), where legend symbols are specified by dot and number (.56) along with its descriptive text.

You can also define legends using items in the feature attribute table (AAT, PAT, etc.). Lookup tables (INFO data file) you create to shade the landuse polygone (LUSE.LUT) can be used to create a legend by adding an item named DESCRIPTION.

This same information can appear and be accessed in the feature attribute table of the coverage.

Once all the preparatory work is done, you can begin creating your map on the computer, using the ARCPLOT (AP) programme and ARC/INFO plot system.

**Using Arc/Info to Create Map**

Once you have established your map design, size and scale, its time to translate this layout into ARC/INFO commands in ARCPLOT program to generate a map composition and a graphic file from which hardcopy plots can be generated.

There are five basic steps for creating your map using ARCPLOT.

1. Indicate the display method for the map on the graphic screen or on a graphic plotter.
2. Specify the portion of the coverage to be drawn on the map or several adjacent coverage (*i.e.* specify map extent).
3. Specify certain parameters about the size and layout of map to translate coverage features from computer to the display surface. This include final size of the map page, position of the geographic features and the scale. This operation is known as *map-to-page transformation.*
4. Draw the geographic features on map, such as landuse area, road and stream lines and specify which symbols to use for drawing and labeling them.
5. Add additional cartographic elements to make map easier to read and understand. These include neatlines, title, legends, scale bar, north arrow, etc.

# 15

# Mathematical Modeling in Grid Analysis

*Dibyendu Dutta*

It is a raster or cell based geoprocessing toolbox that is integrated with ARC/INFO. It represents space from a locational perspective and can accurately portray continuous surfaces.

Grid uses a georelational model for geographic data. It is based on a combined raster based spatial model and a relational attribute model. In Grid, the inherent power of the grid modeling structure is coupled with the capabilities of a relational database that manages all attributes associated with the cell values.

### The Data Structure

Grid is based on hierarchical tile block structure. A grid is divided into uniform square units called tiles. A tile is divided into blocks. Because there are more blocks on the y-axis than on thc x-axis, a block is always rectangular. A block is made up of cells, arranged in a Cartesian matrix consisting of row and columns. Cells are square.

This tile-block structure allows grid to support random access to data—rapid retrieval of information maintained from any sub-section of a grid, regardless of the size of the database. This forms the spatial indexing. Most of the cases all data for a grid resides in a single tile.

**Grid → Tiles → Blocks → Cells**

### Advantages

GRID data is accessible seamlessly.

Data compression using an adaptive run-length encoding scheme—compresses individual blocks or strips of data. It tests each group of data and then decides whether cell-by-cell or run-length code compression. Spatial indexing and compression techniques are applied separately.

Adaptive compression techniques allow for efficient use of a wider variety of tools providing more flexibility while performing spatial analysis. ARL performs well for per cell (LOCAL), per neighbourhood (FOCAL), per zone (ZONAL), and per layer (GLOBAL).

Fast processing speeds through run-length code processing without expansion. The commands that process compressed data directly include all operators, local functions and DOCELL loops.

GRID allows to store and transparently process grids at different resolutions within the same database. If two or more input grids in an expression are at different resolutions, grid automatically resamples them to the coarsest resolution unless otherwise specified.

Automatically optimizes spatial indexing and compression, making them transparent.

**Data Model**

1. GRID supports categorical/discrete data, *i.e.* categorical object has known and definable boundaries. A integer value is associated with each cell in categorical grid. All the integer grids include an INFO table called VAT. It contains at least two items, VALUE and COUNT. Any number of additional items can be added.
2. It supports also the storage and manipulation of continuous data. A continuous surface is usually represented by grid with floating point values, examples are elevation, aspect, slope etc. It does not have a VAT, because most, if not all, cell values are unique and nature of continuous data excludes other associated attributes.
3. Full supports for NODATA when inadequate information exists for a cell, the cell location can be assigned NODATA value in grid. All operators and functions process NODATA cell and return predictable values.
4. Full power of the relational database management system can be applied to VAT, *e.g.* ADDITEM and DROPITEM.
5. Deriving grids: Grids can be derived from other attributes in the VAT, which increase the flexibility and power of spatial analysis.
6. Inputting data into GRID: Grids can easily be produced from ARC/INFO vector coverages. Required inputs are attribute upon which to grid, cell resolution and type of gridding process.
7. An ARC/INFO lattice is a grid in GRID. Synergy is created between GRID and TIN modules. Lattice also uses tile-block spatial indexing.
8. GRID can directly input image files from external image processing and raster based packages, *e.g.* ERDAS files can be converted to GRID.
9. GRID also support other generic raster files, *viz.* TIFF, BIL, BIP and Sun raster files.
10. Map algebra language: GRID is based on map algebra. Map algebra is a data manipulation language designed specifically for geographic cell-based system. It describes cartographic spatial analysis.

11. Through spatial language, GRID furnishes functions specifically designed to process data and information in the grid-cell format. Type of processing can be either operators or/and functions.

**Operators:** They complete computation on one or more input data sets. GRID supports following operators, *viz.*

—Arithmatic
—Boolean (TRUE or FALSE)
—Relational (<< >< =)
—Bitwise
—Combinatorial (overlay of grids while carrying attribute)
—Logical (contained within a set)
—Accumulative (sum, divide, multiply...all value within the grid)
—Assignment (output equals)

***Functions Can be of Four Types***

- **Local (or per cell):** Functions compute an output grid in which the output value at each location is a function of the corresponding input value at each location. The value of a cell determines the result of a local function, *e.g.* sin(x), cos(x), squart(x), exp(x,2), log(x), reclassification and selection function (select all cells in a circle). For multiple inputs, operators that return min, max, majority or minority values.
- **Focal (per neighbourhood):** Functions compute an output grid in which the output value at each cell location is a function of the input cells in the specified neighbourhood of each location. The value of particular location is determined by the values of the cells around it, *e.g.* 3×3, 25×25, circular neighbour, wedge neighbour, annulus neighbour. The functions it can perform are return of mean, standard deviation, sum or range of values within the immediate neighbourhood.
- **Zonal (or per zone):** Functions compute an output grid in which the output value at each cell location depends on the values of all the input cells on an input value grid that share the same input value defined by an input zone grid. All cell values from the input grid that fall within the specified zone of the input zone grid is used to complete output value for each cell.
- **Global (or per grid):** Functions compute an output grid in which the output value at each cell location is potentially a function of all the cells in the input grids.

Four types of functions—

—Euclidean distance
—Weighted distance

—Surface distance
—Others

By applying global function to a weighted (cost) surface, the cost of moving from a destination cell to the nearest source cell can be determined. Surface functions include slope, aspect, analytic hill shading, kriging, inverse distance weighted and trend surface interpolation.

**Problems It Can Solve**

Best address locational problems. Two greatest advantages are: the ability to represent continuous surfaces and the ability to store points, lines, polygons and surfaces uniformly (identical representation). A continuous surface is best represented by a cell based system since the attributes of a location in the cell based system are a function of where the location is relative to a phenomena that is progressively changing as it moves across space.

Because of identical data representation data combination is easier, all data types are treated as same. But due to this some accuracy is sacrificed.

***Advantages of Cell-based Data Processing System***

- When the attributes of a location are influenced by the attributes of the locations that surround it.
- The attributes of a location are influenced by where its position falls within another feature.
- Cell-based systems can be used for continuous surface data modeling.
- Optimum allocation and surface determinations, *e.g.* determining the optimal course of a new road over a non-network surface such as soil map; drainage map creation from elevation data.

**Basic Concepts in Cell Based Processing**

Modeling locational problems is an inherent strength of the cell-based storage and analysis environment.

**Grid:** Store geographic data, but view and store surfaces differently. Grid based system divide the world into discrete uniform cells. Each cell is given a value to correspond to the feature. Location is not defined as an attribute but is inherent to storage structure. Every cell in a grid has a unique row and column.

***Grid and Raster***

**Raster:** It refers to a matrix composed of pixels or cells. Each pixel or cell stores a numeric value.

**Grid:** It is an implementation of generic raster data structure. Uses blocks and tiles for spatial indexing and adaptive run-length compression technique. Value associated with the cells in a grid can be discrete or continuous.

**Grid Resolution:** More homogeneous the area, larger cell size can be used with accuracy. With increase in size of the cell, resolution decreases.

**Values:** Value in a cell is an identifier that defined the class group, category or member of the cell belongs. Value can be integer or floating point. Cell locations with the same value belong to the same zone. There is usually one-to-many relationships between grid cell values (or codes) and the number of cells that are assigned the code.

**Measurements:** Measurement values can be broken into 4 types, *viz.* ratio, interval, ordinal and nominal.

- ***Ratio:*** Values derived relative to a fixed zero point on a linear scale, *e.g.* age, distance, weight etc.
- ***Interval:*** Time of day, pH scale etc. Values on a linear calibrated scale but not relative to a true zero point in time or space.
- ***Ordinal:*** It determines the position, do not establish magnitude or relative proportions, *e.g.* 1st, 2nd, better, stronger etc.
- ***Nominal:*** Values are used to identify one instance from another. They may also establish the group, class, member or category with which the object is associated. The values are qualities, with no relation to a fixed point or a linear scale.

Attribute handling within and between grids is most effective and efficient when using nominal measurements.

**Grid registration:** Each location on the ground is represented by the same x,y cell address on the different grid inputs. Each location of an input grid have a cell address. Processing the grids is the same as processing matrices which is very fast in computer.

Methods of determining cell value:

- Centroid
- Predominant type
- Most important type
- Percentage breakdown

Each method is suitable for certain type of data, choice depends on the type of data to be gridded and the analysis to be preformed.

**Centroid:** Suitable for continuous data, *e.g.* elevation. Each cell is assigned the value of the feature that passes through the center of the cell.

**Predominant (majority weighting):** The value of the feature that fills the majority of the cell is assigned to the location. This is good for non-continuous (discrete) data such as landcover, soils etc. When a grid is overlaid in the gridding process onto a vegetation coverage.

**Most important:** Each cell is assigned the value associated with the features that have been specified as more important to the study (weightage is assigned with the categories).

**Percentage break down:** A cell is assigned several values one per feature, according to per cent each feature occupies within the cell. Difficult and costly method. Useful for statistical data.

Data compression: Two most important types:

- *Cell by cell:* For data that has a unique value for every cell. True for floating point grids or continuous surfaces, *e.g.* 1, 1:0; 1,2:0; 1,3:4......
- *Run-length code:* When adjacent cells have same value, runs are created and data can be compressed. It stores data by row. The column range information is stored as a from-column to a to-column along with the value associated with that cell or group of cells, *e.g.* 1:1-16:0, 2:1-9:0, 10-11:1, 12-16:0......
- *Quad trees:* It first divides the grid into 4 equal smaller squares when cells in the grid have different values. If all the cells within any of the 4 smaller square have the same value, the square will not be broken down any further. If the square is not homogeneous it will further be broken into 4 small squares. The process continues until each square only represents cells with the same values.

**Raster data source:** Raster digital images, Grid cell GIS data, Scanned imagery.

**GRID:** It describes the features and characteristics of an area and their relative positions in space.

**CELL:** Units of grid, square and same size which is defined by the user.

**ROW AND COLUMN:** Cells are arranged in row and columns and produce Cartesian matrix. Each cell has unique row and column address.

**VALUE:** Each cell is assigned value to identify or describe the class, category or group that the cell belongs to. Within the theme which the grid describes. It can also represent magnitude, distance etc. Both integer and FP are supported.

Integer: For categorical data
FP: For continuous surface

**ZONE:** Two or more cells with same value, belong to same zone. Zone is consists of cells which can be connected or disconnected or both.

**REGIONS:** Each group of connected cells in a zone is considered as a region.

**NODATA:** Also known as null value, is treated differently from any other value by all operators and functions. It represents either no or insufficient information available about a particular characteristics. It can be processed in 2 ways.

- By assigning NODATA to the output cell location if NODATA value exists for the location of any of the inputs in an operator or local function, focal function or zonal function.
- Ignoring the cell and continue calculation for other valid values.

- Ignoring not possible with operators between two or with local functions. When NODATA is in a focal function, or zonal function, by default, the sum, median, majority or minority of all cells with known values can be calculated and assigned to outgrid.
- VAT: For categorical (integer grids), similar to PAT first term is value, second term count. Both are mandatory.

### Data Representation

**Point data:** Represented by the smallest unit of a grid, a cell. Smaller the cell size, smaller the area and closer the representation of the point feature.

**Linear data:** Can be represented by a series of connected cells. When both the scale and the resolution are exceedingly fine, with each cell standing for a very small area, the representation is accurate.

**Polygon data:** Best represented by a series of connected cells that best portray their shape. Finer the cell resolution and greater the cell number, more accurate the representations.

**Surface data:** Represented as a matrix of evenly spaced points called lattice. In cell view, each value applies equally to the area, but in lattice view it applies to the center point of cell. Lattice view is used for all surface calculations.

**Cell resolution:** It is the cell size given in map units.

### *Spatial Processing*

1. **Location determination:** GRID stores the origin in map units. Using origin coordinates and the cell size GRID can associate the cell row-column address with any given map x,y coordinates. Cell locations are specified in terms of map coordinates.
2. **Cell by cell processing:** All operations (except zonal and global) as cell-by-cell basis. Starts from top left and proceeds towards right and then top to bottom. The result of each cell processed is written in outgrid before the second is processed. Processing occurs for all operators and local and focal functions and within DOCELL block.
3. **Multigrid calculations:** When using multiple grids, operators and local functions process all values between grids. For zonal and global functions often treat one grid as the main processing grid and use other grid as means for defining the values and parameters necessary for completing calculations.
4. **Neighbourhood processing:** Focal functions also use cell by cell processing but unlike operators and local functions, focal function consider the values of the cells within a specified neighbourhood around the processing cell. Neighbourhood can be square, circle, annulus or donut shape or wedge.
5. **Neighbourhood-notation processing:** Way to create custom neighbours and define the manner in which the neighbourhood should be processed. Following will return same result as that of FOCALSUM.

Grid: outgrid = Ingrid (-1,1) + ingrid1 (-1,0) + ingrid1 (-1,-1) + ingrid1 (0,1) + ingrid1 (0,0) + ingrid1 (0,-1) + ingrid1 (1,1) + ingrid1 (1,0) + ingrid1 (1,-1).

**Zonal calculations:** Same as neighbourhood calculations, except that zone from a input grid decides the shape of the neighbourhood, processing is zone by zone.

**Calculating distance and direction:** Centre of one cell to center of other cell when cells are apart the distance is measured as Euclidean distance. True direction is also calculated from center to center of cells.

**Weight-distance calculation:** Cost path calculations utilize weighted surface grids (cost surface or impedence grids). Weigthted surface assigns a value to each cell that identifies some cost to pass through the cell. Start and destination points assumes cell center.

For horizontal and vertical node a1(cost) = (cost1+cost2)/2
For diagonal cells cost = [(cost1+cost2)×1.421]/2

**Area calculation:** Area of cell × number of cells in a zone. If area to be calculated for each region of a discontinuous region, then REGIONGROUP function has to be run first which will assign new identifier zone value to every continuous area within the same value.

**Surface calculations:** Values associated with a location represent cell center. Aspect and slope is calculated from a cells relationship.

# 16

# Manipulation and Analysis in GIS

*Vinod M. Bothale*

Analysis subsystem is the heart of the GIS; it is what the GIS is really all about. This chapter provides a simple framework for analysis that should provide an ample survey of existing capabilities of most GIS software. GIS can be used for counting and locating objects, making measurements of length, area, shape, of the various entities, measuring distances between the objects, identifying spatial objects, reclassifying the available data into logical groupings, carry out neighborhood operations, studying spatial pattern and arrangement, cartographic overlays of point, line and polygon data, cartographic modeling etc. Using these kinds of functionalities one can solve the problems in different application domains to get fruitful solutions.

The manipulation and analysis functions of GIS need to be used in the combination so as to arrive at the solution of a problem at hand. The functions could be categorized in various groups—

- Spatial join
- Feature extraction
- Feature merging: Reclassification, Sliver removal
- Measurement, connectivity and neighborhood operations
- Map database merging and splitting
- Centroid determination
- Statistical analysis
- Modeling

Geographic analysis allows to study the real world process by developing and applying manipulation and analysis criteria (models). These criteria illuminate underlying trends in geographic data, making new information available. A GIS enhances this process by providing tools which can be combined in meaningful sequence to reveal new or previously unidentified relationships within or between data sets, thus increasing better understanding of real world. The results of geographic analysis can be communicated in the form of maps, reports or both.

For doing any kind of analysis for arriving at desired results, the goals and objective must be defined which will set the sequence of analysis functions to be performed on the data. Generally, following steps are involved:

- Establish objectives and analysis criteria
- Prepare data for spatial operations
- Perform spatial operations
- Perform tabular analysis
- Evaluate and interpret results
- Refine the analysis if necessary
- Produce final maps and tabular reports

The some of the typical applications which can be accomplished using manipulation and analysis functions include:

- Water resources planning
- Land resources development planning
- Waste site selection
- Dam site selection
- Irrigation water management
- Agriculture production modeling
- City planning
- Biodiversity characterization
- Habitat suitability assessment

**Spatial Join**

Spatial join are also called spatial overlay operations. Among the most powerful and most frequently used features of the modern geographic information system is its ability to place the cartographic representation of thematic information of a selected theme over that of another. One process could be just visually overlaying the features of one map on another and other could be actually combining the spatial and tabular information of these maps in a single map. The later process is called spatial join or overlay. This brings the information contained in different themes in a single theme for combined analysis. Any application requires more than one theme (map) data to be analyzed for arriving at the conclusion. In such cases, spatial overlay of the concerned maps is must. The overlay operation could be point-in-polygon, line-in-polygon or polygon-in-polygon type of function. Spatial join operations are nothing but the logical combinations like union, intersection etc.

**Feature Extraction**

Feature extraction refers to operations like clip or erase. The clip kind of operations extracts part of the area from the theme, *e.g.* It can generate a landuse map or taluk from a district landuse map. Similar to clipping operation, erase type of option erases the input map at the areas specified by the "erase map".

**Feature Merging**

Feature merging operations derive new map by merging features in the map. It is generally used to perform following kind of operations:

- Reclassification (Elimination)
- Removal of sliver or unwanted small polygons created during analysis (Dissolving)

Reclassification merges adjacent polygons or lines, which have the same value for specified item. It is used to create a simplified coverage from one, which is more complex. While the input map may contain information concerning many feature attributes, the output map contains information about the item on which reclassification is carried out. For example, Landuse map at level 3 may have kharif, rabi crop land as distinct classes (under level 2 classification CROPLAND) but if one requires a simplified map then the reclassification can be done which will combine kharif and rabi land and show them as simply "cropland".

The spatial join of two or more maps normally generate small polygons with negligible area and these area can be merged with the adjoining relatively bigger polygons. Feature merging can also be used to do this kind of operations.

**Measurement and Neighbourhood Functions**

A wide variety of measurement tools are needed in a GIS. With raster-based data, the precision of a measurement is limited due to raster cell size; vector systems are ultimately limited by the precision of the stored node locations. In general, the measurement include the line length (length of the road), area of polygon (Village area). Shape measurement is also necessary for some typical applications. This normally involves measurement of perimeter and area of the polygon to give the polygon complexity.

Spatial analysis involves operations that consider the spatial arrangement of information in one or more data layers. They may be broken down into two families: operations concerned with connections between location, and operations concerned with local or neighborhood characteristics. One of the classic functions of a geographic information system is to be able to identify items in proximity to each other. This function has wide variety of applications, including impact and corridor analysis and in problems of site selection.

Other common requirements could be measuring the distance between a point and the other feature (How far is village from the road), distance between polygon to polygon (which is the nearest water body for a cropland patch) of line to polygon (which is the nearest canal point from the agricultural area). There are a variety of kinds of spatial analysis that are based on networks. Applications in this general area include optimum corridor or travel selection, and hydrology and flow functions. Interesting example could be to evaluate alternative routes for emergency vehicles, based on a combination of total length of the route plus anticipated congestion on surface streets which is dependent on the time of the day. Network analysis also gives the solution to location-allocation problem to optimize demand supply scenario. Hence path finding or optimal routing, location-allocation and facility management provides solutions to the complex day to day problems.

The buffering is very common analysis function which is used to find what lies in the neighborhood of the feature. Buffering could be point buffering, line buffering or polygon buffering. With the application of point buffering one can find out the area and attributes of features around a location in specified distance. The line buffer could be useful for road or stream related applications.

### Map Database Merging and Splitting

Map database merging operation combines polygon or network features from to or more adjacent maps into single output map. It combines both feature coordinates and attribute table and recreates the topology. Three important edge matching checks that should be performed prior to joining adjacent maps are:

- Edge coordinates should match
- Node coordinates should match
- Polygon item value should match

Map database splitting creates new maps by overlaying two sets of features. It performs series of extract or clip operations, *e.g.* one can generate watershed-wise talukwise landuse map from a single district landuse map. The number of maps created will be equal to number of taluk in the taluk map.

### Centroid Determination

A centroid is a common way to describe the "average" location of a line or polygon. It can be defined physically as the center of mass of a two-or-three dimensional object. There is way to think about a centroid. Consider taking a polygonal area on a rigid map, cutting it out along it is boundaries and then locating the point at which this two-dimensional object will balance on a single point. This point is the centroid of the area. With the centroid as a location key, we can rapidly find objects that are relatively near a specified location. Thus one can use the set of centroid locations as a spatial index for objects in the database.

### *Statistical Analysis*

There are variety of statistical techniques that are common in modern GIS. Whether for quality assurance, or for summarizing a dataset as a data management support or for deriving new data during analysis, several statistical procedures are commonly required. These include:

### *Descriptive Statistics*

The mean, median, and variance of the attribute values in a data layer are often needed for continuous variables.

### *Histogram or Frequency Counts*

The histogram of a dataset provides us with the distribution of attribute values in a region. Histograms and frequency counts can be extremely valuable as data screening tools. Histograms are useful for examining all types of variables

### *Extreme Values*

Locating the maximum and minimum attribute values in a specified area is often useful. As an example we may minimum and maximum population for villages in a given area or to find out the minimum and maximum depth in a water body.

### *Correlations and Cross-tabulation*

In correlation analysis, we wish to compare the spatial distribution of attributes in two or more data layers, usually by calculating a correlation coefficient or linear regression equation when working with interval or ratio variables. For nominal or ordinal variables, a cross-tabulation compares the attributes in two data layers by determining the joint distribution of attributes.

Some GIS provides basic statistical functions but do not have exhaustive options for statistical analysis. In such cases data from the GIS has to be exported to the statistical packages like SPSS, MINITAB etc. and import data back to GIS after statistical analysis.

# 17

# Biodiversity Assessment Using Geoinformatics

*Sarnam Singh*

The most simplistic definition of Biodiversity is the variability among living organisms consisting of flora and fauna. However, Biodiversity is now considered as a very complex and defined as the variety of living organisms considered at all levels of organization, from gene through species, to higher taxonomic levels, and including the variety of habitats and ecosystems, as well as the processes occurring therein. Global Biodiversity Assessment (UNEP, 1995) estimates the total number of animal and plant species to be between 13 to 14 million. UNEP-WCMC (2000) estimate around 270,000 species of Vascular plants, 52,000 animals (vertebrates). Nearly 45 per cent of the world's vascular plant species occur in closed tropical forests of the world (Myers *et al.*, 2000). The vegetation in Indian subcontinent is distributed mainly in four distinct geographical zones, *viz.* Himalayas, Vindhyans, Western and Eastern Ghats. India possesses a rich flora of flowering plants (17,000 species) with a high degree of endemics (33.5%). Western Ghats of India alone constitutes 4,000 species of flowering plants, in which 1500 species are endemic (Nayar, 1989) and it is regarded as one of the biodiversity 'hotspots' of the world (Myers, 2000).

Biodiversity has ecological significance in terms of providing natural services across plant-animal interactions, productivity, soil regulation, ecosystem balance and responses to climate change etc. The processes include biogeochemical cycles, biotic and abiotic disturbances, predatorprey, mutualistic or parasitic relationships, migrations, competitive effects, and so forth. The changes in human civilization and cultural pattern has eliminated competing or threatening species, domesticated plants and animals, cut forests, used fire to alter habitats, indiscriminate use of pesticides, draining and filling of wetlands, destructive fishing practices, air pollution, conversion of wild lands to agricultural and urban uses and recently even significantly changed hydrological and geo chemical cycles. It is estimated that deforestation is occurring at a rate of between 15-17 millions ha per year and 5 to 10 per cent of tropical forest species may face extinction within the next 30 years largely due to human induced land cover changes.

### Regulators of Biodiversity

The relationship between natural and anthropogenic processes and biodiversity is complex. The organisation of biodiversity is a manifestation of the cyclic relationship between the kind and the magnitude of causes, impacts, responses and resulting ecological processes of the system over the past millions of years. In order to understand and quantify the interrelationship among these factors and understand the biodiversity, it is necessary to reliably identify and quantify individually these parameters and their development.

Human interventions are complex in terms of large-scale conversion to other land uses and processes, which do not involve loss of forest but have significant impact on biodiversity. These processes include selective logging, removal of under storey trees for building material, grazing, trampling, burning, wildlife impact, collection of non-timber forest products (NTFPs)—reproductive structures (fruits, nuts, seeds, flowers), non-reproductive structures (bark, latex, branches for firewood, foliage), and whole individuals (ornamentals, hunting, fishing) and associated infrastructure development.

### Impact of Anthropogenic Factors

The natural and anthropogenic impacts/factors both individually and synergistically which regulates and maintain the biodiversity can be characterized through the effects and response of the system. The effects and the responses have both varied spatial and temporal scale.

(a) **Changes in area:** Forests becomes non-vegetation types, in other cases, they are transformed into another vegetation type.
(b) **Fragmentation and neighborhood:** When a forest becomes fragmented, there is a change in the spatial mosaic of the forest. For example, the number, size and/or shape of patches of a vegetation type may change. These changes may result in modifications in patch connectivity across the landscape. Patch edges can change both in their length and complexity. These spatial changes can affect the ability of an organism to move within a landscape, because for some organism's different vegetation types act as either barriers or corridors to movement and dispersal.
(c) **Habitat change:** Changes in interior and core characteristics of a given habitat may lead changes in community formation and species assemblages.
(d) **Loss of species:** Some human interventions cause a direct loss of species. The loss of a certain species, which act as mediator can cause the loss of certain other species (*e.g.*, loss of obligate pollinators).

### Processes for Biodiversity Maintenance

The mediators of human interventions (effects and responses) affect the processes that generate and maintain biodiversity. These processes are:

(a) **Dispersal/Migration:** Human interventions may affect the capacity of the landscape to provide suitable sites for dispersal or migration. For example, in neotropical forests the majority of tree species are dispersed by vertebrates so hunting may affect the dispersal agent. Migration refers to the movement of organisms on which successful completion of the life cycle depends.

(b) **Reproduction:** Impacts on the process of reproduction can have rapid, direct and dramatic consequences. In the case of species with short generation periods, non-overlapping generations or highly specific mutualisms, such as the *Ficus*-fig wasp interactions (Janzen, 1979), changes can be particularly devastating.

(c) **Regeneration/succession:** The consequence of logging has led to reduction in area of mature, or old-growth forest, and replacement with forest dominated by pioneer or early successional species.

(d) **Trophic dynamics:** Trophic dynamic processes refer to the ways that species from different trophic levels interact. These include pollination, predation and herbivory. As each trophic level is dependent on other levels, impacts on trophic dynamics can be very serious.

(e) **Ecosystem processes:** Ecosystem processes are the interactions of nutrients, water and energy that allow the growth and reproduction of species. These processes typically involve a complex mix of species, each influencing the processes in different ways, though not all species present in an ecosystem are essential for ecosystem functioning.

(f) **Local extinction:** In some cases the dominant process determining change in species composition may be local extinction. For example, in a system characterised by small patches of a particular vegetation type, the loss of a patch and the ensuing local extinction of a species dependent on that vegetation type result in a more broad-scale extinction (Lomolino, 1996).

## Geo-Informatics—Tools for Biodiversity Assessment

The holistic understanding of aforesaid complex mechanisms that control biodiversity, their spatial and temporal dynamics requires synergetic adoption of measurement approaches, sampling designs and technologies. Studies have established that long term biodiversity assessment and monitoring requires spatial and non-spatial data at various time scales. The conventional ground measurements approaches don't provide effective solution. In view of this a growing demand and adoption is realized to use Satellite remote sensing, Global positioning system (GPS) aided ground surveys, integrative tool like GIS and development of Information Systems to integrate, collate and analyze various factors for comprehensive understanding and end-to-end solution. The amalgamation of these technologies together forms the basis for Geoinformatics. The various parameters required for biodiversity assessment and their amenability for measurements by different techniques is given in Table 17.1. The details on potential of various technologies in biodiversity assessment are given below:

***Remote Sensing Vs. Biodiversity***

At global to local scales, the only feasible way to monitor the earth's surface to prioritize and assess the success of conservation efforts is through remote sensing. Currently a suite of remote sensing satellites having various resolutions are available to generate spatial information on vegetation and land cover from global to local level. The remote sensing based vegetation and land cover information provides a potential spatial framework and works as one of the vital input layers for the following:

(a) Vegetation and land cover losses and conversion
(b) Stratification base for optimal ground sampling and assessment of diversity
(c) Fragmentation and neighborhood analysis
(d) Delineation of broader vegetation types and analyze species assemblages along with ancillary data
(e) Identification of gregarious and ecological important species
(f) Inputs for species habitat models
(g) Spatial delineation of biological rich zones
(h) Developing conservation strategies.

The potential of satellite data of different spatial and temporal resolutions in generating inputs for assessing the biodiversity are given in Table 17.1 and brief details are given below:

**Table 17.1:** Components of Biodiversity Assessment and Measurement Tools

| *Parameters* | | *Remote sensing* | *Ground Measurement/ GPS* | *GIS Based (Derived/ Integrated Spatial Layer)* |
|---|---|---|---|---|
| **A** | **Human interventions** | √ | √ | |
| 1 | Logging | √ | √ | √ |
| 2 | Grazing | √ | √ | √ |
| 3 | Fire | √ | √ | √ |
| 4 | NTFP resources extraction | √ | √ | √ |
| 5 | Trampling | √ | √ | √ |
| 6 | Plantation | √ | √ | √ |
| 7 | Agriculture | √ | √ | √ |
| 8 | Encoarchment/Clearances | √ | √ | √ |
| 9 | Infrastructure | √ | √ | √ |
| **B** | **Natural Process** | √ | √ | |
| 10 | Climate | √ | √ | √ |
| 11 | Erosion | √ | √ | √ |
| 12 | Topography | √ | √ | √ |
| 13 | Soil | √ | √ | √ |
| **C** | **Structure and Function** | | √ | |
| 14 | Vertical structure | √ | √ | √ |
| 15 | Size class distribution | | √ | |
| 16 | Relative abundance | | √ | |

*(contd.)*

*(contd.)*

| | Parameters | Remote sensing | Ground Measurement/ GPS | GIS Based (Derived/ Integrated Spatial layer) |
|---|---|---|---|---|
| 17 | Gap frequency | √ | √ | √ |
| 18 | Canopy openness | √ | √ | √ |
| 19 | Standing and fallen dead wood | | √ | √ |
| 20 | Trophic dynamics | | √ | √ |
| 21 | Other structural elements | | √ | |
| **D** | **Landscape level** | | | |
| 22 | Vegetation type and extent | √ | | √ |
| 23 | Landscape diversity | √ | | √ |
| 24 | Species diversity | √ | √ | √ |
| 25 | Number of patches per unit area | √ | | √ |
| 26 | Neighborhood | √ | | √ |
| 27 | Patch shape | √ | | √ |
| 28 | Core-edge ratio | √ | | √ |
| **E** | **Habitat level** | | | |
| 30 | Species assemblages/Communities | √ | √ | √ |
| 31 | Species diversity | √ | √ | √ |
| 32 | Interior to exterior habitat | √ | √ | √ |
| 33 | Regeneration | √ | √ | √ |
| 34 | Habitat extinction | √ | √ | √ |
| **F** | **Species level** | | | |
| 35 | Reproduction | | √ | |
| 36 | Dispersal | | √ | |
| 37 | Regeneration | | √ | |
| 38 | Migration | | √ | |
| 39 | Local extinction | | √ | |

*Note*: Presence of ticks in single, two, all columns indicate individual and synergesitic approaches

### *Coarse Resolution Remote Sensing*

Use of satellite image data for mapping and monitoring global land cover, biomass burning, estimating geophysical and biophysical characteristics of terrain features, monitoring continental-scale climate shift is a primary input for biodiversity assessment. The rapid revisit time of AVHRR helps better understanding of land cover, burnt area etc. both at global and regional levels (Eva and Lamin, 1998; Stone *et al.*, 1994; Loveland and Belward, 1997). The global vegetation type maps, land cover changes analysis, burnt areas in conjunction with trends in human disturbance are effectively used to generate coarse scale biodiversity maps and identification of biodiversity hotspots (Figure 17.1). In addition the Moderate Resolution Imaging Spectroradiometer (MODIS) is designed to provide consistent spatial and temporal comparisons of global vegetation conditions that can be used to monitor photosynthetic activity which facilitate understanding the biodiversity function.

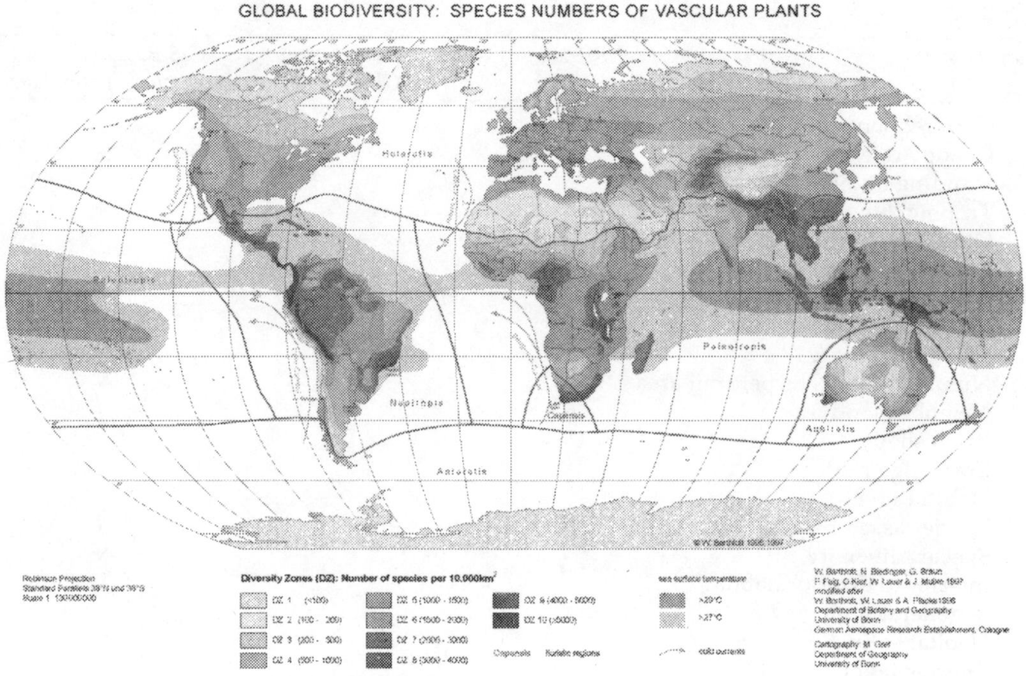


*Source*: Bathlott, W. (1999) http://www.nees.uni-bonn.de/globbiod.gif

**Fig. 17.1:** Global Biodiversity: Species Numbers of Vascular Plants

### *High resolution remote sensing*

Rapid change in land use in tropical areas and the need to map changes in land use over large areas effectively calls for high to very high resolution satellite sensors applications. At the national or local level, IRS, Landsat or SPOT imagery can provide finer scale information on forest type distribution and agriculture expansion. Radar systems such as JERS and Radarsat are not affected by clouds, and are useful for determining the extent of forest and non-forest landscapes where topographic relief is not substantial (<200m).

Vegetation type and land cover mapping of entire North East Region, Western Himalayas and Western Ghats, Andaman and Nicobar of India were mapped at 1:250,000 scale using IRS LISS data. Forests cover has been mapped using LISS III satellite data on 1:50,000 scale in Central India, Eastern Ghats, East Coasts. Tropical evergreen forest along with other phenological types and major disturbed habitats/ grassland, orchards, mangroves, *Myristica* swamps and *Ochlandra* etc. were mapped. The spatial data generated using remote sensing is useful in many ways in biodiversity monitoring and conservation efforts. Data sets from IRS 1C/1D LISS III have been used effectively in mapping the pure plant colonies of *Hippophae rhamnoides* in the Spiti region of India with prior knowledge of their occurrence and vegetation types of the area using remote sensing technique (Roy *et al.*, 2001). IRS 1C/1D LISS-III FCC has been used for stratification of *Ephedra gerardiana* in complex terrain conditions of Lahul and Spiti districts (Porwal *et al.*, 2003) (Fig. 17.2).

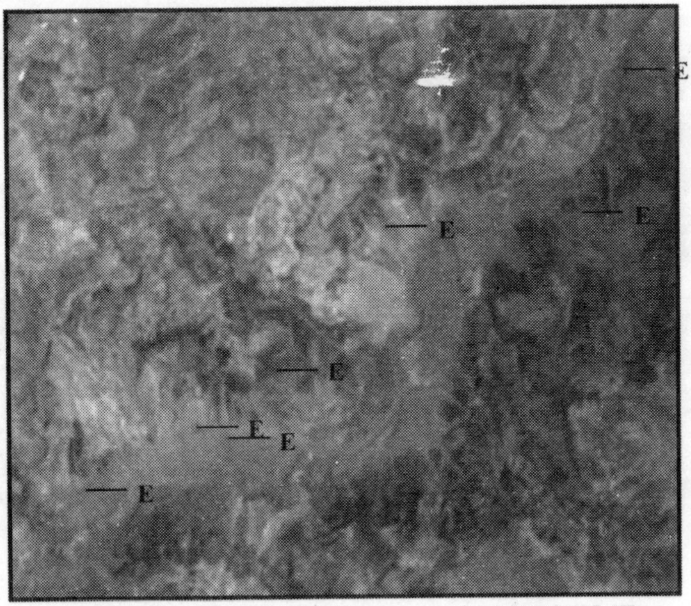


**Fig. 17.2:** *Ephedra gerardiana* on FCC of IRS LISS-III

### *Very High Resolution Remote Sensing*

Applications of very high resolution remote sensing techniques to conservation of biodiversity, assessment of protected areas and species protection show that fine-grain remote sensing is underused in conservation of forest ecosystems. Very high-resolution data (1-m panchromatic and 3-m multi-spectral) that are now available from the commercial IKONOS II and IRS LISS-IV satellite may be useful for determining the actual activities on the ground that have led to forest clearing. Although such data can detect very small clearings, the scientific community as yet has very little experience with these data.

Mapping of diversity estimates is often accomplished by analyzing variation of some spectral signal, and correlating this variation with measure of landscape or taxa diversity (Rey-Benayas and Pope, 1995; Jorgenson and Nohr, 1996). Mapping individual trees using high resolution data poses problems not encountered when mapping associations or habitat patches. Pixels covering different component of a tree, such as bark and leaf, can be extremely variable in intensities. This makes the spectral signature of a species of tree difficult to define (Fig. 17.3).

### *Temporal Monitoring*

The amount of change that is occurring in the tropical part of world has been of considerable interest in the past ten years. Remote sensing offers perhaps the only practical method of analyzing large areas over time. However these studies don't provide information on vegetation type transition and losses, which is primarily necessary for understanding shifts and losses in biodiversity. A few examples of the

**Fig. 17.3:** FCC of FRI Campus Dehradun (IKONOS Data)

studies conducted in southern Western Ghats of India and Vindhyas of Central India and North East region of India details about vegetation type transitions. These transitions when coupled with ground based species databases helps in analyzing and quantifying the biodiversity losses. Prediction of the spatial distribution and relative abundance of wildlife using multi-temporal satellite data and simulation models is also of recent development.

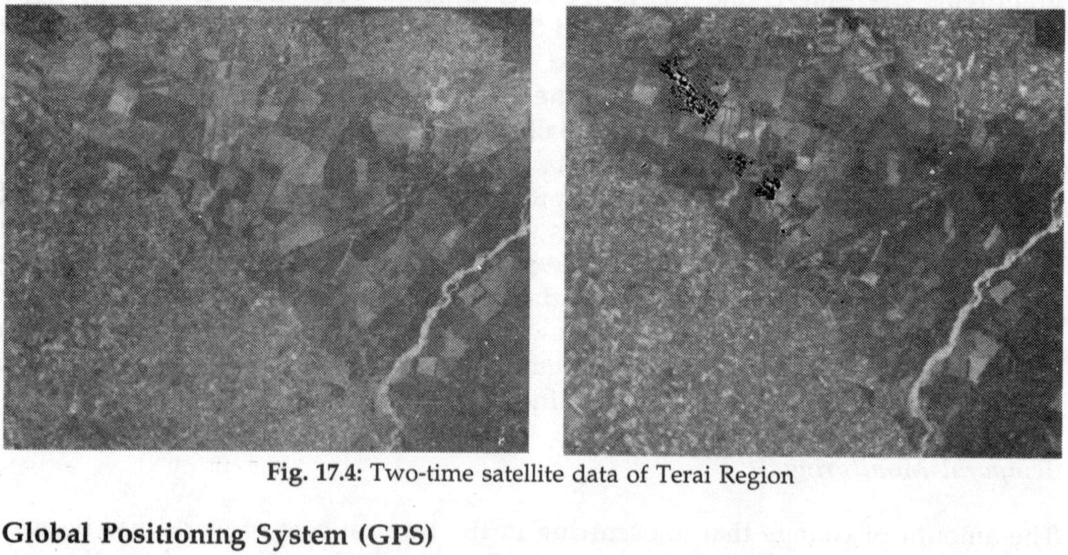

**Fig. 17.4:** Two-time satellite data of Terai Region

## Global Positioning System (GPS)

Ground based measurements of various parameters stand as vital input for effective biodiversity assessment. The parameters that need to be measured on ground are given in Table 17.1. However the translation of this ground measured data into a spatial domain or linking with any other spatial or non-spatial parameters to analyze the relationships and understand the trends, precise locations and areas under consideration assume primary importance. In this regard Global Positioning Systems (GPS) provide powerful tools for acquiring accurate locations and areas (Fig. 17.5). The relatively recent development of GPS and GIS technologies appear ideally suited to conservation effort because they empower ecologist to expeditiously acquire, store, analyze, and display spatial data on organisms and their environment (Johnston, 1998; Wadsworth and Treweek, 1999).

Currently available flora that provides valuable information about the species distribution pattern doesn't indicate specific locations. With the advent of availability of GPS, the recent Phytosociological surveys provided enormous information on species distribution with specific locations. The endemic atlas of western ghats (Ramesh, 1997), mapping of sandal wood etc, species databases of *Agalia bourdillonii* (Meliaceae) with sample point locations is (Figure 17.4) are a few examples. Under DBT-DOS project, studies conducted in North-East, Western Himalayas and Western Ghats region of India (IIRS, 2002) are noteworthy to mention. These databases are helpful in further identifying species—specific habitats by knowing the precise area under a given habitat.

Precise point location aided data on microclimate, topography and soil in association with species distribution helps in understanding the interrelationships and controls of biotic and abiotic factors on species distribution pattern. Such databases can be effectively imported into a biostatistical software packages (Biopro, EstimatesS, SPSS, PCORD) and analyze the species assemblage patterns. Studies conducted in Tirunelveli hills of Western Ghats showing the community assemblages derived through statistical analysis of the point location data on species and ancillary information (Giriraj *et al.* 2003) is shown in Figure 17.5. The application of integrated

**Fig. 17.5:** Acquisition of coordinates using GPS

GPS/GIS technology to habitat utilization models is particularly strong because it is capable of identifying the areas of threat habitats most at risk of human encroachment and works as essential tools for monitoring. GPS aided wildlife survey in terms of presence/absence data is useful in various studies to understand the habitat distribution patterns (Kushwaha *et al.*, 2000; Lele *et al.*, 1998; Tutin *et al.*, 1991; Goldsmith, 2000).

Use of differential GPS survey will help in estimating the accurate area change, type and the kind of species alternation with pinpoint coordinates, demarcation of permanent plots, patches for temporal monitoring. Recently studies were conducted in Vindhyan highlands (Jha *et al.*, 2002) delineating disturbed and undisturbed patches using DGPS survey for assessing temporal patterns of biodiversity. Global research efforts are taken up to develop databases on spatial patterns and dynamics of tropical forests in large permanent plots across tropical countries where GPS survey are effectively used in tree census and other associated information for long term, large-scale ecological research in biodiversity (Plotkin *et al.* 2000, Ayyappan and Parthasarathy, 1999; Pascal and Pelissier, 1996; Pelissier 1998; Pelissier and Goreaud, 2001 etc).

## Geographic Information System (GIS)

The integrated analysis of spatial data generated both from remote sensing and other sources and also point information becomes critical in order to generate information on several aspects of biodiversity, *viz.* landscape processes, habitat evaluation, characterization of disturbance regimes, analysis of forest structure and function in spatial domain. GIS provides a powerful tool to undertake such integrated analysis. The following are the details where GIS plays important role:

### *Landscape Analysis*

Forman and Godron (1986) defined landscape as "heterogeneous land area composed of a cluster of interacting ecosystems that is repeated in similar form throughout." Landscapes are composed of mosaic of patches. *Vegetation,* a dominant expression of natural assemblage of various coexisting plant communities, plays a major role in characterizing a landscape with its biodiversity. Species diversity at any one point in a landscape is determined by multiple factors acting in multiple scales (Turner and Gardner, 1991; Turner, 1989; Wiens, 1989).

Quantification of landscape heterogeneity is done with the help of landscape metrics. Patch characterization is based on the analysis of various parameters like *size, shape, fragmentation, porosity, patchiness, interspersion, juxtaposition* etc. The heterogeneous distribution of communities can be conceived to be controlled by soil, climate and human activities. Hence patch characterization will provide insight into the spatial organization of communities. Various GIS based software packages like Fragstat, BIOCAP, Patch analyst etc. provides customized approaches to analyze these parameters and assessing the impact on spatial biodiversity patterns.

An extensive study was conducted in India subcontinent covering three major bioclimatic region, *viz.* North East India, Western Himalayas and Western Ghats using concepts of landscape analysis to identify biological rich zones (Roy, NRSA, 2003). Customized software "Biocap" was developed which facilitates analysis of landscape parameters like porosity, juxtaposition, interspersion, patchiness etc. These landscape parameters are inturn integrated to develop spatial disturbance index map. The disturbance index map thus generated is integrated with ground based parameters like species richness, terrain complexity, ecosystem uniqueness and biodiversity value to identify biologically richness zones (Figure 17.7).

### *Species Composition and Habitat Analysis*

The factors like crown closure, crown geometry, stand density, topography and soil type etc. regulate the reflectance properties of vegetated surfaces and hence characterizing the individual species, communities and vegetation types is a complex process using satellite remote sensing data. In areas where vegetation structure varies greatly, structure rather than species differences may predominate in imagery. The remote sensing data may then prove less suitable for determining species composition and delineation of specific vegetation types and habitats. Patterns of species distribution on the ground have been shown to be associated with the distribution of environmental variables such as topography, rainfall, soil type and disturbance. In such cases a GIS model based on elevation, slope, aspect and proximity to a water sources etc. in conjunction ground based species databases, and broad vegetation types derived from RS will help in identifying the spatial pattern of the species assemblages and habitats.

Altitude information is effectively used along with remotely sensed derived vegetation map to spatially delineate different species assemblages, which are largely controlled by altitude in Himalayan ecosystems (Roy *et al.* 2001 and Porwal *et al.*, 2003). The tropical evergreen forest of Western Ghats which are largely influenced by spatial and temporal patterns of monsoon rainfall are further subdivided using terrain, bioclimatic and vegetation type maps (Ramesh *et al.*, 1997). Giriraj *et al.* (2003) used multispectral RS data and elevation-slope complexes to delineate different species assemblages in evergreen forest of Tirunelveli hills of Western Ghats, Tamil Nadu and further identified endemic habitat zones based on distribution pattern of endemic species in different Vegetation-Elevation-Slope complexes (Figure 17.5).

### *Geostastical Analysis and Spatial Modeling*

Geostatistical techniques are the best tools to interpolate sample data to create a map of tree species distribution, estimate the possible occurrence, disturbance and effective prediction by spatial information using local variability. Currently the conservation of endemic, rare and endangered species is largely supported by point level information in terms of species and their number. The effects of forest cut, forest fire, grazing, NTFP extraction, wildlife impacts, encroachment, settlements etc. are point specific. In addition the climatic data, terrain information, soil are also broadly available as point data.

The conversion of these kinds of point level database into a spatial domain helps in integrating with other vegetation type layers, species level databases to understand the patterns of diversity and conservation zoning. However, such an effort requires enormous amount of ground data collected over well-designed sampling strategy and interpolation using robust statistical approaches. In the absence of reliable quantitative databases, statistical approaches involving non-parametric models like multi-logistic regression, probit regression, Bayesian conditional algorithms etc. are used to understand the relationship between species richness/diversity and environmental/disturbance variables. These statistical approaches can work on simple "Presence or Absence data" and also rank information. Based on such relationships spatial layers can be generated in GIS domain. In addition geostatistical tools like kriging are also used to generate spatial surface on species distribution pattern.

Ganeshaiah and Umashaanker (2003) generated contours on distribution patterns of *Bamboo, Ochlandra, rattans*, medicinal plants and major NTFP products. Rachel (2003) used geostatisitical techniques *viz.* kriging, sequential gaussian conditional simulation to create an interpolated dataset—a "map" of individual species distribution (10 species in Pennsylvania) from known sample information. Giriraj *et al.* (2003) developed potential disturbance surfaces based on presence-absence data collected on fire, logging, wildlife, grazing, adjacency etc. in Tirunelveli hills of Western Ghats to understand species distribution pattern in relation to disturbance. Pandian *et al.* (2003) developed potential grazing intensity map through geostatistical analysis of cattle movement and land cover pattern and species composition of grass species.

**Biodiversity Information System (BIS)**

Organized databases and information on biodiversity on user friendly format is necessary to facilitate decision makers and researchers, in developing strategic action plans for Biodiversity Conservation. The available vast amount of data need to be collected and represented using internet based technology with advanced user friendly decision tools in order to facilitate future dissemination of the derived spatial and non-spatial information among the user community.

Datasets on spatial and non-spatial information at various spatial scales such as bioclimatic maps, RF boundaries, roads, rails settlements, DEM, terrain complexity, species-information database can be integrated into a single system in digital domain (Figure 17.8). Such a system will enhance querying the spatial and non-spatial information, monitoring and assessment of biodiversity, identification of risk habitats and developing suitable conservation strategies (Fig. 17.6).

Roy *et al.* (2002) have developed Biodiversity Information System (BIS) with an objective of collection and organization of the available but distributed spatial and non-spatial database, into an interactive system, which is capable of presenting a user friendly interface to its clients. It has been developed on the basis of an object-oriented design approach that proceeds from data collection and application process design,

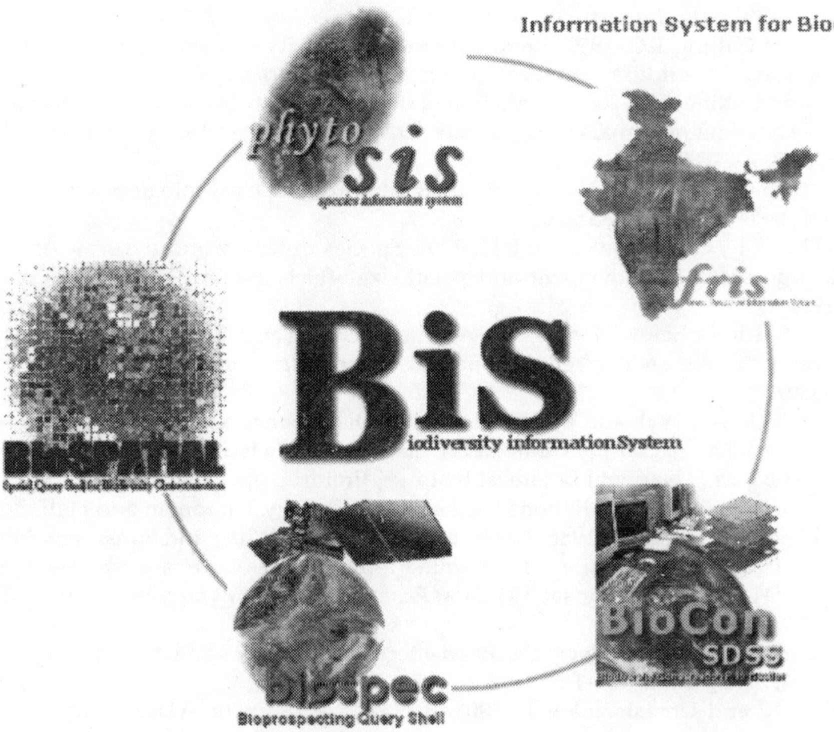


**Fig. 17.6:** Biodiversity Information System portal (*www:bisindia.org*)

navigation and workflow design, web page and web-flow design. The components of the BIS are Biospatial, Biospec, PhytoSIS, FRIS and BioCon. Individually all these components focus on separate but related issues of biodiversity and natural resources management. All the components are scalable and up gradable.

## REFERENCES

Arino, O., and Melinotte, J.M., 1995, Fire index atlas. *Earth Observation Quarterly*, 59,10–15.

Arnold, G.W. and Weeldenburg, J.R. 1990. Factors determining the number and species of birds in road verges in the wheatbelt of Western Australia. *Biological Conservation*, 53: 295-315.

Ayyappan, N. and Parthasarathy, N. 1999. Biodiversity inventory of trees in a large-scale permanent plot of tropical evergreen forest at Varagalaiar, Anamalais, Western Ghats, India. *Biodiversity and Conservation* 8: 1533-1554.

Barthlott, W., Biedinger, N., Braun, G., Feig, F., Kier, G., and J. Mutke, 1999. Terminological and methodological aspects of the mapping and analysis of global biodiversity. In: *Acta Botanica Fennica* 162: 103-110.

Brokaw, N.V.L. and Scheiner, S.M. 1989. Species composition in gaps and structure of a tropical forest. *Ecology* 70: 538-541.

Burnett, M.R., August, P.V., Brown, J.H. Jr, and Killingbeck, K.T. 1998. The influence of geomorphological heterogeneity on biodiversity. I. Patch-scale perspective. Conservation Biology 12: 363-370.

Cochrane, MA (2000). Using vegetation reflectance variability for species level classification of hyperspectral data. *International Journal of Remote Sensing* 10: 2075-2087.

Coops, N.C. and Catling P.C. 1997. Predicting the complexity of habitat in forests from airborne videography for wildlife management. *International Journal of Remote Sensing* 18: 2677-2782.

Coops, N.C. and Catling, P.C. 2002. Prediction of the spatial distribution and relative abundance of ground-dwelling mammals using remote sensing imagery and simulation models. *Landscape Ecology* 17: 173-188.

Debinski, D.M. and Humphrey, P.S. 1997. An integrated approach to biological diversity assessment. *Natural Areas Journal* 17: 355-365.

Debinski, D.M., Ray, C. and Saveraid, E.H. 2001. Species diversity and the scale of the landscape mosaic: do scales of movement and patch size affect diversity? *Biological Conservation* 98: 179-190.

Debinski, D. M., Kindscher, K. *et al.* (1999). A remote sensing and GIS-based model of habitats and biodiversity in the greater Yellowstone Ecosystem. *International Journal of Remote Sensing* 20: 3281-3291.

Everard, D.A., G.F. van Wyk and J.J. Midgley. 1994. Disturbance and diversity of forests in Natal, South Africa: lessons for their utilization. *In*: B.J. Huntley (ed.), *Botanical Diversity in Southern Africa: Strelitzia 1.* National Botanical Institute, Pretoria. pp. 275-286.

Farina, A. 1998. Principles and Methods in Landscape Ecology. Chapman and Hall, London.

Forman, R.T.T. and Godron, M. 1986. *Landscape Ecology.* John Wiley and Sons, New York.

Franklin, S.E. 1994. Discrimination of subapline forest species and canopy density sing digital CASI, SPOT PLA, and Landsat TM data. *Photogrammetric Engineering and Remote Sensing* 60: 1223-1241.

Frelich, L.E. and Reich, P.B. 1999. Neighborhood effects, disturbance severity, and community stability in forests. *Ecosystem* 2: 151-166.

Ganeshaiah K.N. and Umashaanker R. 2003. *A Decade of Diversity,* ATREE and UAS, Bangalore. pp 100.

Giriraj, A., Murthy, M.S.R., Britto, S.J., Rajashekar, G., Dutt, C.B.S. 2003. Diagnostic analysis of conservation zones using remote sensing and GIS techniques in wet evergreen forests of Western Ghats—An ecological hotspot, Tamil Nadu, India. *Biodiversity and Conservation Journal*: In press.

Giriraj, A., Murthy, M.S.R., Dutt, C.B.S. and Ramesh, B.R. 2003. Phytodiversity and endemic habitat analysis in wet evergreen forest of Tirunelveli hills (Tamil Nadu) using remote sensing and GIS. National Remote Sensing Agency report. pp. 1-51.

Goldsmith, M.L. 2000. Effects of ecotourism on the behavioral ecology of Bwindi gorillas, Uganda. *American Journal of Physical Anthropology* [Supplement] 30: 161.

Gong, P., Pu, R. and Yu, B. 2001. Conifer species recognition: effects of data transformation. *International Journal of Remote Sensing* 17: 3471-2481.

Gould, W. 2000. Remote sensing of vegetation, plant species richness, and regional biodiversity hotspots. *Ecological Applications* 10: 186-1870.

Huston, M.A. 1994. *Biological Diversity: The Coexistence of Species on Changing Landscapes.* Cambridge University Press, Cambridge.

Indian Institute of Remote Sensing (NRSA) Dehradun. 2002. Biodiversity Characterization at Landscape level in North East, Western Himalayas, Western Ghats using Satellite Remote Sensing and Geographic Information System.

Janzen, D.H. 1979. How to be a fig. *Annual Review of Ecology and Systematics* 10: 13-51.

Kushwaha, S.P.S., Munkhtuya, S. and Roy, P.S. 2000. Geospatial modeling for Goral habitat evaluation. *Journal of Indian Society of Remote Sensing* 28: 293-303.

Lapin, M. and Barnes, B.V. 1995. Using the landscape ecosystem approach to assess species and ecosystem diversity. *Conservation Biology* 9: 1148-1158.

Lele, S., Rajashekar, G., Venkataramana, R.H., Prevish Kumar, G. and Sarvanakumar, P. 1998. Meso-scale analysis of forest condition and its determinants: A case study from the Western Ghats region, India. *Current Science* 75: 256-263.

Liu, J.G., Linderman, M., Ouyang, Z.Y., *et al.* (2001). Ecological degradation in protected areas: The case of Wolong Nature Reserve for giant pandas. *Science* 292(5514): 98-101.

Lomolino, M.V. 1996. Investigating the cause of nestedness of insular communities: selective immigrations or extinctions? *Journal of Biogeography* 23: 699-703.

Lovejoy, T.E., Rankin, J.M., Bierregaard, R.O. Jr, Brown, K.S. Jr, Emmons L.M. and Van der Voort, M.E. 1984. Ecosystem decay of Amazon forest remnants. In: Nitecki, M.H. (eds.), *Extinctions.* University of Chicago Press, Chicago. pp. 295-325.

McKinney, M.L. 1997. How do rare species avoid extinction? In *The Biology of Rarity* (W.E. Kunin and K.J. Gaston, eds), pp. 110-129. London: Chapman and Hall.

Merriam, G.K., Henein, K. and Smith, S.K. 1991. Landscape dynamics models. In Turner MG, Gardner RH (eds.) *Quantitative Methods in Landscape Ecology.* Springer-Verlag, New York, NY, USA, pp. 399-416.

Murthy, M.S.R., A. Giriraj and C.B.S. Dutt 2003. Geoinformatics for Biodiversity Assessment. *Bio. Lett.* 40(2): 75-100.

Myers, N., Mittermeier, R.A., Mittermeier, C.G., da Fonseca, G.A.B. and Kent, J. 2000. *Nature* 403: 853-858.

Nagendra, H. and Gadgil, M. 1998. Linking regional and landscape scales for assessing biodiversity: a case study from Western Ghats. *Current Science* 75: 264-271.

Nagendra, H. and Gadgil, M. 1999. Satellite imagery as a tool for monitoring species diversity: an assessment. *Journal of Applied Ecology* 36: 388-397.

Nayar, M.P. 1989. In situ conservation of wild flora resources. *Bull.Bot.Surv. India* 29: 319-333.

Nichols, W.F., Killingbeck, K.T. and August, P.V. 1998. The influence of geomorphological heterogeneity on biodiversity. II. A landscape perspective. *Conservation Biology* 12: 371-379.

Opdam, P. 1991. Metapopulation theory and habitat fragmentation; a review of hoarctic breedings birds studies. *Landscape Ecology* 5: 93-106.

Pascal, J.P. and Pelissier, R. 1996. Structure and floristic composition of a tropical evergreen forest in south-west India. *Journal of Tropical Ecology* 12: 191-214.

Pearson, J.E. 1993. Complex patterns in a simple system. *Science* 261: 189-192.

Pelissier, R. 1998. Tree spatial patterns in three contrasting plots of a southern Indian tropical moist evergreen forest. *Journal of Tropical Ecology* 14: 1-16.

Pelissier, R. and Goreaud, F. 2001. A practical approach to the study of spatial structure in simple cases of heterogeneous vegetation. *Journal of Vegetation Science* 12: 99-108.

Peters, D.P.C. and Goslee, S.C. 2001. Landscape Diversity. In Levin SA (eds) *Encyclopedia of Biodiversity.* Vol. 3: 645-658 Academic Press, New York.

Plotkin, J.B., Potts, M., Yu, D., Bunyavejchewin, S., Condit, R., Foster, R., Hubbell, S., LaFrankie, J., Manokaran, N., Seng, L., Sukumar, R., Nowak, M.A., Ashton, P.S. 2000. Predicting species diversity in tropical forests. Proceedings of the National Academy of Sciences 97: 10850-10854.

Porwal, M.C., Sharma, L. and Roy, P.S. 2003. Stratification and mapping of Ephedra gerardiana Wall. in Poh (Lahul and Spiti) using remote sensing and GIS. *Current Science* 84: 208 – 212

Purvis, A., Gittleman, J.L., Cowlishaw, G. and Mace, G.M. 2000. Predicting extinction risk in declining species. Proceedings of the Royal Society, London, Series B, 267, 1947–1952.

Ramesh, B.R. and Pascal, J.P. 1997. *Atlas of Endemics of the Western Ghats (India),* Institut Francias de Pondicherry.

Ramesh, B.R., De Franceschi, D. and Pascal, J.P. 1997. Forest Map of South India, Thiruvanthapuram-Tirunelveli at 1:250,000 (Sheet 6). Institut Français, Pondichérry.

Romme, W.H. 1982. Fire and landscape diversity in subalpine forests of Yellowstone National Park. *Ecological Monographs* 52: 199-221.

Romme, W.H. and Knight, D.H. 1982. Landscape diversity: The concept applied to Yellowstone park. *Bioscience* 32: 664-670.

Roy, P.S., Porwal, M.C. and Sharma, L. 2001. Mapping of Hippophaerhamnoides Linn. in the adjoining areas of Kaza in Lahul and Spiti using remote sensing and GIS. *Current Science* 80: 1107-1111.

Schullery, P. 1989. The fires and the fire policy. *BioScience* 39: 686-694.

Stoms, D.M. 1992. Effects of habitat map generalization in biodiversity assessment. *Photogrammetric Engineering and Remote Sensing* 58: 1587-1591.

Swingland, I.R. and Greenwood, P.J. (eds.) 1983. *The Ecology of Animal Movement.* Claredon Press, Oxford.

Townsend, J.R.G., Justice, C.O., Skole, D., Malingreau, J.P., Cihlar, J., Teillet, P., Sadowski, F., and Ruttenberg, S., 1994, The 1 km resolution global data set: needs of the International Geosphere Biosphere Programme. *International Journal of Remote Sensing*, 15, 3417–3441.

Treitz, P.M., Howerth, P.J., Shuffling, R.C and Smith, P. 1992. Application of detailed ground information to vegetation mapping with high spatial resolution digital imagery. Remote Sensing and Environment 42: 65-82.

Turner, M.G. 1989. Landscape Ecology: the effect of pattern of process. *Annual Review of Ecology and Systematics* 20: 171-197.

Turner, M.G. and Gardner, R.H. 1991. *Quantitative Methods in Landscape Ecology*, Springer-Verlag, New York, USA.

Tutin, C.E., Williamson, E.A., Roger, M.E. and Fernandez, M. 1991. A case of a plant-animal relationship: Cola lizae and lowland gorillas in the Lope Reserve, Gabon. *Journal of Tropical Ecology* 7: 181-199.

UNEP-WCMC (2000). *Global Biodiversity: Earth's living resources in the 21st century.* Cambridge, World Conservation Press.

Van Horssen, P.W., School, P.P. and Barendregt, A. 1999. A GIS-based plant prediction model for wetland ecosystems. *Landscape Ecology* 14: 253-265.

White, J.D., Kroh, G.C. and Pinder, J.E. III. 1995. Forest mapping at Lassen Volcanic National Park, California, using Landsat TM data and Geographical Information System. *Photogrammetric Engineering and Remote Sensing* 61: 299-305.

Whitmore, T.C. 1975. *Tropical rain forest of the Far East.* Oxford: Oxford University Press. 282 p.

Whittaker, R.H. 1960. Vegetation of the Siskiyou Mountains, Oregon and California. *Ecological Monographs* 30: 279-338.

Wiens, J.A. 1989. Spatial scaling in ecology. *Functional Ecology* 3: 385-397.

# 18

# Biodiversity Characterization for Conservation Prioritization Using Geoinformatics in Punjab Shiwaliks

*Sarnam Singh*

## Introduction

The anthropogenic interventions in natural landscape have brought in enormous change species composition and their distribution pattern in time and space. Though, with the technological and human expansion, the similar activities are now flattering progressively more invasive, giving Shiwalik forests little opportunity to recuperate. Understanding landscape spatial pattern is important since it contains all levels of the biological hierarchy, from ecosystems to species and genes, which are targeted for phytodiversity conservation. Tropical communities are often worse susceptible to loss of biological diversity than temperate communities because tropical species are occur in lower densities and are less widely distributed and often have weaker dispersal capabilities. Increasing human intervention and excessive exploitation of resources have resulted in great changes and provide alarming signals of accelerated biodiversity loss.

A significant change in the understanding the priorities of biodiversity conservation and management has resulted in a policy shift from conservation of single species to their habitats through interactive network of species at landscape level (Orians, 1993; Edward *et al.*, 1994). Calls for the conservation of biodiversity are an explicit recognition that biological loss occurs at all levels, and that attempts to maintain this diversity-conservation effort must be applied to all levels and not just to endangered species (Noss, 1991; Scott *et al.*, 1991). Species composition, abundance and assemblage structure changes with forest disturbance. The rapid biodiversity assessment techniques for sampling are designed with a view to identify the rich sites in order to investigate the relationship between biodiversity and forest ecosystem processes. There is a growing need for better understanding of the biodiversity distribution pattern *vis-à-vis* human interventions. India have very varied environmental conditions and are among the countries with high biodiversity. The flowering plants, which provide maximum direct benefit to mankind, comprise about 19395 taxa, which is about 7 per cent of the described species in the world (Karthikeyan, 2000). It has resulted in the formation micro-endemic centres of plants in the country. The great heights and complex terrain of the Himalayan region, which change frequently, provide endless microclimatic conditions suitable to the species to grow and evolve. The Himalayas have more than 5 micro-endemic centres. Shiwalik ranges are one such mirco-endemic centre. About 125 wild relatives of crop plants have been reported in the western Himalayas, and Shiwaliks ranges are part of these. These ranges are among the youngest hills in the world and are active as well as fragile. Shiwalik hills of Punjab state have rich biological diversity and act as major natural green belt of the state. The state is well known for agricultural produce and industries.

Satellite remote sensing has been used to map and classify land use and vegetation cover classes in various remote, inaccessible areas and mountainous regions (Frank, 1988; Lal *et al.*, 1991). Remote sensing technology is being widely used world over for the quick assessment of the Earth resources. In this study, vegetation type map derived from satellite data was considered as prime input for landscape ecological analysis of forest ecosystem. Phytosociological data collected from field sampling was analyzed to derive species richness, biodiversity value and ecosystem uniqueness of various forest types. Ancillary databases such as proximity from the roads/villages, terrain complexity etc. were derived in GIS domain.

A geospatial approach for phytodiversity conservation also addresses some of the limitations of conventional random sampling. To overcome this limitation, stratified random sampling with probability proportion to the size (PPS) was adopted for analyzing vegetation composition of all the types encountered. In the present study, vegetation cover type map derived from satellite remote sensing data have been considered as prime input for phytodiversity analysis of forest ecosystem. Geographic Information System (GIS) has been used to derive landscape indices such as fragmentation, porosity, patchiness, patch density, interspersion and juxtaposition, which depict landscape characteristics. Phytodiversity richness map generated for the Shiwalik hills of Punjab state is based on the disturbance index, terrain complexity, species richness, biological value and ecosystem uniqueness. The resultant maps highlight areas that are rich in phytodiversity.

## Study Area

The study was carried out in the Shiwalik hills of Punjab state (Fig.18.1) having geographical area of 9448.97 km$^2$ and situated in north western part of the state. It lies between latitude 30° 34′ and 32° 33′ N and longitude 74° 50′ and 76° 52′ E. It is broadly divided into sub-mountainous Himalayas and the eastern and western alluvial plains. The important rivers draining the region are the Sutlej and the Beas. The average annual rainfall varies between 400 to 600 mm and the mean annual temperature ranges from 22.50° C to 25.0° C.

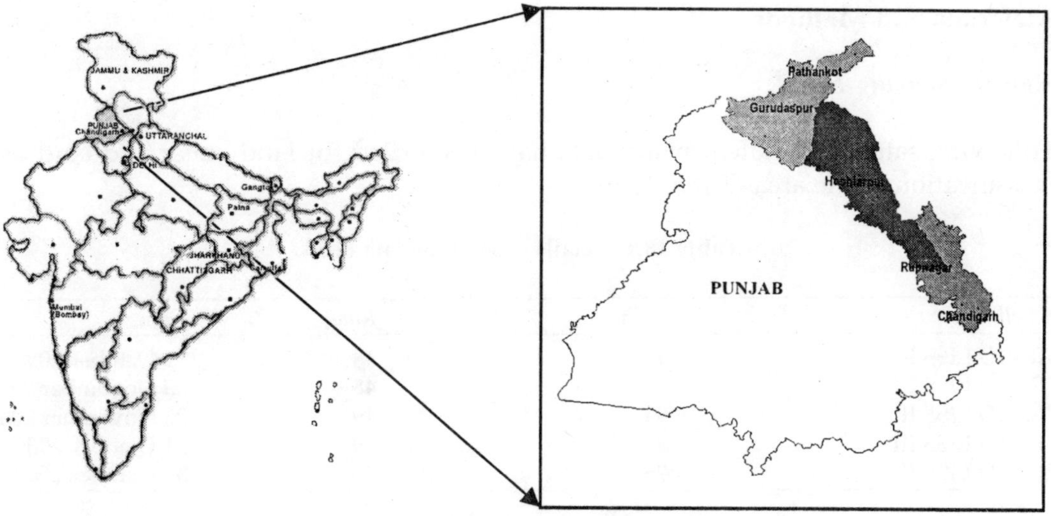


**Fig. 18.1:** Location of the Study area

## Land Use Pattern

The recorded forest area (including dry deciduous scrub) of Shiwalik hills of Punjab state is 1599.42 km$^2$, which constitutes 16.93 per cent of total geographic area. The major forest types are dry deciduous, moist deciduous, dry deciduous scrub and coniferous forest. The non-forest area such as agriculture, grassland, water body, canals, settlements, riverbed and barren land contributes 7849.55 km$^2$ which constitutes 83.07 per cent of the total geographical area.

### *Vegetation type*

Deciduous forest, moist deciduous forest, dry deciduous scrub and pine in small packets are the main vegetation of the region. Champion and Seth (1968) described 6 forest types, *viz.*, Northern dry mixed deciduous forest (5B/$C_2$), Dry bamboo brakes (5$E_9$), Dry deciduous scrub ($DS_1$), Khair-Sissu forests (5/1$S_2$), Shiwalik chirpine forest (9/$C_1$) and Subtropical *Euphorbia* scrub (9/$C_1$/$DS_2$).

## Approach

Ground observations are taken through stratified random sampling in all the forest types. Their economic uses have been found from literature. Total Importance Value (TIV) of each plant is established for its value for food, fuelwood, charcoal, timber, medicine etc. Ecosystem uniqueness is established from the list of the species found during survey based on its representativeness, species endemism etc. Biological richness is obtained after integrating species richness, biological value, disturbance index, ecosystem uniqueness and terrain complexity.

## Materials and Methods

### *Remote Sensing Data*

Following satellite remote sensing data have been used for land cover and land use classification of the area (Table 18.1).

**Table 18.1:** Details of satellite data used

| *Satellite ID* | *Path* | *Row* | *Date* |
|---|---|---|---|
| IRS-1D LISS III | 93 | 48 | 12 October 2000 |
| IRS-1D LISS III | 94 | 48 | 03 November 2000 |
| IRS-1D LISS III | 94 | 49 | 03 November 2000 |
| IRS-1D LISS III | 95 | 49 | 31 October 2000 |
| IRS-1D LISS III | 95 | 50 | 31 October 2000 |

### *Preprocessing of Satellite Data*

IRS-1D LISS-III data (October 2000 and November 2000) were used to prepare vegetation cover type map. Total five scenes were loaded and each scene was rectified with respect to 1:50,000 scale SOI toposheet (Total 32 toposheets were used, geometrically corrected and mosaicked to a single image). A second order transformation was followed. Average root mean square error within one pixel was maintained while preparing transformation model. Lambert Conformal Conic projection (LCC) was used during rectification of image. Each rectified scene was subjected to radiometric correction before mosaicing it to a single mosaic image. After extraction of required area from this single mosaic image, it was subjected to Supervised Maximum likelihood classification using the ground truth information collected during the fieldwork.

### *Ground Truthing*

Reconnaissance survey was carried out in the area to acquire the knowledge of the vegetation and other broad land uses. During reconnaissance information on the correlation of image elements with that of ground features was also obtained. Interpretation key was formulated and classification was performed.

### *Field Data*

Information on plant species is further processed for evaluating other parameters like Total Importance Value, Ecosystem Uniqueness, Biodiversity value etc. There it is important that well distributed enough sample are taken for information on species occurrence. Classified vegetation cover type has been used for finding the sample size. Sampling intensity of 0.021 per cent has been done. Higher sample intensity is adopted in view of variability in the area.

### *Sampling Design*

The probability proportionate stratified random sampling was adopted and the optimal sample plots for each floristic type were calculated @ 0.002 per cent sampling intensity. Detailed inventory was done in 74 sample plots covering four major vegetation cover classes for trees, shrubs, seedlings, saplings, epiphytes, climbers and other growth forms including herbs (Table 18.2). Cumulative species-area curves were plotted for all forest types sampled by sequential arrangement of plots. For sampling, various strata of vegetation, nested quadrat sampling mode was followed. A 20 × 20 m plot for trees (CBH ≥ 15 cm), within which a 10 × 10m nested plot at the center for shrubs were laid. For herbs/seedlings 1×1 m plots of which, five were laid at the four corners and one at center of the 20×20 m plot (Fig. 18.2). The epiphytes, creepers, climbers and other lianas and their host/symbiotic plants were also been noted as a special attribute in a view to take an account of all the aboveground floral components present in a particular site of sampling pertaining to that forest type.

**Table 18.2:** The distribution of sample points in each of the forest type

| *Forest Type* | *No. of sample plots* |
|---|---|
| Moist deciduous | 32 |
| Dry deciduous | 31 |
| Deciduous scrub | 7 |
| Pine forest | 4 |
| **Total** | **74** |

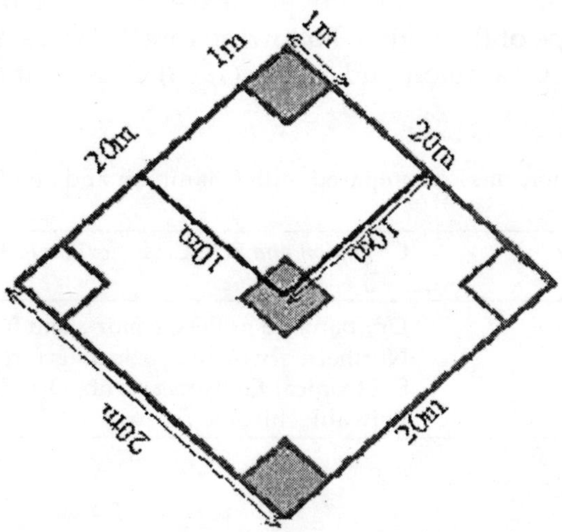


**Fig. 18.2:** Layout of nested quadrat sample plot

The data was collected on following parameters in each of the sample plot:

- Description of ecosystem and forest type including phenology

- Species name and number of individuals for every species
- Girth at breast height in centimeters
- Economic importance such as grazing, medicinal, human food, fuel, timber, charcoal and other uses such as industrial use, rope making, tanning leather etc. This importance value was collected by interviewing local people wherever possible and from literature.

### *Database Creation in GIS*

In geo-spatial analysis integration of spatial and non-spatial data or vector data is important. As discussed earlier the biotic disturbance had played a very significant role in existing biodiversity of toady. Database in GIS domain provides opportunity to analyze their impact zones. Therefore, village locations (point and polygon features) transport networks (Road and railway) and contour lines with 20m intervals were digitized in ERDAS 8.4 software. The road and settlement maps were used as input in further analysis for deriving disturbance gradient.

### Vegetation Classification

Based on the prior knowledge supervised classification method was followed. Training sites were selected and processed. The classified output was finally subjected hybrid classification approach to prepare vegetation type map of the study area showing various vegetation types (Fig. 18.3). The accuracy of the image was evaluated using field knowledge and the ground truth information. Along with the different types of forest, other general lands use/land cover classes were also classified so as to understand the landscape of the region. Following forest classes have been delineated and a comparison with Champion and Seth's (1968) classifications scheme is given below (Table 18.3).

**Table 18.3:** Vegetation classes compared with Champion and Seth's Classification

| *Satellite based classification of vegetation types* | *Champion and Seth Classification (1968)* |
|---|---|
| Moist deciduous forest | Dry bamboo brakes, Khair-sissu forest |
| Dry deciduous forest | Northern dry mixed deciduous forest, Dry deciduous forest |
| Dry deciduous scrub | Subtropical *Euphorbia* scrub, Dry deciduous scrub |
| Pine | Shiwalik chirpine forest |

### Phytodiversity Analysis

Phytodiversity analysis was carried out to understand the floristic and vegetation pattern in the region. For the purpose the vegetation types were grouped into four major types. The phytosociological database was created and computed the basic structural parameters, *viz.* frequency, basal area and density etc. Importance value index (IVI) was calculated to assess the ecological importance of the species with respect to the community structure.

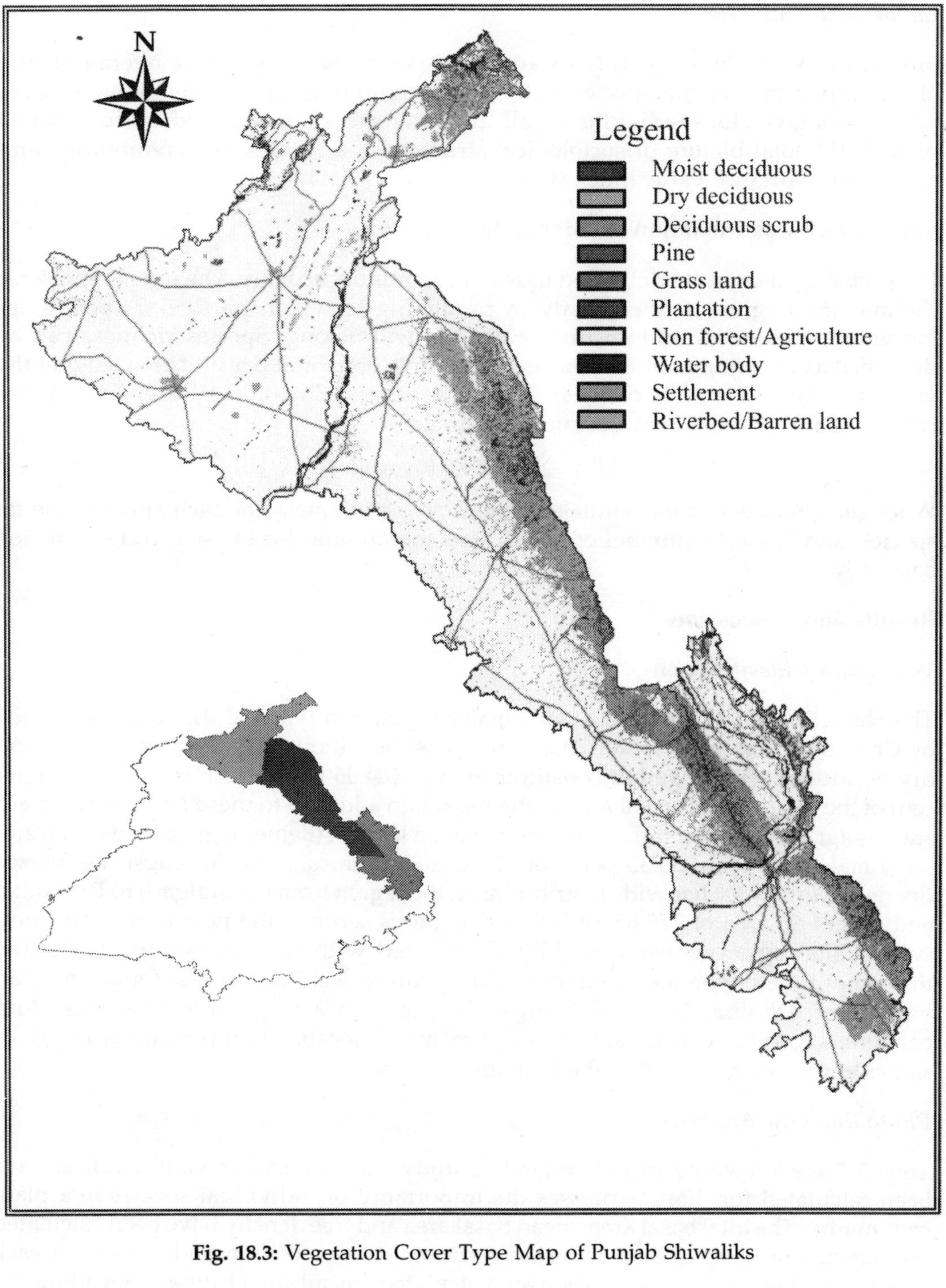


**Fig. 18.3:** Vegetation Cover Type Map of Punjab Shiwaliks

### *Importance Value Index*

Importance Value Index (IVI) is a statistical quantity, which gives an overall picture of the importance of the species in the plant community. Since the above relative parameters give clues individually, all the parameters are summed up in order to provide the total picture of sociological structure of a species in a community, and called as importance value index (IVI).

### Species richness (Shannon-Wiener Index)

It is probably the most widely used index in community ecology. The index represents the average degree of uncertainty in predicting to which particular species, an individual chosen at random from a sample will belong. Species richness can be described as the number of the species in a sample or habitat per unit area. Higher the value greater the species richness. Species richness (Shannon Wiener Index) was calculated for all forest types using the formula:

$$H' = -\Sigma\ [(ni/N)^*\ \log_e(ni/N)]$$

Where *ni* = number of individuals or amount (*e.g.* biomass) of each species (the *ith* species) and N = total number of individuals (or amount) for the site, and e = the log base of 10.

## Results and Discussion

### *Vegetation Classification*

The Shiwalik hills of Punjab has four major vegetation types of the seven described by Champion and Seth (1968). These are, moist deciduous, dry deciduous, pine and dry deciduous scrub together constitute about 1404.06 km², which is about 14.65 per cent of the total geographical area of the region. In addition to these non-forest classes such as agriculture, plantation, riverbed, barren land, settlement, grassland and water body makes up about 85.35 per cent of the geographical area. Amongst the forests, dry deciduous forest has wide distribution in the region from Chandigarh to Pathankot and covers an area of 775.85 km². Dry deciduous scrub is the next dominant forest type of the region which is mainly constituted with Lantana scrub distributed throughout the region and then followed by moist deciduous forest found in Dhar, Pathankot, Dholba, Talwara, Nangal, Noorpur in a fragmented patches. And coniferous forest covers an area of 6.51 km² and is localized on the higher ridges or slopes in the northern part of the Pathankot district.

### *Phytodiversity Analysis*

Total 315 species were encountered in this study. The importance values indices have been calculated for those expresses the importance of individual species in a plant community. The total basal area, mean basal area and tree density have been calculated for each forest types clearly defines the structure, composition and density of each forest type. Species diversity has been calculated for all forest types prevailing the region.

**Table 18.4:** Area under different Land cover/land use classes in the region

| *Land use/cover class* | *Area in km²* |
|---|---|
| Moist deciduous forest | 276.46 |
| Dry deciduous forest | 775.85 |
| Dry deciduous scrub | 345.24 |
| Coniferous forest | 6.51 |
| Grass land | 38.24 |
| Plantation/Avenue trees | 211.04 |
| Agriculture | 7443.22 |
| Water body | 78.94 |
| Settlement | 178.46 |
| Riverbed/Barren land | 238.19 |
| Total | 9592.15 |

*Moist Deciduous Forest*

Out of 74 sample plots 32 were laidout in this forest type. Total of 161 individuals was encountered of which 42 are trees, 24 are shrubs and rest belongs to herbaceous categories. The total basal area including trees and shrubs occurring in moist deciduous was calculated to be 22.95m²/ha. This forest type is most predominated with *Acacia catechu, Mallotus pilippensis.*

*Dry Deciduous Forest*

31 sample plots were laid in this forest type. A total of 363 species were encountered of which 141 are trees, 75 are shrubs and rest belongs herbaceous vegetation. The total basal area of the trees was calculated to be 38.41 m²/ha. The tree density was observed to be 916 per ha. This forest type is most prominently dominated by *Acacia catechu Willd.* (IVI = 108.86) of which relative density contributes a major share of 30.72 followed by relative dominance of 69.83. Major association of dry deciduous was composed of *Anogeissus latifolia, Lannea coromandalica, Aegle marmelos, Mallotus philippensis etc.*

*Deciduous Scrub Forest*

Out of 74 plots 7 plots were laid in this forest type. A total of 77 species were encountered of which 7 are trees, 12 are shrubs and 58 herbaceous species. The total basal area of the trees was calculated to be 8.133 m²/ha. Deciduous scrub forest is dominated by *Lantana camara* L., *Woodfordia fruiticosa, Carrissa opaca* Stapf, *Capparis decidua* (Forsk.) Edgew. with the some association of *Acacia modesta* Wall *Dodonaea viscosa, Aegle marmelos* (L.) Corre etc.

*Pine Forest*

Pine forest was distributed only in northern part of the Gurudaspur district of the region with small packets in ridges and side slopes. Only 4 plots were laid in this type. The total basal area of the trees was calculated to be 6.531 $m^2$/ha. A total of 58 species were encountered of which 7 are trees, 15 are shrubs and 36 herbaceous species. The vegetation is dominated by *Pinus roxburghii* (IVI=183.61 and relative density: 68.57) is associated with *Syzygium cumini* (L.) Skeel, *Wendlandia heynei* (R. and S.) Sant. and Merch. *Pyrus pashia, Syzygium cuminii.*

***Species Diversity***

Dry deciduous forest shows highest diversity (3.5361) with total number of 363 species followed by moist deciduous (3.0959) then dry deciduous scrub (2.2666) having 77 species and coniferous forest shows least diversity (1.6207) with 58 species.

**Table 18.5:** Biodiversity status in the Shiwalik hills of Punjab state

| *Forest Type* | *No. of Families* | *No. of Species* | | | *Total no. of Species* | *Total Importance Value* |
|---|---|---|---|---|---|---|
| | | *Trees* | *Shrubs* | *Herbs* | | |
| Moist deciduous | 36 | 42 | 24 | 95 | 161 | 10.46 |
| Dry deciduous | 31 | 141 | 75 | 147 | 363 | 10.53 |
| Deciduous scrub | 25 | 7 | 12 | 58 | 77 | 9.75 |
| Pine | 11 | 7 | 15 | 36 | 58 | 8.01 |

**Table 18.6:** Forest types-wise Shannon Wiener Index and mean basal area

| *Forest Type* | *Mean Basal Area ($m^2$)* | *Shannon Wiener Index (SWI) (H')* |
|---|---|---|
| Moist deciduous | 22.948 | 3.0959 |
| Dry deciduous | 38.412 | 3.5361 |
| Deciduous scrub | 8.133 | 2.2666 |
| Pine | 6.531 | 1.6207 |

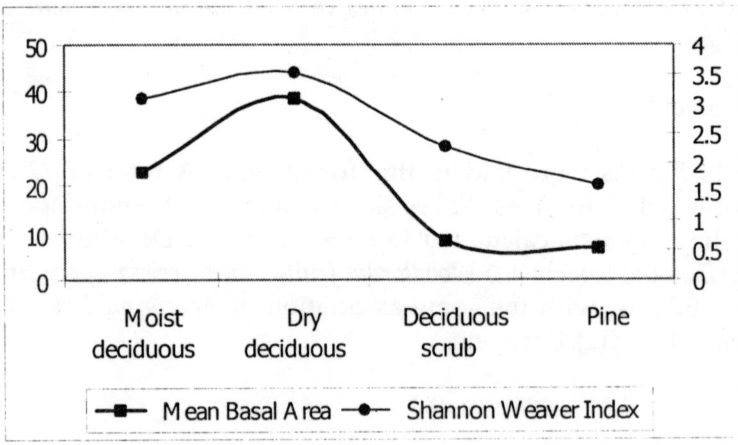


**Fig. 18.4:** Graph shows positive correlation exists between mean basal area and species diversity.

### *Economically Important Species*

Economically Important plants are the species, which have social and economic value. In the Shiwalik hills of Punjab state 240 economically important plants were recorded. The total importance value (TIV) for each species was calculated considering 10 important uses. The parameters considered are (1) Food, (2) Fuel, (3) Fodder, (4) Fiber, (5) Timber, (6) Medicinal, (7) Oil, (8) Gums/Resins, (9) Tannin and (10) Others. These 10 parameters have been weighted for a scale of 1 to 10 wherein maximum value represents highest economic value. Maximum total importance value was observed in dry deciduous type (TIV of 10.53) and coniferous type has the least value (TIV of 8.01). Some of the economically important species are *Acacia catechu*, *Achyranthes aspera*, *Justicia adhatoda*, *Ageratum conyzoides*, *Azadirachta indica*, *Cannabis sativa*, *Moringa oleifera*, etc.

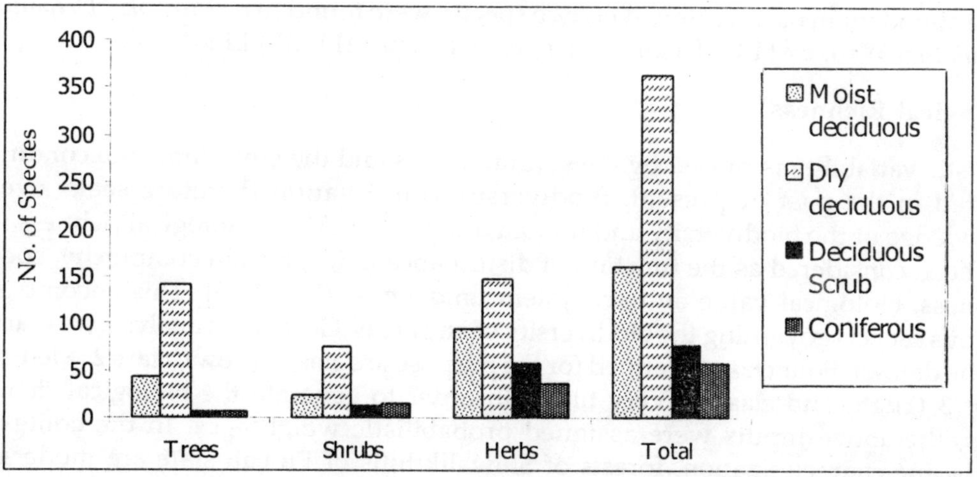


**Fig 18.5:** Species distribution in each habit type

**Table 18.7:** Total Importance Value of different vegetation types

| *Forest Type* | *TIV %* |
|---|---|
| Moist deciduous | 10.46 |
| Dry deciduous | 10.53 |
| Deciduous scrub | 9.75 |
| Pine | 8.01 |

### *Medicinal Plants*

About 132 medicinally important species have been recorded during the sampling. Medicinal usage of these plants occurring in Shiwalik hills of Punjab have been compiled from available literature sources. Some of the important medicinally important plants are *Justicia adhatoda*, *Aegle marmelos*, *Azadirachta indica*, *Bacopa monnieri*, *Cordia dichotoma*, *Terminlaia chebula*, *Terminalia bellirica* etc. Table 18.8 provides overview of the per cent utilizable species.

**Table 18.8:** Per cent utilizable species for Total Importance Value (TIV)

| *Forest type* | *Uses* | | | | | | | | | |
|---|---|---|---|---|---|---|---|---|---|---|
| | *Food* | *Fuel* | *Fodder* | *Fiber* | *Timber* | *Medicinal* | *Oil* | *Gums/Resin* | *Tannin* | *Others* |
| DD | 11.15 | 0.79 | 9.09 | 9.8 | 10.2 | 31.66 | 5.02 | 3.5 | 5.18 | 9.83 |
| MD | 12.7 | 2.36 | 6.94 | 7.91 | 2.6 | 32.1 | 0.65 | 0.86 | 1.3 | 8.45 |
| DS | 10.05 | 2.21 | 9.06 | 9.31 | 9.55 | 31.61 | 6.37 | 3.18 | 6.61 | 8.09 |
| PN | 0 | 0 | 8.52 | 0 | 0 | 20.78 | 0 | 0 | 0 | 2.35 |
| **Total** | 33.9 | 5.36 | 33.61 | 27.02 | 22.35 | 116.15 | 12.04 | 7.54 | 13.09 | 28.72 |

### *Ecological Importance*

The species recorded during the field data collection were screened for their uniqueness with help of RED DATA BOOK and many other references. All the species recorded were abundant in nature. However, two species were found to be rare, *viz., Delphinium danudatum* Wall. ex HK.f.Th *and Peristylus constrictus* (Lindl.) Lindl.

### Biological Richness

Floristic variability is caused by the several factors and the environmental conditions existed in the past or present. Biodiversity conservation therefore seeks overall knowledge of the biodiversity and human dimensions. Thus, Biological richness (BR) has been considered as the function of disturbance index, terrain complexity, species richness, biological value and ecosystem uniqueness (Fig. 18.5). This encompasses various aspects governing the biodiversity of any areas. Geospatial analysis was carried on the dataset. Four classes defined for the purpose are class 1 (Low); class 2 (Medium); class 3 (High) and class 4 (Very high). In order to generate the biological richness map, the above inputs were assigned probabilistic weightages. In the context of landscape characterization, forests of Shiwalik hills of Punjab state are moderately rich in some fragmented packets. Deciduous forest showed high degree of richness (55.09 per cent and 12.86 per cent in high and very high categories respectively) followed by moist deciduous forest (17. 92 in high and 16.19 in very high categories. Deciduous scrub shows least richness (13.96 per cent in high and 1.61 per cent in very high categories) as compared to pine forest.

### Conclusion

Biodiversity of Punjab Shiwaliks is facing threat due to various developmental activities. Satellite remote sensing data provide much needed qualitative information on the land cover and land use pattern of the region. Efforts directed towards conservation of one or a few species have limitations and therefore, it is essential to consider biodiversity conservation in its entirety, *i.e.* at landscape level. Disturbance is one of the major factors for biodiversity loss, and the forest patches represent biodiversity depending on the existing environmental conditions and associations. Landscape principles like fragmentation, porosity, interspersion, juxtaposition etc. allow us to establish the disturbance gradient. The analysis done through remote sensing and GIS and phytogeographical analysis revealed that majority of the area is highly disturbed and therefore, it is matter of great concern for biodiversity conservation. Shiwalik hills are faced with increasing anthropogenic activities and humans in the name of development invade forest landscape. Large areas are under scrub and need protection to avoid further site degradation. The region has a large number of medicinal plants. Biorich areas are restricted to certain areas and fragmented pockets. These biodiversity 'refugia' in the unique and fragile ecosystem of Shiwaliks need to be protected on priority for future prosperity (Fig. 18.6).

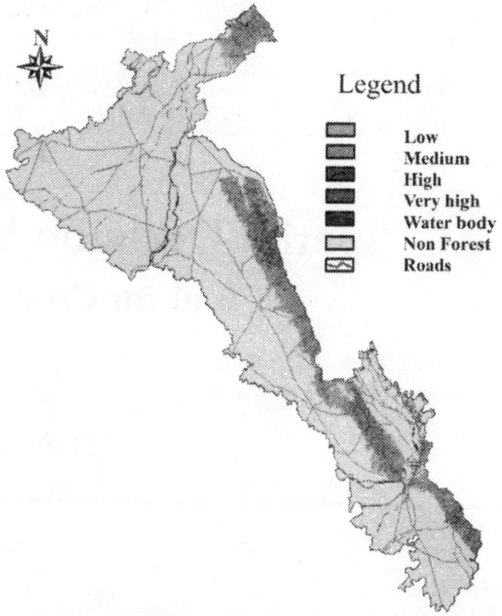


**Fig. 18.6:** Biological Richness Map of Punjab Shiwaliks

**REFERENCES**


Champion, H.G. and S.K. Seth, 1968. *Revised Forest Types of India.* Govt. of India Publications, New Delhi.

Chandrashekhar, M.B., S. Singh and P.S. Roy (2003). Geospatial modeling techniques for rapid assessment of Phytodiversity at landscape level in Western Himalayas, Himachal Pradesh. *Current Science* 84(5): 663-670.

Edwards, P.J., N.R. Webb, and R.M. May (eds.). 1994. Large-Scale Ecology and Conservation Biology. Blackwell: Oxford. *Environments, Nature and Resources* 32 (1): 33-39.

Jeganathan, C., Diwakar, P. G., Nagajyothi, B. and Sastry, T. R. S. V. S., 1999. *Bio_CAP*–User Manual for landscape analysis and Modelling Biological Richness. DOS-DBT, Indian Institute of Remote Sensing (NRSA), Dept. of Space, Govt. of India, 4-Kalidas Road, Dehra Dun, India

Karthikeyan, S. 2000. A Statistical Analysis of Flowering Plants of India. In N.P. Singh, D. K. Singh, P.K. Hajra and B.D. Sharma (eds.). *Flora of India Introductory volume,* Part II, 201-217, New Delhi.

Lal, J.B., Gulati, A.K. and M.S. Bist, 1991: Satellite mapping of alpine pastures in the Himalayas. *Int. J Remote Sensing.* 12 (3): 435-443.

Noss, R.F. 1991a. From endangered species to biodiversity. pp. 227-246 in K. Kohm, editor. *Balancing on the brink of extinction.* Island Press, Washington, DC.

Orians, G.H. 1993. Endangered at what level? *Ecological Applications*, 31: 206-208.

Scott, J.M., B. Csuti, K. Smith, J.E. Estes, and S. Caicco. 1991. Gap analysis of species richness and vegetation cover: an integrated biodiversity conservation strategy. *In* K. Kohm, ed. *Balancing on the brink of extinction: the Endangered species Act and lessons for the future.* Inland Press, Washington, D.C.

Singh, S., P.S. Roy, M.B. Chandrashekhar, D.K. Singh, Surendra Singh and B.P. Uniyal and P.K. Joshi (2004). Phytodiversity analysis: a geospatial approach. *Bull. Bot. Surv. India* (Seminar Volume) 46(1-4): 19-33.

# 19

# Spatial Decision Support System

## A Tool for Crop Management

*N.R. Patel*

### Introduction

*"Spatial Informations Systems provide the platform of integrated information and science from which all future land and environmental monitoring, evaluation and management decisions will be made."*

In the rapidly developing spatial industry, such a statement reflects an almost "given" concept. However in Indian agriculture, spatial information systems are still regarded as "new technology" because by history- remote sensing in the form of satellite data was prompted very heavily as a useful information source for agricultural monitoring purposes in late eighties and nineties but did not live up to expectations. This "failure" of remote sensing was mainly because the resolution, timeliness, and frequency of data at an appropriate cost (and still is), a major issue. The lack of a simple product that could be used by farm manager or the lay-person to help solve a problem has also been seen as poor technology transfer. Geographical Information System (GIS) is seen as coming out of the "stable" (high tech, high expense) and in consequences, the barriers to the adoption of these technologies is long standing. Despite this, Indian agriculture as an enterprise is unforgiving of technologies that do not work. This is primarily exists within the framework of an extremely variable climate and fragile soils which puts extreme pressure on the ability of an enterprise to survive. The need for mechanisms to increase profitability at the same time maintaining sustainability of the land is of paramount importance. A farmer or a grower will always ask "What does it cost and what do I get out of it over and above what I already have?" To date, answer has rarely been favorable enough to use these technologies for practical agricultural management.

Precision farming may be the catalyst that will awaken the Indian agricultural sector to the power of remote sensing and GIS technologies for spatial data manipulation and integration. Precision crop management has been defined as "information and technology based agricultural management system to identify, analyze and manage site specific spatial and temporal variability within field for optimum profitability, sustainability and protection of the environment" (Robert *et al.*, 1995). In particular, the role that such technologies play together with process based models in creating land assessment and management tools such as Spatial Decision Support System. For many years we had the technological capability to vary the rate of planting density, of fertilizer applications, of irrigation applications, herbicides and insecticides. What has been lacking has been the remote sensing as source of spatial information of agriculture resource and the integrating technology of geographic information system which allows producers and farm managers to analyze crop performance on an area basis and to make decision on the basis of yield maps. But in recent times, some spatial decision support systems have come up to in order to help growers to make decision concerning to irrigation scheduling, fertilization, use of crop growth regulators and other chemicals.

**Spatial Decision Support Systems (DSS)**

- Many spatial problems are complex and require the use of analysis and models.
- Many spatial problems are semi-structured or ill-defined because all of their aspects cannot be measured or modeled.

Spatial decision support systems (SDSS) are designed to help decision-makers solve complex spatial problems. Spatial decision support systems have evolved in parallel with decision support systems (DSS). DSS developed for business applications (corporate strategic planning, scheduling of operations, etc.). Many definitions of DSS require the presence of certain characteristics, *e.g.* Geoffrion's definition requires 6 characteristics: (1) designed to solve ill- or semi-structured problems, *i.e.* where objectives cannot be fully or precisely defined; (2) have an interface that is both powerful and easy to use; (3) enable the user to combine models and data in a flexible manner; (4) help the user explore the solution space (the options available to them) by using the models in the system to generate a series of feasible alternatives; (5) support a variety of decision-making styles, and easily adapted to provide new capabilities as the needs of the user evolve; (6) problem solving is an interactive and recursive process in which decision making proceeds by multiple passes, perhaps involving different routes, rather than a single linear path. These characteristics also define a SDSS. In addition, in order to effectively support decision-making for complex spatial problems, a SDSS will need to:

- provide for spatial data input
- allow storage of complex structures common in spatial data
- include analytical techniques that are unique to spatial analysis
- provide output in the form of maps and other spatial forms

GISs stanalone fall short of the goals of SDSS for a number of reasons:

- analytical modeling capabilities often are not part of a GIS
- many GIS databases have been designed solely for cartographic display of results—SDSS goals require flexibility in the way information is communicated to the user
- the set of variables or layers in the database may be insufficient for complex modeling
- data may be at insufficient scale or resolution
- GIS designs are not flexible enough to accommodate variations in either the context or the process of spatial decision-making

SDSS provide a framework for integrating: (1) analytical modeling capabilities, (2) database management systems, (3) graphical display capabilities, (4) tabular reporting capabilities, (5) the decision-maker's expert knowledge. GISs normally provide 2, 3 and 4. The addition of 1 and 5 create a SDSS.

## DSS Architecture

Armstrong and Densham (1990) suggest that five key modules are needed in a SDSS: (1) a database management system (DBMS), (2) analysis procedures in a model base management system (MBMS)—defined later, (3) a display generator, (4) a report generator, (5) a user interface.

### *Database Management System*

- GIS database management systems are designed to support cartographic display and spatial query
- database of an SDSS must support cartographic display, spatial query and analytical modeling by integrating three types of data: (1) locational (spatial primitives such as coordinates and chains), (2) topological (attribute-bearing objects, *e.g.* points, nodes and lines, and relationships between them), (3) thematic (attributes of the topological objects, including population, elevation, and vegetation)
- database must permit the user to construct and exploit complex spatial relations between all three types of data at a variety of scales, degrees of resolution and levels of aggregation
- database management systems found in many GIS use the relational data model, however, alternative data models have proved effective in applications of DSS

### *Model Base Management System*

- one approach to incorporating analytical models in geoprocessing systems is to develop libraries of analytical sub-routines

—permits large numbers of models to be made accessible very quickly, because existing programs can be patched into a system
—wasteful in terms of replicated code

- second approach, used in business applications of DSS, is to develop a model base management system (MBMS)

—consists of small pieces of code, each of which solves a step in an algorithm
—as many of these steps are common to several algorithms, this approach saves large amounts of code
—the system developer only has to modify one piece of code to update a step in several algorithms

*Graphical and Tabular Report Generator*

- should provide the following capabilities:

—high-resolution cartographic displays
—general-purpose statistical graphics, including two and three-dimensional scatter plots and graphs
—specialized graphics for depicting the results from analytical models and sophisticated statistical techniques
—the full range of tabular reports normally associated with each of the above

*User Interface*

- must be easy to use if they are to be effective in decision-making
- interfaces of many current GIS systems are modelled on those of business systems, using command lines, pull-down menus and dialogue boxes
- the move to graphical interfaces for operating systems provides an opportunity for system designers to develop more intuitive interfaces for geoprocessing systems
- by using a graphical display for communication between the decision-maker and the system:

—icons can be used to represent system capabilities
—the user can select parameters, data, output, etc., easily and intuitively
—the user may be able to more easily visualize the processes represented within the model

## SDSS for Agriculture

The SDSS is a tool for use in precision farming, also called site-specific farming. The hypothesis of site-specific farming is that agricultural growing environment varies spatially, and that by understanding the spatial variability in the parameters influencing the growing environment, decision can be made that optimize inputs by varying them spatially on a site specific basis. The general methodology of the decision support system is driven off a spatial databases characterizing the growing environment on a spatial basis. The optimum solution produced in an economic evaluation of cost/benefit if prior production records are available, or is a maximum production if no prior data is available.

### *Information Needs of SDSS for Input Optimization*

There are three basic types of information required are:

- Information on seasonally stable conditions
- Information on seasonally variable conditions
- Information required to diagnose the cause of the crop yield variability and develop a management strategy

***Mapping of seasonally stable management units***: Seasonally stable conditions are those that are relatively constant through the crop growing season such as soil-based management units, and only need to determined preseason and simply updated. It is well known fact that soil variability influences the productive potential of agricultural lands. Maps of soil fertility and physical attributes are being used to determine the responsive and non-responsive parts of field. The most important soil fertility and physical attributes that could be mapped and managed are soil nitrogen, some other macro or micro nutrients, relative position and slope of the terrain and soil organic matter. There are three approaches for mapping soil management units:

- Soil survey at 1:5000 or 10,000 scale
- Geostatistical interpolation techniques (*e.g.* kriging) to map soil properties from a grid of point samples
- Use of soil/landscape models with input from either remote sensing or digital elevation map

***Mapping seasonally variable management units***: Though, many DSS for input optimization based only on seasonally stable management units defined by maps of soil fertility or yield, there are other seasonally variable information on such condition as weed or insect infestation, crop phenology, crop stress (due to water or nitrogen), crop disease, soil moisture and evapotranspiration. For example, within field soil moisture throughout the season is relavent to decision made about nitrogen application and amount of irrigation applications. There are two approaches for mapping variable management units are:

- Grid sampling—not good for quick and large area coverage needed for mapping seasonally variable management units
- Remote sensing—Multispectral images is promising for monitoring seasonally variable soil and crop conditions

***Information on causes of crop yield variability***: Remote sensing has a variety of role in determining the cause of spatial and temporal crop and soil variability. One of promising role is the use of remote sensing information to improve the capacity and the accuracy of DSS and agronomic models by providing accurate input information or as a means of model calibration or validation.

- Remote sensing could provide important information for agricultural DSS
- Integration of remote sensing and agrometeorologic models
- Hyperspectral sensors for large scale variability

***Need for SDSS in Agriculture***

- Where are the major growing areas of particular crop?
- How many hectares are under particular crop?
- What is the expected yield of particular crop for this year?
- Where to expand the cultivated areas of high yielding varieties?
- What is the best management strategy for particular crop?

These are some most common questions that have been raised by the policy makers as well as researchers on regional or national scale. The answers rely on a system that can integrate the power of spatial information with the ability of a crop model to simulate different scenarios based on production environments and resources in the target areas with the management and policy imposed. However, estimating crop yield at the field and regional levels involve different types of complexity and efforts. The following table outlines the issues:

| | *Field scale* | *Regional scale* |
|---|---|---|
| Landscape complexity | simple | complex |
| Data Layers | few | many |
| Spatial variation | less | more |
| Data management | low (MB) | high (GB) |
| Importance of spatial information | low | high |
| Link to policy | less | |

Considering the need of spatial decision support system to optimize input applications in agriculture, a system should be able to:

- Store and manage spatial information
- Accurately estimate and timely predicting crop yield
- Provide good interface between spatial information, crop and user and
- Incorporate different scenario analysis

***Crop Models for Decision Making***

Many simulation models have been over last few decades to investigate the relations between soil and crop conditions. Well calibrated and validated models simulation models can be used to simulate past growing seasons by defining what would have been the ideal form of management once weather conditions are known. The results can be compared with actual management and differences can be analyzed by considering weather, crop, soil conditions at any particular time during the growing season. Weather forecast in combination with simulation models can be used to predict crop conditions, providing information on which management can be best. However, these kind of traditional decision support tools based on process based models may end up being used (and misused) in range of situations, across many spatial and temporal scales, and with data of varying quality. To implement such scientifically accepted models and avoid poor decision making by a diverse group of user based on inaccurate results derived by applying a model at inappropriate scale or by using data of inappropriate precision and accuracy, it is critical to develop a scientifically sound spatial decision support systems. With increasing availability of geo-spatial data management tools such as GIS and public access to geo-spatial data sets through the internet, it now common to extend site specific models to large areas for evaluating management strategy or varying inputs on a spatial scale.

***Components of SDSS for Input Optimization***

- Spatial database development based on GIS and image processing softwares to generate spatial data as required by crop model
- Field calibration and validaton of crop models and the modification of the model if required
- A graphic user interface development to facilitate the interface between spatial data and crop model and the display the results of different scenario analyses.

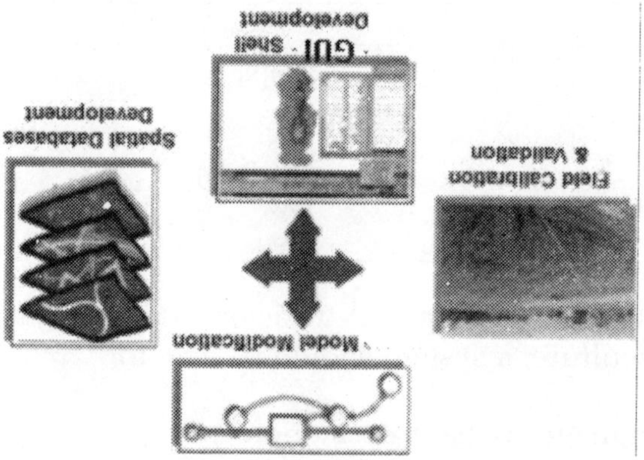


**Fig. 19.1:** A framework for SDSS

***Spatial data base***: Many spatial data layers are required in the SDSS development. An example of spatial database used for Rice decision support system in Thialand is shown in Fig. 19.2. Among them, soil and weather data is considered to be a significant input for the crop model. The soil spatial data can also overlaid with the weather data layer to form simulation mapping unit (SMU) within which crop yield will be simulated. A spatial database can be designed to store and mange soil data at the series level. The spatial data can be stored as as Arc/INFO coverages, the attribute tables of which are linked to relational tables which store data for each horizon of all soil pedons found in a region (Fig. 19.2). A structure of soil database is shown in Fig. 19.3. It is flexible to allow for making a query on specific soil characteristics and it can be transformed and exported as an soil input data file in the format required by crop model. As most of the crop model needs daily step weather data, coarse resolution or monthly data can be converted into actual daily data by using weather generator within SDSS framework. Weather data are interpolated to generated grid based climate surfaces. All spatial data are organized in GIS in unique grid format which are linked through relational database.

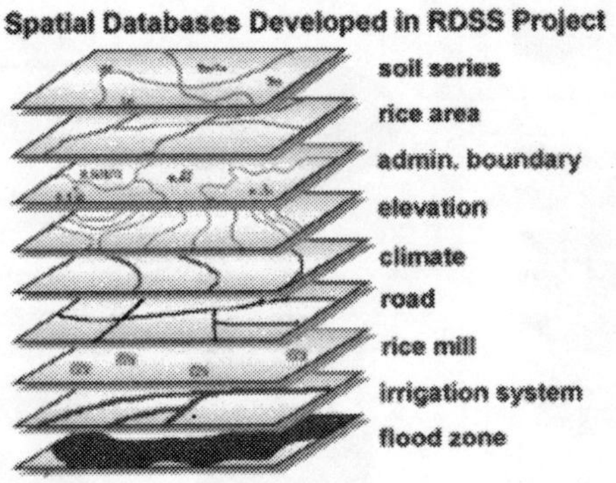


**Fig. 19.2:** Spatial database for Rice decision support system

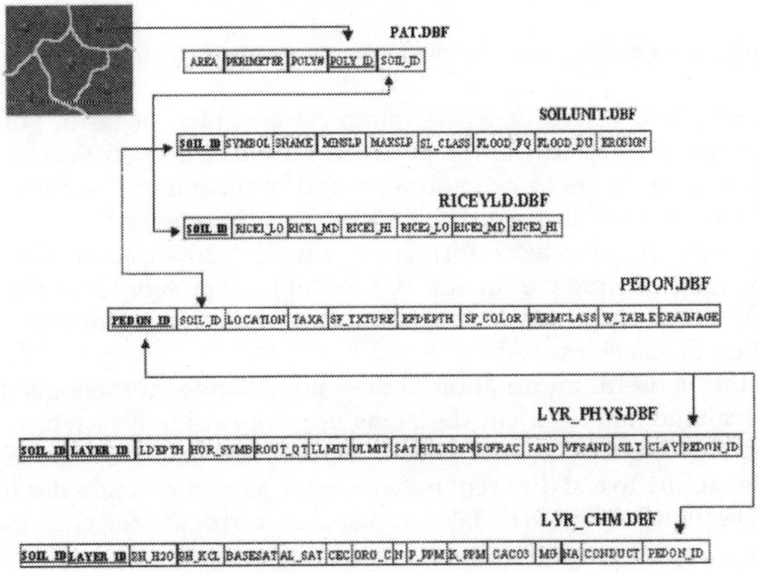


**Fig. 19.3:** Structure of soil database

***Graphical user interface***: GUI play a key role in communicating effectively between the model developer and user in describing a data and model scales, as well as GIS methods for transformation of information between scales, that produce useful assessment results at the user's scale of interest. For successful implementation and acceptance requires the use of widely available datasets and the automatic preparation of model default input to begin and reliable model predictions.For example, ThaiRice is a graphic user interface (GUI) that is designed to link spatial databases with CERES-Rice model in order to facilitate the selection of target area, management strategies and various scenarios for rice yield prediction and mapping. It is a customized ArcView GIS application using Avenue script that enable local language in the display mode (Fig. 19.4).

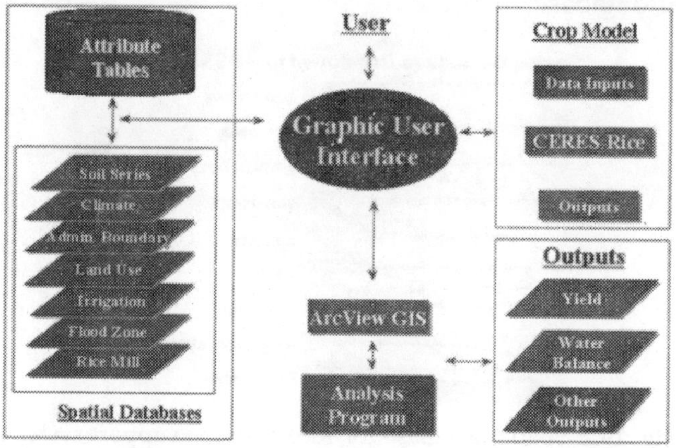


**Fig. 19.4:** A graphical user interface for rice

## Remote sensing based decision support for precision farming

Remotely sensed data which provides complete coverage of farm. For temporally consistent, quantitative relationships between remotely sensed measurements and crop conditions, data needs to be calibrated and atmospherically corrected. Precise georeferencing of satellite data so data can be directly integrated into a geographic information system. A corrected information is used with a data model to relate the reflectance to an agronomic parameter. For example, remotely sensed data has been found useful to detect crop water stress, estimate leaf area index and APAR as well as to map nitrogen deficiencies.

Though this is useful information, it does not provide all the tools necessary for a grower to evaluate management decisions nor does it identify which alternatives best satisfies multi-objective criteria. Thus it requires fourth component as crop model which provides ability to test different management scenarios before it is implemented in the field. The remotely sensed data are used as surrogate for crop growth in the model. For example, use of remotely sensed estimates of leaf area index or evapotranspiration to adjust the crop model's parameters so that its prediction match the field conditions. Once the various management alternatives (*e.g.* rate of fertilizers or timing and frequency of irrigations) have been simulated with the crop model, the resulting information is then input to a decision model. The decision model should be capable of processing previously set multiple criteria. For example, the prediction of yield from the crop model can be combined with ancillary data of production cost and crop price to establish the profitability of different management approaches. Data on nitrogen leaching and required inputs for various management scenarios provide the decision model with information on sustainability and environmental protection. The framework for integrating remote sensing, crop model and decision support id as shown in Figure 19.5.

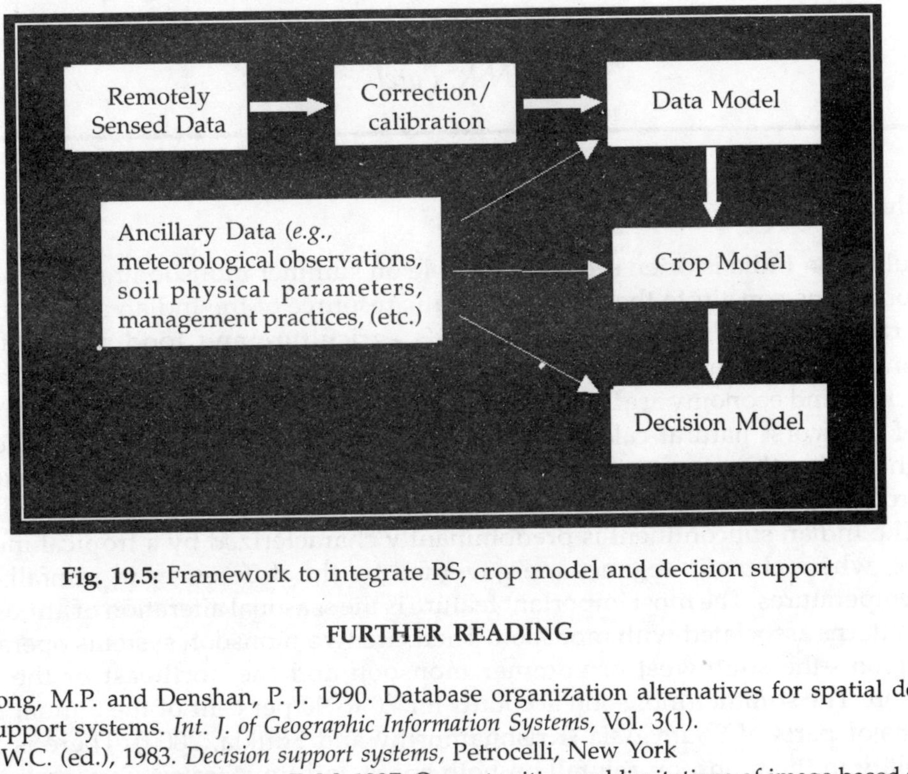


**Fig. 19.5:** Framework to integrate RS, crop model and decision support

## FURTHER READING

Armstrong, M.P. and Denshan, P. J. 1990. Database organization alternatives for spatial decision support systems. *Int. J. of Geographic Information Systems,* Vol. 3(1).

House, W.C. (ed.), 1983. *Decision support systems,* Petrocelli, New York

Moran, M.S. Inoue, Y. and Barnes, E. M. 1997. Opportunities and limitations of image based remote sensing in precision crop management. Remote Sensing of environment, Vol. 61 No. 3, pp. 319-346.

Goodchild, M.F., Parks, B.O. and Steyaert, L.T. 1993. *Enviornmental modeling with GIS,* Oxford University Press, Oxford.

*Precision Agriculture 1997* © 1997 BIOS Scientific Publishers Ltd.

# 20

# Drought Monitoring by Satellite Remote Sensing

*N.R. Patel*

## Introduction

Agriculture in India is often seen as a gamble on summer monsoon rainfall. Summer monsoon rains constitute the greatest climatic resource of the Indian subcontinent as these rains support not only the country's agriculture and food production but substantially contribute to power generation (H.P. Das, 2000). Thus success or failure of the crops and economy are intimately linked with prospects of good or bad monsoon. One of the worst natural calamities that affect India is the large-scale incidence of drought during the summer monsoon season (June to September) wherein extensive and prolonged droughts have cumulative effects, which are often disastrous.

The Indian subcontinent is predominantly characterized by a tropical monsoon climate, where climatic regimes are governed by the differences in rainfall, rather than temperatures. The most important feature is the seasonal alteration of atmospheric flow patterns associated with monsoon. There are two monsoon systems operating in the region—the southwest or summer monsoon and the northeast or the winter monsoon. The summer monsoon accounts for 70 to 90 per cent of the annual rainfall over major parts of South Asia (Krishnamurthy and Shukla, 2000). There is a large variability in the monsoon rainfall on both space and time scales. Consequently the Indian region experiences drought or flood in some parts of the country or the other almost every year during the monsoon period (June-September).

### *Impact of Drought*

Drought is a slow-onset, creeping natural hazard and a recurrent feature of climate which occurs in virtually all regions of the world; it results in serious economic, social, and environmental impacts (Wilhite, 2000). Drought is a natural hazard originating from a deficiency of precipitation that results in a water shortage for some activities or some groups and is often associated with other climatic factors. Large portion of India approximately 68 per cent perennially reel under recurrent drought due to erratic monsoons. In India, droughts of varying magnitude and spatial spread were witnessed recently as well as in last century. The 1987 and 2002 drought were by far the worst drought hits in the country with more than 50 per cent reduction in crop area and nearly 30,000 crores of rupees in agricultural losses. The drought of 1987 was one of the worst in the century. The monsoon rainfall was normal only in 14 out of 35 meteorological sub-divisions in the country. The overall deficiency in rainfall was 19 per cent as compared to 26 per cent in 1918 and 25 per cent in 1972 being worst years. Agricultural operations were adversely affected in 43 per cent (58.6 million ha) of cropped area in 263 districts in 15 States and 6 Union Territories. In the two worst affected states of Rajasthan and Gujarat, the rainfall was less than 50 per cent from normal. In these states, the drought of 1987 was the third or fourth in succession resulting in distress to an unprecedented level.

Gujarat is one such state where drought occurs with unfailing regularity. The most recent, the drought of 2002, ranks fifth in terms of magnitude but is unique when examined in overall terms of magnitude, spacing, dispersion and duration. In July 2002, rainfall deficiency dropped to 51 per cent, surpassing all previous droughts. The impact of the drought spread over 56 per cent of the land mass and threatened the livelihoods of 300 million people across 18 states. The drought-prone areas of the country are confined to arid, semi-arid and sub-humid parts of peninsular and western India. These regions experiences almost every third year being a drought year (Table 20.1).

**Table 20.1:** All India and Gujarat State Drought Years

| *1901-1910* | *1911-1920* | *1921-1930* | *1931-1940* | *1941-1950* | *1951-1960* | *1961-1970* | *1971-1980* | *1981-1990* | *1991-2000* |
|---|---|---|---|---|---|---|---|---|---|
| **Gujarat state** | | | | | | | | | |
| 1901 | 1911 | 1923 | 1931 | 1942 | 1951 | 1962 | 1972 | 1982 | 1991 |
| 1904 | 1915 | 1924 | 1936 | 1948 | 1952 | 1963 | 1973 | 1985 | 1993 |
| 1905 | 1918 | 1925 | 1938 | | 1955 | 1965 | 1974 | 1986 | 1995 |
| | 1920 | 1927 | 1939 | | 1957 | 1966 | | 1987 | 1998 |
| | | 1929 | 1940 | | 1960 | 1968 | | 1990 | 1999 |
| | | | | | | | | | 2000 |
| **All India** | | | | | | | | | |
| 1901 | 1911 | | | 1941 | 1951 | 1965 | 1972 | 1982 | |
| 1904 | 1918 | | | | | 1966 | 1974 | 1987 | |
| 1905 | 1920 | | | | | 1968 | 1979 | | |

*Source:* Gore and Ponkshe, 2004.

## *Drought: Definitions*

Despite drought impacts and consequences are well documented, the definition of drought is not yet fully described owing to complexity of drought events with respect to its timing, intensity, duration and spatial extent. Wilhite and Glantz (1985) have reviewed definitions of drought and classified them into four distinct categories as, namely, meteorological, agricultural, hydrological, and socio-economic drought.

***Meteorological Drought***: defined usually on the basis of the degree of dryness (in comparison to some "normal" or average amount) and the duration of the dry period.

***Agricultural drought***: refers to situations in which the moisture in the soil is no longer sufficient to meet the needs of the crops growing in the area. Orr A climatic excursion involving a shortage of precipitation sufficient to adversely affect crop production or range production

***Hydrological drought***: refers to deficiencies in surface and subsurface water supplies. It is measured as streamflow, snowpack, and as lake, reservoir and groundwater levels. There is usually a delay between lack of rain or snow and less measurable water in streams, lakes and reservoirs. Therefore, hydrological measurements tend to lag other drought indicators.

***Socio-economic drought***: occurs when physical water shortages start to affect the health, well-being, and quality of life of the people, or when the drought starts to affect the supply and demand of an economic product.

## Drought Monitoring: Meterological Drought Indicators and Their Limitations

Operational definitions help in specifying the degree of departure from average of precipitation over a time period and this can be done by comparing the current conditions with historical climatic data, usually over a 30-year period of data. This definition used when dealing with agriculture, to tell things such as the impact the drought is having on crops and the rate of soil depletion. Drought severity, frequency, and duration for a historical period can be established operationally, but requires weather data from various time scales (such as hourly, daily, monthly, etc.). Many indicators and indices of drought exist and these may disagree as to the severity of drought conditions. Over the last five decades, several drought indices have been formulated by integrating meteorological parameters like rainfall, evapotranspiration (ET), runoff and water supply into a single number and used extensively to quantify moisture condition of a region and estimate severity and spatial extent of agricultural drought. Drought indices have therefore become an important tools for decision making and planning during times of drought episodes. The most commonly used drought indices are per cent rainfall departure, Aridity index, Palmer Drought Severity Index (PDSI), Crop Moisture Index (CMI), and Standardized Precipitation Index (SPI). Each of these indices has recognized strengths and weaknesses. Indices are often used to trigger both response and mitigation programs by local, state, and federal government. The PDSI, a meteorological drought index, was the first comprehensive drought index developed in the United States [Palmer, 1965]. The PDSI provides a measure of the departure from normal of the moisture supply. The CMI is an indicator of soil moisture in the topsoil. The SPI is a simple calculation solely based on rainfall with a temporal flexibility that is theoretically much better suited to the quicker responses in vegetation detected by satellite imagery. It is a statistical measure on the surplus or lack of precipitation during a given period as a function of the long-term average precipitation [McKee *et al.*, 1994]. Whereas drought indicators may assimilate information on rainfall, stored soil moisture, or water supply, typically they do not express much local spatial detail (that is, one value may be used to indicate climate conditions over an entire county). Alternatively, drought indices may also be calculated at one location where the input data are collected (that is, a climate station). This information is spatially discrete but only valid for a single location. Thus, a significant drawback of climate-based drought indicators is their lack of spatial detail. In addition, meteorologically based indices are dependent on data collected at weather stations. Some areas have very sparsely distributed stations and this affects the reliability of the drought indices. Recently, it has become clear that no one indicator or index is adequate for monitoring drought on a regional scale; instead, a combination of monitoring tools integrated together is preferable for producing regional or national drought maps (Brown, 2002).

## Drought Monitoring: Satellite Remote Sensing

Utility of remote sensing data especially satellite data in drought assessment has long been proven and needs no reiteration. It is far superior to conventional methods at an optimal spatial extent. Remote Sensing technology in its current state-of-art can help in predicting, mitigating and monitoring all the five different types of drought. Data from various satellites can be utilized for the purpose depending on the perspective that a researcher has towards drought, whether it is agricultural, meteorological, hydrological, socio-economic or ecological. It enables to understand the manifestations of drought in a larger area more directly than the conventional methods, which used to utilize indirect methods for assessing the various impacts of drought. Drought monitoring mechanisms exist in most of the countries that use ground based information on drought related parameters such as rainfall, weather, crop conditions and water availability. Earth observations from satellites are highly complementary to those collected by *in-situ* systems. Satellites are often necessary for the provision of synoptic, wide-area coverage and provision of the frequent information required putting *in-situ* information into broader spatial monitoring of drought conditions.

### *Normalized Difference Vegetation Index (NDVI)*

Tucker first suggested NDVI in 1979 as an index of vegetation health and density (Thenkabail *et al.*, 2004). NDVI is defined as:

$$NDVI= (NIR-RED)/(NIR+RED)$$

Where, NIR and RED are the reflectance in the near infrared and red bands. NDVI is a good indicator of green biomass, leaf area index, and patterns of production (Thenkabail *et al.*, 2004; Wang *et al.*, 2004). NDVI is the most commonly used vegetation index. It varies from +1 to -1. Since climate is one of the most important factors affecting vegetation condition, AVHRR-NDVI data have been used to evaluate climatic and environmental changes at regional and global scales (Ji and Peters, 2003; Singh *et al.*, 2003; Li *et al.*, 2004). It can be used not only for accurate description of continental land cover, vegetation classification and vegetation vigour but is also effective for monitoring rainfall and drought, estimating net primary production of vegetation, crop growth conditions and crop yields, detecting weather impacts and other events important for agriculture, ecology and economics (Singh *et al.*, 2003). NDVI has been used successfully used to identify stressed and damaged crops and pastures but only in homogenous terrain. In more heterogeneous terrain regions their interpretation becomes more difficult (Vogt *et al.* 1998; Singh *et al.*, 2003). Many studies in the Sahel Zone (Tucker *et al.*, 2005), South Africa (Unganani and Kogan, 2004) and Mediterranean (Vogt *et al.*, 1998), and Senegal (Li. *et al.*, 2004) indicate meaningful direct relationships between NDVI derived from NOAA AVHRR satellites, rainfall and vegetation cover and biomass.

### *Vegetation Condition Index (VCI)*

It was first suggested by Kogan (1997) and subsequently used elsewhere (Thenkabail *et al.*, 2004; Vogt *et al.*, 1998). VCI is an indicator of the status of the vegetation cover as a function of the status of the vegetation cover as a function of the NDVI minimum and maxima encountered for a given ecosystem over many years. VCI is defined as:

$$VCIj = (NDVIj - NDVImin)/(NDVImax - NDVImin) *100$$

Where, NDVImax NDVImin is calculated from long-term record for a particular month and j is the index of the current month. The condition of the ground vegetation presented by VCI is measured in per cent. The VCI values between 50 per cent to 100 per cent indicate optimal or above normal conditions whereas VCI values close to zero per cent reflects an extreme dry month.

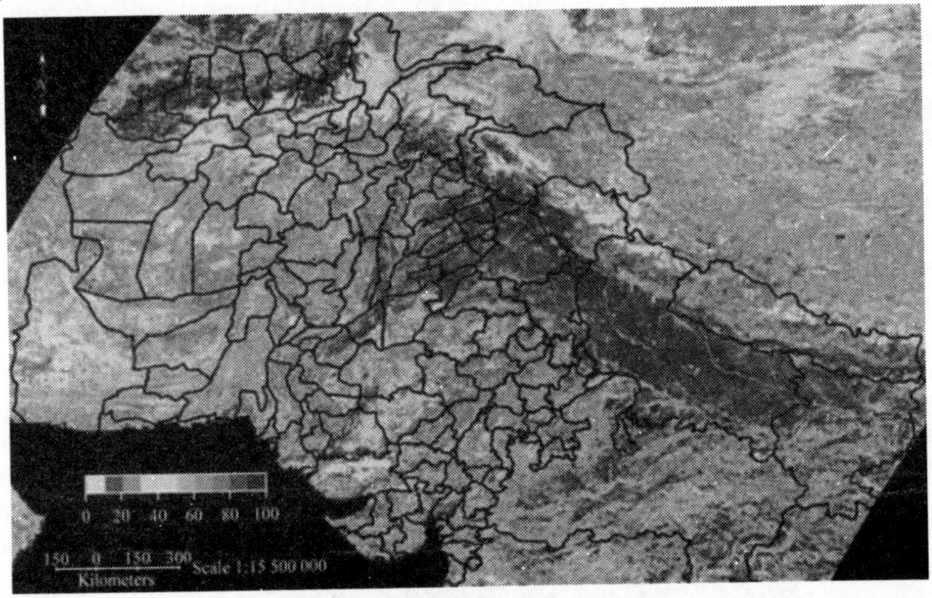


**Fig. 20.1:** VCI (12 September, 2004)

VCI has been used by Kogan and Unganani for estimation of corn yield in South Africa drought monitoring over India (Singh *et al.*, 2002); monitoring droughts in the southern Great Plains, USA (Wan *et al.* 2004); drought detection and monitoring in the Mediterranean region (Vogt *et al.*, 2000) and drought assessment and monitoring in Southwest Asia (Thenkabail *et al.*, 2004). These studies suggest that VCI captures rainfall dynamics better than the NDVI particularly in geographically non-homogeneous areas. Also, VCI values indicate how much the vegetation has advanced or deteriorated in response to weather. It was concluded from the above studies that VCI has provided an assessment of spatial characteristics of drought, as well as its duration and severity and were in good agreement with precipitation patterns.

***Temperature Condition Index (TCI)***

TCI was also suggested by Kogan (1997), (Thenkabail *et al.*, 2004). It was developed to reflect vegetation response to temperature, *i.e.* higher the temperature the more extreme the drought. TCI is based on brightness temperature and represents the deviation of the current month's value from the recorded maximum. TCI is defined as:

$$TCIj = (BTmax - BTj)/(BTmax - Btmin) *100$$

Where, BT is brightness temperature. Maximum and minimum BT values are calculated from the long-term record of remote sensing images for a particular period j. Low TCI values indicate very hot weather. TCI has been used for drought monitoring in the USA, China, Zimbabwe and the Former Soviet Union. A study in Argentina for drought detection revealed that TCI was useful to assess the spatial characteristics, the duration and severity of droughts, and were in good agreement in precipitation patterns (Seiler *et al.*, 1998). TCI has been related to recent regional scale drought patterns in South Africa (Kogan, 1998) and India (Singh and Kogan, 2002).

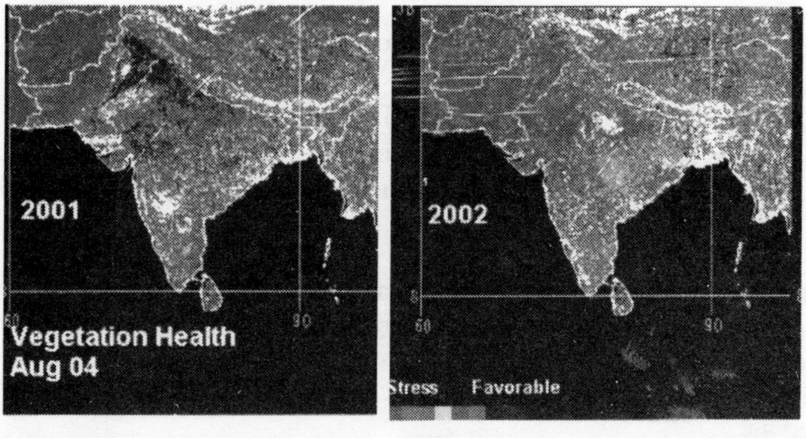


**Fig. 20.2:** VT image of non-drought year-2001 and VT image of drought year-2002

By integrating VCI and TCI for particular period, vegetation health (VT) is formulated as,

$$VT = a*VCI + b*TCI$$

Where, a and b are coefficients quantifying a share of VCI and TCI contribution in the combined condition. For example, if other conditions are near normal, vegetation is more sensitive to moisture during canopy formation (leaf appearance) and to temperature during flowering. Therefore, the share of moisture contribution into the total vegetation condition (health) is higher than temperature during leaf canopy formation and lower during flowering. If moisture and temperature contribution during a vegetation cycle is currently not known. It can be assume that the share of weekly VCI and TCI is equal. The VT reflects indirectly a combination of chlorophyll and moisture content in vegetation and also changes in thermal conditions at the surface. The VCI and TCI both provide information about vegetation stress due to excessive wetness and drought conditions, in such case VCI < 35 and TCI > 95.

***Standardized Vegetation Index***

The Standard Vegetation Index (SVI) is based on the fact that vegetation conditions are closely linked to weather conditions in the atmosphere closest to the ground. It shows us the effects of climate on vegetation over short-time periods. Low SVI values indicate poor vegetation condition that could be the result of climate conditions. High SVI values might reflect ideal crop condition so that vegetation greenness is higher than encountered in other years.

The Standardized Vegetation Index (SVI) is based on the calculation of a t-score (Student's T) for each AVHRR pixel location. The t-score is calculated from the NDVI values for each pixel location for each month for each year, during the years 1981-2003 as:

$$t_{ijk} = \frac{\left(NDVI_{ijk} - \bar{x}_{ij}\right)}{\frac{s_{i,j}}{n^{0.5}}}$$

Where:

$NDVI_{ijk}$ = highest NDVI value for pixel *i* during month *j* for year *k*,
$\bar{x}_{ij}$ = mean NDVI for pixel *i* during month *j* over *n* years
$s_{ij}$ = standard deviation of pixel *i* during month *j* over *n* years, and
$n$ = No. of years used

A t score was calculated for each land pixel location over Indian subcontinent (NDVI image). Monthly values were determined by taking the maximum-pixel value if images for two composite periods were available.

After calculation of the t-score for each pixel, the probability of that score was determined as:

$$SVI = Prob\ (t_{i,j,k} < t_x, \nu)$$

Where,

$\nu = n - 1$ (degrees of freedom)

Intuitively, the SVI is an estimate of the "probability of occurrence" of pixel greenness. This per-pixel probability estimate constitutes the Standardized Vegetation

Index. Thus, the values of the SVI range between greater than zero and less than one. "Zero" is the condition in which a pixel NDVI value is lower than all possible NDVI values for a pixel for a month in all other years of this study (1981-2003). The value "one" is the condition in which the pixel NDVI value for the respective month is higher than all the NDVI values of the same month in the other years. For mapping purposes, SVI values can be grouped into 5 classes, each of which comprises a different and consecutive range of values. SVI values were grouped into 5 classes, each of which comprises a different and consecutive range of values. These classes are average, good, very good, poor, and very poor. Pixel classification into probability class 1 (0 - .025) indicates the pixel NDVI value is lower than the average NDVI value for that same pixel for the same month in the nine years of the study period, indicating very poor vegetation condition relative to that in the other years. Pixel classification into probability class 5 (.975 - 1.0) indicates the pixel NDVI value for the respective month is higher than the average NDVI values of the same month in the nine year period indicating very good vegetation condition relative to that in the other years.

### *Vegetation Temperature Condition Index*

The most commonly used normalized difference vegetation index (NDVI) from remote sensing often fall short in real time drought monitoring (Wang *et al.*, 2004). Due to a lagged vegetation response to drought, NDVI cannot detect drought events instantaneously. On the other hand, surface temperature (Ts) is sensitive to water stress and has been identified as good indicator of water stress (Jackson, 1981; Goetz, 1997). Thus, accurate and real time drought monitoring needs combination of the thermal and visible/near infrared wavelength which provide information on vegetation and moisture condition simultaneously.

This index has been used as an effective agricultural drought index to monitor the spatial pattern of vegetation over a region. The VTCI approach (Wan *et al.*, 2004) for agricultural drought monitoring integrates the remotely sensed land surface reflectance and thermal properties, and gives the emphasis on changes in both LST and NDVI based on Ts-NDVI space relation. It can be calculated for drought monitoring at a regional level for specific time period. This index has been used to monitor the drought occurrences in 8 days composite basis in Gujarat (Patel *et al.*, 2006). Mathematically it can be written as:

$$\mathrm{VTCI} = \frac{\mathrm{LST}_{\mathrm{NDVIi\,max}} - \mathrm{LST}_{\mathrm{NDVIi}}}{\mathrm{LST}_{\mathrm{NDVIi\,max}} - \mathrm{LST}_{\mathrm{NDVIi\,min}}}$$

Where $LST_{NDVIimax} = a + b\,NDVIi$

$\mathrm{LST}_{\mathrm{NDVIimin}} = \mathrm{a}' + \mathrm{b}'\ \mathrm{NDVIi}$

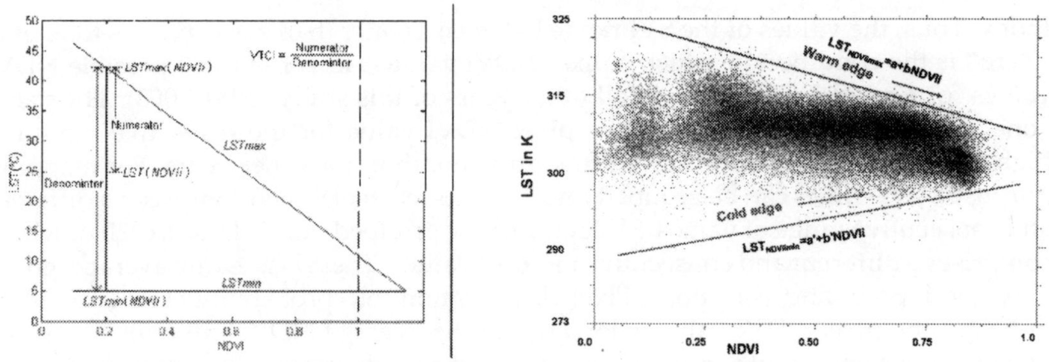


**Fig. 20.3:** Parameterization of $LST_{NDVImax}$ and $LST_{NDVImin}$ from LST/NDVI triangle

The $LST_{NDVIimax}$ and $LST_{NDVIimin}$ are maximum and minimum LSTs of pixels, which have same NDVI value in a study region on each ith date or period of image, respectively, and $LST_{NDVIi}$ denotes actual LST of one pixels whose NDVI value is NDVIi. Coefficients a, b, a′ and b′ can be estimated from an area large enough where soil moisture at surface layer should span from wilting point to field capacity at pixel level. The shape of the scatter plot is normally triangular at a regional scale (Gillies, 1997) and (Wang, 2001), provided the study area is large enough to provide a wide range of NDVI and surface moisture conditions, where in $LST_{NDVImax}$ and $LST_{NDVImin}$ represents "warm edge" (no water limitation) and "cold edge" (water stress restriction). The value of VTCI ranges from 0 to 1. In general, the lower the value of VTCI, the higher the magnitude of drought stress. This index was found to have positive relationship with crop moisture index. It was observed that the VTCI is an ideal index to monitor agricultural drought because it is highly sensitive to short-term changes in crop moisture status in terms of CMI. Besides this, the VTCI was found to be related crop yield anomalies occurs due to drought conditions. Furthermore, interpretation of drought duration from time series of VTCI can clearly depicts severity of drought stress effects on crop performance. The major advantage of VTCI is that it can captures information about drought stress condition solely on satellite measurements. However, this index has limited applicability in presence of cloudy condition since surface temperature is highly sensitive to cloud cover.

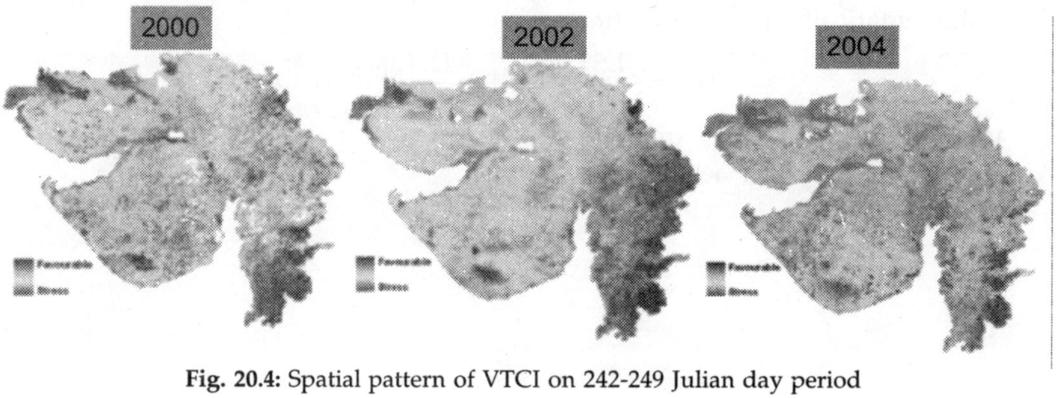


**Fig. 20.4:** Spatial pattern of VTCI on 242-249 Julian day period

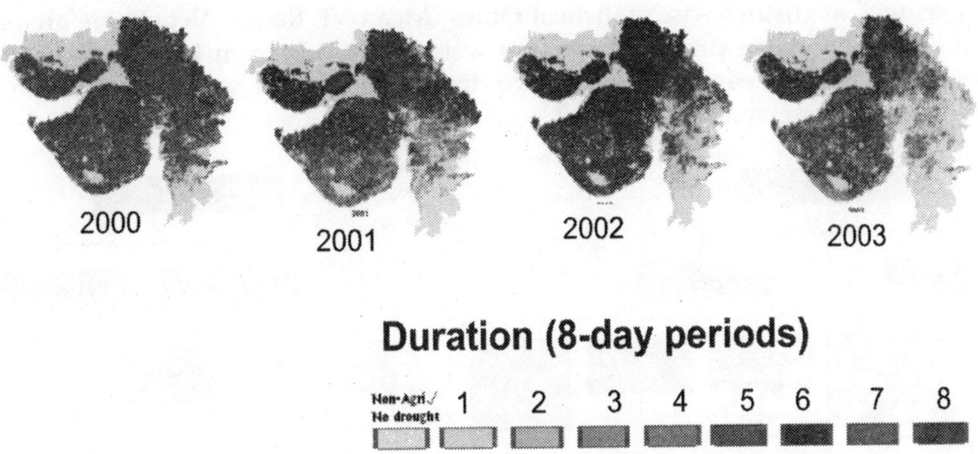


**Fig. 20.5:** Spatial pattern of drought duration based on VTCI

## National Agricultural Drought Assessment and Monitoring System (NADAMS)

In the context of limitations in current ground based drought monitoring system, the Department of Agriculture and Cooperation, Government of India sponsored the Remote Sensing Application Mission on drought which is being executed by Department of Space/National Remote Sensing Agency, with participation by Indian Meteorological Department (IMD), Central Water Commission (CWC) and concerned State Government Agencies.

Drought assessment with district as the reference unit and monitoring through the Kharif season (June-December) is primarily based on Normalised Difference Vegetation Index (VI) derived from NOAA satellite AVHHR (Advanced Very High Resolution Radiometer) sensor data, acquired daily at the earth station operated by NRSA.

The NOAA VI is given by:

$$VI = \frac{CH2 - CH1}{CH2 + CH1}$$

where, CH1 and CH2 are the reflected radiation in visible and near IR channels of NOAA-AVHHR sensor.

In view of coarse spatial resolution of NOAA-AVHHR sensor (1.1 km at Nadir) vegetation type cannot be discriminated and total green vegetation is monitored for drought conditions. Ancillary data on rainfall, aridity anomaly, cropping pattern, crop alendar, land utilization and irrigation support has also been collected through State Government field agencies to support interpretation of VI data. Drought conditions are assessed based on comparative analysis of two weekly VI image and the statistics with those of similar period in previous year. In addition, the profile of vegetation development/condition till this period in the reporting year is also compared with previous years. For comparative analysis, a VI data base of country/state VI maps, as well as district-wise statistical tables (Mean VI, Range, Vegetative area and cloud cover) has been prepared for two weekly periods from June to December, covering the Kharif seasons. The relative drought severity level is assessed on the basis of criteria as given in Table 20.2.

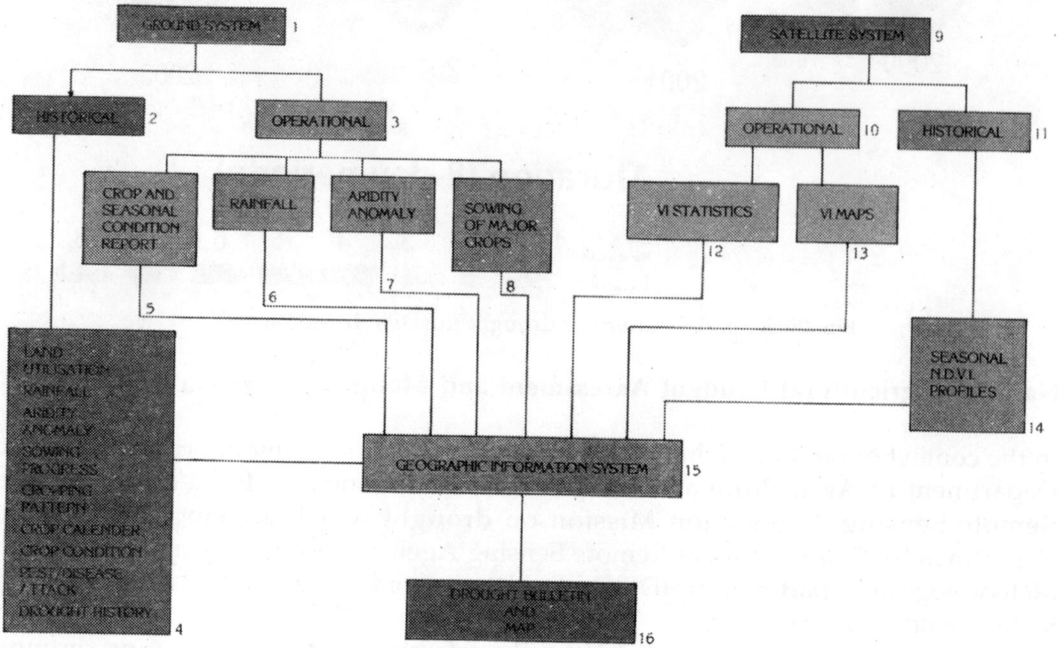


**Fig. 20.6:** Flow diagram of methodology of NADAMS

**Table 20.2:** Drought severity level

| *Delay in vegetation growth* | *VI anomaly compared to normal year (%)* | *Drought severity level* |
|---|---|---|
| Upto 1 fortnight | Upto 10 | Normal |
| 1-2 fortnights | Above 10, but below 25 | Mild |
| 2-4 fortnights | Above 25, but below 50 | Moderate |
| More than 4 fortnights | Above 50 | Severe |

## Global Scenario of RS Application

The Normalised Difference Vegetation Index (NDVI) and temperature condition index (tci) derived from the satellite data is accepted worldwide for regional monitoring.

The ongoing Program: Africa Real-Time Environmental Monitoring using Imaging Satellites (ARTEMIS) is operational at FAO uses METEOSAT rainfall estimates and AVHRR NDVI values for Africa.

The USDA/NOAA Joint Agricultural Weather Facility (JAWF) uses Global OLR anomaly maps, rainfall map, vegetation and temperature condition maps from GOES, METEOSAT, GMS and NOAA satellites.

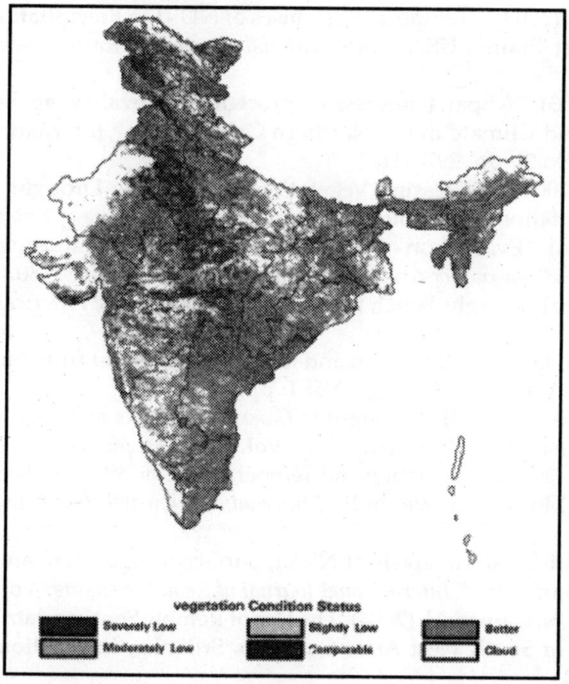


**Fig. 20.7:** NOAA based comparison of vegetation condition of June 2002 with June 2001 (NADMAS)

Joint Research Centre (JRC) of European Commission (EC) issues periodical bulletin on agricultural conditions under MARS-STAT (Application of Remote Sensing to Agricultural Statistics) project which uses vegetation index, thermal based evapo-transpiration and microwave based indicators.

Agricultural Division of Statistics, Canada issues weekly crop condition reports based on NOAA AVHRR based NDVI along with agro-meteorological statistics.

## REFERENCES

F. Brown, J., B.C. Reed, *et al.* (2002). A Prototype Drought Monitoring System Integrating Climate and Satellite Data. Percora 15/Land Satellite Information IV/ISPRS Commission I/FIEOS 2002.

Gillies, R.R., Carlson, T.N., Cui, J., Kustas, W.P. and Humes, K.S., 1997. A verification of the 'triangle' method for obtaining surface soil water content and energy fluxes from remote measurement of the Normalized Difference Vegetation Index (NDVI) and surface radiant temperature. *International Journal of Remote Sensing*, 18: 3145-3166.

D.A. Wilhite (2000). Drought as a Natural Hazard: Concepts and Definitions. Drought: A Global Assessment. W. D.A., Routlegde. **Vol. 1:** pp.1-3.

J.V. Vogt, S. Niemeyer, *et al.* (2000). Drought Monitoring from Space. Drought and Drought Mitigation in Europe. J. V. V. a. F. Somma, Kluwer Academic Publishers: pp. 167-183.

Jackson, R.D., Idso, S.B., Beginato, R.J. and Pinter, P.J., JR., 1981. Canopy temperature as a crop water stress indicator. *Water Resources Research*, 17: 1133-1138.

J. Wang, P.M. Rich, *et al.* (2003). "Temporal Responses of NDVI to Precipitation and Temperatures in the Central Great Plains, USA." *International Journal of Remote Sensing,* **Vol. 24** (No.11): pp. 2345-2364.

Ji, L. and A.J. Peters (2003). "A Spatial Regression procedure for evaluating the Relationship between AVHRR-NDVI and Climate in the Northern Great Plains." International Journal of Remote Sensing **Vol.25** (No.2): pp. 297-311.

Ji, L. and A.J. Peters (2003). "Assessing Vegetation Response to Drought in the Northern Great Plains using Vegetation and Drought Indices." *Remote Sensing of Environment*: pp. 85-98.

Li, J., J. and Lewis (2004). "Evaluation of land performance in Senegal using multi-temporal NDVI and rainfall series." *Journal of Arid Environments* **Vol.59**: pp. 463–480.

Kogan, F.N., 1997. Global Drought Watch from Space. *Bulletin of the American Meteorological Society,* 78: 727-636.

Kogan, F. (2000). Global Drought Detection and Impact Assessment from Space. Drought: A Global Assessment. D.A.Wilhite, Routledge, **Vol.1:** pp.196-209.

P.G. Gore and A.S. Ponkshe (2004). "Drought in Gujarat Districts and Sate as Key Indicators to All India Drought." *Journal of Agrometeorology,* **Vol. 6** (No.1): pp. 47-54.

P. Singh, R., S. Roy, *et al.* (2003). "Vegetation and Temperature Condition Indices from NOAA AVHRR data for Drought Monitoring over India." *International Journal of Remote Sensing,* **Vol. 24** (No.22): pp. 4393-4402.

S.J. Goetz (1997). "Multi-Sensor analysis of NDVI, Surface temperature and Biophysical variables at a mixed grassland Site." *International Journal of Remote Sensing,* **Vol.18** (No.1): pp. 71-94.

Thenkabail, P.S., M.S.D.N. Gamage, l. (2004). The Use of Remote Sensing data for drought assessment and monitoring in South West Asia. Colombo, Srilanka, International Water Management Institute: pp.1-23.

V. Krishnamurthy and J. Shukla (2000). "Intraseasonal and Interannual Variability of Rainfall over India." *Journal of Climate,* **Vol.13**: pp. 4366-4377.

V. Vogt, J., A. A.Viau, *et al.* (1998). Drought Monitoring from Space using Empirical Indices and Physical Indicators. International Symposium on Satellite Based Observation: A Toll for the Study of Mediterranean Basin, Tunis, Tunisia.

Z. Wang, P. Wang, *et al.* (2004). "Using MODIS Land Surface Temperature and Normalized Difference Vegetation Index Products for Monitoring Drought in the Southern Great Plains, USA." *International Journal of Remote Sensing,* **Vol.25** (No.1): pp. 61-72.

Jeyaseelan, A.T.; Suresh, B.A.V.; and Chandrasekhar, K. (1999). Improvement in agricultural drought using IRS-WiFS in Andhra Pradesh State during 1998. Proc. ISRS National Symposium on RS applications of Natural Resources—Retrospective and Perspective, Bangalore, pp. 53-62.

Thiruvengadachari, S.; Jeyseelan, A.T., Harikishan, J. and Krishna Rao, P.V. (1991). Satellite Surveillance of Agricultural Drought Condition in India. In book on *Applications of Remote Sensing in Asia and Oceania—Environmental Change Monitoring* (Ed. Shunji Murai)—pp. 37-50.

# 21

# Remote Sensing and GIS Application in Agro-ecological Zoning

*N.R. Patel*

## Introduction

Sustainable agricultural development requires a systematic effort towards the planning of land use activities in the most appropriate way, apart from several other institutional and policy programmme initiatives. Agro-Ecological Zoning (AEZ) is one of the most important bases for agricultural developmental planning because survival and failure of particular land use or farming system in a given region heavily relies on careful assessment of agro-climatic resources. A practical zoning approach thus arises because climate represented by thermal and moisture regimes forms small geographic areas, resulting in a variable mosaic of specialized areas, capable of supporting varied land use system (Troll, 1965). The approach is used to categorize agroclimatically uniform geographical areas for agricultural developmental planning and other interventions. A framework of agro-ecological zoning describing concepts, methods and procedures was conceptualized for the first time by FAO (1976). Agro-ecological zoning refers to the division of an area of land into land resource mapping units, having unique combination of landform, soil and climatic characteristics and or land cover having a specific range of potentials and constraints for land use (FAO, 1996). The particular parameters used in the definition focus attention on the climatic and edaphic requirements of crop and on the management systems under which the crops are grown. Each zone has a similar combination of constraints and potentials for land use and serve as a focus for the targeting of recommendations designed to improve the existing land use situation, either through increasing production or by limiting land degradation. The addition of further layers of informations on such factors as land tenure, land availability, nutritional requirement of human and livestock populations, infrastructure and costs and prices, has enabled the development of more advanced applications in natural resource analysis and land use planning. AEZ can be regarded as a set of core applications, leading to an assessment of land suitability and potential productivity. An output of AEZ studies includes maps showing agro-ecological zones and land suitability, quantitative estimates on potential crop yields and production. Such information provides the basis for advanced applications such land degradation assessment, livestock productivity modeling, population support capacity assessment and land use optimization modeling.

### Importance of AEZ in Sustainable Agricultural Development Planning

The ability of the world's natural resources to provide the needs of its growing population is a fundamental issue for the international community. World's population is increasing rapidly and at the same time, essential natural resources, such as land and water, are declining both in quantity and quality due to such factors as competition with industrial and urban demands. The basic problem in that limits to the productive capacity of land resources are set by climate, soil and land form condition. In this context AEZ can be regarded as a set of applications, leading to an assessment of land suitability and potential productivity in terms of climate, soil and land forms condition.

Agro-Ecological Zoning (AEZ) is one of the most important bases of sustainable agricultural development planning of a region. It is applicable in micro or local level planning mainly for rainfed agriculture. It assesses the basically the yield potentialities of various crop conditions; evolves future plan of action involving crop diversification; determines suitability of different crops for optimizing land use, disseminates research results and agro-technology. As a result sustainable agricultural development planning is increasingly being based on agro-ecological zones. In this process agro climate zoning has become very popular (Verma and Partap, ARDU 1989, Carson, Beg, *et al.*, 1985). The initial focus of the FAO on Agro-Ecological Zoning System was to assess the suitability of different types of landuse for selected land uses. It is an important starting point for land for selected land use planning with an overview of the whole region. It diagnoses the present situation with regard to farming and land use by categorizing, describing and analyzing, farming systems components.

### Definitions

***Agro-Ecological Zoning (AEZ)*** refers to the division of an area of land into smaller units, which have similar characteristics related to land suitability potential production and environmental impact.

***Agro-Ecological Zone*** is a land resource mapping unit, having unique combination of landform, soil and climatic characteristics and or land cover having a specific range of potentials and constraints for land use (FAO, 1996).

***Agro-Ecological Cell (AEC)*** is defined by a unique combination of land form, soil and climatic characteristics

### Traditional Approach

Several attempts have been made to classify the land area into climatic regions. Many of the earlier efforts to delineate agro-climates used manual overlay of isolines representing either potential evapotranspiration or temperature or their combinations and superimposed on soil resource maps. G. Carter (1954) divided India into six climatic regions, ranging from arid to perhumid, based on the criteria of Thornthwaite system of climate classification.

Sehgal *et al.* (1987) prepared a computerized bio-climatic map of North-West India, based on the criteria of dry month. Krishna (1988) delineated 40 soil climatic zones based on major soil types and moisture index. Murthy and Pandey (1978) brought out a 8 agro-ecological region map of India on the basis of physiography, climate, soils and agricultural regions. The approach depicts a good beginning of agro-ecological zoning in the country, but it suffers from several limitations due to over generalization such as grouping together the areas having different physiography, temperature and soil in a zone.

Subramanian (1983) based on the data of 160 meteorological stations in the country and using the concept of moisture adequacy index, delineated 29 agro-ecological zones with the possible 36 combinations of IMA and dominated soil groups as per FAO/UNESCO Soil Map (1974). The Planning Commission, as a result of mid-term appraisal of the planning targets of VII Plan (1985-1990)(Sehgal *et al.*, 1992) , divided the country into 15 broad agro-climatic zones based on physiography and climate.

### New Tools for AEZ

Modern tools such as satellite remote sensing and GIS have been providing newer dimensions to effectively monitor and manage natural resources. It has been well conceived that remote sensing and Geographic Information System (GIS) have great role to play in agro-ecological zoning for sustainable development due to multi-stage character of the comprehensive approach to agro-ecological zoning (Pratap *et al.*, 1992). Several approaches of AEZ in past involves manual integration of agro-climatic and other natural resource data (Mavi, 1984; Venkateswaralu *et al.*, 1996). As a result, large amount of agro-ecological data could not be handled easily and aggregation was required at an early stage in the analysis. This led to loss of information on spatial variability. On the other hand, GIS technology is very useful for automated logical integration of bio-climate, terrain and soil resource inventory information (Patel *et al.*, 2000a). The system is capable of containing all data required to solve resource management problems. Topographic maps, land resource map and contour map having physiographic, geographic and bio-climatic information forms primary input for GIS for agro-ecological zoning activities. The system also facilitates the enlargement of a particular geographic pocket to render more details on retrieval. After collecting the basic data on zonal resource information, the data can be manipulated to create relavent profiles of applied use that can be retrieved on demand. A zonal database can also be integrated with non-geographic information such as socio-economic data, that is relevant for making decision on development priority interventions about the sustainable management of zonal resources. Remote sensing provides digital or hard copy data base information on natural resources. These information can be stored and retrieved as and when required and also data can be classified and aggregated for any number of planning exercises. This AEZ concept involves the representation of land in layers of spatial information and combination of layers of spatial information using geographic information system (GIS).

**Structure of AEZ**

The structure of AEZ includes the comprehensive framework for the appraisal and planning of land resources (Fig. 21.1). The nature of analysis, which involves the combination of layers of spatial information to define zones, lend itself to application of a GIS. The major requirements of computerized GIS for an activity like agro-ecological zoning and zonal resource information of mountain areas are topographic maps, land resource maps, and contour map. These maps, containing physiographic, geographic, and bioclimatic information which forms primary inputs. Various outputs are generated in both tabular and map form. Till date, good progress have been made in developing GIS based tools for land resources planning, management and monitoring at different scales.

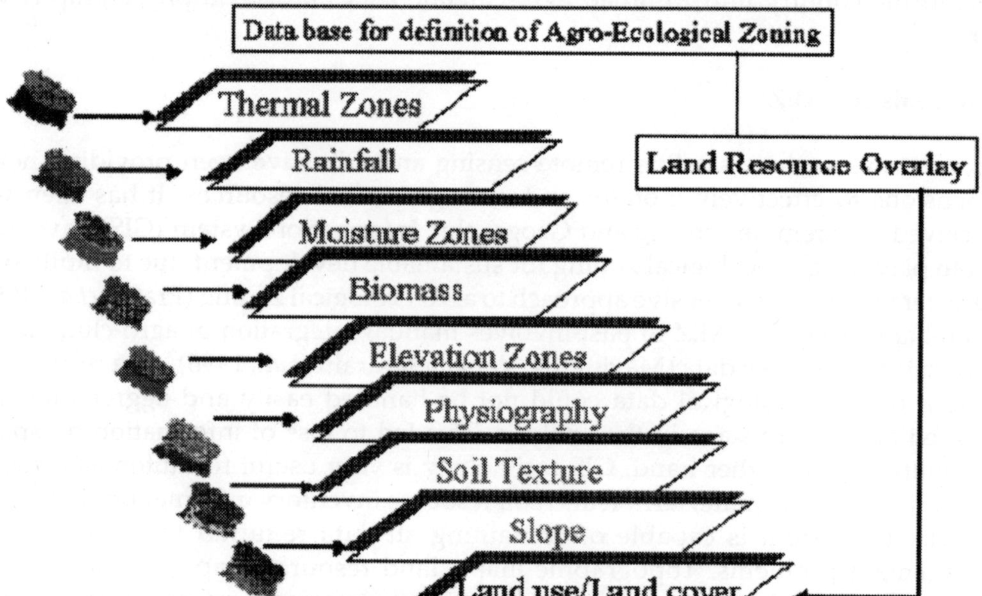


Information in computerised GIS form for each cell. Thermal regimes (3 zones) soil moisture (8 zones) Rainfall (5 zones) Soil Texture (3 classes) Slope (4 classes) Physiography (3 types) Elevation (5 zones) Soil unit (47 types) Land use (10 classes)

**Fig. 21.1:** Structure of land resource

**Elements of AEZ**

The essential elements of the core application s of AEZ includes:

- ❑ Land resource inventory, comprising
  - Analysis of length of growing period or moisture availability index
  - Defining thermal zones
  - Compilation of climatic resource inventory
  - Compilation of soil and landform resource inventory
  - Compilation of present land use inventory
  - Combination of above to make land resource inventory based on agro-ecological zones or agro-ecological cells.
- ❑ Inventory of land utilization types and crop requirements
- ❑ Land suitability evaluation, including
  - Potential productivity computations
  - Matching of constraints and requirements

**A Case Study on Agro-Ecological Zoning in Mountain Ecosystem**

Sustainable development of mountain regions is a challenging task because the areas have highly diverse and fragile ecosystems. One of the most striking characteristics of mountains is their spatial variability. This makes the planning of the use of natural resources in the mountains more complex than any other area. In view of this, the present study was conducted in part of Kumaon Himalaya (latitudes 28°45′ to 30°00′N, longitude 78°45′ to 80°15′) to demonstrate the use of remote sensing and GIS as a tools for agro-ecological zoning with mountain perspective (Patel *et al.*, 2002a). The methodology used in this study is outlined in the flow diagram in Fig. 21.1. This methodology is further described as following sub-heads. The methodology used in this study is outlined in the flow diagram in Fig. 21.2. This methodology is further described as following sub-heads.

*Climate*

Long term (Approximately 10 years) monthly temperatures both maximum and minimum were collected from six meteorological stations falling in the western Himalaya. However, monthly rainfall for eight years were collected from eleven rain gauge stations lies within the study area. The details about location of meteorological and rain gauge stations are shown in Table 21.1. Digital elevation data with one kilometer grid size was taken from Global Digital Elevation Model (USGS GDEM) and geometrically registered in UTM projection. Validation and accuracy check for digital elevation data derived from Global DEM was done with spot height observation from Survey of India toposheets on 1:250,000 scale. A close agreement was observed

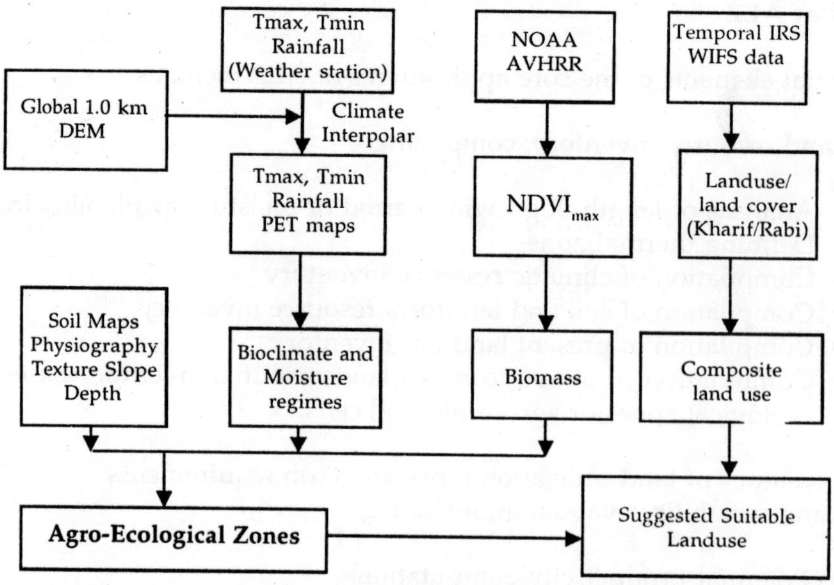


**Fig. 21.2:** Flow diagram of the method for agro-ecological zoning

between spot height observations and Global DEM based elevation data ($R^2 = 0.98$). Long term monthly and annual averages of mean temperatures of six meteorological stations were regressed against corresponding elevation using MICROSTA statistical software (Table 21.2). A good agreement was also observed between annual mean temperature and elevation (annual mean temperature = 24.443 - 0.0045 × elevation, $R^2 = 0.97$). Similarly long term average annual rainfall recorded at different rain gauge stations were regressed against elevation for developing rainfall-elevation relationship (annual rainfall = 515.1 + 0.3843 × elevation, $R^2 = 0.75$) representing the region under study. The empirical relations thus developed were used to utilize inherent spatial quality of digital elevation model in GIS environment for depicting spatial variation in normal monthly and annual mean temperatures as well as annual rainfall condition over Kumaon region. These monthly spatial distribution of mean temperatures were used for computation of spatial potential evapotranspiration (PET) based on method described (Thornthwaite, 1948) as:

$$PET = 1.6 \left[ (10\, T_{ijk}/I_{jk})^{ajk} \right]$$

Where,

$$I_{jk} = \sum_{i=Jan}^{Dec} (T_{ijk} / 5)^{1.54}$$

T = Mean air temperature (°C)

i = Month of a year (i = Jan, Feb, ......Dec)

j = Pixel value of ith row

k = Pixel value of jth column

$ajk = 67.5*10^{-8}(I_{jk})^3 - 7.71*10^{-5}*(I_{jk})^2 + 0.01792(I_{jk}) + 0.4923$

**Table 21.1:** Data fields and location of meteorological and rain gauge station

| No. | *Met/rain gauge station* | *Data fields Monthly* | *Period (years)* | *- Latitude - Longitude* | *Elevation meter)* | *Source* |
|---|---|---|---|---|---|---|
| 1. | Mukteswar | Rainfall, Temperature | 10 | 29° 27′ 28.7" N<br>79° 39′ 27.2" E | 2275 | Institute Temperate Horticulture Station |
| 2. | Hawalbagh | Rainfall, Temperature | 10 | 29° 36′ 00.0" N<br>79° 40′ 00.0"E | 1250 | Met. Station |
| 3. | Almora | Rainfall, Temperature | 10 | 29° 35′ 22.4" N<br>79° 38′ 42.2" E | 1528 | Vivekanand ICAR Institute |
| 4. | Pantnagar | Rainfall, Temperature | 10 | 29° 02′ 27.2" N<br>79° 24′ 30.5" E | 232 | Agriculture University, Pantnagar |
| 5. | Nainital | Rainfall, Temperature | 10 | 29° 21′ 30.7" N<br>79° 27′ 26.3" E | 1945 | Astronomy State Observatory, Nainital |
| 6. | Dehradun | Rainfall, Temperature | 10 | 30° 19′ 00.0" N<br>78° 02′ 00.0" E | 682 | Met Station |
| 7. | Mussoorie | Rainfall, Temperature | 10 | 30° 27′ 00.0" N<br>78° 05′ 00.0" E | 2024 | Met Station, CSW-CRII Dehradun |
| 8. | Chaukutia | Rainfall | 8 | 29° 52′ 32.1" N<br>79° 22′ 15.6′ E | 976 | Forest conservation Department, Raniket |
| 9. | Kedar | Rainfall | 8 | 29° 47′ 07.8′ N<br>79° 15′ 26.8" E | 958 | Forest conservation Department, Raniket |
| 10. | Naula | Rainfall | 8 | 29° 44′ 13.5" N<br>79° 15 11.8" E | 886 | Forest conservation Department, Raniket |
| 11. | Tamadhaun | Rainfall | 8 | 29° 50′ 49.0" N<br>79° 12′ 05.4" E | 912 | Forest conservation Department, Raniket |
| 12. | Sauni | Rainfall | 8 | 29° 37′ 47.9" N<br>79° 22′ 05.8" E | 1599 | Forest conservation Department, Raniket |
| 13. | Deolikhet | Rainfall | 8 | 29° 38′ 51.1" N<br>79° 27′ 00.6" E | 1715 | Forest conservation Department, Raniket |
| 14. | Binta | Rainfall | 8 | 29° 47′ 10.0" N<br>79° 28′ 14.5" E | 1887 | Forest conservation Department, Raniket |

**Table 21.2:** Mean Temperature *versus* Elevation Relationship

| *Month* | *Regression Equation* | $R^2$ |
|---|---|---|
| January | y = - 0.0031 x + 14.106 | 0.89 |
| February | y = - 0.004 x + 17.012 | 0.95 |
| March | y = - 0.0047 x + 22.122 | 0.97 |
| April | y = - 0.0051 x + 27.95 | 0.96 |
| May | y = - 0.0057 x + 31.485 | 0.98 |
| June | y = - 0.0059 x + 31.925 | 0.96 |
| July | y = - 0.0058 x + 30.642 | 0.99 |
| August | y = - 0.0054 x + 29.755 | 0.98 |
| September | y = - 0.0053 x+ 28.855 | 0.99 |
| October | y = - 0.0044 x + 25.133 | 0.95 |
| November | y = - 0.003 x + 19.284 | 0.89 |
| December | y = - 0.0018 x + 15.045 | 079 |

These monthly potential evapotranspiration were summed over twelve months in a year to obtained spatial distribution of annual PET for use in computation of moisture index (MI). The moisture index with positive and negative values indicates moist or dry climate and seasonal variation of effective moisture. The assessment of moisture index (MI) which stands for a balance between moisture availability and extent of dryness. The revised moisture index of Thornthwaite and Mather (1955) method based on annual rainfall and potential evapotranspiration was calculated as:

$$MI = [(P - PET)/PET] * 100$$

Where, MI = Moisture Index
P = Rainfall (mm)
PET = Potential Evapotranspiration (mm)

This information on moisture index is vital to congenial biotic environment and has been used to classify the climatic types. To arrive at homogeneous zones, the limits of moisture index of the various climatic types was scaled as shown in Table 21.3.

**Table 21.3:** Scaling of moisture index into different agro-climate types

| *Climatic type* | *Moisture Index* | *Symbol* |
|---|---|---|
| Semi arid | -66.7 to – 33.3 | D |
| Dry sub-humid | - 33.3 to 0 | C1 |
| Moist sub-humid | 0 to 20 | C2 |
| Humid (4 classes) | 20 to 100 | B1, B2, B3 and B4 |
| Per-humid | > 100 | A |

### *Vegetation Biomass Variability*

Using NDVI to estimate standing green biomass proved to be a reliable source of biomass data. A existing functional relationship between monthly cutting of green dry matter (DM) and maximum normalized difference vegetation index (NDVI) derived from NOAA AVHRRR (Advanced Very High Resolution Radiomater) was used. Monthly NDVI images of NOAA AVHRR during year 1999 were used to derive the maximum NDVI in a year for estimating biomass or dry matter (DM) as per equation:

$$DM = (1.615 * NDVI_{max})^{1.318} ; R^2 = 0.90$$

DM = Dry matter
$NDVI_{max}$ = Maximum NDVI in a year

### *Land Use/Land Cover*

Land use/land cover was derived from coarse resolution IRS WiFS satellite data. Ground truth was collected through integrated use of previous year IRS LISS III hard copy (1:250,000 scale) satellite data, [Survey of India (SOI)] toposheets and handheld Global Positioning System (GPS). Combination of satellite data acquired during *kharif*

(September and October, 2001) and *rabi* (January and March, 2002) seasons were digitally classified to land use/land cover information classes for *kharif* and *rabi*, respectively using MXL classifier. Agricultural land use classes in *rabi* season were refined with respect to land use information in *kharif* season and crop calendar of major crops cultivated in the region. Finally, classified land use/land cover information of *kharif* and *rabi* seasons were logically integrated pixel by pixel basis in raster GIS for deriving cropping system or composite land use/land cover (Fig. 21.6).

### *Soils*

Forty-six soil mapping unit along with their characteristics such as depth, texture, slope, erosion status, and drainage condition for the study area were obtained from soil map (1:250,000 scale) prepared by National Bureau of Soil Survey and Land Use Planning , India. These spatial and non-spatial data on soils were converted into digital soil resource databases for AEZ. In general terms, coarse loamy and skeletal soils are in side slope and top of Lesser Himalayas and piedmont plain while fine textured soils mainly found in alluvial plain and fluvial valleys. The soils are mostly moderately deep to deep, however, approximately 25 per cent of the area having shallow soils mainly found in lesser Himalayas and piedmont plain (Fig. 21.4).

All the land resource databases and characteristics (Fig. 21.1) described above as layer or combination of layers of spatial information were integrated or overlay to derive different unique agro-ecological cells. These agro-ecological cells were further aggregated to arrive at agro-ecological zones and sub zones based on their potential to support agriculture and vegetation patterns.

### *Delineation of Agro-climatic Zones*

Agro-climatic zones are the paramount importance for defining or delineation of agro-ecological zoning for sustainable use of land resource. The essential elements in demarcating or defining of an agro-climatic zones are bioclimates based on thermal regimes, moisture regime and biomass variability (Fig. 21.3). Thermal regimes indicates to the amount of heat available for plant growth and development during the growing period. Moisture regimes represent water availability for crop production and hence they are the vital to classify the agro-climatic zones. Nine different agro-climatic zones were delineated by GIS aided integration of thermal regimes, moisture regimes and biomass map layers (Fig. 21.3).

### *Delineation of Agro-ecological Zones and Sub-zones*

Thirty agro-ecological sub zones (AEZIa to AEZXIIc) were delineated in the study area by GIS aided integration of nine agro-Climatic and eight agro-edaphic zones (Fig. 21.4). Results revealed that the majority of area falls in XIa where as minimum area is occupied by Via (Patel *et al.*, 2002a). The other larger sub-zones are Ib and VIIIa, respectively. AEZIc and AEZ IIc are the most potential zones for intensive

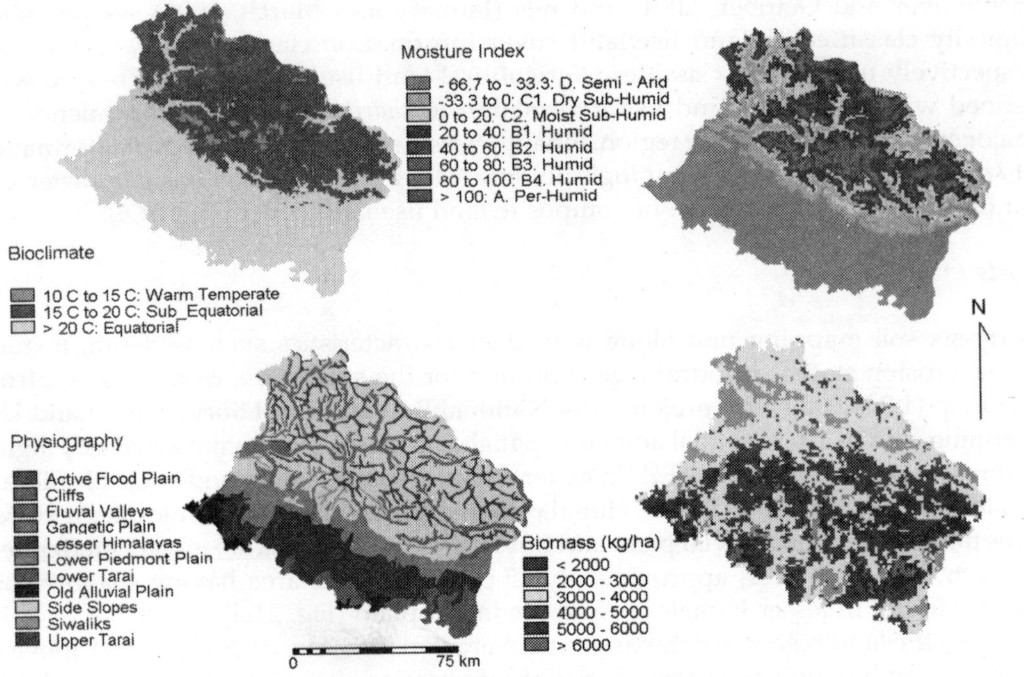


**Fig. 21.3:** Input layers for agro-ecological zoning

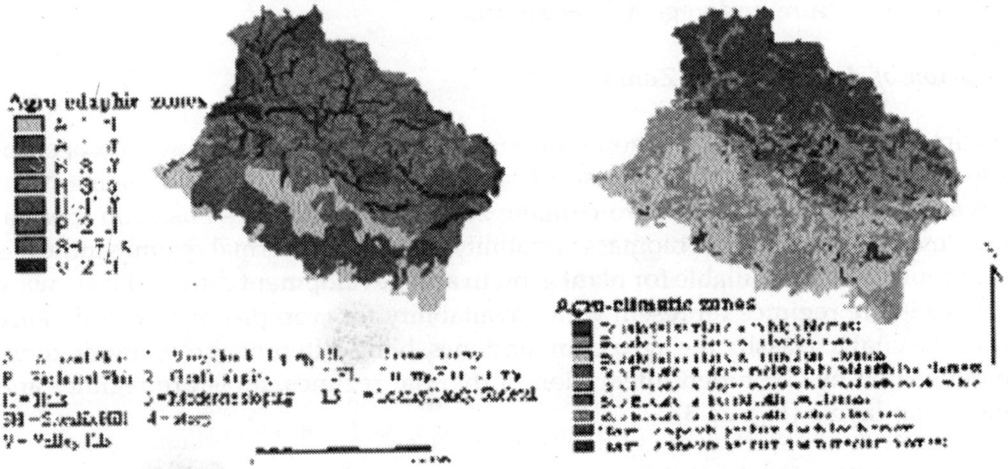


**Fig. 21.4:** Characteristics of agro-edaphic and agro-climatic zones

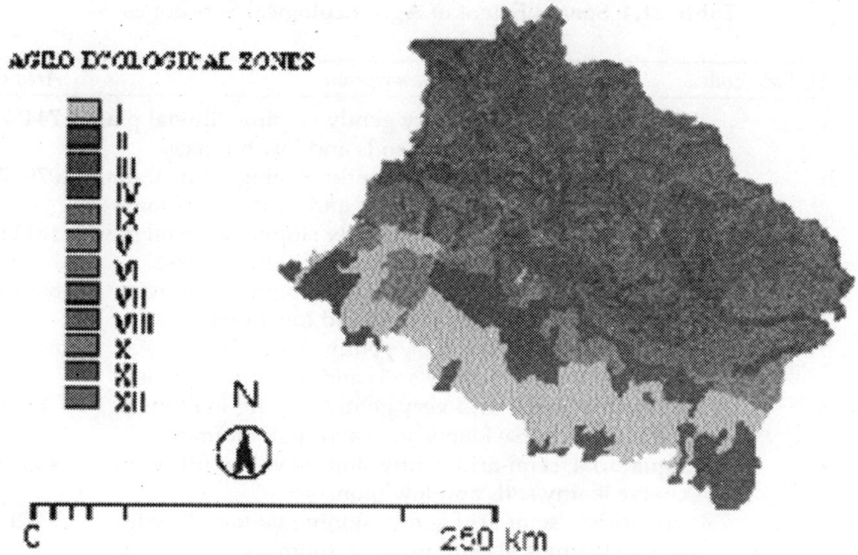


**Fig. 21.5:** Agro-ecological zones

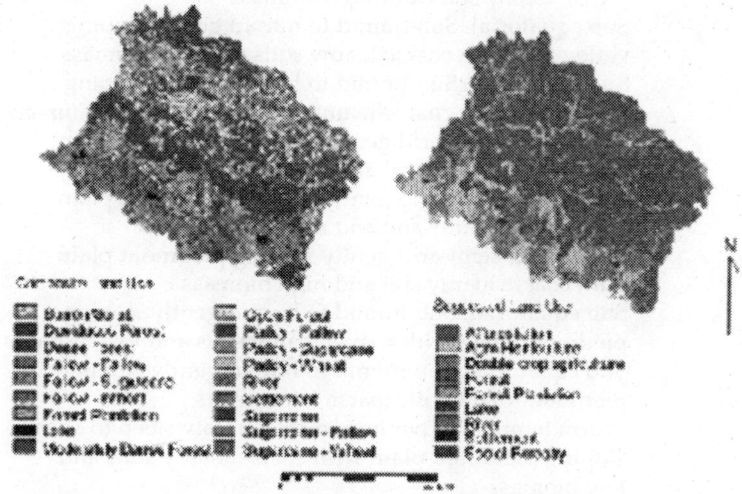


**Fig. 21.6:** Suggested land use based on AEZs and present land use

cropping with possibility of two and three crops such as paddy—wheat or sugarcane—wheat (Table 21.4). Further sub-ecological zones are reclassified by GIS aided integration in which sub-zones are clubbed into main agro-ecological zones. Therefore, twelve agro-ecological zones (AEZI to AEZXII) are identified in the study area. The spatial distribution of these zones are presented figure 21.5. The area covered ranges from 0.54 per cent in AEZ X to 25.15 per cent in AEZ XI. The whole hilly portion falls in AEZ VIII whereas lower alluvial plain in AEZ I and AEZ II (Table 21.5). A suitable land use (Fig. 21.6) plan for sustainable use of land resource for the Kumaon region was suggested. based on characteristics of AEZs and existing landuse pattern.

**Table 21.4:** Spatial Extent of Agro-Ecological Sub-Zones

| *Sl.No.* | *AEZ* | *AE Sub-Zone* | *Description* | *Area (ha)* | *(%)* |
|---|---|---|---|---|---|
| 1. | I | a | Equatorial, semi-arid very gently sloping alluvial plain with loamy to fine loamy soils and low biomass | 74487.48 | 6.50 |
| 2. | I | b | Equatorial, semi-arid very gently sloping alluvial plain with loamy to fine loamy soils and medium biomass | 107997.1 | 9.42 |
| 3. | I | c | Equatorial, semi-arid very gently sloping alluvial plain with loamy to fine loamy soils and high biomass | 10111.92 | 0.88 |
| 4. | II | a | Equatorial, semi-arid very gently sloping in alluvial plain with coarse loamy soils and low biomass | 80015.28 | 6.98 |
| 5. | II | b | Equatorial, semi-arid very gently sloping in alluvial plain with coarse loamy soils and medium biomass | 64135.22 | 5.59 |
| 6. | II | c | Equatorial, semi-arid very gently sloping in alluvial plain with coarse loamy soils and high biomass | 2371.58 | 0.21 |
| 7. | III | a | Equatorial, semi-arid gently sloping valley fills with coarse loamy soils and low biomass | 46335.98 | 4.04 |
| 8. | III | b | Equatorial, semi-arid gently sloping valley fills with coarse loamy soils and medium biomass | 24758.47 | 2.16 |
| 9. | III | c | Equatorial, semi-arid gently sloping valley fills with coarse loamy soils and high biomass | 77.76 | 0.01 |
| 10. | IV | a | Sub equatorial, Sub-humid to humid gently sloping valley fills with coarse loamy soils and low biomass | 34531.08 | 3.02 |
| 11. | IV | b | Sub equatorial, Sub-humid to humid gently sloping valley fills with coarse loamy soils and medium biomass | 11631.71 | 1.01 |
| 12. | V | a | Equatorial, semi-arid gently sloping piedmont plain with coarse loamy soil and low biomass | 42151.25 | 3.68 |
| 13. | V | b | Equatorial, semi-arid gently sloping piedmont plain with coarse loamy soil and medium biomass | 34266.01 | 2.99 |
| 14. | V | c | Equatorial, semi-arid gently sloping piedmont plain with coarse loamy soil and high biomass | 968.43 | 0.08 |
| 15. | VI | a | Sub equatorial, Sub-humid to humid gently sloping piedmont plain with coarse loamy soils and low biomass | 7.07 | 0.00 |
| 16. | VI | b | Sub equatorial, Sub-humid to humid gently sloping piedmont plain with coarse loamy soils | 1180.48 | 1.10 |
| 17. | VII | a | Warm temperate, per humid moderately steep to steep sloping piedmont plain with coarse loamy soils and low biomass | 5444.59 | 0.57 |
| 18. | VII | b | Warm temperate, per humid moderately steep to steep sloping piedmont plain with coarse loamy soils | 6976.9 | 0.61 |
| 19. | VIII | a | Sub equatorial, Sub-humid to humid moderate steep to steep sloping Hills with loam to fine loam soils and low biomass | 123103.1 | 10.75 |
| 20. | VIII | b | Sub equatorial, Sub-humid to humid moderate steep to steep sloping Hills with loam to fine loam soils | 65662.08 | 5.72 |
| 21. | IX | a | Equatorial, semi-arid moderate steep to steep sloping in Hills with loam to fine loamy soils and low biomass | 35354.6 | 3.08 |
| 22. | IX | b | Equatorial, semi-arid moderate steep to steep sloping in Hills with loam to fine loamy soils and medium biomass | 15561.97 | 2.67 |

*(contd.)*

*(contd.)*

| Sl.No. | AEZ | AE Sub-Zone | Description | Area (ha) | (%) |
|---|---|---|---|---|---|
| 23. | IX | c | Equatorial, semi-arid moderate steep to steep sloping in Hills with loam to fine loamy soils and high biomass | 498.35 | .05 |
| 24. | X | a | Warm temperate, per humid moderately steep to steep sloping Hills with coarse loamy skeletal soils and low biomass | 2286.76 | 0.20 |
| 25. | X | b | Warm temperate, per humid moderately steep to steep sloping Hills with coarse loamy skeletal soils and medium biomass | 3990.33 | 0.34 |
| 26. | XI | a | Sub-equatorial, Sub-humid to humid moderate steep to steep sloping Hills with loamy skeletal soils and low biomass | 182201.9 | 15.88 |
| 27. | XI | b | Sub-equatorial, Sub-humid to humid moderate steep to steep sloping Hills with loamy skeletal soils and medium biomass | 106272 | 9.27 |
| 28. | XII | a | Equatorial, semi-arid moderate steep to steep sloping Hills with loamy skeletal soils and low biomass | 2940.62 | 0.26 |
| 29. | XII | b | Equatorial, semi-arid moderate steep to steep sloping Hills with loamy skeletal soils and medium biomass | 43830.09 | 3.82 |
| 30. | XII | c | Equatorial, semi-arid moderate steep to steep sloping Hills with loamy skeletal soils and high biomass | 353.44 | 0.03 |

**Table 21.5:** Spatial Extent of Agro-Ecological Zones

| Sl.No. | AEZ | Description | Area (ha) | (%) |
|---|---|---|---|---|
| 1. | I | Equatorial, semi-arid very gently sloping in alluvial plain with loamy to fine loamy soils | 192596.5 | 16.8 |
| 2. | II | Equatorial semi-arid very gently sloping in alluvial plain with coarse loamy soils | 146522.1 | 12.78 |
| 3. | III | Equatorial, semi-arid gently sloping in valley fills with coarse loamy soils | 71172.21 | 6.21 |
| 4. | IV | Sub-equatorial, Sub-humid to humid gently sloping valley fills with coarse loamy soils | 4842.13 | 4.03 |
| 5. | V | Equatorial, semi-arid gently sloping piedmont plain with coarse loamy soil | 77385.69 | 6.75 |
| 6. | VI | Sub-equatorial, Sub-humid to humid gently sloping piedmont plain with coarse loamy soils | 1187.55 | 1.10 |
| 7. | VII | Warm temperate, per humid moderately steep to steep sloping piedmont plain with coarse loamy soils | 12421.49 | 1.18 |
| 8. | VIII | Sub-equatorial, Sub-humid to humid moderate steep to steep sloping Hills with loamy to fine loamy soils | 188765.2 | 16.47 |
| 9. | IX | Equatorial, semi-arid moderate steep to steep sloping in Hills with loam to fine loamy soils | 51414.92 | 6.80 |
| 10. | X | Warm temperate, per-humid moderately steep to steep sloping Hills with coarse loamy skeletal soils | 6277.09 | 0.54 |
| 11. | XI | Sub-equatorial, Sub-humid to humid moderate steep to steep sloping Hills with loamy skeletal soils | 288474.2 | 25.15 |
| 12. | XII | Equatorial, semi-arid moderate steep to steep sloping Hills with loamy skeletal soils | 47124.15 | 4.11 |

**REFERENCES**


Carter, D.B. (1954). Climates of Africa and according to Thornthwaiters (1948) Classification; John Hopkins University Publication (in) *Climatology,* 7(14)

FAO (1996) Guidelines: Agro-ecological zoning; *Soils Bulletin.* Rome, FAO

Krishnan, A. (1988). Delineation of soil climatic zones of India and its practical applications in Agriculture; *Fertilizer News,* 33 (4).

Mavi, H.S. (1994). *Introduction of Agrometeorology,* Indian Indian edition, Raju Primlani for onboard and IBH Publishers Co. Pvt. Ltd.

Pratap, T., Pradhan, P., Lotta, P.K., Mya, S., Karim, Z. and Nakarmi, G. (1998). *Sustainable Mountain Agriculture,* MENRIS Division, ICIMOD, Nepal.

Pariyar, M.P. and Singh, G. (1994). GIS based model for agro-ecological zoning: a case study of Chitwan district, Nepal. Proc. 15th Asian Conference Rem. Sens., Bangalore, India. Vol. 1: A4-1 to A4-6.

Patel, N.R., Mandal, U.K. and Pande, L.M. (2000). Agro-ecological zoning system. A Remote Sensing and GIS Perspectiive, *Journal of Agrometeorology* 2 (1): 1-13.

Subramanian, A.R. (1983). Agro-ecological Zones of India; *Arch. Met. Geoph. Biocl. Ser* B32; 329 - 333.

Sehgal, J.L.; Vernemmen, C. Tavernier, R. (1987). Agro-climatic Engironments and Moisture Regimes in NW India - Their Applications in Soils and Crop Growth; *Research Bull.* NBSS Publ. 17, Nagpur, India, NBSS and LUP.

Sehgal, J.L., Mandal, D.K., Mandal, C. and Vadivelu, S. (1992). *Agro-ecological Region of India,* NBSS and LUP (ICAR) Publication 24, Nagpur.

Thornthwaite, C.E. and Mathew, J.R. (1955). *The Water Balance. Publications in Climatology,* Vol. 8, No.1, Drexel Institute of Technology, Laboratory of Climatology, Centerton, N.J. pp 104.

Thornthwaite, C.W. (1948). An Approach towards a rational classification of climate. *Geographical Review,* 38: 55-94.

Troll, C. (1965). Seasonal Climates of the earth. *World maps of Climatology.* ed. E. Rodenwalt and H. Jusatz Berlin: Springer – Verleg, pp 28.

Venkateshwarlu, J.; Ramakrishna, Y.S. and Rao, A.S., 1996. Agro-climatic zones of India. *Annals of Arid Zone,* 35 (1); 1-8.

# 22

# National Agricultural Market Atlas

*Hema Yadav*

## Introduction

Agricultural Marketing System involves activities and functions of movement of the produce from producing area to the final consumption. The logistics that are required between production and consumption are of dynamic nature. These logistics of different kinds relating to space and time are real determinants of the marketing costs. The quantification of the spatial movement of the produce from one location to another can improve the whole scenario of agricultural marketing. This is an important activity for efficient, innovative and modern market planning. Thematic presentation of spatial movement and the related data on geographical locations helps understanding the grassroots level problems of marketing.

The Government of India constituted an Expert Committee on strengthening of agricultural marketing in the country under the chairmanship of Shri Shankarlal Gugu. Expert Committee on Agricultural Marketing as well as the sub-group of Inter-Ministerial Task Force on Agricultural Marketing, Government of India (2002) has proposed I.T. Application in agricultural marketing. Sub-group has proposed following major recommendations on I.T. Application in agricultural marketing. These are (a) Setting up of value added network services, Information Kiosks in rural areas; (b) promotional E-Catalogue for Commodity Profiles; (c) Farmer advisory services in the fields of agricultural marketing, (d) National Atlas of Agricultural Markets.

Accordingly, the Institute initiated the pilot research on the project of preparation of Atlas was taken up. The atlas encompasses various dimensions of data directly or indirectly related to agricultural marketing.

National Atlas of Agricultural Marketing would be "data intensive" and informative model for planning and decision-making. The Atlas is a cartographic and thematic exercise of the quantified data. It has the advantage of presenting the dynamics of Information in visual form. Since "seeing is believing" the visual impact of placement of data on maps sounds more clarity of the data and leaves long lasting impressions. This all together help dissemination of information in more remembrable and friendly environment.

The "Information Revolution" fueled with high speed, low cost, user-friendly software, helps remove of geographical barriers. Inflow of information, thanks to Internet, has changed the landscape of Information Technology. Application software like Geographical Information System (GIS) has percolated down to various fields of agricultural marketing, particularly in movement identification of commodities. The GIS technology and Global Positioning System (GPS) with input of real time data from remotely sensed gadgets would be the backbone of the proposed Atlas.

**Information for Atlas**

Efficient Agricultural Marketing System needs strong backward and forward linkages. The backward linkage means inter-sharing of information in an integrated manner at different stages, like the production, seeds, fertilizers and market. Forward linkages comprise the information with respect to infrastructure available, *e.g.* market and its facilities, means of transport, storage, processing, pledge-finance, location of the markets, ports, price realization, etc. Hence, the back-end database will have diversity with vast base. Various socio-economic variables pertaining to rural areas are also important to be included. Proposed Market Atlas model will have following domains:

- Multi-Database (Socio-Economic, Spatial, Non-Spatial)
- Relational Database (for all secondary data)
- Geomatic Technology (RS, GIS, GPS)
- Distributed System for Internet

***Multi-Database***: This kind of database requires a systematic and inter-sectoral approach. The Meta database standards are simply a common set of terms and definition that describe the spatial and non-spatial data.

- What data is available?
- From where to find the data?
- How to access the data?

The information needed to create a metadata is often readily available, when the data is collected. A small amount of time invested in making metadata base strong, in the beginning of the project, may save time, resource and material for future. Details of information required for proposed Atlas are as under:

- Agricultural Production
- Marketable Surplus
- Facilities like Godowns and Cold Storage, Grading etc.
- Various Systems of Sales
- Demographic Features of Agriculture and Agricultural Marketing
- Credit Facilities

- Trends in Arrival and Prices
- Market Location Details
- Shortest Route for Transportation
- Distances from other Markets
- Position of State and National Highways
- Position of Road Links
- Status of Transport Network
- Level of Processing and Details of Units
- District Boundaries *vis-à-vis* Market Area
- Details of Market Functionaries
- Future and Forward Markets
- Commodity Exchanges
- Market Trend Analysis
- All Other Functional Aspects

**WEB-GIS Based Agriculture Information System**

The system provides a new approach to agricultural marketing applications. This approach involves development of tools that will strengthen marketing and bringing efficiency in disposal of commodities. Market related information and tracking of loaded transport vehicles through WEB application will make marketing modern. Key component to this approach is the application of GIS technology in various forms. GIS provides visual integration of all the data sources as well as the markets and allows farmers to identify cost effective and highest paying alternative. This approach of GIS incorporating spatial information of markets including areawise tracking, online prices, where in-house information, electric bidding, etc. is unique in itself.

**Performance of Internet GIS**

Generally instructions required by the client to initiate GIS processing are transmitted across the Internet in a compact manner. A major drawback of current Internet GIS technology is with slow performance. It takes a long time to transfer vector and image data. This can become more evident if additional analysis functions are added. A significant amount of time is spent waiting for data. Slow response usually causes loss of interest among the users.

Slow performance can be sorted-out in two ways: (a) increasing the speed of Internet connection and (b) developing more efficient Internet GIS programs. The speed of the Internet connection can be improved by using faster modems and faster communication connections. Conversely, the efficient design of the Internet GIS program will make it feasible to run even at a slower speed. The modularized design of GIS analytical tools/data, and the just-in-time delivery mechanism can allow the Internet GIS user to initially download the minimum GIS functions and data. Additional data and analytical tools can be delivered to the user as needed.

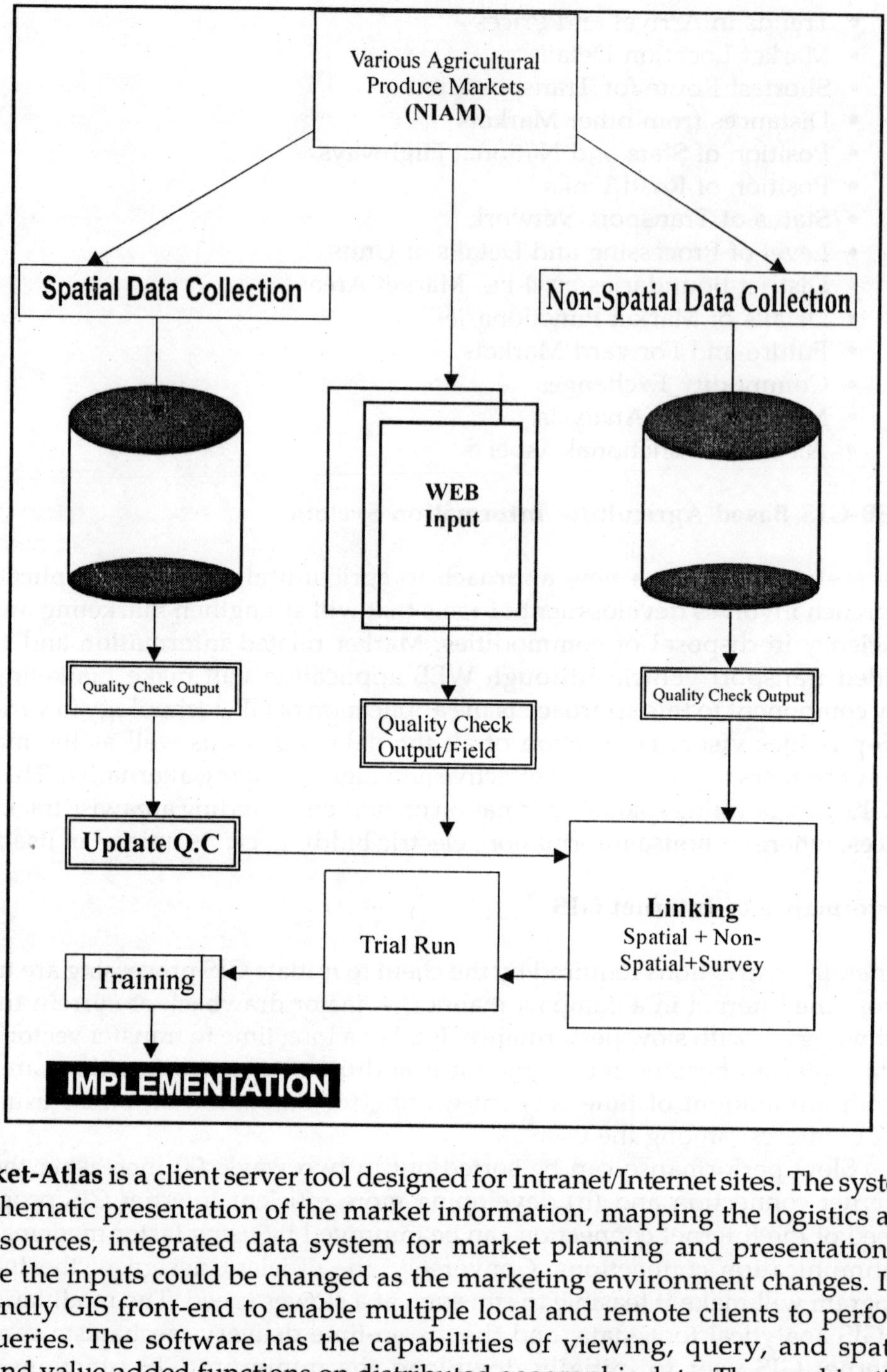


**Market-Atlas** is a client server tool designed for Intranet/Internet sites. The system provides thematic presentation of the market information, mapping the logistics and flow of resources, integrated data system for market planning and presentation of data where the inputs could be changed as the marketing environment changes. It is a user friendly GIS front-end to enable multiple local and remote clients to perform routine queries. The software has the capabilities of viewing, query, and spatial analysis, and value added functions on distributed geographic data. The combination of Web Technologies and the power of commercial GIS software enable land use and natural resource managers to analyze GIS data that resides across the Internet.

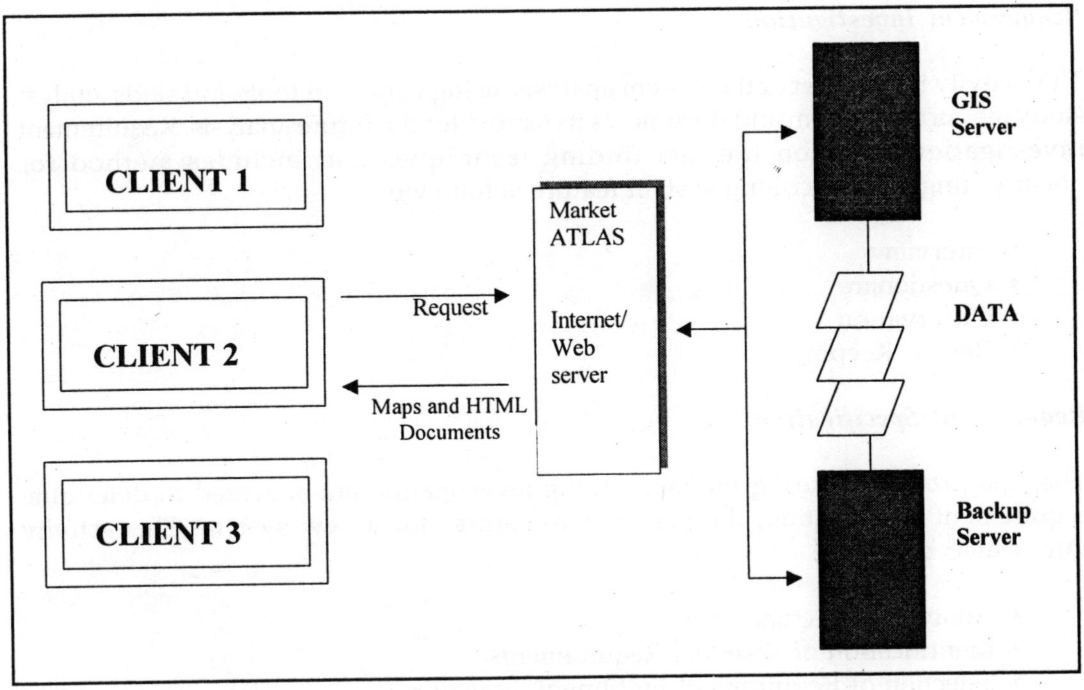


**Model Designing**

Requirement analysis involves studying the current business system to find out how it works and where improvement should be made. System studies result in an evaluation of how current methods are working and whether adjustments necessary are possible or not. A requirement is feature that must be included in the system. It may include a new way of capturing or processing data, producing information control business activity, or supporing management.

The determination requirement thus entails studying the existing system and details about it to find about what this requirement is.

**Activities in Requirement Determination**

***Requirement Anticipation***

Having had a particular business area or having encountered system in an environment similar to the one currently under investigation will influence system analysis study. Requirement anticipation can be mixed blessing on one hand, experience from previous studies can lead to investigation of areas that would otherwise be unnotices by inexperienced analyst. Having a background to know what to ask or which aspect to investigate can be substantial benefit to the organization.

***Requirement Investigation***

This activity is the heart of the system analysis, using variety of tools and skills analyst study the current system and documents its feature for the future analysis. Requirement investigation relies on the fact finding techniques and includes method for documenting and describing system feature is following:

- Interview
- Questionare
- Observation
- Record Keeping

***Requirement Specification***

The data produced during the fact finding investigation are analyzed to determine requirement specification, the description features for a new system. This activity interrelated parts:

- Analysis of Factual Data
- Identification of Essential Requirements
- Selection of Requirement Fulfilment Strategies.

**Existing System**

This is second activity of the analysis phase. In this activity, the existing system is carefully examined. The assignment of the system is done on the basis of a number of factors like what we are already having and where we want to improve, what has to be done from the scratch etc.

The present MIS system comprises the information in the form of reports. The marketing personnel daily collects the price but this information is not easily accessible to the producers. Though in our country trader community are well connected. They are well equipped with latest technology like internet, e-mail, fax, telephone etc. traders is playing with information only. The trader community also does not share the information for the benefit of the farmers and only other way our farmer community is highly unorganized and illiterate. Language is also largest barrier in dissemination of such information among the farmers.

The problem with the information which is collected daily is that there is no systematic way of dissemination of information. The directorate of marketing state agricultural marketing board and national horticultural board for horticultural commodities are collecting information and then compiled in the form of weekly, monthly reports. This information is a post mortared data having a very little value and not to percolate to the farmers. The staff for the collection of such information is also not well versed about the techniques of data collection. The information which is being collected covers a very few parameters like maximum, minimum and average price and arrivals. Price alone cannot be the only factor for better marketing of a product, other factors are also required to reduce the marketing cost like transportation, packaging, storage, grading etc.

**Proposed New System**

Project planning is very important aspect of the analysis phase. Details study activities are planned and outline of the remaining system, analysis phase activities are noted. Planning in fact is an ongoing process of system development. After having seen the need for such a system, we planned for the Web Market Atlas: The basis planning process includes planning regarding various types of database, which were to be used. Once the planning for the procedure file is done, then we established the relationship among them.

**Integrated System**

The online market information is perceived to be national data communication network where by farmers intending to sell a commodity can know the prevailing prices of the commodity in all the market yards of the country through internet. Farmers undoubtly have a need for information about probable supplies and prices in order to make decisions when planning there production and sales. With the help of information traders help growers to grow with the growth of trade. This reduces their business risk and enables them to operate profitable on lower margins. Thus it brings benefits to producers and consumers. Consumers purchases also can be influenced by market news. They can be encouraged to leave products that are in short supply and by alternatives that are plentiful. This helps in equitable distribution; universal flow pattern and reduction in fluctuation in prices.

The recent development in internet and communication has important applicability in agricultural marketing. Marketing of any produce requires fully equipped and latest market trends. This information is useful to have an access to price prevailing in the market. The markets in turn increase the bargaining power of the producers and it also enhances the efficiencies of the market. The networking concept is applicable to the wide networks of the regulated market. The networking would facilitate the flow of information and this information can be easily updated.

The MIS can have the following impact:

- It can facilitate efficient allocation of productive resources.
- It improves the bargaining power of the farmers with the traders.
- Farmers with timely and reliable information and the ability to interpret it can decide to which market they should send their produce to maximize their returns.
- The essence of the good MIS is that it should provide commercially useful information on a timely basis. Information produced on MIS is also useful for the policy makers. This should in the long run improve policy formulation as the functioning of market comes to the better understood.

Market information system is also an important component of Early Warning System for food security as it can assist in identifying areas of possible shortage and can highlight whether prices are below or above normal seasonal trends.

***Time Constraints***: We decided to complete the software by the end of December 2002 so that it could be used as quickly as possible. We were 2 software professionals and 1 map digitization experts on the team. We had to complete the project in 130 days to meet the deadline.

***Resource Constraints***: We had 3 computers, one A0 size scanner and one A0 size plotter. One computer was needed for digitization and two for programming. On the software side we had Dreamweaver, MS Access, MSDN Library, Internet Explorer, IIS, Intergraph's Geomedia Professional and Integraph's Geomedia Web Enterprise.

***Decisions***: After analyzing the constraints we found that there were over 28 maps for covering Karnataka and its 27 Districts. Other maps that we covered were road, categorised by National Highway, State Highway and other roads, Railways etc. need to be prepared for the software.

The following maps were prepared:

**Karnataka (one map)**

| *S.No.* | *Description* | *Feature* |
|---|---|---|
| 1. | State Boundary | Polygon |
| 2. | District Boundary | Polygon |
| 3. | District Headquarters | Point |
| 4. | National Highways | Line |
| 5. | Major Roads | Line |
| 6. | Roads | Line |
| 7. | Railways | Line |
| 8. | APMC's | Point |

**For Each District (27 maps)**

| *S.No.* | *Description* | *Feature* |
|---|---|---|
| 1. | District Boundary | Polygon |
| 2. | District Headquarters | Point |
| 3. | National Highways | Line |
| 4. | Major Roads | Line |
| 5. | Roads | Line |
| 6. | Railways | Line |
| 7. | APMC's | Point |
| 8. | Block Headquarters | Point |
| 9. | River | Line |
| 10. | Sub-Markets | Point |
| 11. | Town | Point |

***Various related terms used***

**Map Window:** This refers to the area on the screen on which the map is displayed.

**Feature**: Objects represented on maps, whether nature or man-made are called map features, or simply features. Each feature has a location, a representative shape, and a symbol that represents one or more of its characteristics.

**Attributes:** Information about each feature is stored in the database. This information is referred to as attribute information, or simply attributes. For example, the attributes of a Market include its Id, name, district id and so on.

**Themes:** Themes represent collection of sets of features. On the same map window we can link sets of features and their attributes and manage them together in units called theme is a collection of geographic features such as Market (Mandi), Roads, Railways, District Headquarters, towns etc.

**Legend:** Legend is known as display control center of the map window. It allows you to dynamically control the map. Through this you can control which feature class, labels appear in the map window.

**Various tools used:** Various tools have been provided. Each has a specific function as defined below:

| *S.No.* | *Name* | *Description* |
|---|---|---|
| 1. | Zoom In | This tool is used to view a small area in more detail. When you click this tool, the map expands. |
| 2. | Zoom Out | This tool is used to view a large area in small map window. It is useful when you are interested to cover greater area in a single view. |
| 3. | Fit to Normal | If this tool is clicked the map window is restored to its normal state. |
| 4. | Zoom by Rectangle | This tools is used to zoom a particular area of a map. Just click this tool and draw a rectangle at the desired area. The selected area is shown in detail. |
| 5. | Pan | This tool is useful when you want to focus attention on some other part of the map. Click the pan tool. Place this on the map window, click and drag up the cursor to any area on the map and release it. The view redraws and the point where you release the mouse becomes the center of focus. |
| 6. | Magnify | When you click this tool, a new window is displayed where you can see the details of any particular area where the mouse moves. |
| 7. | Refresh | This tool is used to bring back the map window to its default state. |

## Concept

Some of the salient features involved in application designing are:

### *Requirement Analysis*

Before the designing of any application the most important feature related is the analysis of the requirements of the application. The analysis involves the user requirement analysis, software requirement analysis and hardware requirement analysis as well. The user requirement involves the analysis of the basic requirement of the user, as to what he wants complying with feasibility and alleviate. The software requirement includes the analysis of the software provisions available with the user and the feasibility of the application being run on them and hardware requirements involve the hardware available with the user and the viability of the application being run on the system available.

### *Data Flow*

Data flow is a very imperative concept that involves the study of the data flow in the application. It principally includes the analysis of the flow of data during the various transactions and operations performed.

### *Front End*

The front end of an application is the software used for building its interface with which the user interacts. The application interface should be friendly, informative and easily navigable. The decision to use Web Pages to design the interface for the application was based on the ease and comprehensive basis that it provides for application development.

### *Back End*

The back end, which is the tool used for the designing of the database required in the application was chosen to be Microsoft Access, which provides powerful tools for managing and analyzing data.

### *Database Design*

The design of the database should be such that it provides the requisite information along with minimizing data redundancy and inconsistency.

## Design Features

### *ActiveX Data Objects (ADO)*

The ActiveX Data Objects (ADO) programming model represents the best of the existing Microsoft data access programming models. The ADO objects provides with the fastest, easiest and most productive means for accessing all kinds of data sources.

ADO is Microsoft's strategic, high-level interface to all kinds of data. ADO provides consistent, high-performance access to data, whether one is creating a front-end database client or middle-tier business object using an application, tool, language, or even an Internet browser. ADO is the single data interface one needs to know for 1- to n-tier client/server and Web-based data-driven solution development.

ADO is designed as an easy-to-use application level interface to Microsoft's newest and most powerful data access paradigm, OLE DB. OLE DB provides high-performance access to any data source, including relational and non-relational databases, e-mail and file systems, text and graphics, custom business objects, and more. ADO is implemented with a small footprint, minimal network traffic in key Internet scenarios, and a minimal number of layers between the front-end and data source—all to provide a lightweight, high-performance interface.

### *ADO Programming Model*

The various ActiveX Data Objects are:

#### *The Connection Object*

The Connection object represents a connection to the data source and allows one to execute commands. To execute any kind of command, one uses the Execute method of the Connection object. If the command returns rows, a default Recordset object is created and returned. To specify a more complex Recordset, one creates a new Recordset object, associates it with the Connection, and opens the cursor.

#### *The Command Object*

The Command object represents a command (also known as a query or statement) that can be processed by the data source. Commands can return rows or not, and if the provider is capable, can also handle parameters. The Command object is actually optional in the ADO model because some data providers cannot supply command execution, but the object is supported if the provider supports commands.

Commands can be simple SQL statements (or some other language the data provider recognizes) or calls to stored procedures in the database. Commands can then be executed using the Command's Execute method, or one can create a Recordset object and associate it with the Command object when opening the cursor.

The Command object includes a collection of Parameter objects, which is described below. If the provider can support commands with parameters, the Parameters collection will contain one parameter object for each parameter in the command. As opposed to past models, one can create Parameter objects and explicitly add them to the Parameters collection, thus allowing one to use well-known parameterized commands to avoid the sometimes very expensive operation of having the provider populate the Parameters collection automatically based on the system catalog.

#### *The Parameter Object*

The Parameter object represents a parameter of a Command. As noted in the Command description, one can explicitly create Parameter objects and add them to the Parameters collection to avoid the often unnecessary and expensive task of going to the system catalog to automatically populate the parameter binding information.

*The Recordset Object*

The Recordset object is by far the most complex (the others are simplified considerably). This is because all the cursor functionality is represented in this object.

*The Field Object*

The Field interface represents a column in a Recordset that one can use to obtain values, modify values, and learn about column meta-data.

*The Error Object*

The Error object represents an error returned from a data source. This object is actually optional because it is only needed when data sources can return multiple errors for a single method call. If a provider does not return multiple errors for a single function call, the provider just raises the error through the normal COM mechanisms that all COM servers do when called from languages like Visual Basic.

Following is the diagram showing the objects and how they relate to one another:

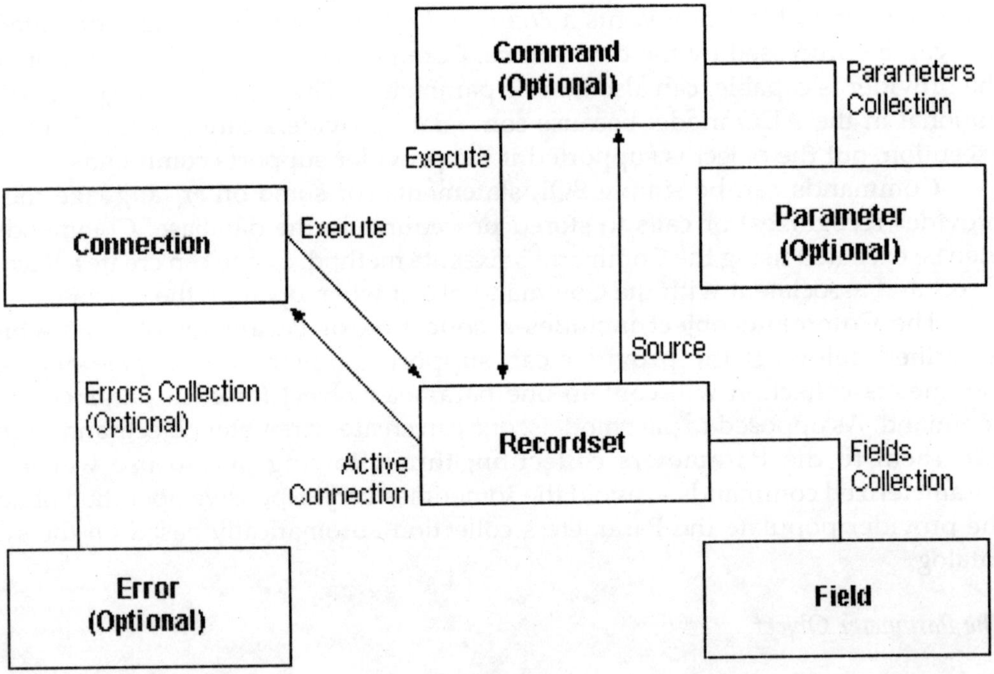

## Data Flow Diagrams

### *(i) Generating a Map*

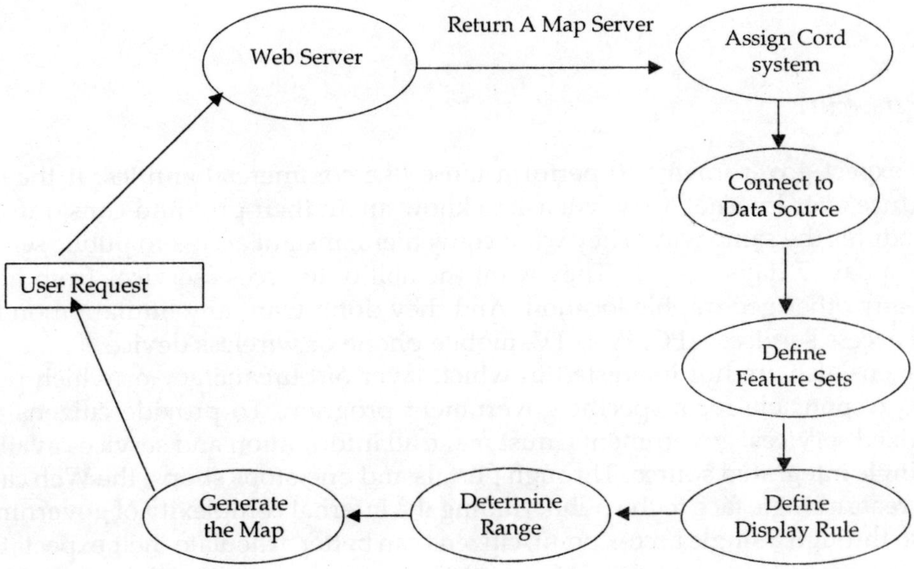


### *(ii) Online Enquiry System*

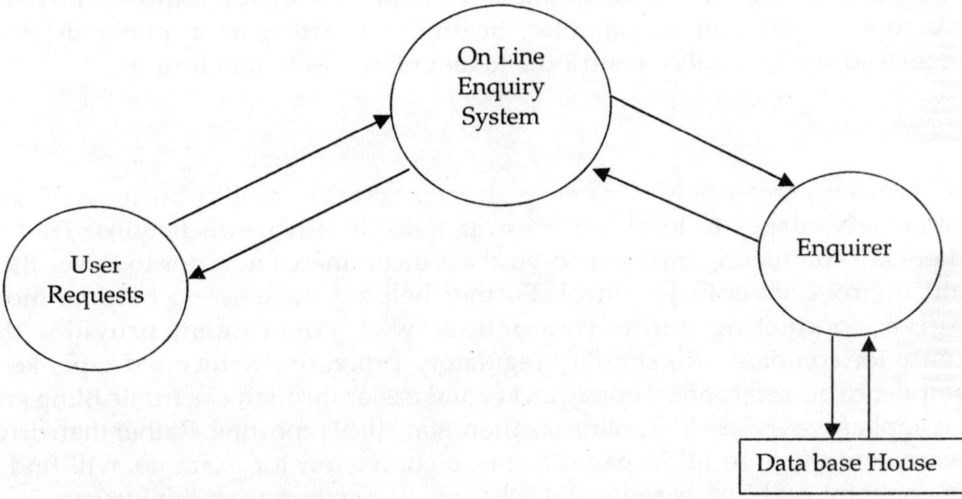


## Future Enhancemets

- Along with shortest distance, path should be traced so as to give a route also between the two APMCs.

- Comparitive study of crops arrival, maximum price, minimum price, average price etc. can be done in more ways.
- Retail prices of commodities is also to be linked with each commodity.
- Designing a control panel for modifying static entries is to be made.

### *Benefits*

#### *Citizen Perspective*

Citizens expect governments to perform more like commercial entities. If they can buy produce over Internet, they will ask to know about their pros and cons or follow the procedures the same way. They want convenient, instant access to public services 24 hours a day, 7 days a week. They want the ability to access services from home, work or any other geographic location. And they don't want any limitation on how they can access services—PC, Web TV, mobile phone or wireless device.

Citizens also are not interested in which layer of bureaucracy or which public official is responsible for a specific government program. To provide citizens with personalized services, governments must make all information and services available from a single integrated source. Through portals and one-stops shops, the Web can be used to create a single face to the public, hiding the internal complexity of government.

Also through a single access point, citizens can better articulate their expectations and needs from government. It reinforces their participation in local community life and the democratic process since they can interact with government and access public information, official documents and administrative proceedings. For those who don't have time to go to city hall or committee hearings to participate in public debates, they can instead send e-mail or contribute to an online discussion forum.

#### *Business Perspective*

When governments create new efficiencies, they also create a healthy business climate and provide advantages to local traders over those in other jurisdictions. Traders everywhere are conducting business-to-business e-commerce in order to lower their costs and improve inventory control. Further helping business to become more competitive, conducting online transactions with government provides the opportunity for companies to simplify regulatory processes, reduce red tape, keep legal compliance and start operations quicker and easier through electronic filing and various compliance services like online taxation, statistical reporting. Rather than drive to a government office to fill in paper forms, a contractor, for example, will find it easier to apply for building permits and schedule inspections over the Internet.

Governments can further create a healthy business environment by ensuring the right infrastructure is in place to make it easy for traders to go online. Traders operating in jurisdictions with high-speed bandwidth Internet connection at a reasonable price will have advantage over others that don't. And with the right level of consulting and financial support, local traders can conduct online transactions, leveraging their high-speed connections to create new business opportunities.

The delivery of integrated, single-source public services creates opportunities for business and government to partner together. The accounting industry and tax office, for example, could build on their existing relationship and work together to provide added value services for citizens and businesses filing online tax returns. Partnering with private sector can also help government establish a Web presence sooner and cheaper. The most important e-government projects are funded by Public Private Partnerships where there is a shared approach to the provision of services, and to the risks and rewards involved.

*Government Perspective*

Governments can change citizens' perceptions of poor quality public service and regain public trust and confidence by putting the citizen at the center of any service improvement initiative. Rebuilding the customer relationship requires the provision of services in an altogether different way, without long waits and cumbersome procedures. Customer-centric organizations achieve greater success both within the government and in serving the public. They are better able to provide easier public access to services, increase service volume and reduce employee's time spent on non-customer activities.

Recognizing that a single person rarely performs an entire public service process, citizen-focused organizations combine Customer Relationship Management (CRM), workflow and Internet technologies to empower government employees as knowledge workers. Employees must be able to use case management tools, understand any given situation and the governing laws and regulations, and then they must be able to deal with the case and take decisions. This involves having concurrent access to files on their 'electronic desks', ensuring a uniform processing of cases, shorter response times and less burdensome administrative duties.

Knowledge workers can work as team and move smoothly between different documents and databases on a variety of back-end systems. Desperate legacy networks are characteristic of the traditional stovepipe approach to government, resulting in single services and single systems. The difficulties of integrating service delivery across agencies can be overcome through the exploitation of open technologies, developing new integrated service processes on the Internet to virtually mirror agencies and, finally, through proper business process re-engineering of government organizations.

## REFERENCES AND BIBLIOGRAPHY

Awad M. Elias: *System Analysis and Design*
Black Book: Asp 3.0
Evangelos Petroutsos: *Mastering in VB 6.0*
Korth F. Henry: *Database System Concepts*
Press Man S. Roger: *Software Engineering*
Sarang G. Poornachandra: *ASP* (Hand Book)

# 23

# Land Resource and Land Capability Analysis

## Role of Geomatics

*Ali Mohammad*

The innovation and diffusion of computer technology at large scale has created a healthy impact on the well-being of mankind. Computer has provided a new dimension to information processing specifically related to the processing of information of the earth and its natural resources. New technologies have emerged because of capability, *i.e.* GIS (Geographical Information System) which is a tool which allows synergism of map data and tabular data in the most efficient manner. Remote Sensing Observations from satellites provide data on the earth and its natural resources in a spatial format. The easy availability of data in temporal domain from RS techniques provides a new dimension to spatial information processing and monitoring the features of the Earth and generates a large volume of information.

The technology over the last two decades, has matured to provide valuable and timely information for a variety of resources themes/areas such as yield information, drought monitoring and assessment, flood monitoring and damage assessment, land use—land cover and related changes mapping becomes possible, marine resources survey, urban planning, mineral targeting and environment and environmental impact assessment. The integration of information derived from RS techniques with other datasets—both in spatial and non-spatial format provides tremendous potential for characterization and analysis of earth surface features which is needed for planning and development purposes.

Land Capability classifications processes is highly complicated but needed for the balanced land use planning. Land capability survey before the emergence of RS/GIS was a process not to be completed within time and within the spatial scale for planning purposes. The major processes of land capability classification is related with following major components:

(1) Gradient and slope analysis on higher and lower elevations is needed be causes relief and elevations are not only the criteria for the determination and evaluation of the region for various purposes such as agriculture, forestry,

grazing land, settlement, construction of transport network and the land to be left for recreation purposes etc. Slope analysis either through the H.H. Bennet or Raisz method or any other techniques is a time taking, difficult and practically impossible for planning purposes in view of the time and space. Since land capability is a dynamic aspect, hence the completion and collection of data should be in time and for the whole space under planning, which is not possible through the slope analysis of Bennet method.

(2) Soil profile, structure, texture, nutrients value, soil moisture retaining capacity survey is highly needed for the analysis of land for the use of special purposes. The methods being used by the Bureau of soil survey for land use planning is now more or less failed to give the reliable and authentic results. With the emergence of RS/GIS sources the problem is solved and an authentic planning can be done in a highly reliable manner.

The usefulness and practicability of land capability classification has been done for the Kashmir valley with the final result that for a small region like Kashmir valley the traditional method (Bennet) is no doubt suitable but practically not suitable in other regions of the country where heterogeneity is more.

## Land Capability Classification

The land in Kashmir is proving inadequate for the burgeoning population that is dependent on it. It is now being realized that all wasteful uses of land should be discouraged and rational land policy should be chalked out to face the challenge. More and more emphasis is now being laid on using land according to its best capability. This is especially significant in view of the growing competition between different uses of land, such as residential, recreational, industrial and agricultural. An overemphasis on one use might have a chain reaction on the other. Besides the different competitive uses, the land in the Valley is continually menaced by severe erosion and water logging, both seriously inhibiting its productive uses. A hopeful feature is that a large chunk of this land is, reclaimable provided a rational strategy is chalked out in this respect.

For all this, and for ensuring rational use of land in the future, a regular survey to establish the capability of different types of land for optimal uses is badly needed. An empirical exercise is, however, being attempted here to identify the generalized capability classes based on site, properties of soil, proportion of land under different slope categories, exposure to erosion hazards and dominant land use. Various methods have been developed to categorize land into capability classes by different authorities. These include some of the most sophisticated techniques, such as the one developed by the US National Resources Planning Board which integrates the whole gamut of physical, economic and institutional factors into a single scheme, as well as most rudimentary ones. The present study is based on a method developed by Bennet which is based on site (altitude, degree of slope and drainage) climate, soil type and major land use. It is suited to such areas as the Kashmir Valley where non-availability of classified information on specific aspects of land inhibits the application of more rigorous methods.

*Factor in Land Capability.* According to Bennet, the land capability classifications are based on the following criteria:

(i) Soil type;
(ii) Degree of slope;
(iii) Erodability of surface soil or degree of erosion;
(iv) Drainage; and
(v) Predominant land use pattern.

The soils of the Kashmir Valley reveal great variation in texture, permeability and fertility status. These typological differences have been used as a variable in the identification of land capability classes. Areas characterized by steep slopes are liable to erosion the intensity of which will depend on the nature of terrain and vegetal cover.

*Land Capability Classes:* The land of the Kashmir Valley has been classified according to its capability, using Bennet's methods based on site peculiarities and physical factors. Primarily, two major categories have been distinguished lands suited to cultivation, and lands, not suited to cultivation.

The first category can further be grouped into four capability classes. The lands unsuitable for cultivation, on the other hand, lend themselves to a classification into three groups. The general characteristics of these seven land capability classes are described.

### A. Lands Suited to Cultivation

*Class I:* The soil of class I lands is deep, highly fertile and mostly consists of best quality loams and clayey loams. The texture, however, gets heavier with increasing depth. The soil has a high retention capacity and is rich in humus. Class I lands are found in areas which are either flat or characterized by gentle slope. These lands are by and large free from the hazards of erosion or water-logging and the physical environment favors their maximal utilization.

The area occupied by class I lands, although it extends over the entire length of the Valley on either side of the Jhelum, has its main expanse in the central part consisting of parts of Srinagar, Pulwama, Badgam and Sonawari Ganderbal tahsils.

The fertility status of these lands can be further raised if farmers are Induced to take to new methods of farming and land management and their capacity use inputs enhances.

*Class II*: The class II lands are characterized by coarse-textured soil: The subsoil is heavy and gets heavier with increasing depth. The surface soil has low to moderate permeability; low at the subsoil levels and very low at the substratum. These lands are not liable to water logging or erosion, although lands in sloping areas suffer from moderate erosion. Substantial areas in Kulgam, Sopore and Handwara tahsils are dominated by class II lands. They occur in two compact blocks—the southern one lies in the Kulgam tahsil while the northern extends over parts of Sopore and Handwara tahsils. Terrace cultivation is a common phenomenon on the periphery of the northern block.

*Class III:* The class III lands form a narrow belt along the karewa uplands. The land is dominated by soils with a coarse texture and there is a marked increase in the degree of slope. The permeability decreases with depth. This class of land is bordered by extensive marshy tracts in the northern part of the Valley. Both erosion and water logging impose serious limitations on its use. The utility of these soils can be improved if erosion is controlled and suitable drainage methods are introduced to combat the problem of water logging.

The main concentration of class III land is found in Sonawari, Baramulla, Badgam, Pulwama and parts of Kulgam tahsils.

*Class IV:* The class IV lands are found along the karewa slopes with their tongues extending higher up in the side valleys of the Jhelum. The slope increases rapidly with the result that cultivation is possible only on terraces using rigorous measures of soil conservation and drainage. The soil is shallow with variable texture and permeability. The depth of the soil decreases as stoniness increases with increasing altitude.

These four classes of land under cultivation differ vastly in their cropping pattern. Rice is the dominant crop if class I lands and is alternated by maize on higher areas. Among other crops grown are barely and wheat mainly on lands irrigated by wells. Rice continues to be important on class II land as well with maize as close associate on drier tracts. Wheat and barley sharply decline in importance. Maize emerges as a principal crop on class III land with barely and wheat flourishing on lands provided with ensured water supply. A major proportion of the class IV land is also devoted to maize, although rice is also grown extensively on well-watered terraces.

### *B. Lands not Suited to Cultivation*

*Class V:* Lands with predominant uses such as grazing and forestry have been categorized as class V. They are characterized by steep slopes and contain shallow, stone-studded soils. The low-lying sloper on rainy aspects are thickly forested. Above the triclinic lie grazing lands which are sued as summer pastures by transhumant groups. The soil of these margs is fairly fertile with a high moisture-holding capacity.

*Class VI*: This class consists of lands with steeper slopes and poorer soil which has no capability even to support the growth of vegetation. They consist of which remain covered with perennial snow have been rocky wastes mainly in the higher precipices of the Pir Panjal and the Great Himalaya ranges.

*Class VII:* The higher slopes of the mountain ranges which remain covered with perennial snow have been subjected to rigorous glaciations in the past and are occupied by glaciers even today.

## NOTES AND REFERENCES

Notable among these are S.P. Raychaudhuri, *et al.*, Final Report of All India Soil Survey Scheme, ICAR Bull, 73, 1957, and Soils of India, ICAR, 1963, pp. 105-110: Generalized information on the soils of Kashmir Valley and the surrounding mountains is inserted in a number of soil maps of India such as Z.J. Schokalskya, "The Natural Conditions of Soil Formation in India," in B. Polynov (ed), *Contributions of the knowledge of the Soils of Asia,* No.2, Leningrad, 1932, pp. 53-153; D.N. Wadia, M.S. Krishnan and M.P. Mukherjee, Mem, GSI, 1935, plate XXV; S.P. Raychaudhuri, *NIS Bulletin*, No. 3, 1954; and the soil map of the National Atlas of India.

"Stray information on soils is available in Bate's *Gazetteer* as well as in Drew and Lawrence. The work done by Lawrence during his settlement operation in Jammu and Kashmir is exceptionally useful and is available in the fifteen assessment reports. These reports cover, among other things, "rates of assessment, the mode of classifying and valuing soils, and many facts bearing on the past revenue administration of Kashmir."

# 24

# Environmental Pollution: Land and Water

## A Threat to Food Security

*Ali Mohammad*

In all the predominantly agricultural countries, no other environmental crisis affects our survival as that of water and soil degradation. Water and soils are our basis for existence and if the productive soils and water are lost, at the accelerated rate at which they are degraded, the human survival may be at stake.

Soil degradation can be defined as the rate of adverse changes in soil quality resulting in decline in productive capacity of land due to processes induced mainly by human intervention (UNEP, 1992). Oldeman (1988) defined it as process, which lowers the current and/or future capacity of the soil to produce. There are various estimates of the extent of soil degradation. At global level soil and land degradation affects about one-fifth of the world's population, 70 per cent of all dry lands amounting to 3-6 billion hectares and one-quarter of the total land area of the world. According to UNEP (1986), it is estimated that over the millennia as much as 2 billion hect. of land that was once biologically productive have been rendered unproductive through soil degradation. Further more, the current rate of soil degradation is estimated at 5 to 7 million hect./year. On the whole among all the resources available, soil is found as the most degraded and posing a serious threat for the survival of human beings. Since soil degradation is accepted as a human induced phenomenon, in addition to its estimation of the extent, it is of interest to know, the reasons for degradation and the use at which these degraded lands are being put to.

An attempt has been made to assess the present land utilization patterns and degradation level of the Indo-Gangetic divide area of India, which is characterized as semi-arid. In this region the production process cannot be started in an useful manner without the human interference. As it is observed that human activities leads to unfavorable change in the physical, biological and hydrological resources and leads to the certain state of degradation in resource scarcity region in a much faster manner as compared to the tropical-sub-tropical and temperate regions. The region under study is termed as semi-arid where without human interference it is impossible to start the crop-agriculture except of pasturing activities. With the introduction of irrigation system and Green Revolutionary measures the region is highly developed as compared to other regions of India but at the cost of high level of soil degradation. The 'soil fertility rating index' of the region is better as compared to other regions of India but today without the chemical fertilizer supplement and plenty of water agricultural performance is not possible in a sustainable manner.

Within the last 50 years doses of fertilizer has increased to the extent that input-output ratio is going to be equal and the farming community is in doldrums either to continue with such an agricultural practices or not. Since the region is very significant in maintaining the present food security of India, therefore, an alternative is needed and planning should be based on checking the land degradation on priority bases and a model should be developed for the adoption in most of the regions of the world.

The productivity level of the study area is the highest in India comprising 30 districts of India occupying eight per cent of the gross cultivated area, providing 16 per cent of the total food grain production of the country.

From agricultural point of view the region in characterized as follows:

(a) Highest level of productivity ranging between 3000-4000 kg/hect.
(b) Occupying 8 per cent of the cultivated area (GCA) providing 16 per cent of total requirement of food grain of India.
(c) All the cultivated area under irrigation and flood irrigation is the major characteristics—which is a major source of soil degradation.
(d) Crop-rotation is (Rice-wheat) the major cause of soil degradation.
(e) Both vertical and horizontal fertility of the soil is badly affected.
(f) Fertilizer intake per hectare is the highest and productivity output per kg of fertilizer intake has declined from 7 kg to 3 kg through per kg input of fertilizer from the last two decades.
(g) Spread of high yielding variety seeds has reached to the saturation point with major drawback *i.e.* rice and wheat in rotation exploiting the specific soil nutrients.
(h) Input output ratio is reaching towards a dangerous turn, *i.e.* both are going to meet together if such practices are continued.
(i) Farmers are facing the problem of profit and loss and thinking to adopt the traditional pattern of agriculture.

These consequences are largely related with the environmental degradation—soil and water. Water use and management is another aspect to be studied with special reference to its sustainability and continuation of the existing cropping pattern.

The depredation and pollution is a major concern for the developing countries because of the rapidly growing population, low level of technology and shortage of resources. The rapid increase in greenhouse gases in the atmosphere, large-scale deforestation and its impact on bio-diversity, land degradation and pollution have become local as well as global concern. Locally, the impact is felt in the changes in climate, agricultural productivity and loss of biodiversity, social patterns and culture etc.

**Role of Remote Sensing and Geomatics**

The term Geomatics relates to the technology dealing with the character and structure of spatial and non-spatial information, its methods of acquisition and qualification, analysis, management, display and dissemination, as well as the infrastructure necessary for the optimal use of the information.

Geomatics is a synergism of various disciplines—Geographical information system (GIS), computerized data basis and applications, computer science, graphical processing, cartography, photogrammetry, statistics, remote sensing etc. The applications of geomatics pertain to real world problems of management of natural and man-made environment and of the objects related to it. This would encompass the fields of natural resources management, resources planning and decision-making etc. Geomatics has to be at the core of sustainable development efforts with specific utilities for:

(a) Organizing integrated spatial and non-spatial data bases using GIS tools in a systematic manner. The spatial data consisting of maps from remotely sensed data and also conventional sources would have to be input and organized on a standard cartographic reference. The non-spatial data consisting of numeric attributes in respect of socio-economic characteristics from census and other sources—most of which would be on the administrative hierarchy of the region, say village-taluk-district-ward-municipality etc.

(b) Integration or the synthesis of the spatial and non-spatial information within the framework of a coherent data model and linkages between the different datasets. This involves the bringing together of diverse information from a variety of sources, requires the effective matching of similar entities and demands information consistency across the datasets.

(c) Generation of spatial outputs, supported by table charts, to help the developmental planning and decision making.

# 25

# RS-GIS Application in Road Mapping

## Examples from Thiruvananthapuram District, Kerala

*Mahamaya Chattopadhyay*

### Introduction

Advances in space science have facilitated extraction of earth related information easier. Laborious field surveys are replaced by inputs from satellite derived data. Improvements in resolution of imaging have helped tracking small areal/linear features of great public importance. Road transport network development is considered to be one of the keys to rapid modernisation and development, especially for better traffic efficacy. Other than the dense network of roads in cities, roads are very often built in suburban areas to accelerate the development and economic growth of these areas. The initial planning of a road route is usually dictated by political, social, and economic factors and is not well balanced by geo-technical feasibility, environmental factors or route efficacy. As a consequence, problems are often encountered at the time and after road construction. Efficacy of road transport is ensured by selection of terrain-friendly alignments selection and scientific traffic-routing. In terrains of undulations and thick canopy like in Kerala, remote sensing products remain the only dependable tool for extraction of road network, canal system etc. with sufficient precision. Absence of a dependable road map was a constraint in the preparation of computerised database of the road network of the district. The Kerala Highway Research Institute approached us with the idea of preparing a digitized road map of the district using latest remote sensing technique. The work has been accomplished through an exercise of digital road mapping of the Thiruvananthapuram district using PAN images of 1:25,000 scale (1999) along with concurrent field verification. Utility of remote sensing data for alignment correction have also been proved in the case of some segments of the proposed Express Highway from Kasaragod to Thiruvananthapuram. Based on analysis of Geographic Information System (GIS) and interpretation of aerial photographs, physical suitability of the terrain was evaluated and alternative route corridor was suggested from a stretch extending from Nediyasala to the south of

Pizhaku. This study demonstrates the importance of remote sensing and GIS application in road mapping and in road alignment correction.

**Study Area**

Trivandrum district in Kerala has an area of 2192 $km^2$ and a total road length of 1842 km according to the Kerala Public Works Department (PWD). Road density amounts to 0.84 $km/km^2$. Road network development is less in the eastern part where terrain is not hospitable. In order to elucidate the terrain-road network interrelationship, a sample area near Vellanad, 22 km east of Thiruvananthapuram city was selected for detailed investigations. The district has an average annual rainfall of 1943 mm and average temperature of 28°C. Although, 9 months are climatically wet (Evaporation is less than rainfall). 80 per cent of the monsoonal rainfall precipitates in a span of 6-7 days.

Geologically, Trivandrum district forms a part of the south Indian granulite terrain. The area is covered by Precambrian crystalline rocks, sedimentary rocks of tertiary age, laterites and recent to subrecent sediments. The Precambrian rocks include the charnockites and the khondalite group of rocks. They are unconformably overlained by the sedimentary rocks of Warkalli formation. Laterites cap both the crystallines and the sedimentary rocks. The low lying areas and the river valleys are covered by recent and subrecent sediments.

**Study Components (using RS)**

(a) Preparation of base map in 1:25,000 scale from Survey of India (SOI) toposheets (1967-69) including coordinates, important roads and road junctions, railwayline, airport, agglomerated settlements/townships and major drainage.
(b) Incorporation of detailed inputs from the latest IRS-IC PAN (1999) imagery of 1:25,000 scale, resolution of 5.8 metre.
(c) Preparation of quadrant maps.
(d) Designation of NH, SH, Bypass, MDR (Major District Roads), ODR (Other District Roads) and their labelling. Demarcation of road segments in abbreviated formats deriving their names from the original PWD list like Nmd section for Nedumangad, Vka for Varkala section, Kzm for Kazhakuttam and so on (Table 1).
(e) Preparation of PWD section-wise road map.
(f) Verification of roads of individual segments with the KHRI and PWD officials.
(g) Field verification.
(h) Draft map preparation.

**Using GIS**

(a) Digitization of maps
(b) Integration
(c) Supply of data in different map sheet quadrants as well as map join for the district in Arc/Info format/sectionwise.

**Table 25.1:** PWD road network in Trivandrum district

| *Segments/Section* | | *No. of roads* | | | |
|---|---|---|---|---|---|
| | | *SH* | *MDR* | *ODR(includes VR*)* | *Length (km)* |
| City road-I S | CR I | — | 2 | 35 | 42.732 |
| City road-II | CR II | 1 | 1 | 51 | 77.402 |
| City road-III | CR III | 1 | — | 47 | 90.710 |
| Cantonment | Cnt | — | 16 | 17 | 64.629 |
| Kazhakuttam | Kzm | — | 12 | 20 | 141.990 |
| Malayinkizh | Mlh | — | 8 | 9 | 70.720 |
| Attingal | Atl | 1 | 4 | 20 | 99.871 |
| Kilimanoor | Kmr | 1 | 5 | 16 | 125.570 |
| Varkala | Vka | — | 2 | 33 | 124.728 |
| Nedumangad | Nmd | 4 | 9 | 13 | 145.090 |
| Palode | Pld | 1 | 6 | 8 | 107.960 |
| Venjaramoodu | Vjd | 1 | 5 | 17 | 133.305 |
| Aryanad | Ard | 1 | 2 | 22 | 151.140 |
| Kanjiramkulam | Kjm | — | 16 | 12 | 124.590 |
| Kunnathukal | Kkl | 1 | 14 | 12 | 165.268 |
| Parassala | Psa | — | 9 | 23 | 85.394 |
| Neyyattinkara | Nta | " | 10 | 16 | 79.915 |
| **Total** | | | | | **1831.014** |

VR: Village Road

* Discrepancy in length of PWD roads in Eco.Rev.1999 and the enclosed Table is due to non-inclusion of certain roads as suggested by PWD officials.

*Source*: Kerala Public Works Department, Road Register.

## Methodology

Various work components were successfully attempted through judicial usage of technique of remote sensing and GIS. In this background it is apt to describe RS and GIS in short.

***Remote Sensing (RS)*** literally means sensing from a distance. It may be defined as the collection of information about an object without being in physical contact with the object. Remote sensing data (acquired from various sensors onboard the orbiting satellites) because of its repetitive, multi-spectral and synoptic nature, have been proved to be extremely useful in number of application projects such as mapping forest land, preparation of hydrogeomorphological maps including the work under discussion. The successful launching of IRS series of satellites (IRS-1A/1B, P2/1C/1D) have made it possible to sustain all these activities.

***Geographic Information System (GIS)*** is an information system designed to work with data referenced by spatial or geographic coordinates. It is also defined as "an organised collection of computer hardware, software, geographic data and personnel designed to effectively capture, store, update, manipulate, analyze and display all forms of geographically referenced information". It is meant for preparing, presenting and interpreting facts that pertain to the surface of the earth. Comprehensive GIS operations require means or devices for:

- Data input from maps, aerial photos, satellite imagery, survey and other sources, *i.e.* data sources and input devices (digital files, scanner, digitizer)
- Data storage, retrieval and query, *i.e.* computers
- Data transformation, analysis and modeling including spatial statistics, *i.e.* specialised software.
- Data reporting, such as maps, reports and plans, *i.e.* output devices (plotter, printer...)

***Integration of RS and GIS*** as amplified above RS provides synoptic, multi-spectral data which is capable of studying varied inhospitable terrain while GIS is capable of analysing, integrating spatial data and above all can implement criteria based models for the management and development in various applications.

## Output

Eighteen map quadrants covering the district featuring road network have been digitized in Arc/Info environment. Transformation and projection of the coverage have been attended to and the coverages were formatted. Roads, NH, railway, state highway and waterbodies have been labelled and annotations have been shown as different layers. Map joining has been done with edge matching. Final output has been prepared in four forms: (a) map showing road network for the entire district, (b) map showing city and cantonment sections, (c) maps of individual quadrants and (d) section-wise road map. Separate thematic maps on drainage, road network, slope and geomorphology were prepared for a sample area near Vellanad using imagery. These themes were digitized. Digital terrain model (DTM) of the study area was created using PC-TIN software based on 10 m—interval contour from the Survey of India toposheets of 1:25,000 scale. Overlay of selected themes was accomplished on two-dimensional and three-dimensional surfaces to establish the terrain-road network interrelationship. Road network has been overlayed on the geomorphology map. Alternative route has been suggested for a sample road to ensure minimal valley filling. Road network has been draped over 3-dimensional surface created from TIN. Greater concentration of settlement in a linear pattern discerned from PAN imagery along these road sides, especially in the valley crossings indicates accentuated reclamation consequent on road development. Express Highway alignment from Kasargod to Trivandrum has been accomplished for two segments using imagery and application of GIS.

## Conclusion

Apart from road mapping the study documents that a general relationship between terrain features and road alignment could be deciphered from suitable satellite imagery. PAN images were found highly useful in identification of the road network of Thiruvananthapuram district and preparation of the first ever digital atlas, enabling PWD to create an authentic database on roads for maintenance, repair and better utilisation. This is an example where the integrated approach of remote sensing and GIS could be utilised effectively for monitoring, management and development of road network.

## SUGGESTED READINGS

Akinyede, J.D. (1990): A geotechnical concept for highway route planning. *ITC Jour.* Spl. Issue, No. 3, Remote Sensing and GIS. Enschade, The Netherland, pp. 262-269.

CESS Report (2001): Preparation of section-wise digitized road map of Trivandrum district using PAN imagery. Submitted to the Kerala Highway Research Institute, Thiruvananthapuram, Centre for Earth Science Studies, Thiruvananthapuram, p. 78.

Chattopadhyay Mahamaya (2002): Application of remote sensing and geographic information system in infrastructure development. *Photonirvachak,* Jour. Indian Soc. of Remote Sensing, Vol. 30.

Chattopadhyay, S. and Mahamaya Chattopadhyay (1995): Terrain analysis of Kerala, Concept, Method and Application. Tech. Monograph No. 1/95, State Committee on Science, Technology and Environment, Government of Kerala, Thiruvananthapuram, p. 62.

# 26

# Application of Fractal in Geomorphology

*Srikumar Chattopadhyay*

## Introduction

Fractal concepts are increasingly being applied in earth science research across the world. Earth's topography evolved through tectonic activities modified by erosion and sedimentation. It is complex, chaotic and yet there is orderliness as shown by the applicability of fractal statistics. There were studies on fractal dimension of various geographic features like coastline, drainage basin perimeters, sink holes etc. These studies demonstrated that many relations in geomorphology had a fractal nature.

It was in 1967 that Mandelbrot wrote an article "How long is the coast of Britain?—Statistical self-similarity and fractional dimension" in *Science* (vol. 156, pp. 636-638). Subsequently he published several articles on fractals and in 1982 he published the book *"Fractal Geometry of Nature"* (Freeman, New York, NY, p. 468). Mandelbroot's work brought out that as a subject "fractal" is concerned, at least superficially, with spatial phenomena. His book dealt in part simulation of terrain and in part with measures of length and area of geographic features. In 1980s, general interest articles also appeared in variety of journals and magazines in USA dealing with the term 'fractals' albeit loosely. For geomorphology also this decade of 1980s witnessed considerable expansion of literatures specifically applying fractal concepts. Several topical and methodological studies were conducted on fractal geomorphology and by 1992 a special issue of *Geomorphology* (an international journal of pure and applied geomorphology) was published on "Fractals in Geomorphology".

In India we are yet to start any work on application of fractals in geomorphology, although, Dr. Dimri of NGRI, Hyderabad initiated several studies on application of fractals. He edited a book on "Application of fractals in earth sciences" and currently editing a special issue of the *Indian Journal of Marine Sciences* devoted to fractal applications. It is high time that geomorphologists in our country take interest in this branch.

### *What is Fractal?*

According to Oxford Dictionary of Earth Sciences, fractal is "A geometric entity which has basic pattern that is repeated at ever decreasing sizes. Fractal patterns are not able to fill spaces and are hence described as having fractal dimension. Fractals occur frequently in nature, such as in forked lightning or in chaotic system". Terming something fractal implies a distinctive relationship among structures observed in different scales although the fractal is scale invariant. **Fractal dimension is a measure of roughness of geographic features or it is the descriptor of the complexity of surfaces.** It differs from other measures of 'roughness' in that it provides a description theoretically independent of the sample—most other measures of roughness are sample dependent. Thus a consideration of fractal models provides broader benefit for geomorphic study: comparison of features observed in different scales; to question why a particular form should appear the same in all scales of inspection; and to ask why that is not the case for other particular forms. The numerical value of fractal dimension (D) may be the most important single parameter of an irregular cartographic feature, just as the arithmetic mean and other measure of central tendency are often used as the most characteristic parameters of a sample.

### *Calculating Fractal Dimension*

Many different methods have been used in the earth sciences to determine fractal dimensions. We discuss here the commonly used divider method. The divider method based on a technique of measuring length with a fixed step length (G) and counting the number of steps (N) taken to cover the entire length is widely used in geomorphology. The measured length L (G) is equal to N * G. The fractal dimension D of a line can be derived from the equation:

$$L(G) = MG^{1-D} \qquad (1)$$

Where L(G)—the estimated length of line measured with a unit length of G (step length),

M—positive constant.

D must exceed 1 for a line to be fractal. This indicates that as step length G decreases the measured length L(G) increases as a power function of G. The complexity of the line increases with larger value of D and when D value approaches 2 the line becomes so complex that it fills the plane.

With only two step lengths D can be estimated using the equation 2.

$$D = \log (N_2/N_1)/\log (G_1/G_2) \qquad (2)$$

Where $N_1$ and $N_2$ are the number of steps of lengths $G_1$ and $G_2$ needed to trail the line, and $G_1 > G_2$.

When the step lengths are more than two D is estimated by a commonly used method known as Richardson plot in which L(G) is plotted against G in a log-log paper and a best fit line is drawn through the scatter of points in case of linear distribution. D is equal to 1 minus slope of the regression line. Another method to estimate D when more than two step lengths are used is to plot log N against log G. If the plot appears linear, a best fit line is drawn through the scatter. In this case D is equal to the absolute value of the slope of the regression line.

## Fractal Dimensions of Selected Coastal Water Bodies in Kerala—A Case Study

Coastal water bodies in Kerala are either coast parallel or coast perpendicular. This orientation is partly linked to their genesis. The coast parallel water bodies are situated in the coastal alluvium (Recent sediment) belt and coast perpendicular water bodies are foundered river mouth mostly encircled by laterite surfaces. The present study is one of the trial efforts to work out fractal dimension of perimeters/shorelines of four selected coastal water bodies in Kerala. One of these four water bodies is completely surrounded by laterites. The objectives of this study are (i) to examine the scope of using fractal dimension to classify the coastal water bodies as linked to their genesis and (ii) to select a suitable method for calculating fractal dimension based on the results obtained from this analysis.

### *Study Area*

Kerala is located in the south western corner of Indian peninsula. More than 60 per cent of Kerala's geographical area is covered by laterites. The narrow coastal plain of Kerala is characterized by a series of estuaries and lagoons. These water bodies cover an area of around 460 sq. km. Four water bodies, namely, Paravoor (area 5 sq.km), Ashtamudi (54 sq.km), Kayamkulam (20 sq.km) and parts of Vembanad (160 sq.km) were taken up for the analysis. The Vembanad, running parallel to the coast, is the largest lagoon in the west coast. Its formation is linked to the emergence of barrier bar, an unique feature of Kerala coast, and transgression and regression of sea. Conversely, the Ashtamudi estuary is a foundered river mouth controlled by horst and graven structure. Kayamkulam is similar to the Vembanad. Paravoor is genetically closer to the Ashtamudi, however, this water body has a coast parallel northern arm.

### *Methodology*

At the present instance, we followed all three methods discussed under section 1.2 and worked out the fractal dimensions of four brackish water bodies in the coastal belt of Kerala. The rationale behind applying all three methods is to compare the results and suggest the appropriate one for undertaking similar studies. Perimeters of all four water bodies considered for this study were drawn from the Survey of India topographical maps in 1:50,000 scale. The step lengths used were 250m, 500m, 750m and 1000m.

### *Results and Discussion*

Fractal dimension (D) of perimeters of all four water bodies calculated based on two-step length method showed that the D values were 1.01, 1.03, 1.17 and 1.37 for the

Vembanad, Paravoor, Kayamkulam and Ashtamudi respectively. D values exceeded 1 in all four cases indicating fractal nature. However, in case of the Vembanad and Paravoor the values are only marginally above 1 and therefore calling them fractal may not be very appropriate. In view of this observation we applied other two methods to work out D values for examining fractal nature of the perimeters.

Following Andrle both log N-log G and Richardson plots [log L(G) - log G] have been constructed for each of the four water bodies. All four log N-log G plots appeared linear (Fig. 26.1). Therefore, least square regression analyses were performed (Table 26.1). The high $R^2$ (coefficient of determination) values (0.99) of the regressions seemed to indicate that the log N-log G relations were indeed linear and hence the lines were statistically self-similar.

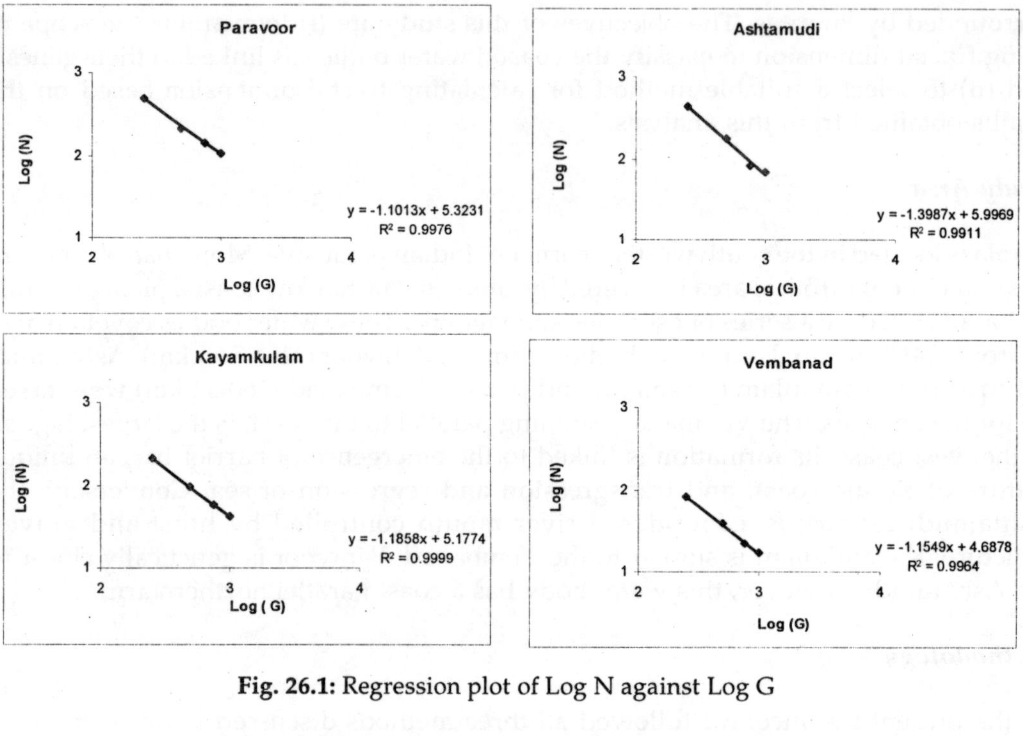


**Fig. 26.1:** Regression plot of Log N against Log G

**Table 26.1:** Regression equations for all four waterbodies

| *Waterbody* | *Regression equation* | $R^2$ | *D value* |
|---|---|---|---|
| Paravoor | Log N = 4.69 - 1.15G | 0.996 | 1.15 |
| | Log L(G) = 4.63 – 0.14G | 0.851 | 1.14 |
| Ashtamudi | Log N = 6.00 – 1.40G | 0.991 | 1.40 |
| | Log L(G)= 6.00 – 0.40 G | 0.891 | 1.40 |
| Kayamkulam | Log N = 5.18 – 1.19G | 0.999 | 1.19 |
| | Log L(G)= 5.14 – 0.18G | 0.972 | 1.18 |
| Vembanad | Log N = 5.32 – 1.10G | 0.998 | 1.10 |
| | Log L (G) = 5.19 – 0.09G | 0.701 | 1.09 |

In case of Richardson plot, the trend was also linear for all four cases with some variations (Fig. 26.2). The $R^2$ values here are lower than those under the log N-log G plot for all the waterbodies and it is the lowest (0.70) for the Vembanad. It is observed that the Vembanad and the Ashtamudi recorded the lowest and the highest D value respectively under all three methods. The origin of Ashtamudi is distinctively different from the other three water bodies. Paravoor, also a foundered mouth has a northern arm developed by barrier bar formation. This waterbody is of mixed origin. The Vembanad, Kayamkulam and northern arm of Paravoor are confined to recent sediments dominated by sand and clay material and therefore, their perimeters/ shorelines are not so complex like Ashtamudi, which is surrounded by laterite cliffs, a result of block faulting. In case of Paravoor, D value increases from 1.03 to 1.13 when northern arm confined to the sandy belt is excluded from calculation in the two step method. It may be inferred that coast perpendicular water bodies have a tendency to register high D values. These waterbodies are surrounded by laterites. Therefore, an apparent relationship between roughness and material composition of shorelines of water bodies is evident. These observations illustrate the importance of studying fractal dimension of coastal water bodies.

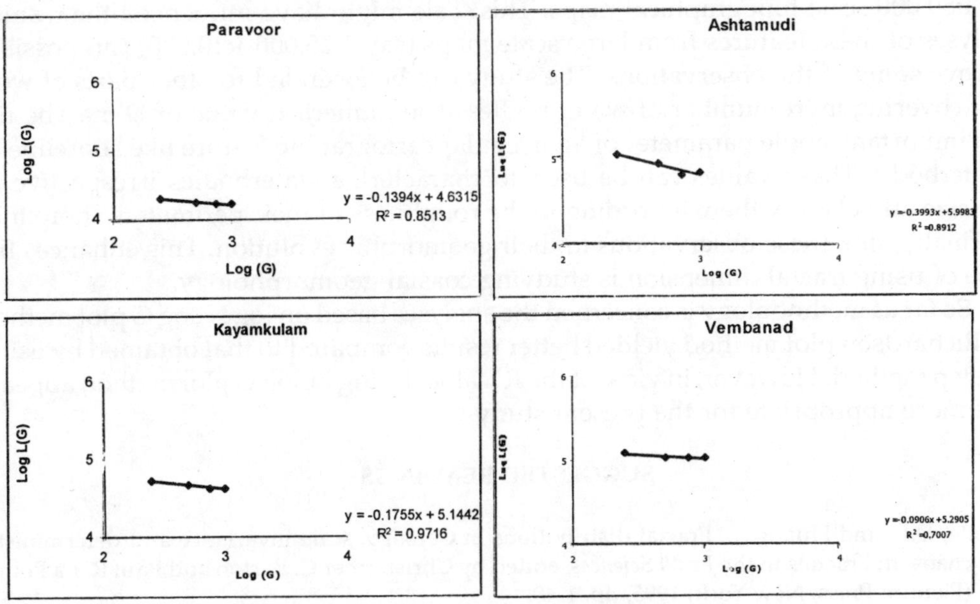


**Fig. 26.2:** Regression plot of Log L(G) against Log G

Perimeters corresponding to different step lengths provided in Table 26.2 indicate that in general, perimeter increases with decrease in step lengths as is usual for a feature to be fractal. However except Kayamkulam in all other three cases perimeters decreased when step lengths were reduced from 1000m to 750m. Perimeters increased again for the step lengths of 500m and 250m. Lower $R^2$ values corresponding to three water bodies (Paravoor, Ashtamudi and Vembanad) in case of Richardson's plot may be attributed to this distribution.

**Table 26.2:** Perimeters of the water bodies corresponding to different step lengths (Values in metres)

| *Step length* | *Paravoor* | *Ashtamudi* | *Kayamkulam* | *Vembanad* |
|---|---|---|---|---|
| 250 | 20,250 | 110,250 | 53,000 | 121,250 |
| 500 | 17,500 | 87,000 | 48,000 | 106,500 |
| 750 | 16,500 | 63,000 | 42,750 | 105,750 |
| 1000 | 17,000 | 68,000 | 42,000 | 108,000 |

## Conclusion

Perimeters/shorelines of coastal waterbodies, irrespective of their size, appear to be of fractal nature. D value ranges from 1.09 to 1.40. The Ashtamudi estuary has the rougher edges compared to other three as indicated by higher D value. Geologic factors might have contributed in this context. Although data set is smaller, there is a clear trend. It is suggested that the possibility of utilizing fractal dimension in differentiating coastal waterbodies according to their genesis may be explored. There is a need to use larger data set, large scale map and image. The base map used for the present analysis was 1:50,000 scale topographical maps. This scale might have influenced the results. Analyses of these features from large scale maps (say 1:25,000/1:10,000) can possibly improve some of the observations. The study can be extended to other parts of west coast covering more number of water bodies. The numerical value of D may be the most important single parameter of an irregular cartographic feature like shoreline of a waterbody. These values can be used to characterize waterbodies irrespective of their size and classify them according to the roughness of their perimeters/shorelines and finally, link these observations to their geomorphic evolution. This enhances the scope of using fractal dimension is studying coastal geomorphology.

So far as methodology is concerned the analyses based on log N-log G plot method and Richardson plot method yielded better results compared to that obtained by using two step method. However, in view of the $R^2$ value the log N-log G plot method appears to be more appropriate for the present study.

### SUGGESTED READINGS


Turcotte, D.L. and Huang, J., Fractal distributions in Geology, scale invariance and deterministic chaos. In Fractals in the *Earth Sciences,* edited by Christopher C. Barton and Paul R. La Pointe (Plenum Press, New York) 1995, pp. 1-40.

Dimri, V.P. (ed). *Application of Fractals in Earth Sciences* (A.A. Balkema, USA/Oxford and IBH Publishing Co., New Delhi), 2000.

Vedanti, N. and Dimri, V.P., Fractal behavior of electrical properties in Oceanic and Continental crust. *Indian Journal of Marine Sciences,* Vol. 32 (2003) pp. 273-278.

Snow, R.S. and Mayer, L. (ed). Special Issue: Fractals in Geomorphology, *Geomorphology,* Vol. 5 (1992).

Mandelbrot, B.B., How long is the coast of Britain?—Statistical self-similarity and fractional dimension, *Science,* 156 (1967) pp. 636-638.

Mandelbrot B.B. The Fractal Geometry of Nature, *Freeman,* New york, 1982

Goodchild, M.F., and Mark, D.M., The fractal nature of geographic phenomena. *Annals for the Association of American Geographers,* Vol. 77 (1987) pp 265-278.

27

# Remote Sensing and Natural Resource Management

*S.R. Singh Yadava*

## Introduction

The growing importance of resources in university curricular and in the planning of natural resources have created a demand for a systematic introduction to the subject. There is at present time a pressing need for considerable planning of natural resources of the world, a need created by two factors:

1. In the first place, there is entirely internal problem of population increasing at a greater rate then the means of production are able to satisfy the increased demand. The burden on land has reached its limits. Unless and until we create alternative sources of employment, it will not be possible to withdraw a portion of sui plus population from land. In view of this, if in the interim stage we aim at improving their standard of living, the remedy lies in providing additional opportunities for supplementary occupation.
2. Secondly, practical for planning of natural economy in particular and the full use of natural resources, the response to adjustments of nature depends essentially on the technical skill and degree and civilization of the human groups living in various regions of the world.

## Development of Resources

In 1953 the American scholar, E.W. Zimmermann wrote a book *'World Resources and Industries'* and defined resources and estimated the mutual relations between industries and resources.

Resources, in fact, throws light upon the following: distribution and conservation of resources of the world in one area from the another, practical relationship of economic activities, distribution of resources, their sufficiency and utility, and the various aspects of protection from them. In fact, it studies the part of economic action.

E. Huntington has divided the economic acts of man into four classes known as material needs, main occupation, efficiency and higher needs and economic activities of man depend upon the progress of civilization.

***Resource—Introduction***

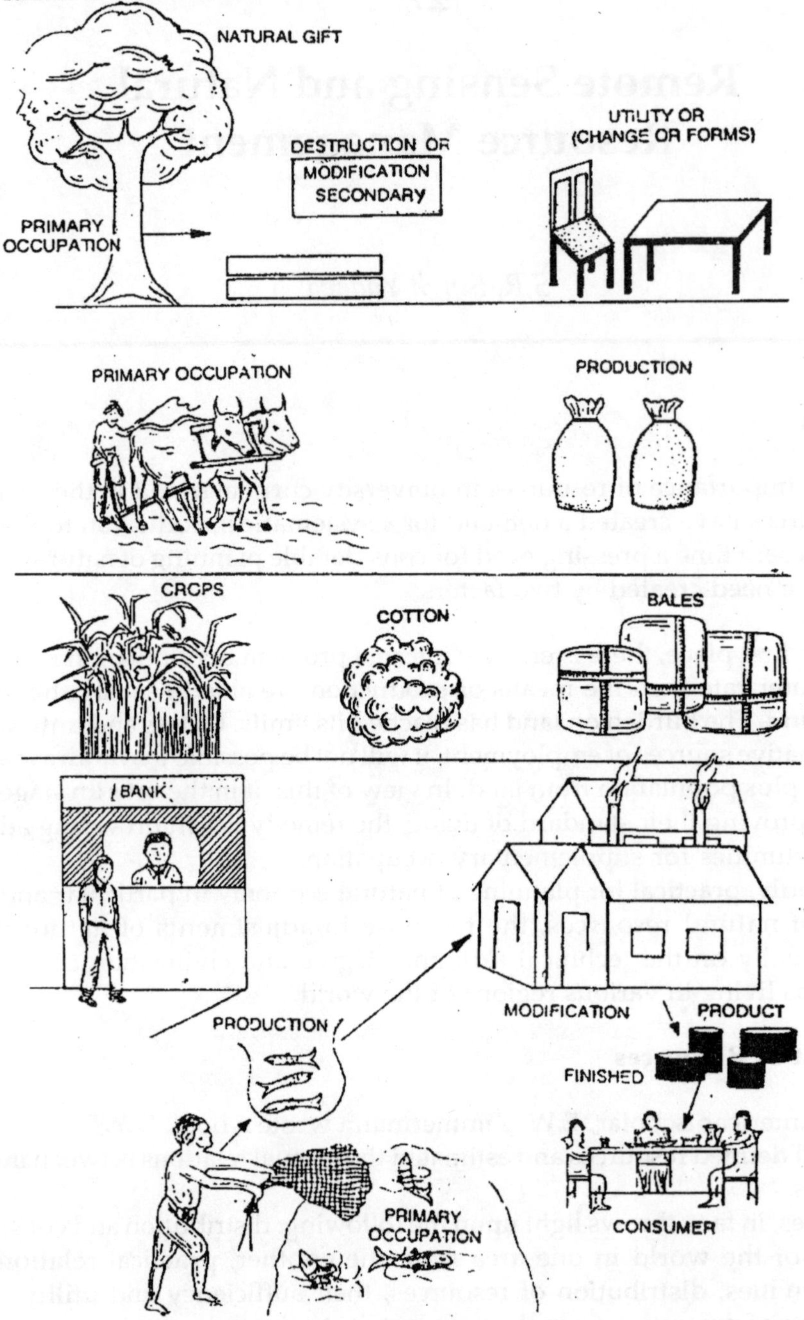


**Fig. 27.1:** Occupational Cycle from Primary to Tertiary Stages

Under the resources we discuss the distribution of all kinds of organic and inorganic matter, resources activities, institution customs, capability and the various means of livelihood. Agriculture and trade are the chief means of livelihood. So the resources have three stages based on productivity and development of culture and raw materials.

1. Primary Production or sometimes also called primary occupation where man have direct relation to the production-chief of which are: agricultural, pasturing, lumbering, fishing, mining hunting etc.
2. Secondary occupation is the occupation where man modified the original product such as paper and pulp is the modified form of forest, bridge or pig iron is the product of raw iron etc.
3. The third occupation is called Tertiary occupation. With the help of the tertiary occupation we changed or modified the first and secondary occupation such as banking, transport facilities or skilled labours etc. all changed the form of first occupation and secondary occupation. Fig. 27.1 shows the development of occupational cycles from primary occupation to tertiary occupation.

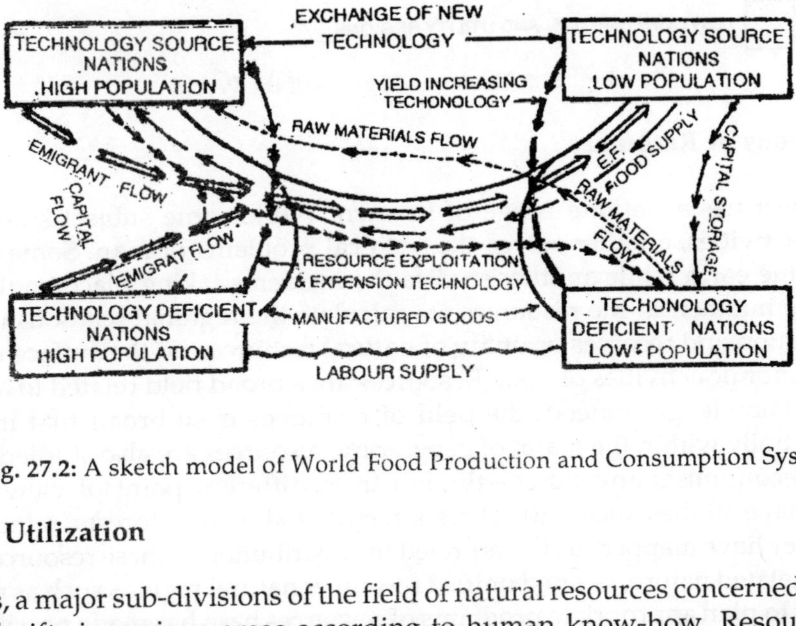


**Fig. 27.2:** A sketch model of World Food Production and Consumption System

## Resource Utilization

Resources, a major sub-divisions of the field of natural resources concerned with utility of natural gifts in various areas according to human know-how. Resources are the study of distribution and characteristics of resources which distinguish one region from another, with interest focused on utility of these natural resources rather than specific objects or processes. It is the study of differences between one region to the other regions in terms of their resources development which effects their economic characteristics. Resources means literally the description of all the accessible and available wealth of the universe. Resources are those aspects of man's environment which facilitate the satisfaction of human wants and the attainment of social objectives.

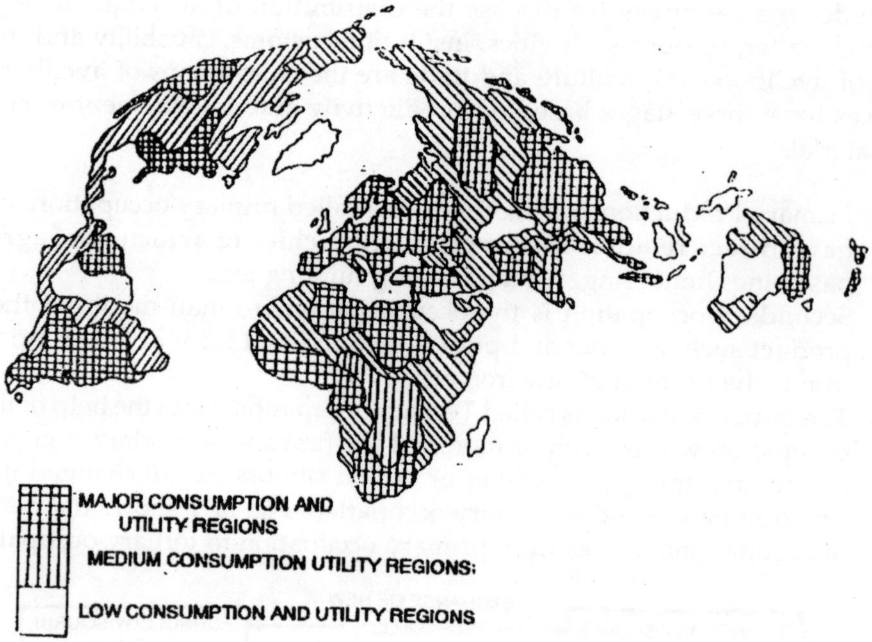


**Fig. 27.3:** Resource Regions of the World

## The Divisions of Resources

Every subject has a definite range of its own. While some subject studies human economic activities, another solves the political problems of man. Some studies the surface of the earth while another studies the incidents taking place on that surface. In the same manner, in the resources we calculate the regional relationship between the distribution and reserves or utility of natural resources on the surface of the earth and the economic activities of man. Resources are a broad field related to all branches of human knowledge. Indeed, the field of resources is so broad that it cannot be included wholly within the realm of geography; resources are also studied by natural scientists, economists and other—though from different point of view. Primarily resources have studies such natural resources as soil, water, forests, minerals etc. In addition they have mapped and interpreted the distribution of these resources, clarified their inter-related nature, defined unified resources natural regions such as river basins and helped to plan appropriate programs of resources base has made possible realistic development programs in developing countries of the world.

## Methods of Analysis of Resources

Among the several methods of studying resource, the two most widely followed are the Principle of Resource Adequacy on the one hand and the Principle of Resource scarcity on the other hand, are popular in studying the resources.

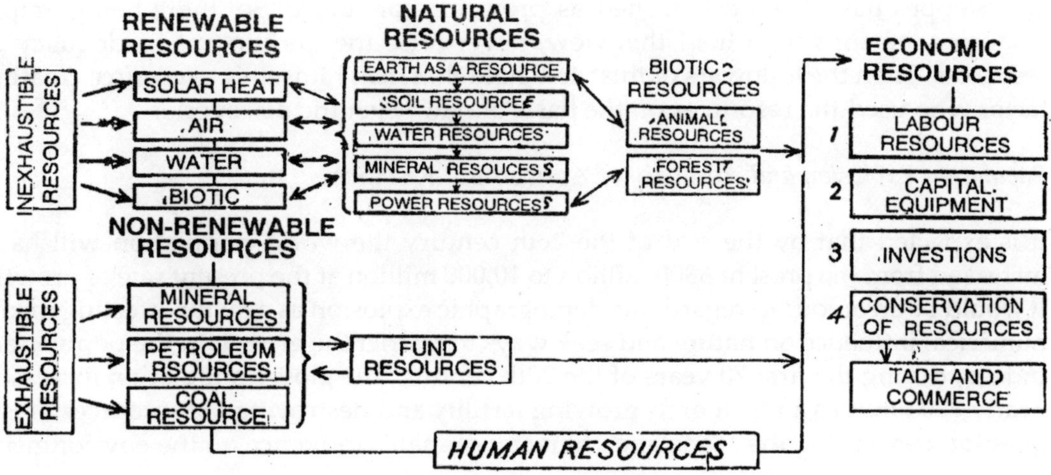


**Fig. 27.4:** Subject matter of Geography of Resources

### *The Principle of Resource Adequacy*

Russian economists and ecologists are the chief follower of this view. They maintain that there is an ample amount of resources on the earth and as there are move of new scientific inventions, artificial or substitute things will take the place of these resources. So the man of today need not worry or think that there will be dearth of resources for future generations. In fact, the area of Russia being vast, there has never been scarcity of land, nor the production is less. The density of population per km$^2$ is between 150 to 200. Crops are grown in only 15.3 per cent land of the whole area, the remaining area is left for future use. There is enough land for supporting the growing population of Russia, and the vast jungles of Siberia and the areas in Russian Khirzkistan Republic

**Fig. 27.5:** Interlinked chain of biotic communities

and Steppes have been established as provision for future. So, there being ample resources, persons who hold this view, never raise the question of inadequacy of resources. Then the followers of this view hold that man himself is a resource creating factor who used the resources on the basis of new scientific discoveries.

*Population Explosion and Adequacy of Agricultural Resources*

It is expected that by the end of the 20th century the world population will have increased from the present 6800 million to 10,000 million at the present rate of growth. It would be erroreous to regard this demographic explosion as a factor affecting man's numerical influence on nature and seek ways to restrict the growth in the population. Indeed, during the first 70 years of the 20th century, the global population increased nearly 150 times as a result of its growing fertility and destroying the resources. It is a question concerning the scope and character of man's influence on the environment.

*Adequacy of Water Resources*

There is another problem facing mankind, is that of providing an adequate supply of water. True, water resources in the form of annual river flow are fairly large and reach 7,400 cubic kilometres per annum. The share which can be taken into account for distribution is equal to 400 cubic kilometres. This should be enough to satisfy the demands of the population for 100 years or more. At the same time, some regions have a surplus of water, while other, suffer from an acute water shortage. With a population of 70 billion, the water deficient will reach 2,000 cubic kilometres. It is possible to compensate for this by controlling the river flow, extending the uniform use of water resources, utilizing purified pump water repeatedly, diverting surplus water from rivers with excessive flow to regions suffering from water shortage, developing production processes which do not require high water consumption, desalinating sea water and precipitating evaporated moisture on the ground. Work

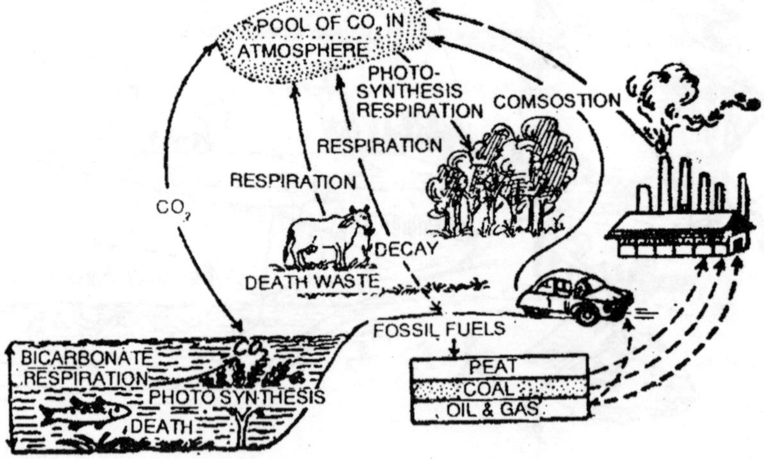


**Fig. 27.6:** Carbon cycle

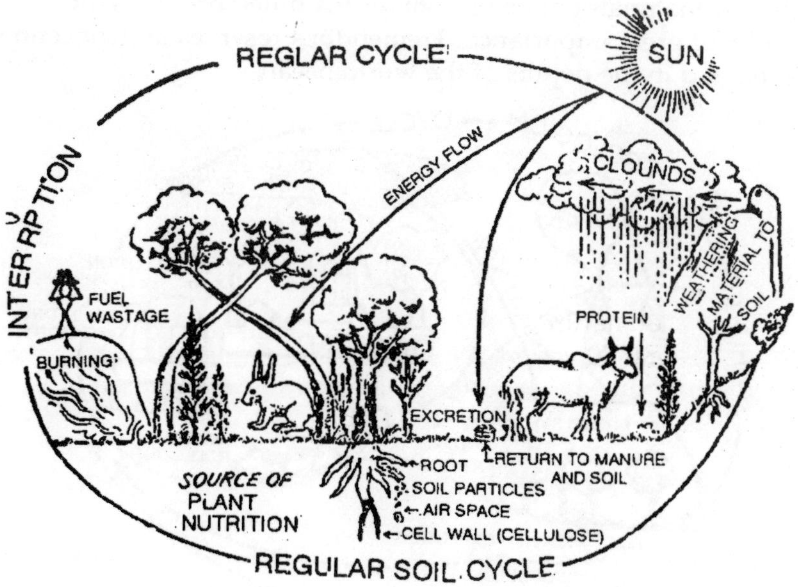


**Fig. 27.7:** Soil Cycle

in this field has already been initiated in various parts of the earth by various government agencies.

*Adequacy of Power Resources*

Population growth leads to one more problem—that of generation of power with reduced use of combustion processes. The estimates of scientists indicate that fuel combustion releases tremendous amounts of heat as result of which the heat and oxygen cycles on our planet may reach a critical stage as early as the middle of the 21st century. Although with thermonuclear power development the generation of power will be large enough to fully satisfy the demands of the population, it will be necessary to restrict its use as well as that of other traditional fuels which above all, are valuable raw materials. The use of everlasting sources of power, such as the energy of the sun, wind and tides, which do not affect the heat and oxygen cycles of the earth and do not consume water, will be extended.

*Adequacy of Mineral Resources*

There is also problem of mineral resources with the ever increasing rate of utilizing the earth's mineral wealth, they will reach their estimated life-term as the beginning of the 21st century. Different estimates have been made for the life expectancy for major minerals on the basis of different rates of consumption. However, there are other resources, such as the discovery of new deposits, fuller use of the existing ores, all-round extraction of all the useful components of rocks, utilization of waste products, etc. Secondary raw materials obtained from reconstituted products (nothing is wasted in nature) will be of great importance. Tremendous reserves are concentrated in the continental shelf and in the depths of the world ocean.

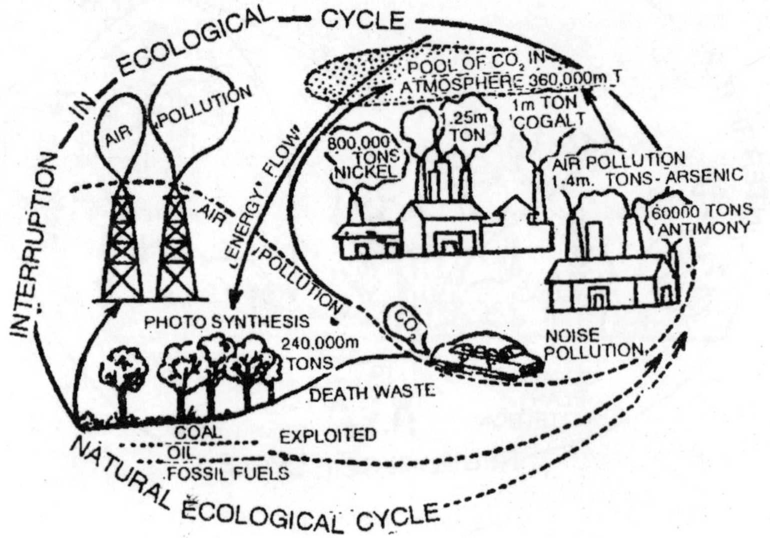


**Fig. 27.8:** Air Pollution

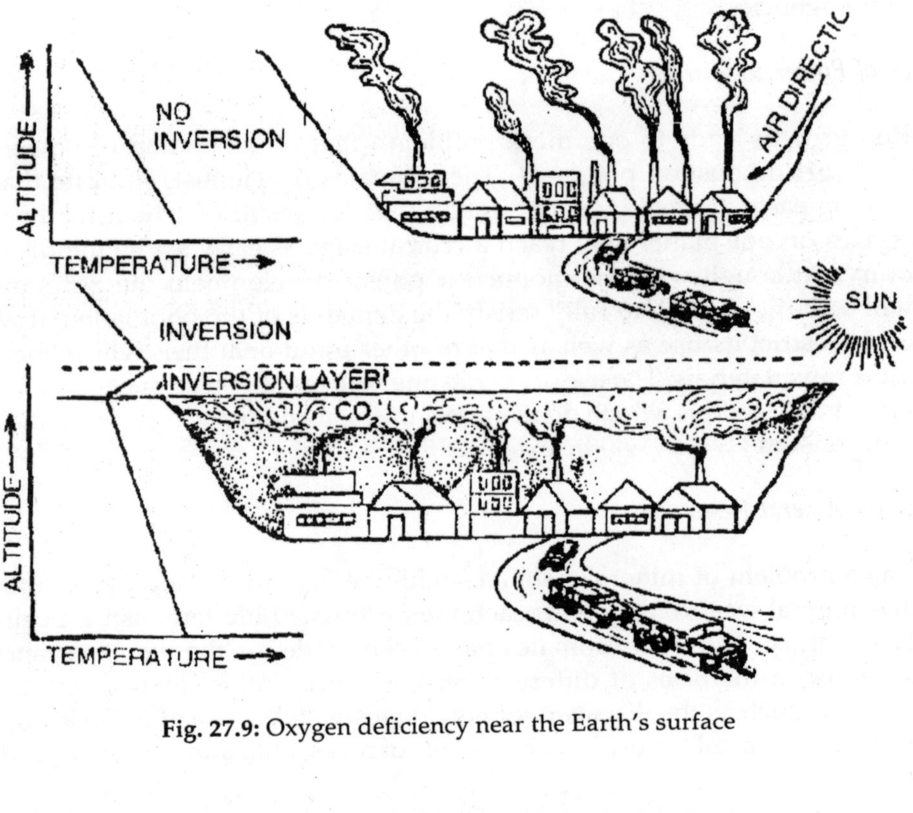


**Fig. 27.9:** Oxygen deficiency near the Earth's surface

### *Principle of Resource Scarcity*

Western scholars are the main propounders and followers of this view. The followers of this view believe that the earths area is limited and if population goes on increasing at the rate of which it is increasing today, a time is sure to come when a scarcity of mineral resources, agricultural resources, energy resources along with that of other resources will begin. These scholars believe in the principle of resource scarcity.

The problem of scarcity of resources had existed even before Thomas Malthus who wrote about it and David Ricordo analysed the effect of scarcity in terms of Diminishing Returns, while Zimmermann called it phantom pile. The resource scarcity has always been central problem in Max's sicio-political thought. Pessimists achieved respectabily when the entire question came up for a detailed analysis particularly with reference to the availability of minerals for a sustainable economic growth before the Paley Commission in the USA during the early 1950s.

### Resource Management, Eco-System and Ecological Crisis

The U.N. Environmental Conference at SIPRI (Stockholm International Peace Research Institute) brought together a large number of scientists and thinkers who were deeply concerned about the ecological degradation of the world and related problems. Experts and politicians gathered earlier for environmental crisis in effect warned all governments that between reckless wastage and thoughtless pollution mankind was moving inexorably towards ecological and economic disaster.

Environmental scientists the world over are profoundly concerned over man's abuse of nature in the name of human progress. Under the influence of the stimuli provided by nature, or as a result of the efforts man makes for satisfying his wants, the material progress is created. Land is cultivated, irrigation is provided, industries develop, rivers are bridged, roads and railways are built, towns grow and there is the whole paraphernalis of modern civilization that is born simply out of man's efforts for satisfying his wants.

Industry is belching more than 800 million tonnes of pollutants, like soot, noxious fumes, gases and chemical substances, per year into the air, and letting out millions of tonnes of chemical effluents into rivers, lakes and the seas. Over the last seventy years it is estimated 1.25 million tonnes of flint, 1.4 million tonnes of arsenic, 600,000 tonnes of antimony, one million tonnes of cobalt and about 800,000 tonnes of nickel—all extremely poisonous substances have got onto the atmosphere, Fig. 27.8 shows the imbalanced ecological cycle created by man.

# 28

# Waste Land Management and Geomatics

*M.B. Singh*

By the year 2020, the world will have around 7.7 billion people, of whom 84 per cent will be in developing countries (Scherr, 1999: 31). These people will need to be fed and as populations grow and inequalities in land distribution continue, the amount of cultivable land per capita will decline. If the world's presently cultivated land area is maintained at about 1.45 billion ha, the per capita arable land will fall from approximately 0.25 ha to 0.15 ha by 2050 (Lal, 1991).

The most serious problems faced by the country are the increase in wastelands, deterioration in the quality of arable land and decline in availability of per capita agricultural land. India has vast tracts of wastelands, which have been lying barren for ages. Decline of per capita arable land in India is much faster than the total world. Presently it is 0.14 ha and by 2020 it would be 0.07 ha.

### Waste Land

The concept of wasteland is sometimes used as a synonym of land degradation but according to dictionary meaning, "wasteland is that which is unfit for use, that is uncultivable, barren or without vegetation". Literally, waste land means land not used for any purpose or a land incapable of habitation or cultivation producing little or no vegetation, barren or desert. The Technical Task Group Report of the National Wastelands Development Board (Anonymous, 1985) defined "wastelands as the lands, which are presently lying unutilized due to different constraints". These include culturable and uncultivable wastelands. But according to ICAR (Anonymous, 1987a, c) wastelands are lands, which, due to neglect or degradation are not being utilized to their full potential. The Wasteland Survey and Reclamation Committee (1961) defined "Wastelands as those lands which are either not available for cultivation or left out as fallows and cultivable wastes". Officially, areas that have remained fallow for at least five years are one type of wasteland. The wastelands are the degraded lands which can be brought under vegetative cover with reasonable efforts and which are currently underutilized and the land which is deteriorating for lack of appropriate water and soil management or on account of natural causes (Report of Technical Task Group, 1987).

**Types of Wastelands**

Wastelands are broadly grouped into culturable and unculturable wastelands (National Wasteland Development Board, 1987).

***Culturable Wastelands***

The lands which are capable or have the potential for the development of vegetative cover and is not being used due to different constraints of varying degrees, such as erosion, waterlogging, salinity, etc. Most of these lands can be put to some productive use after proper treatment and reclamation measures. Actually these lands are problematic lands instead of wastelands.

1. Eroded lands—Gullied and/or Ravinous land
2. Undulating Upland
3. Waterlogged land
4. Salt affected areas—Saline and alkali soils
5. Shifting cultivation areas
6. Degraded forestlands
7. Degraded non-forest plantation land
8. Desert land, sand dunes, sand bar and coastal land
9. Mining and industrial wastelands
10. Strip lands
11. Degraded pasture and grazing land
12. Road, rail and canal side areas.

***Unculturable Wastelands***

The lands that cannot be developed for vegetative cover are called as unculturable wastelands.

1. Barren rocky/stony wastes/sheet rock areas
2. Steep sloppy area
3. Snow covered/glacial area

**Distribution and Estimation of Waste Land**

The four States, namely Rajasthan, Gujarat, Madhya Pradesh, and Maharashtra together share more than 58 per cent of the total waste land of the country. Rajasthan possesses about 5.04 million ha waste land followed by Madhya Pradesh (2.25 m ha), Gujarat (1.97 m ha), Maharashtra (1.46 m ha), Manipur (0.89 m ha) and Andhra Pradesh

(0.72 m ha). It is remarkable to note that Manipur has roughly 64 per cent of the total geographical area under this category.

The waste land estimate made by NRSA using Landsat data at the time of waste land mapping of the country on the scale 1:1 million accounts for 53.30 million ha (32.84 mha culturable waste land and 20.46 m ha unculturable waste land) in 1980-82. The second estimate of NRSA using LISS-I and LISS-II data on scale 1: 250,000 puts wastelands at 75.53 million ha. In the context of India, National Wasteland Development Board (NWDB) has reported 129.57 million ha of land (approximately 40%) under different types of wasteland out of 329 million hectares of total geographical area. Of this 93.69 million ha are non-forest wasteland. Geographically, India is the seventh largest country in the world but unfortunately 45 mha of land falls under cultivable wasteland out of the total wasteland. Several contributing factors like deforestation, scarcity of food, fuel, fodder, loss of common property resources, poor agricultural and pastoral practices aggravate the problem. Increasing pressure from commercial interests and human and livestock populations has led to encroachment on and increasing degradation of the common lands (Jodha, 1986). On the other hand per capita land availability is decreasing at a rapid rate.

## Reasons of Degradation of Waste Land

The most of the waste land is degraded. Only because of this reason many have described the waste land as degraded land. The degradation of waste land has been caused by soil erosion, soil nutrient depletion, salinization, acidification, agrochemical pollution, soil compaction, deforestation and desertification.

### *Soil Erosion*

Soil erosion due to water or wind is one of the main reasons of land degradation. Erosion of exposed soil leads to the loss of fine topsoil along with organic matter and nutrients depletion like nitrogen, phosphorous, potassium and calcium. These are essential ingredients for crop production. As a result of erosion, soil's water holding capacity, effective rooting depth and plant available water reserves are reduced. Further it exposes infertile subsoil and affects plant growth adversely. According to Stocking (1995) since 1945, about 1.2 billion ha areas (roughly equivalent to combined China and India size) have been eroded to the point where their original biotic functions are impaired.

Table 28.1 shows the seriousness of soil erosion problem. Without knowing the rate of erosion, planning for bringing down the soil loss within acceptable level is not possible. Presently at world level about 1094 million ha and 548 million ha are eroded by water and wind respectively making total eroded areas as 1642 million ha.

**Table 28.1:** Global extent of soil degradation (million ha) due to erosion

| Region | *Area Eroded by Water Erosion* | | | | *Area Eroded by Wind Erosion* | | | | |
|---|---|---|---|---|---|---|---|---|---|
| | *Light* | *Moderate rate* | *Strong and Extreme* | *Total* | *Light* | *Moderate rate* | *Strong and Extreme* | *Total* | *Total Area Eroded* |
| Africa | 58 | 67 | 102 | 227 | 88 | 89 | 9 | 186 | 413 |
| Asia | 124 | 242 | 73 | 441 | 132 | 75 | 15 | 222 | 663 |
| South America | 46 | 65 | 12 | 123 | 26 | 16 | Negl. | 42 | 165 |
| Central America | 1 | 22 | 23 | 46 | Negl | 4 | 1 | 5 | 51 |
| North America | 14 | 46 | Negl. | 60 | 3 | 31 | 1 | 35 | 95 |
| Europe | 21 | 81 | 12 | 114 | 3 | 38 | 1 | 42 | 156 |
| Oceania | 79 | 3 | 1 | 83 | 16 | Negl. | Negl. | 16 | 99 |
| World | 343 | 526 | 225 | 1094 | 268 | 254 | 26 | 548 | 1642 |

## Human Activities

Human activities are second important reason of land degradation. These activities include deforestation, cultivation of marginal lands (cultivation on steeplands, poor or moderately fertile lands, and on less soil depth lands), unscientific irrigation, excessive and indiscriminate use of chemicals and pesticides, etc. and overgrazing. Soil nutrients depletion is also caused when the same crops are raised on the same land year after year. About 1966 million ha lands worldwide are degraded by this reason. This accounts for 15 per cent of the total land area or 38 per cent of agricultural land.

Factor-wise land degradation has been given in Table 28.2 which indicates that overgrazing, deforestation and agricultural activities are principal factors responsible for land degradation. Further it is remarkable to mention that in Australasia and Africa overgrazing singly accounts for 80 per cent and 49 per cent of land degradation. South America and Asia are witnessing land degradation by deforestation. Agricultural activities contribute more than 50 per cent of land degradation in North and Central America.

**Table 28.2:** Continentwise degraded land in per cent

| *Continents* | *Overgrazing* | *Deforestation* | *Agricultural Activities* | *Overexploitation of Vegetation* | *Bio-industrial Activity* |
|---|---|---|---|---|---|
| Africa | 49 | 14 | 24 | 13 | — |
| N/C America | 24 | 11 | 57 | 7 | — |
| South America | 28 | 41 | 26 | 5 | — |
| Asia | 26 | 40 | 27 | 6 | — |
| Australasia | 80 | 12 | 8 | — | — |
| Europe | 23 | 38 | 29 | — | 9 |
| World | 35 | 29 | 28 | 7 | 1 |

Table 28.3 shows the types of land degradation which clearly evinces the loss of top soil as most disastrous aspect of land degradation as it alone encompasses 70 per cent of the total degraded area followed by terrain deformation and nutrients loss.

**Table 28.3:** Worldwide land degradation types

| *Types of Degradation* | *% of total area degraded* |
|---|---|
| Loss of topsoil | 70 |
| Terrain Deformation | 13 |
| Loss of Nutrients | 6.9 |
| Salinisation | 3.9 |
| Compaction | 3.5 |
| Pollution | 1.1 |
| Overblowing | 0.6 |
| Waterlogging | 0.5 |
| Acidification | 0.3 |
| Subsidence | 0.2 |

## Impact of Degradation of Waste Land

FAO study (1995) on agriculture estimated that, at least 700 to 800 million people are likely to be undernourished by the end of the decade. In otherwords, about 400 million tons of grain stock and over 60 million hungry people are co-existing on our planet today. The degradation of waste land would further aggravate the food security problem if adequate measures are not adapted timely. The following table clearly evinces the reduction in global food grain production during last five years period.

**Table 28.4:** World Food Grain Production (million tonnes)

| | |
|---|---|
| 1997 | 1880 |
| 1998 | 1872 |
| 1999 | 1871 |
| 2000 | 1836 |
| 2001 | 1843 |

Impact of degradation of waste land on yield/productivity has been measured at regional and local level. Yield reductions of 20 to 40 per cent have been measured for row crops in Ohio (Fahnestock *et al.*, 1995) and elsewhere in Midwest U.S.A. The productivity of some lands in Africa has declined by 50 per cent as a result of soil erosion and desertification. There are serious productivity losses (20%) caused by erosion in Asia, especially in India, China, Iran, Israel, Jordan, Lebanon, Nepal, and Pakistan. Soil compaction is a worldwide problem, especially with the adaption of mechanized agriculture. It has caused yield reductions of 25 to 50 per cent in some regions of Europe and North America and between 40 and 90 per cent in West African countries. In Ohio, reductions in crop yield are 25 per cent in maize, 20 per cent in soyabean and 30 per cent in oats over a seven year period.

**Indian Scenario of Waste Land Degradation**

The cultivable crops in India today remove annually on an average 3 million tonnes of nitrogen, 1.5 million tonnes of phosphorous oxide and 3.5 million tonnes of potash. Through organic sources the plant foods returned to the soil are hardly 1.8 million tonnes if nitrogen, 0.6 million tonnes of phosphorous oxide and 1.8 million tonnes of potash. This is the main reason of low yield in India. The quantities of nitrogen loss varies from crop to crop. For example, loss of nutrients by the sugarcane, maize and paddy per acre is much greater than any other crops.

Another serious aspect of degradation of waste land is displacement of people at all geographical levels. In India it was estimated (1990-91) that about 8 million hectares of land were damaged by waterlogging or salinity from irrigation and that as many as 1.5 million farmers had been displaced by those problems since Independence.

1. The seriousness of soil erosion problem can be realized from the fact that in India 6000 million tonnes of top soil are lost every year causing nutrients loss of Rs. 700 crores per annum.
2. In the country the available land is being eroded at an average rate of 16.35 tonnes/ha/year which is far more than the highest tolerance limit of 12.5 tonnes/ha/year.
3. According to Bali and Kanwar (1977), about 167 million ha lands of the country have been suffering from different kinds of degradation problems, such as water erosion (90mha), wind erosion (50 mha), salinity and sodicity (7 mha) and flooding (20 mha), another 20 mha especially in the canal irrigated areas are under risk of becoming chemically degraded. The Ministry of Agriculture estimated that, of the 329 mha of the geographical area of India, nearly 175 mha (53.2%) are subject to varying kinds and degree of degradation.

**Management of Waste Land**

The traditional techniques to manage land from erosion are construction of live barriers, rockwalls, terraces and earth bunds along with other physical structures such as drainage channels and vegetated waterways. Now-a-days efforts are being made to retain as much rainfall as possible by contour cultivation, strip cropping, and tied ridging. Another important technique is to modify slope in one shot by creating bench terraces that convert a steep slope into a series of steps and to modify slope progressively over time by trapping soil on site with the help of earth banks, trash lines from crop residues; live barriers of grass and woody species. Now the use of cover crops to protect the soil surface from the impact of high intensity raindrops is considered sound practice.

### Farmer Adoption of Technology

The success of technical recommendations made for managing degraded lands depends upon the level of farmer adoption. Adoption may reflect the genuine interest of the farmer in a particular technology though there may be many reasons for adoption other than that of halting erosion (Bunch, 1982). One such reason may be temporary incentives like subsidies. Once the subsidies are withdrawn, farmer starts discarding the erosion control measures. Similarly, adoption is also affected by negative incentives such as the threat of resettlement, social ostracism or peer pressure which force farmers to adopt soil management programmes against their better judgement. Thus, it is argued that the success of such program is partly based on the degree of adoption rather than adoption of technologies. The record shows that there is wide reluctance on farmers' part to adopt recommended land management technologies.

Farmers should not be addressed as **targets**; they should to be treated as **collaborators** and **controllers** (Shaxson, 1997). They should be involved in decision making through expressing their priorities, skills, indigenous knowledge and through participation to direct research and extension which support their needs.

Many argues in favour of **direct** and **indirect incentives** for promoting land management. Direct incentives include cash payments for labour, grants, subsidies, loans, and in kind payments like provision of food aid (food-for-work) and agricultural implements. Indirect incentives include fiscal and legislative measures, namely tax concessions, secure access to land and the removal of price distortions.

### Farmers' Perception about Soil Erosion

A worldwide study in the 1980s (10,000 farmers) says that almost all the farmers knew that their lands were declining in fertility, few of them associated this decline with erosion (Hallsworth, 1987:84). 1994 reports (240 farmers) of northern Thailand indicated that farmers were not seriously concerned about soil erosion even though they were aware of a decline in soil fertility and productivity due to continuous farming of the same land. In Zululand, South Africa farmers only consider erosion as a problem when gullies were formed. Farmers tendency not to identify soil erosion as a problem is not confined to the developing world. Osterman and Hicks (1988) report that in the Missouri Flat Creek area in USA, farmers' perception of highly erodible land represented only 28 per cent of what the United States Department of Agriculture defined as highly erodible. A survey of 197 farms in New South Wales, Australia (Hallsworth, 1987:150) observes that 90 per cent of farmers did not consider erosion as problem. Ericksen (1998) study reveals that Honduran farmers do not identify soil erosion as a cause of reduced productivity even though they are aware of the factors that favour erosion.

## Farming Practices Leading to Infertility/Land Degradation

Improper agricultural practices also leads to land degradation. In order to save arable land from natural and man induced effects, crop rotation is being popularized in every parts of the world. Crop rotation is used in order to promote:

(i) adequate biomass levels of permanent mulch cover
(ii) assist in control of weeds, pests and diseases
(iii) recycle nutrients
(iv) ameliorate soil physical conditions

Crop rotation is used with zero tillage (minimum tillage) practices. Zero tillage has several on-farm as well as off-farm benefits.

### *On-farm Benefits*

(i) Increase of organic matter in upper soil layer;
(ii) Increase in biotic diversity such as earthworms, fungi, bacteria, etc.;
(iii) Better soil structure and stability of soil aggregates leading to higher infiltration rates;
(iv) Reduced soil erosion (over 80%) and runoff (over 50%);
(v) Increase in nutrients level leading to less fertilizer use;
(vi) Less variation in yields from year to year;
(vii) Better resilience of crops in drought conditions due to increased water holding capacity;
(viii) Economies of 10-20 per cent in use of water in irrigation;
(ix) Higher sustainable yields—maize >20%, beans > 37%, soya >27%, onions >26%;
(x) Reduced costs for labour, fuel, and machinery hours; and
(xi) Heightened environmental awareness among farmers.

### *Off-farm Benefits*

(i) Conservation of biodiversity in soil, terrestrial and aqatic fauna and flora;
(ii) Reduced flooding risk due to greater rainfall infiltration;
(iii) Less sedimentation and infrastructure damage, *e.g.* silting of waterways and large dams;
(iv) Reduced carbon emissions by comparison with conventional cultivation. It has been estimated to be about 1 tonne of carbon fixed per ha; and
(v) Elimination of cultivation-induced dust clouds in towns and cities.

Green manure cover crops have proved to be very popular and are a fundamental components of minimum and zero-tillage system. Waste land Survey and Reclamation Committee (1961) has recommended that Dhaincha seeds for green manuring should be supplied to the cultivators at subsidized rates. Black oat and pigeon pea are other green manure crops used as cover crops.

The cultivation of steeplands is very disastrous as it has less resistance to degradation and higher degree to soil erosion. Steeplands also have soil fertility problems in terms of low nutrient status and aluminium toxity. Degradation of irrigated lands through salinisation and waterlogging poses second threat because these lands play a central role in commercial food supply in Asia.

**Use of Geomatics for Managing Waste Land**

Remote sensing technology is able to measure extent and types of waste lands quickly and cheaply. Satellite data has been found quite useful for interpreting waste land information, using computer aided image processing techniques. Waste land maps of the entire country have been prepared on 1:1,000,000 and 1:2,50,000 scale. But some district level waste land maps have been made on 1:50,000 scale. Some waste land maps especially for eroded land, salt affected soils, water logged areas and shifting cultivation have been drawn on 1:12,500 scale.

The Landsat, Spot and IRS imageries could be used for interpretation of waste lands. However, their use for village level waste land map and updating topographical map had limitation due to their lower resolution. High resolution satellite data obtained from IKONOS, QUICKBIRD, and ORB VIEW-3 (U.S.A.); KOMPSAT-2 (South Korea); EROS B (Israel); PLEIADES (France); CARTOSAT-2 etc. having ground resolution from 0.7 to 1 metre will provide opportunity to collect spatial data to map in a fairly large scale (1:4000) with increased frequency of data availability. A large volume of data can be easily handled by using digital photogrammetry technique for waste land mapping. Geomatics including Remote Sensing, GPS and GIS, can be used for making inventory, mapping and suggesting suitability of waste land for the following aspects:

- Mapping of waste land areas and change.
- Mapping of waste land types.
- Monitoring of severely degraded waste land.
- Waste land boundary survey and demarcation by using GPS.
- Creation of query based waste land maps for decision support system using GIS (Wasteland GIS at village level).
- To examine the waste land reclamation potentiality and utilization.
- To identify waste land suitability for agroforestry, forestry, fodder, fuel and economic plantations.

The GPS supported survey system of waste land enables making of boundaries and various field points efficiently. Jammu and Kashmir Government has been experimenting the GPS based survey system for mountainous terrain land survey. No better survey system compared to GPS for a smaller piece of land in the form of waste land is available for cheaply and timely survey.

The waste land development planning at village level can be made by using satellite remote sensing data and integrating various types of data with Geographical Information System. With the help of IRS geo-coded images basic data related to land use, vegetation, soil, waste land, geology (structures, bed rocks, lineaments, etc.), geomorphology (landforms, overburden, landslide, position of clay, sand and gravel, boulder fields, unconsolidated deposits, well, moderate and less drained areas, water logged areas, high salinity areas, etc.) may be obtained. Road, drainage, contour, etc. data are obtained from the topographical survey sheets. Extensive fieldwork survey will provide information pertaining to vegetation structure and biomass, soil depth, soil fertility (physico-chemical properties), soil texture groundwater, evapotranspiration, and soil loss. Present level of fuel wood and fodder consumption may be estimated by using socio-economic population of various economic strata through interviews. Suitable species for survey of village fuel wood, fodder, economic plantation and for other land amelioration purposes can be obtained from concerned state forest departments. The socio-economic data especially population, cattle population, are obtained from census handbook.

The following thematic maps can be prepared with the use of Remote Sensing data:

- Land use map
- Vegetation type map
- Waste land map
- Soil map
- Physiographic map
- Geological map
- Hydrogeomorphological map

Similarly, following maps can be prepared from the topographical sheets on 1:50,000 scale:

- Village boundaries map
- Road map
- Drainage map
- Contour map

In this process by using GIS computerized data base (spatial and non-spatial) **village level waste land inventory** can be prepared for queries to extract information at village level and theme basis. Later on the **land capability classes** are decided on the basis of soil depth, soil texture, permeability of soil, soil erosion, slope of land, drainage condition (wetness) and fertility parameters, climatic conditions including rainfall, etc. Now by integrating all types of data in GIS, waste land suitability and utilization analysis for following uses can be made:

- Waste land suitability for fuel and fodder
- Waste land suitability for agro forestry
- Waste land suitability for economic plantations
- Waste land suitability for forestry
- Waste land suitability for cultivation after reclamation

## REFERENCES

Bunch, R., 1982: Two Ears of Corn: A Guide to People-Centered Agriculture, World Neighbours, Oklahoma, USA.

Ericksen, P.J., 1998: An Evaluation of Sustainable Land Use in a Hill Side Agroecosystem in Central Honduras, Ph.D. dissertation, University of Wisconsin-Madison, USA

Hallsworth, E.G. 1987: *Anatomy, Physiology and Psychology of Erosion*, The International Federation of Institutes of Advanced Study, John Wiley and Sons Ltd, Chichester, UK.

Hellin John, 2004: *Better Land Husbandry*, Science Publishers, Enfield, U.S.A.

Lal, R., 1991: Soil Structure and Sustainability, *Journal of Sustainable Agriculture*, 1(4): 67-92.

Osterman, D.A. and Hicks, T.L., 1988: Highly Erodible Land: farmer perceptions versus actual measurements. *Journal of Soil and Water Conservation*, 43(2) pp. 177-181.

Porwal, M.C., 2005: Wasteland Development Planning Using Satellite Remote Sensing and Geographical Information System – An Integrated Approach, in Siya Ram Singh Yadav (ed.), *Application of GIS, GPS and Remote Sensing in Development of Planning and Management*.

Scherr, S.J., 1999: *Soil Degradation: A Threat to Developing Country Food Security By 2020?* International Food Policy Research Institute, Washington D.C., U.S.A.

Shafi, M., 1968: The Problem of Waste land in India, *The Geographer*, No. XXI, Vol. XV.

Shaxson, T.F., *et al.*, 1997: Better Land Husbandry: re-thinking approaches to land improvement and the conservation of water and soil, *Natural Resource Perspectives* 19, Overseas Development Institute, London, U.K.

Singh, S.N. *et al.*, 2005: Economics of Sustainable Development of Waste Land in India in M.B. Singh (ed.): *Sustainable Management of Natural Resources*, Tara Book Agency, Varanasi.

Stocking, M., 1995: Soil erosion and land degradation, in O. Riordan, T. (ed.), *Environmental Science for Environmental Management*, pp. 223-242, Longman, Harlow, U.K.

Yadav, H.R., 1985: *Waste land of India*, New Delhi.

29

# Modeling in Transport and Topology Using Geomatics

*M.B. Singh*

A model is an idealized representation of the real world built in order to demonstrate its certain properties. Model cannot represent all facts of reality. According to **Skilling** (1964), a model can be *a hypothesis* or *a theory* or *a law* or *a structured idea*. It can be *a role*, or *a relation* or *an equation* or *a map*. According to **Apostel** (1961) models are necessary to constitute a bridge between observational and theoretical levels and are concerned with simplification, deduction, concretization, experimentation, action, extension, explanation etc. Thus, the modeling of transport system means depiction of its entire system.

In modern era, infrastructure is considered as a sine qua non—for the socio-economic development of a region as well as the country. Boosting up of agricultural modernization, industrialization, urbanization and tourism, has been possible through the means of infrastructure especially transport system and its efficiency. The effective transport system accelerates the growth of the economy by integrating markets, reducing the cost of production, enhancing the overall productivity, transforming the primitive economy (as happened in case of Konkan railway, Ranade, 2001), removing industrial backwardness by attracting large-scale industrial investment. Transport also helps in maintaining uniformity in prices, removing scarcity of goods during the time of crises, in minimizing the effects of natural calamities, maintaining law and order and in promoting economic self-reliance.

## (A) APPRAISAL OF TRANSPORT SYSTEM IN INDIA

Presently India consisting of over 2.44 million kms of road (2001), has the second largest road networks in the world only after the USA. In this the National Highways constituting merely 2 per cent, carry 40 per cent of traffic and suffer from severe capacity constraints as most of them have two lanes and around 15 per cent have only single lane and this causes a large number of road accidents. It has been realized that this bottleneck is retarding the economic growth of the country. Looking into this the hon'ble Prime Minister Atal Bihari Vajpayee in 1998 undertook the building of massive **Golden Quadrilaterals** expressway—5952 kms (linking of four metro cities—Delhi, Mumbai, Chennai and Kolkata) and East-West (Silchar to Porbander) and North-South **Corridors—7300** (Srinagar to Kanya Kumari) with 4 to 6 lanes highways and the network of 400 km National Highways connecting 11 major ports with an estimated cost of Rs. 54,000 crores.

According to Birla Economic Research Center, the country still needed 0.83 million km additional new roads. This can be viewed with the fact that the road length per 1000 persons has increased only three fold from 1.11 km in 1951 to about 4 km in 2001 as against 36 times increase in the number of registered vehicles/1000 persons and 60 times increase in cargo transport.

Since the states and Union territories of India have varying sizes in context of area and population, the computation of state-wise road length/100 sq.km and/1,00,000 population will be a real indicative of transport scenario prevailing in the country. Owing to small size all union territories show better position in terms of area but they do not reveal sound position in terms of population. Among the states, Kerala tops the list followed by Goa, Orissa, Tripura, Nagaland, Punjab, Assam, U.P. and West Bengal. In terms of population Arunachal Pradesh comes on the top followed by Nagaland, Goa, Orissa, Mizoram, Himachal Pradesh, Manipur and Kerala.

**Table 29.1:** State-wise Density of Roads—2001

| *State* | *Density/ 100 sq.km* | *Density/lakh population* | *State* | *Density/ 100sq.km* | *Density/lakh population* |
|---|---|---|---|---|---|
| A.P. | 69.4 | 252.2 | Nagaland | 126.7 | 1061.4 |
| Arunachal Pradesh | 21.8 | 1680.9 | Orissa | 151.6 | 643.2 |
| Assam | 115.6 | 340.7 | Punjab | 121.6 | 252.4 |
| Bihar | 81.6 | 92.7 | Rajasthan | 41.2 | 249.8 |
| Chhattisgarh | 25.03 | 162.7 | Sikkim | 26.9 | 353.9 |
| Goa | 256.7 | 709.2 | Tamil Nadu | 122.8 | 257.1 |
| Gujarat | 70.03 | 271.3 | Tripura | 141.1 | 463.9 |
| Haryana | 63.5 | 133.3 | Uttaranchal | 57.8 | 380.9 |
| H.P. | 52.8 | 484.3 | U.P. | 100.8 | 144.9 |
| J and K | 10.4 | 230.4 | W.B. | 100.07 | 110.7 |
| Jharkhand | 0.87 | 2.6 | Union territories | | |
| Karnataka | 79.2 | 288.4 | A.N. Island | 14.3 | 336.3 |
| Kerala | 381.2 | 465.4 | Chandigarh | 1758.7 | 222.8 |
| M.P. | 52.6 | 268.8 | Dadra and Nagar Haveli | 114.6 | 255.9 |
| Maharashtra | 84.1 | 267.5 | Daman and Diu | 369.6 | 276.0 |
| Manipur | 51.2 | 480.4 | Lakshadweep | 421.8 | 225.0 |
| Meghalaya | 41.7 | 405.9 | Pondicherry | 513.2 | 260.3 |
| Mizoram | 22.4 | 531.6 | Delhi | 1738.7 | 187.1 |
| **India** | **73.5** | **235.2** | | | |

The increase in population coupled with steady rise in per capita income, had triggered off an unprecedented rise in vehicle population in the country. In 2001 the total number of vehicles stood at 54.99 million compared to 0.31 million in 1951. The percentage growth in vehicles has been found above 100 per cent in every decade. Coping to that vast number there should be remarkable growth in road length. But the decadal analysis of road length shows much lower growth compared to vehicles growth. Most disheartening fact related to growth in road length is very slow growth after 1991 (around 5%).

**Table 29.2:** Growth of Population, Roads and Vehicles

| *Year* | *Population (in million)* | *% growth* | *Road length (in lakh km)* | *% growth* | *Vehicles (in million)* | *% growth* |
|---|---|---|---|---|---|---|
| 1951 | 361.08 | — | 4.00 | — | 0.31 | — |
| 1961 | 439.23 | 21.51 | 5.24 | 30.99 | 0.66 | 117.32 |
| 1971 | 548.15 | 24.80 | 10.22 | 95.03 | 1.86 | 180.65 |
| 1981 | 683.32 | 24.66 | 14.91 | 45.89 | 5.39 | 189.06 |
| 1991 | 846.30 | 23.85 | 23.27 | 56.09 | 21.37 | 296.47 |
| 2001 | 1027.01 | 21.34 | 24.42 | 4.95 | 54.99 | 157.27 |

The National Transport Policy Committee suggested a model split in which the share of long distance freight for railways should be 72 per cent and the rest for road transport system. However, at present the road transport has accounted for 60 per cent of the freight traffic. In 2001 the total rail route length was 81,865 km, which is largest in Asia and second largest in the world. In the same year railways transported 4832.7 million passengers and 504.2 million tones goods from one place to another. The growth in rail route length is much slower (below 13%) in every decade between 1951 and 2001. This is not in conformity with the population growth of the country because that marks higher growth than 20 per cent in each decade. Another painful fact regarding railway is declining trend in growth of railway wagons after 1951 and negative growth during 1981-91 and 1991-2001.

**Table 29.3:** Growth in Rail Route Length and Railway Wagons

| *Year* | *Rail route length (in km)* | *% Growth* | *No. of Wagons* | *% Growth* |
|---|---|---|---|---|
| 1951 | 59315 | — | 205596 | — |
| 1961 | 63602 | 7.22 | 307907 | 49.76 |
| 1971 | 71669 | 12.68 | 383990 | 24.70 |
| 1981 | 75860 | 5.84 | 400946 | 4.41 |
| 1991 | 78607 | 3.62 | 346102 | -13.67 |
| 2001 | 81865 | 4.14 | 222147 | -35.81 |

In terms of rail route length/1000 sq.km among major states of India, Punjab ranks first followed by West Bengal, Haryana, Tamil Nadu, Assam and U.P.

The country has a very long coastline with 11 major and 148 minor ports. The inadequate facilities at ports and the lack of vessels are main constraints of Indian ports. As a result of insufficient facilities, the country was able to handle only 29.78 per cent cargo by Indian vessels in 1996-97.

**Table 29.4:** State-wise Railway Route Length, 1998-99

| *Sl. No.* | *State* | *Length (kms)* | *% Share to All-India* | *Density per 1000 sq. km* |
|---|---|---|---|---|
| 1. | Andhra Pradesh | 5057 | 8.05 | 18.43 |
| 2. | Assam | 2392 | 3.81 | 30.49 |
| 3. | Bihar | 5178 | 8.24 | 29.78 |
| 4. | Gujarat | 5312 | 8.46 | 27.10 |
| 5. | Haryana | 1548 | 2.46 | 35.01 |
| 6. | Karnataka | 2974 | 4.73 | 15.51 |
| 7. | Kerala | 1050 | 1.67 | 27.02 |
| 8. | Madhya Pradesh | 5922 | 9.43 | 13.35 |
| 9. | Maharashtra | 5447 | 8.67 | 17.70 |
| 10. | Orissa | 2340 | 3.73 | 15.03 |
| 11. | Punjab | 2102 | 3.35 | 44.74 |
| 12. | Rajasthan | 5917 | 9.42 | 17.29 |
| 13. | Tamil Nadu | 4181 | 6.66 | 32.17 |
| 14. | Uttar Pradesh | 8893 | 14.16 | 30.21 |
| 15. | West Bengal | 3786 | 6.03 | 42.66 |
| | **All-India** | **62807** | **100.00** | **19.11** |

## (B) ANALYSIS OF TRANSPORT NETWORK SYSTEM

This infrastructure is modeled as networks and the **forms, capacity** and **efficiency** of these networks have a definite impact on our standards of living and our perception of the world around us. Transportation networks provide the essential means and channels for the movement of goods and people from one specialized area to another. A transportation network links urban places together into a system of cities (Berry, 1964). Towns , villages, transportation links are the set of objects, related through the circulation of money, goods (freight), people, services and other movements (energy/ideas/innovations) and the energy inputs are derived from the biological and social needs of the community.

By considering transportation networks in generalized form as **points** and **lines** (a graph) it is possible to apply notions from graph theory which describes the relationships of the various network elements to each other. The terrestrial surface does not permit free access in every direction as hills, water bodies and similar irregularities serve to restrict movement to particular paths, which offer the least line of resistance.

*Topology* is a form of geometry, which is concerned with the position and relationships between points and lines and areas, but not with the distance between points, the straightness of lines or size of areas (Briggs, 1972: 9). The topology is sometimes called rubber sheet geometry. The topological graphs (transport networks) are composed of sets of points, linked together by lines, which may completely enclose areas of space. Points on a graph are referred to as vertices or nodes; lines are referred to as edges, arcs or links; areas enclosed by edges are referred to as regions or faces.

When a plan is being drawn to construct the roads directly or to improve the transport networks for the development of a region, aspect of connectivity; accessibility; efficiency, density of network, network pattern etc. should be taken into account.

**Measures of Connectivity**

The connectivity is the degree of completeness of the links between the vertices. It can be measured through a number of measures, which have been inferred from the concepts of graph theory for measuring the relative cohesiveness of the network. In a transportation network, the more edges are there the more complete are the links between the vertices, that is, the higher its level of connectivity. Connectivity is measured in terms of Beta index, Cyclomatic number, Alpha index and connectivity index.

The *Beta index* is a simple measure of connectivity and is calculated by dividing the number of *edges* (e) by the number of *vertices* (v). But it is less useful for a complex network. Normally it ranges between 0.5 and 3.0 but its upper limit may be higher than 3 in some special cases. High value of Beta index indicates well developed network.

$$\beta = e/v$$

The *Cyclomatic number* (number of fundamental circuits) is a different way of measuring connectivity and it is calculated as follows:

$$\text{Cyclomatic number} = e-(v-1) \text{ or } (e-v)+1$$
$$\text{Maximum possible Cyclomatic number} = 2v-5$$

The *Alpha index* is best measure of connectivity for fairly complex network. This avoids the disadvantage that different levels of connectivity may have the same cyclomatic number by making allowance for the number of vertices in the network. The Alpha index is the cyclomatic number expressed as a fraction of the maximum possible cyclomatic number for the particular network. In other words, it is the number of fundamental circuits possessed by the network expressed as a fraction of the maximum possible number. The value of Alpha index may vary between 0 and 100. High value of Alpha index indicates well developed network.

$$\alpha = \text{cyclomatic number}/2v-5$$
$$= e-v+1/2v-5$$

**Connectivity Index:** For getting the connectivity index one has to know first the maximum number of routes between number of places (vertices—v). If 5 places are connected to each other, the maximum possible number of routes would be ½ $(v^2-v)$ =1/2 (25-5) = 10. Second, observed number of routes are computed which is actually existing.

$$\text{Connectivity Index} = \frac{\text{Observed number of routes}}{\text{maximum possible number of routes}}$$

## Measure of Accessibility

The accessibility of a place is reflected in its relative accessibility to other places via the route ways of the network. In terms of graph network, a vertex which is well connected by edges to the other vertices of the network is said to be accessible. In a complex network, it may not be possible to assess relative accessibility easily. Various measures have been used to quantify the concept of accessibility. One such way is measurement of the *associated number. The associated number is computed by determining the longest distance for each place.* For this purpose the *shortest-path matrix* is calculated. Low value in shortest path matrix is indicative of well-developed network. Another simple measure is *the mean associated number* which is average of all the associated numbers and dividing this sum by the number of vertices. A low mean associated number (near to 1) suggests a high level of accessibility and *vice-versa.*

More reliable measure of accessibility is Shimbel index. It is derived from the shortest path matrix (sum of the values in the row of shortest-path matrix). It is able to exhibit small differences in accessibility more clearly. This index is defined as the sum of the values in a row of the shortest-path matrix and indicates the number of edges needed to connect any vertex with all the other vertices in the network by the shortest-path. Further Shimbel also suggested to calculate dispersion index which is sum of all the values of the shortest-path matrix. This can be obtained by adding the Shimbel indices. Dispersion index can be calculated by using the following formula.

$$D(N) = \sum_{i \text{ and } j = 1}^{n} \text{distance}(ij)$$

Where N is network, distance is the value associated with the minimum paths from i to j. It is in fact a summation of the values associated with the minimum paths connecting a place i with all others in the network N. Knowledge of such minimum paths is necessary for deriving the accessibility measure outlined above.

Places located centrally within the region are likely to be more accessible to all others than are places located on the periphery of the region using Shimbel measure. At favourable locations one would expect the places to be large and to contain a wide variety of activities demanding ready access to external population. This interpretation fails to take into account interaction that crosses the border of the region. Peripheral places may be strongly oriented to the exterior rather than to other internal places No regional highway network system should be studied in isolation. Some sectors of the regional economy are bound to demand contact with the outside world.

In order to ascertain accessibility of the places on the transport network the shortest-path matrix and the associated number are computed.

## Measure of Efficiency

The ideal path between vertices is a *straight line* (direct distance) joining the vertices This path is seldom achieved and the shortest-path between two vertices is usuall somewhat longer than the direct distance. The efficiency of an edge in terms of directness can be measured by calculating the *Detour index* or index of directness.

$$\text{Detour Index} = \frac{\text{Shortest road distance}}{\text{Direct distance}} \times \frac{100}{1}$$

This index is multiplied by 100 to get rid of decimals. By measuring accessibility in terms of distance, this index indicates the spatial efficiency of the network. This index is useful measure for comparing the *efficiency of separate routes* within the area. And this can also be used to *compare the overall directness of routes in one area with that of another one.* For calculating this kind of accessibility, it is convenient to prepare a matrix and that matrix is called *distance matrix.*

The efficiency can also be measured in terms of *time* or *cost*. It may be more fruitful for such assessment. Legal speed limits are often ignored on particular stretches of highway, which would account for some discrepancies between estimated and actual travel time. For this purpose travel time matrixes can be prepared. The measures of accessibility in terms of *distance, time* and *cost* are better measures of effectiveness because the people are not interested in topological accessibility but they are interested in how far it is and how long and how much cost it takes them to travel from place to place. The topological accessibility can be applied to study/know the network pattern.

The *degree of development of transport network* is another measure to know the degree of development of network *i.e.* high or low level of network development; and to compare the network of one area to another area. It is computed by using *Pi index* (Π). Its lower limit is 1 while upper limit is not fixed.

Pi = Total length of the network/actual distance along the diameter = c/d
= total length/length of diameter.

Here total length of transport routes can be taken from published or recoded data (road length or rail length as the case may be). Diameter length is the longest shortest path in the network. In the above shortest path matrix 6 will be the length of diameter.

## (C) ROLE OF GEOMATICS IN TRANSPORT MANAGEMENT

Geomatics does include Remote Sensing apart from Geographic Information System, Global Positioning System, Photogrametry, Cartography and Surveying. One calls it as a science while other as a technology. Technically it involves a systematic acquisition, integration and management of spatial data required for scientific, administrative, legal and technical operations involved in the process of production and management of spatial and non-spatial information. Geomatics is also defined as the integration of different disciplines (computer science, information technology, telecommunication, statistics and geography, etc.). Groot (1989) describes it *as the science and technology dealing with the structure and character of spatial information, its capture, its classification and qualification, its storage, processing, portrayal and dissemination, including the infrastructure necessary to secure optimal use of this information.* It is used synonymously with geoinformatics. It was originally introduced in Canada and became very popular in French speaking countries. The term geomatics, however, was never fully accepted in U.S. where the term *Geographical Information Science* is preferred.

The role of Geomatics in Transport Management can be summarized in the following lines:

- Application in new route location, relocation of existing routes and design plan.
- Updating of existing road and rail maps.
- Assessment of temporal and spatial change in transport system.
- Optimal route analysis in cities using GIS.
- Monitoring of accidents.
- Monitoring of highway impact on ecology.
- Of the area.
- Monitoring of Urban traffic on environment.
- Monitoring of Truck or Bus dispatch using GPS.

**Application in New Route Location, Relocation of Existing Routes and Design Plan**

Photogrammetry, remote sensing, GPS and GIS can be employed in new route location and relocation of existing routes. A proper route location by above mentioned tools need the perfect knowledge about the following aspects:

1. Alignment possibility
2. Grade possibilities
3. Construction-condition possibilities

A pre-field photo-interpreted map for highway location should contain the following elements:

1. Topographical and Hydrological Information
2. Geological Information
3. Information regarding slope stability

**Stages of Route Location**

Potential routes can be selected more efficiently by photo-interpretation than by ground techniques. Reconnaissance in highway engineering through LIDAR produces quick results and the photo-interpreter often can carry out preliminary planning without having to leave the office. The general sequence of steps to be followed are:

1. Area study to select route corridors (first stage reconnaissance)
2. Corridor study to select route strips (second stage reconnaissance)

3. Analysis of route strips and selection of final center line (final reconnaissance)
4. Design

For surface elevation data collection EDM (Electronic Distance Measurement) and GPS methods are highly accurate, time and cost saving. But for a large area these methods are impractical because workers must move with equipment in the field. For a large area digital photogrammetry is most accurate for surface information collection. In this case no aerial photos are produced but high resolution scanner is used to produce digital image. The digital nature of data allows terrain mapping in efficient manner through automation. But photogrammetry used for acquiring surface terrain information, has several limitations. For instance it is useful when trees are without leaves, ground is free from snow, sun is at above 30° angle and sky is free from clouds. It is costly and time consuming too.

Thus experiment has been carried out to integrate LIDAR and Photogrammetry for surface elevation data collection. LIDAR (Light Detection and Ranging) collects terrain information more rapidly than the existing data collection technique. LIDAR is an active remote sensing system that utilizes *a laser beam* as the sensing carrier. Laser scanners measure three dimensional points on the surface of the earth. In this airplane (aerial platform) has a laser ranging system mounted on board, along with other equipment including a precision GPS receiver and accurate Inertial Navigation System (INS). The airplane is flown over the area in which data are to be collected. Lasers utilized emit thousands of pulses (up to 25,000) per second. The travel time of these pulses is timed and recorded round trip along with position and orientation of the airplane to determine distance (range). Elevations are derived from the distance measurements.

By integrating LIDAR and Photogrammetry in highway location, time and cost both are saved. LIDAR developed terrain products and digital imagery have enough accuracy for planners to decide the *route corridors* (several miles wide) and *route strip* (narrow than corridors). After the decision of route strip, final photographic control and processing is completed to finalize the *central line* (final highway location). IKONOS and QuickBird imageries supplement the LIDAR by providing visual base for reference purpose.

LIDAR digital elevation data are collected in the form of a point cloud consisting of an easting, northing and elevation (XYZ) with an average spacing of 2 meters. Three data sets are collected by taking the help of first return pulse, last return pulse and bare earth pulse. Later on a gridded digital elevation model of 5 feet is produced.

## Existing Process for Photogrammetric Mapping

### *Once a Study Corridor has been finalized*

(i) The first task of photogrammetric mapping is the placement of photo control. In some cases existing features (manholes, etc.) are used for this purpose while in other cases actual targets (fabric Xs) are placed in the field. *Photo control* serves as a known location (XY) for georeferencing of aerial photos.

(ii) Next step is to fly the corridor and collect aerial photography of adequate resolution which depends on accuracy requirements of the project.

(iii) Once aerial triangulation is completed, break lines and mass points can be produced. The combining of these two products gives Digital Terrain Model (DTM). DTM is used to produce additional products including orthophotos, contours at regular interval such as 2 m or similar. DTM are prepared either by using DEM method or TIN method. DEM is prepared at regular interval height or gridded height. Tringulated Irregular Networks (TINs-photogrammetric products useful to designers) are also used to produce digital elevation model but not at regular interval like in DEM. In both cases contours are also drawn at some regular vertical interval like at 2 m or 5 m.

(iv) On the basis of above photogrammetric products, designers identify a final , preferred alignment. Once the development of an alignment is approved, additional field survey and photogrammetric work are preferred to densify the existing network.

(v) Terrain elevation data can also be collected by digitizing the existing topographic maps but in this case accuracy standard is poor.

**Case Study:** In USA for 10 sq. mile corridor mapping, LIDAR took 598 hours while photogrammetric method took 2670 hours in 2001 so saving 70 per cent cost. Similarly, second project completed for 46 mile long corridor. In this LIDAR cost was estimated as $ 1,50,000 and photogrammetric mapping costed $ 5,00,000. Finally the project completed with a cost of $ 2,50,000 means saving of 50 per cent when LIDAR integrated with photogrammetric mapping (Veneziano *et al.* 2003).

## REFERENCES

Agrawal, M.L., *et al.* 2005: Ecological Impacts of Highway Project Using GIS, GIS @ development,Pp.32-33.

Briggs, K., 1972: *Introducing Transportation Networks,* University of London Press Ltd.

Chorley, R.J. and Haggett, P., 1976: *Integrated Models in Geography,* Methuen and Co. LTD., London.

Dalton Roser *et al.*, 1978: *Network in Geography,* George Philip and Son Ltd., London.

David, Veneziano, *et al.*, 2003: Integrating LIDAR and Photogrammetry in Highway Location and Design, TRB Annual Meeting.

Kamalasudhan, A. *et al.*, 2002: *An Analysis of Expressways Accidents in Singapore,* Vol. VI, pp. 30-32.

Sandeep, M. *et al.*, 2002: *Environmental Effects of Urban Traffic: A Case Study of Jaipur City,* Vol. vi, pp. 3434-36.

Thirumalaivasan, D. *et al.*, 2006: Optimal Route Analysis using GIS, GIS@development, Vol. pp. 1-2.

Vasanthakumaran, T. *et al.* 1976: The Transportation Network (Road) of Karur Taluk: An Application of the Theory of Graphs and Some Recent Geographical Approaches, in the Proceeding of the Symposium on "Resource Development and Planning", during 5-7 November, 1977, Department of Geography, University of Madras, Chennai.

Verma, K. *et al.* 2001: GIS@development, Vol. V, Issue 11, pp. 24-26.

# Index